The fourth R

THE REPORT OF THE COMMISSION ON
RELIGIOUS EDUCATION IN SCHOOLS

appointed in 1967 under the chairmanship of
THE BISHOP OF DURHAM

LONDON

National Society

SPCK

1970

First published in 1970
National Society and S.P.C.K.
Holy Trinity Church
Marylebone Road
London N.W.1

Made and printed in Great Britain by
William Clowes and Sons, Limited
London and Beccles

SBN 281 02359 X

Contents

Foreword

The Church of England Board of Education and the National Society decided in 1967 to set up an independent commission to inquire into religious education. The National Society agreed to finance the Commission, and appointed its then Educational Adviser as Secretary. The decision to establish the Commission arose from a widely felt need to examine the whole field of religious education at a time when hitherto accepted presuppositions were being questioned, the aims of religious education reconsidered, and methods of teaching transformed.

The Church of England Board of Education and the National Society express their very great gratitude to all those who have given so liberally of their time and expertise to make the Commission's report the comprehensive and thorough document it is. They thank all those who gave evidence, all who worked on the subsidiary groups and, chiefly, the members of the Commission, the Secretary, and the Bishop of Durham who, as Chairman, contributed to the Commission's work his distinguished personal and academic qualities.

The report is offered as a major contribution to the Church's thinking on religious education. We commend for study the sustained argument of the first seven chapters, and the recommendations which ensue from them.

ROBERT LONDIN:
Chairman, Church of England Board of Education

GEORGE WHITBY
Chairman, National Society for Promoting Religious Education

The Members of the Commission

CHAIRMAN
The Rt Rev. I. T. Ramsey, D.D., Bishop of Durham

SECRETARY
The Rev. A. G. Wedderspoon, M.A., B.D.

The Rev. Professor P. R. Ackroyd, M.A., PH.D., M.TH.	Samuel Davidson Professor of Old Testament Studies, University of London, King's College
Mr C. Alves, M.A.	Head of Department of Religious Studies, Brighton College of Education
Mr G. Benfield, B.D.	Religious Education Adviser, Hampshire County Council
The Rev. J. Bowker, M.A.	Fellow of Corpus Christi College, Cambridge
Mr J. R. Bradshaw, M.A.	County Education Officer, Dorset
Mr E. Burwell	Head of Christian Education Department, Bishop Stopford Secondary School, Kettering
The Rev. Canon F. C. Carpenter, M.A.	Canon of Portsmouth, Diocesan Director of Religious Education
The Rev. Canon D. G. Childs, B.A.	Principal of Trinity College of Education, Carmarthen
The Rev. C. P. Gordon Clark, M.A.	Rector of Keston, Kent (formerly Chaplain of Tonbridge School)
Mr D. V. Day, B.A.	Head of Religious Education Department, Bilborough Grammar School, Notts.
The Rev. Canon F. W. Dillistone, D.D.	Fellow of Oriel College, Oxford
The Rev. Canon J. Gibbs, B.A., B.D.	Principal of Keswick Hall College of Education, Norwich
Miss A. Golden, M.A.	Head of Department of Religious Education, North London Collegiate School, Edgware

1*

Mrs J. C. Graves

Headmistress, Mundella County Primary School, Folkestone

Miss M. Gray, B.A.

Headmistress, Merrywood Grammar School for Girls, Bristol

Professor F. H. Hilliard, B.D., PH.D.

Professor of Education, University of Birmingham

Dr P. W. Kent, M.A., PH.D., D.PHIL., D.SC.

Dr Lee's Reader in Chemistry, Christ Church, Oxford

The Rev. H. M. Luft, M.A., M.LITT.

Headmaster, Merchant Taylors' School, Crosby, Lancs.

Professor B. G. Mitchell, M.A.

Nolloth Professor of the Philosophy of the Christian Religion, University of Oxford

Mr M. H. A. Roberts, B.A.

Headmaster of Bishop of Llandaff High School, Cardiff

The Rev. Canon E. Rothwell, M.A.

Rector of Chorley, Lancs.

The Very Rev. M. S. Stancliffe, M.A.

Dean of Winchester

The Rev. S. W. Sykes, M.A.

Dean of St John's College, Cambridge

The Rev. Professor E. J. Tinsley, M.A., B.D.

Professor of Theology, University of Leeds

Dr B. M. W. Trapnell, M.A., PH.D.

Headmaster of Oundle School

The Venerable E. Wild, M.A.

Archdeacon of Berkshire

Mrs T. R. Wilkinson, M.A.

Assistant Mistress, Birkby County Infants' School, Huddersfield

ASSESSORS

For the Church of England Board of Education—The Rev. G. J. N. Whitfield, M.A., A.K.C.

For the National Society—The Rev. Canon R. T. Holtby, M.A., B.D.

Chairman's Preface

In October 1967 we were set a two-year task of producing a Report on Religious Education in Schools and I am glad to record that all our formal meetings have been completed within that predicted period. It would, however, be utterly misleading to suggest that no other hard work then needed to be done. In fact, such were the detailed suggestions and comments made by members of the Commission on the preliminary final draft that three further months elapsed before the manuscript could be sent to the printer.

Even that bald statement will make it clear how much we owe to the devoted and conscientious work of the Secretary, the Reverend Alexander Wedderspoon, who not only shared fully in our discussions, but whose planning of our business and preparation of our papers was done with meticulous care and incredible patience. In all this he was greatly helped by Mrs Marjorie Brand who was, in turn, assisted by Miss Christian Stranack, and the Commission is much indebted to these two ladies.

The best tribute I can pay to my colleagues on the Commission is to say that we all began as members and finished as friends, who had learned much from one another. We were in many ways sorry when our task concluded; indeed I even had the suspicion in later meetings that some points were being raised from an unconscious desire to keep us longer together. Meanwhile, apart from producing the Report, we have ample experience to do a comparative study of the numerous Conference houses at which we have stayed, should any-one wish it!

Besides being deeply grateful to members of the Commission for the ready, generous, and entirely selfless way in which they have shared in the work, I am also greatly indebted to those who have given of their time, their thought, and their specialist knowledge to the various sub-groups, and whose names are listed elsewhere, along

---

with others who have helped us in a consultative capacity. A very special burden has fallen on those members of the Commission who were also Chairmen of the sub-groups, and an extra word of gratitude is certainly due to Mr Bradshaw, Professor Hilliard, Professor Mitchell, and Dr Trapnell for helping us in this way.

Chapters 1–7 and part 1 of chapter 8 have emerged from drafts discussed and amended in both the sub-groups and the Commission, and give the background to the Commission's recommendations. In signing the Report, members of the Commission commend these chapters to the reader as representing broadly their corporate thinking in the various areas. Religious Education is a subject so intricate and complex, and our backgrounds and experience so varied and wide-ranging, that it will be no surprise to the reader to be told that not everyone attaches precisely the same importance or significance to every point of the argument or to every detail of the discussions. At the same time, all of us are agreed that in relation to the complex and far-reaching issues with which we have been concerned, these chapters represent as clearly as possible the collective thinking of the Commission. Our recommendations are contained in part 2 of chapter 8 and these recommendations, I am glad to say, have been agreed unanimously.

We naturally hope that our Report will be helpful to all who are concerned for the theory and practice of Religious Education and especially to teachers, parents, educationists, and clergy. We hope that it will help to remove prejudices and misunderstandings on all sides; we hope that it will correct, where they are erroneous, expectations and criticisms alike; and that it will point the way forward to a view of Religious Education as an activity which is sound in its intellectual basis, creative in its actual practice, and effective in its concern for maturity and fulfilment; an education which combines openness and commitment, exploration and conviction.

Those who find our Report helpful should, along with the Commission, have a due sense of gratitude to the National Society who provided the generous financial support without which our work would have been wholly impossible. We now offer our Report to the Church of England Board of Education, to the National Society, and to a wider public with gratitude for having been given a task which has proved at once so difficult and so worth-while; but a topic of such range, complexity, and importance that we judge ourselves merely to have begun what others must now continue and carry for-

ward. The Report will be worth little unless it stirs to consequential
action and further thought those in schools, in departments and
colleges of education, in Parliament, in local authorities, in our
universities, and in our Churches, who share with the Commission
a concern that Religious Education should be worthy of its name—
both adjective and noun. If our Report does this, we shall be well
content, and 1970 might then inaugurate changes no less significant
than those which have characterized the whole century since Mr
W. E. Forster's Elementary Education Act of 1870.

IAN DUNELM:

Introduction

Authority of the Report

The Commission was set up in the Autumn of 1967 under the joint sponsorship of the Church of England Board of Education and the National Society to inquire into *Religious Education in schools*. Its sponsors gave the Commission full independence so that the publication of its Report in no way depended on prior authorization and approval. It follows therefore that this Report carries no "authority" beyond that of its own members and it is offered by them to the Church of England Board of Education, to the National Society, and to the general public as a contribution to the current controversial debate about the future of religious education.

Procedure

The membership of the Commission is set out on pp. ix–x. As will be apparent, care was taken to ensure a full representation of serving teachers. The Commission met in full session or in sub-groups on forty occasions. Of these twenty-three were two-day residential sessions. There was one residential session of the Full Commission which extended over three days.

Much of the Commission's work was done in sub-groups set up to consider specific topics and each member of the Commission was a member of one or more of these groups. The sub-groups also benefited from the contribution made by a number of co-opted members whose names are listed below. We wish to make clear that these co-opted members are not bound to any statement contained in the Report, for which the full members of the Commission are wholly responsible. Members of the Commission also sought to remain sensitive to pupil opinion both by study of the research evidence on this subject and by individual contact with pupils in schools.

Chapters 2, 3, 4, 5, and 7 have emerged from drafts discussed and revised in the various sub-groups, further discussed and revised by the Full Commission, and finally submitted to all the members for private study and written comment. In several instances drafts were referred back by the Full Commission to sub-groups for extensive redrafting.

The sub-groups were as follows:

1. THEOLOGY (ch. 2)

CHAIRMAN   The Bishop of Durham

MEMBERS   Rev. Professor P. R. Ackroyd, Rev. J. Bowker, Canon F. W. Dillistone, Dr P. W. Kent, Professor B. G. Mitchell, Rev. S. W. Sykes, Rev. Professor E. J. Tinsley, Rev. A. G. Wedderspoon (Secretary).

CO-OPTED
MEMBERS   Rev. Professor G. W. H. Lampe, Ely Professor of Divinity, University of Cambridge; Professor H. D. Lewis, Department of the History and Philosophy of Religion, King's College London; Professor W. R. Niblett, Professor of Higher Education, University of London Institute of Education. Miss M. Saunders, Principal of Whitelands College of Education was present at one session of the group.

The Chairman, Mr Bowker, Dr Dillistone, and Mr Sykes contributed to the initial drafting. The Group also studied with profit a draft prepared at its request by the Rev. Dr J. W. D. Smith, formerly Principal Lecturer in Religious Education, Jordanhill College of Education, Glasgow.

2. MORALS (ch. 3)

CHAIRMAN   Professor B. G. Mitchell.

MEMBERS   Canon D. G. Childs, Mr D. V. Day, Canon F. W. Dillistone, Canon J. Gibbs, Miss A. Golden, Professor F. H. Hilliard, Rev. Professor E. J. Tinsley, Rev. A. G. Wedderspoon (Secretary).

CO-OPTED
MEMBERS   Rev. Professor G. R. Dunstan, Professor of Moral and Pastoral Theology, King's College London; Rev. Dr W. D. Hudson, Reader in Philosophy, University of Exeter; Mr John Wilson, Director of Farmington Trust Research Unit, Oxford; Lady Helen Oppenheimer, Oxford; Dom Illtyd Trethowan, Downside Abbey.

Professor Mitchell and Professor Hilliard contributed to the initial drafting.

3. EDUCATION (ch. 4)

CHAIRMAN   Professor F. H. Hilliard.

MEMBERS   Mr C. Alves, Mr G. Benfield, Rev. J. Bowker, Mr E. Burwell, Canon D. G. Childs, Rev. C. P. Gordon Clark, Mr D. V. Day, Canon J. Gibbs, Miss A. Golden, Mrs J. C. Graves, Miss M. Gray, Rev. H. M. Luft, Mr M. H. A. Roberts, Rev. S. W. Sykes, Mrs T. R. Wilkinson, Rev. A. G. Wedderspoon (Secretary).

CO-OPTED MEMBER   Professor P. H. Hirst, Professor of Education, King's College London.

Professor Hilliard, Mr Alves, Mr Benfield, Mr Burwell, Mr Day, Canon Gibbs, Miss Golden, Mrs Graves, Mrs Wilkinson, and the Secretary contributed to the initial drafting.

4. INDEPENDENT SCHOOLS (ch. 5)

CHAIRMAN   Dr B. M. W. Trapnell.

MEMBERS   Mr G. Benfield, Canon F. C. Carpenter, Rev. C. P. Gordon Clark, Miss A. Golden, Rev. H. M. Luft, Very Rev. M. S. Stancliffe, Rev. A. G. Wedderspoon (Secretary).

CO-OPTED MEMBERS   Rev. A. A. K. Graham, Fellow and Chaplain, Worcester College, Oxford; Mr D. R. G. Seymour, Headmaster, Bloxham School, Banbury.

The Rev. C. P. Gordon Clark contributed to the initial drafting and was responsible for the drawing up, circulation and assessment of the questionnaires which the group sent to a large number of independent and direct grant schools.

5. CHURCH (ch. 7)

CHAIRMAN   Mr J. R. Bradshaw.

MEMBERS   Rev. Professor P. R. Ackroyd, Mr C. Alves, Canon F. C. Carpenter, Mrs J. C. Graves, Miss M. Gray, Mr M. H. A. Roberts, Canon E. Rothwell, Very Rev. M. S. Stancliffe, Ven. E. Wild, Rev. A. G. Wedderspoon (Secretary).

CO-OPTED MEMBERS   Prebendary R. P. Johnston, Vicar of St Mary's, Islington, Chairman, Islington Clerical Conference; Canon W. Fenton Morley, Vicar of Leeds; Dr G. L. Barnard, Principal, St Katharine's College, Liverpool.

Mr Bradshaw, Mr Alves, Canon Carpenter and Archdeacon Wild contributed to the initial drafting. The group also benefited on a number of occasions from the advice of Mr B. L. Thorne of Messrs Lee, Bolton, and Lee, London, S.W.1. The Commission is indebted to him for his legal appendix on "Independent School Chapels".

Chapters 1, 6, and 8 emerged from drafts prepared by the Secretary and discussed and revised by the Full Commission. The substantial assistance of a number of other persons in the preparation of certain sections of ch. 6 is acknowledged within that chapter.

Evidence presented to the Commission

A listing of the evidence, together with a brief description of the procedure relating to its assessment and some examples of the material submitted, is set out in Appendix A, pp. 287–352 below.

Ecumenical Relations

The twenty-nine full members of the Commission were all members of the Church of England apart from the two members of the Church in Wales. The principal reason for this was that a major subject under examination was the future of Anglican voluntary schools, which is largely a matter of domestic concern for the Church of England and the Church in Wales. We were, however, greatly indebted to those members of other Churches who served as co-opted members of the various sub-groups. As the Report will make clear, the Commission in no way conceived of its task in any narrowly denominational spirit and sought to engage in as much ecumenical discussion as was practicable within the limits of time, finance, and staff.

The Commission had one full day's consultation with representatives of the Catholic Education Council, the British Council of Churches, the Free Church Federal Council, and the Christian Education Movement. Drafts of the Commission's documents were, at two important stages, made available to representatives of these bodies for their study and written comment, and the Commission's work benefited from their comments. It is scarcely necessary to emphasize that this measure of consultation in no way commits any of these bodies to any statement contained in this Report.

Assessors

The Reverend G. J. N. Whitfield and Canon R. T. Holtby were associated with the Commission as Assessors for the Church of England Board of Education and the National Society respectively. The assessors received all the Commission's papers and were free to attend all its meetings. Their association with the Commission in this way commits neither the Church of England Board of Education nor the National Society, nor they themselves, to any statement contained in this Report. The fact that they were not full members of the Commission means that they are not signatories of the Report.

Acknowledgements

Thanks are due to the following for permission to quote from copyright sources.

Church of England Children's Council: *All Children are Special*.

Longmans, Green & Co. Ltd.: *Christian Education*, by Spencer Leeson.

Routledge & Kegan Paul Ltd.: *Reasons and Faiths*, by Ninian Smart.

Colin Smythe Ltd: *Looking Forward to the Seventies*, edited by Peter Bander.

The Editor of *Studies in Philosophy and Education*: an article entitled "Indoctrination as a Normative Concept" which appeared in volume IV, number 4.

1

The Origin and Development of Religious Education in England

From the Earliest Times to 1870

1 "Our English schools were the creation of the Church, and took their rise at the same time as the introduction of Christianity to this island." The opening words of S. J. Curtis's *History of Education in Great Britain*[1] receive support from A. F. Leach: "In England from the first, education was the creature of religion, the school was an adjunct of the Church, and the schoolmaster was an ecclesiastical officer."[2] For close on a thousand years from the seventh to the seventeenth century, educational institutions were for the most part under ecclesiastical control.[3] The law of education was a branch of canon law. The church courts had exclusive jurisdiction over schools, universities, and colleges and, until 1650, all schoolmasters were clerks or clergy, and in orders, though not necessarily holy orders.

In a report of this kind we are not able to go into historical detail. It is sufficient to make the point that from the earliest days of the conversion of the English people until the nineteenth century the history of the Christian Church and the history of education were essentially interconnected.

2 During the medieval period most study was conducted within an overall theological setting, and the Church was the most important educational agency. The population was numerically small, predominantly rural, and economically poor. "Education" for most meant little more than religious belief, learnt through the rites, the teaching,

---

1 (U.T.P. 1948), p. 1.
2 A. F. Leach, *Education Charters and Documents* (C.U.P. 1911), p. xii.
3 J. Simon, *Education and Society in Tudor England.*

and the imagery of the Church, together with vocational skills, learnt in field or workshop. Formal education was the privilege of a small minority of boys usually destined for the Church, the law, or the landowning classes. Such schools as existed were cathedral schools, chantry schools, grammar schools, or other private schools of varying degrees of quality. Any organized system of primary education for all was unknown. Village priests were supposed to teach the young of the parish, and extant records suggest that occasionally they did so. Archbishop Peckham in 1281 laid down a programme of basic religious instruction which every parish priest was due to expound to his flock.[1] It consisted of the fourteen articles of faith, the ten commandments, the two evangelical precepts of charity, the seven works of mercy, the seven deadly sins, the seven chief virtues, and the seven sacraments; in addition, by the fifteenth century vernacular reading was taught in many of these "petty" or primary schools. The grammar schools taught the Latin necessary for an understanding of Bible and liturgy, but, though these increased in number, their geographical distribution was unequal.

3 The Renaissance and the Reformation, theological, economic, and social changes, as well as the introduction of the printing press, resulted in the development and extension of educational provision. The number of schools gradually increased and the curriculum widened. Nevertheless, the curriculum of the average grammar school was still largely based on Latin grammar and literature. Religious teaching was also afforded an important place by a State which saw the schools as an important means of establishing the new state religion. The catechism drawn up by Alexander Nowell, Dean of St Paul's, was widely used in schools from 1570 onwards, and remained in use for nearly 200 years. During the medieval period education was thus conducted in a religious setting. From the earliest times religious teaching had a place in the curriculum of English schools: in some schools it had a place in normal classroom work; in others it took the form of regular attendance at the cathedral or other ecclesiastical institution to which the school was attached.

4 The first moves towards the development of a national educational system providing for the needs of all children may be seen in the

---

[1] J. Lawson, *Mediaeval Education and the Reformation* (Routledge 1967), p. 27.

educational developments of the late seventeenth century. Hitherto formal education had been the privilege of a minority. In 1698 the Society for Promoting Christian Knowledge began to establish charity schools in parishes throughout England. These schools provided education of a kind in the three Rs, "Habits of Industry", and religious instruction for the children of the poor. By 1760 they were educating about 30,000 children, but they declined in number and efficiency as the eighteenth century progressed.[1] Their decline was aggravated by the demands of the Industrial Revolution for child labour, but they paved the way for later nineteenth-century developments. It is also worth noting the Sunday School movement associated with the work of Robert Raikes in Gloucester in 1780. This was strengthened by the Evangelical revival of the period and was popular with both parents and employers alike. On Sundays these schools provided a certain minimal instruction in reading and in religion: on weekdays the children were free for paid employment. Children could thus obtain an education, of sorts, while remaining economically useful. The schools had a rapid success, and by 1787 were providing an education for 250,000 children.[2] The Charity School and Sunday School movements are important. They served to promote the idea that education was for the children of all and not just for a privileged minority, and that the provision of such education was the responsibility of the Churches.

5 The economic, sociological, and political developments of the early nineteenth century pointed to the need for more extensive educational provision. Two voluntary church organizations took the necessary initiative. In 1808 the British and Foreign School Society was founded by a group of Free Churchmen to establish schools on the monitorial system developed by the Quaker, Joseph Lancaster. This was a system whereby a cheap elementary education could be provided for large numbers of children. One master was employed to teach a lesson to a group of monitors—older pupils—who then taught the same lesson to the younger pupils. In 1811 a group of Anglicans headed by Joshua Watson founded "The National Society for the Education of the Children of the Poor in the Principles of the Established Church". This body also set about establishing monitorial schools on the broadly similar system developed

---

[1] H. C. Barnard, *Short History of English Education* (U.L.P. 1947), p. 7.
[2] Ibid., p. 11.

by Andrew Bell. Between them these two societies largely created English elementary education in the nineteenth century. Their success in opening schools was rapid and extensive. By 1830 the National Society alone had established 3,678 schools educating approximately 346,000 children.[1] By modern standards these schools provided an education which was mechanical and uninspired—basic instruction in the three Rs and religious teaching. Little, however, is to be gained by comparing the standards of an earlier century with those of a later. Churchpeople of all denominations contributed largely of their time and money to build an elementary educational system in accordance with their principles and beliefs. It would be naive to assert that they were all angels of light and apostles of progress. But neither were they obdurate obstructionists. They were nineteenth-century English churchmen with the assumptions, principles, and prejudices of their time. It would be churlish to minimize or mock their contribution to English education. Even if their financial contribution alone is examined, the debt is great. Between 1839 and 1869, £24 million was spent on public elementary education. Of this amount, £15 million was provided by voluntary contributions through the Churches.[2] Transposed into modern values, this represents a massive financial contribution, and hard cash is an effective test of serious intent.

6 1833 saw the first move by the State into the field of public education. A government grant of £20,000 was distributed between the two societies to assist with school building. In 1836 was passed the first of a series of Acts of Parliament, known as the School Sites Act, to facilitate the granting of school sites and the establishment of schools. In 1839 a committee of the Privy Council was set up "for the consideration of all matters affecting the education of the people". Between 1839 and 1870 there was a steady growth in school building. There was also increasing tension between the societies and the State, often over the question of a conscience clause in trust deeds. Progress was also impeded by controversy within the Church of England provoked by the early stages of the growth of the Oxford Movement. The voluntary societies were also active in the field of teacher training and in the development of a school

---

[1] H. J. Burgess, *Enterprise in Education* (N.S.:S.P.C.K., 1958), p. 43.
[2] M. Cruickshank, *Church and State in English Education* (Macmillan 1963), p. 12.

inspectorate. As early as 1833 the National Society had drawn up plans for a "normal school".[1] By 1840 colleges for the training of teachers had been opened at Chelsea and in the dioceses of Chester, Exeter, Oxford, Chichester, Gloucester, and Norwich. By 1846 the State was offering financial aid for teachers in training, e.g. scholarship payments based on examination results. The State also had developed a system of school inspection.

7 Thus, in the years leading up to 1870, the initiative in the development of English public elementary education lay with the voluntary church societies. The State had also entered the field and had established its right to promote and extend elementary education and to inspect its secular efficiency. Its effectiveness was hampered by the lack of any system of central and local administration. This was still provided by the voluntary church societies, and in particular by the Church of England through the National Society and the diocesan education committees. The Newcastle Commission in 1858 showed that only one child in seven was receiving full-time education. This report finally revealed that, even with increasing state aid, the voluntary societies could no longer adequately provide for the educational expansion of the late nineteenth century.

8 The influence of the Church of England was also strong in the nineteenth-century development of the boys' and girls' public schools. Circumstances favoured rapid expansion, and Thomas Arnold, appointed headmaster of Rugby in 1828, was the man who met the hour. His educational programme was firmly based on a strict religious and moral training. He sought to produce Christians, gentlemen, and scholars—and in that order. His views received widespread support from the middle-class parents who supplied his pupils. New public schools were founded at the rate of one a year between 1841 and 1881 and the "Arnold tradition" was of profound influence on their aims and their curriculum. Many of these schools, e.g. the Woodard schools, were Church of England foundations. In all of them, school worship and religious teaching was the accepted norm. Even the broadening of the curriculum which followed the work of Edward Thring at Uppingham still gave a central place to the teaching of the Christian faith.

[1] I.e. a school designed for educational experiment and as a place where pupil teachers could obtain experience in teaching practice.

9 The above paragaphs illustrate briefly the following points which we believe to be important and relevant to our later discussion:

(*a*) that the Church's institutional presence in English education is the direct consequence of long historical development;
(*b*) that religious teaching had a place on the curriculum of the majority of English schools for many centuries before the passing of the 1870 Education Act.

1870–1944

10 It is not possible for us to set the problems of religious education and church schools within the full context of the complex political, theological, social, and economic upheavals of this period. We concentrate strictly on points of central importance. The increasing inability of the voluntary church societies to meet the educational needs of the pre-1870 period led to widespread discussion of future developments. There was, from the first, a wide disparity of views. The Voluntaryists consisted mainly of Free Churchmen who advocated the non-intervention of the State in education. All should be left to private or voluntary enterprise; *laissez-faire* should be the rule in education as in economics. The Radicals advocated a wholly secular system of education, with religious teaching as the responsibility of the Churches and their Sunday schools. Anglican opinion was divided. Some held to the Tractarian High Church view that education was entirely the responsibility of the Church. Others held to the Evangelical–Broad Church view that education was a field in which Church and State should co-operate to their mutual advantage. These divided opinions can be seen in many vigorous local disputes, e.g. in Birmingham between the Radical National Education League and the Anglican National Education Union. Compromise was essential if any progress was to be made and this can be seen embodied in the *Elementary Education Act of 1870*.

11 Voluntary schools[1] were allowed to continue, and were to receive grants-in-aid. Local school boards were to be set up, to build their own schools in these areas where voluntary school provision was inadequate. The board schools were therefore intended to "fill the gaps" in the voluntary school system.

---

[1] I.e. church schools founded by one or other of the voluntary societies.

12 Religious teaching in the voluntary schools was to continue to be fully denominational, as before. In board schools, it was to be non-denominational instruction in accordance with the "Cowper-Temple clause" which required that "no religious catechism or religious formulary which is distinctive of any particular denomination shall be taught".[1] The London School Board gave the lead in interpreting this requirement. It approved the teaching of the Bible together with "such explanation and instruction therefrom in the principles of morality and religion as is suited to the capacities of children".[2] On this whole development Disraeli observed that a "new sacerdotal class" was being set up—schoolmasters teaching the Bible and the rudiments of the Christian faith. Recent studies in the sociology of religion have done much to substantiate the shrewdness of Disraeli's observation.[3] These were developments of far-reaching importance. Voluntary schools were given a place of partnership within the educational system, and their right to give denominational instruction was recognized. Religious teaching was given a place in the curriculum of the board schools, and its educational significance was also recognized.

13 The 1870 settlement did not satisfy all parties—no compromise ever does. It also sowed the seeds of much later confusion in religious education. In the voluntary schools the aim of the religious teaching was both instructional (to teach the children the Christian faith) and "ecclesiastical" (to encourage them to go on to full church membership). In the board schools the aim was strictly instructional and any "ecclesiastical" purpose was legally prohibited. Although the schools were in this respect different, the teachers were similar and very frequently worked both in voluntary schools and in board schools in the course of their career. Over the years a gradual but increasing confusion of aim became apparent, as teachers carried over the aims and assumptions about religious teaching from the voluntary schools to the board schools and *vice versa*. This is a confusion which is still apparent and has indeed been much aggravated by later developments.

14 The voluntary schools grew in number until by 1880 there were

---

1 Elementary Education Act 1870, s. 14(2).
2 On this see H. F. Matthews, *Revolution in Religious Education* (R.E.P., 1966), p. 8.
3 E.g. D. Martin, *Sociology of English Religion* (S.C.M. 1967).

over 14,000 educating approximately two million children. The
working of the Act was, however, carried on between the
voluntary societies and the school boards not so much in a spirit of
co-operation as of competition, and the administrative arrangements
very much favoured the board schools. By the 1880s the voluntary
schools were experiencing increasing financial difficulty. In 1885,
for example, whereas the school boards spent 19s 0¼d p.a. on each
child in school, the voluntary societies spent 8s 6½d p.a.[1] It was
apparent that some further legislation would be required if the
voluntary schools were not to become sub-standard.

15 *The 1902 Education Act* extended the compromise of 1870.
Educational administration was taken out of the hands of 2214
school boards and invested in 333 local education authorities. The
board schools were redesignated "Provided" schools. Religious
teaching was to continue in accordance with the Cowper-Temple
clause. Voluntary schools were redesignated "Non-provided" but
were to receive rate-aid to assist with the costs of their upkeep and
maintenance.[2] This very important innovation provoked a violent
storm of opposition from Free Churchmen. Many refused to pay
rates, and some even suffered short periods of imprisonment. Dr
Clifford, the Baptist leader, raised his cry of "Rome on the rates".
This has been criticized as an absurd exaggeration when the vast
majority of non-provided schools were Anglican. Dr Clifford was
indeed protesting against rate-aid to Roman Catholic schools, but
his protest has a wider significance. What lay behind his violent
protests during this period was the fear that some quite fundamental
constitutional and theological principles were at stake in that the
state educational system appeared to be becoming an agency of the
State Church. Enough has been said to show that between 1902
and 1914 a wide diversity of views was still apparent. The Dual
System had its advocates and its opponents. Herbert Hensley Henson,
later to be Bishop of Durham, looked to a future in which education
would be wholly the responsibility of the State, with religious
teaching in all schools in accordance with the basic elements of the
Christian faith.[3] "Cowper-Templeism" in the board schools had its

[1] Cruickshank, op. cit., p. 55.
[2] The 1902 Act thus established what has come to be known as "The Dual
System". This term is used throughout this report to denote the arrangements
whereby county and voluntary schools exist together as parts of the one public
educational system, both kinds of school being maintained by L.E.A.s.
[3] H. H. Henson, *The Education Act and After* (Methuen 1903).

advocates and its opponents. Some Anglicans and Free Churchmen criticized it as tending to indifferentism—a vague Bible/hymnbook theism associated with school and childhood, unrelated to the on-going life of the Church and largely abandoned on leaving school. Others regarded it in the same way as Archbishop Randall Davidson when he said that "it lays foundation on which an ampler teaching of the Christian faith can be laid".[1]

16 If the Churches were unable to agree about the varied problems of religious teaching, the secularist organizations were unable to produce any coherent alternative. The Moral Instruction League began work in 1897 in an attempt to draw up a syllabus of ethical and moral teaching which could take the place of religious teaching. The pre-1914 era was, however, a time of passionate conviction on issues of belief and unbelief—facile agreement was as foreign to the atheist as to the churchman. The impetus of the league was from the start rationalist and anti-religious. In its protest against the poor quality of much Bible teaching in board schools and in its emphasis on the need for moral education in these schools the League had much justification. Where the League failed was in its inability to make common cause with Christians in developing some system of moral education which respected the insights of Christian theology as well as those of natural reason and human experience. The League's efforts lapsed in 1919 after the organizing secretary entered the ministry of the Unitarian Church.[2]

17 What lay behind the controversies of the pre-1914 era was a consciousness that the issues at stake were of fundamental importance. Was the English educational system to be based on principles which enshrined the Christian personal, spiritual, and moral values, or was it to become wholly secularized? Churchmen of all denominations were in the main agreed about the end, but they were quite unable to agree about the means. Under the circumstances, *solvitur ambulando* became the guiding rule of politicians, educationists, and churchmen alike. Then (as now) educational policy was not the outcome of any coherently thought-out educational scheme: it developed

[1] B. Sacks, *The Religious Issue in the State Schools of England and Wales* (University of New Mexico Press 1961), p. 102.
[2] F. H. Hilliard, "The Moral Instruction League", *Durham Research Review*, Sept. 1961.

from the continuing dialogue between those who were partners in
the educational system.[1]

18 Between 1914 and 1944, religious teaching continued to have its
place in English schools, and the Dual System likewise continued in
spite of the Churches' increasing financial difficulty. An abortive
attempt was made to introduce a unitary system of education at the
time of the Fisher Education Bill in 1921. The problems of religious
teaching did not, however, loom large in the minds of men who were
distracted by more pressing issues of war and economic crisis. By
the Education Act of 1936 local authorities were empowered to enter
into agreements with the Churches to assist financially towards
the erection of church senior schools. Few schools were in fact
erected before the outbreak of war in 1939, but a number of agreements were made and it was part of the 1944 Settlement that these
agreements could be revived.

19 Nevertheless, there was one development of great significance
during this period. In 1910 the World Missionary Conference was
held in Edinburgh. This event did much to stimulate the later growth
of the Ecumenical Movement which has been so striking a feature
of the development of the Christian Church in this country. The new
spirit of co-operation between the Churches, and more constructive
movements in theology and biblical studies, were among the factors
which enabled the Cambridgeshire L.E.A. to produce in 1924 the
first "Syllabus of Religious Instruction". Many counties adopted
this syllabus; others were quick to draw up their own. This development went some way to improve the quality of religious teaching in
the county schools. It was also one of the signs of a new era—that of
co-operation rather than competition between the Churches in this
field. The continuing importance of religious teaching found expression in the educational reports during the later part of this period
and most significantly in the Spens Report of 1938, which stated
very clearly that "no boy or girl can be counted as properly educated
unless he or she has been made aware of the fact of the existence of
a religious interpretation of life".[2]

20 In outlining these developments, the very rapid and substantial
growth in the educational work of the Roman Catholic Church must

[1] On this general point see W. Alexander, *Education in England* (1965).
[2] Op. cit. (H.M.S.O.), p. 208.

be recognized. The Catholic Poor Schools' Committee was formed in 1847, and after some delay was recognized as an authority which could receive grants for the building of schools. The classic formula for the Roman Catholic system has been "Every child from a Catholic home to be taught by Catholic teachers in a Catholic school". As the Roman Catholic Church in England has grown in numerical strength since the middle of the nineteenth century, so its system of schools and colleges of education has increased in proportion. In 1905 the Catholic Education Council was established to represent the Hierarchy and the Catholic body in matters concerning education and to maintain general oversight of the development of Catholic education. The Roman Catholic Church has also been active in founding Independent Schools and schools for pupils in need of varying types of special education. The significance of the Roman Catholic schools within the Dual System is a subject to which we return in ch. 7.

Religious Education and the 1944 Education Act

21 The Butler Act was a major piece of English social legislation. It restructured the whole of the educational system, and was seen at the time as a vitally important contribution to the rebuilding of the civilization for which the war was fought. Mr Butler, as he then was, realized from the very beginning that the religious issue was of crucial importance since it was the rock on which the efforts of many previous educational reformers had foundered. Negotiations began as early as 1941 and continued for the next three years. Butler and Chuter Ede were the main political architects of the Bill; Archbishop Temple and Dr G. F. Fisher (then Bishop of London) spoke for the Church of England, Dr J. S. Whale and Dr Scott Lidgett for the Free Churches, and Cardinal Hinsley and Archbishop Griffin for the Roman Catholic Church.

22 The many factors which influenced the religious settlement will be examined below. We believe it important at this stage to stress that the religious education clauses of the Act have to be seen within the context of an attempt to settle the wider problem of the "religious issue" which, as has been said, was a snag to educational reformers from 1870 onwards. "Secondary education for all" was one of the Act's central requirements. To make this effective, a very large number of schools would need to be extended, modernized, and re-equipped. Approximately one-half of the existing schools were voluntary schools which the State could not afford to buy, and which it scrupled merely to annex. On the other hand, the Churches could not afford to maintain these schools or to bring them up to the new standards laid down by the Ministry of Education regulations. In working out the necessary compromise solution, possession of these schools placed the representatives of the Churches in a strong position. Archbishop Temple began by insisting on the importance of preserving voluntary schools, but when Butler pointed out the dilapidated condition of many voluntary schools it is recorded that the Archbishop was "visibly impressed".[1] (Of 753 schools on the then Board of Education's blacklist, no less than 541 were Church of England voluntary schools.) Anglican opinion remained divided, as it had been since 1870. Some, like Archbishop Temple himself, saw the value of voluntary schools and the need to accept a working arrangement which would enable at least a proportion of voluntary schools to continue. Others, such as Bishop Cockin, advocated the abandonment of voluntary schools and the concentration of the Church's resources in the training of teachers. Others agreed with the Free Churches in advocating an end of the Dual System, and supported the idea of a unified state system with an agreed syllabus and the Cowper-Temple clause. We note that these positions still have their advocates at the present time. The prolonged negotiations resulted in a further compromise much in the spirit of the Acts of 1870 and 1902.

23 The Dual System was continued, even strengthened. The church authorities had to choose for their schools either voluntary aided status (which approximated to the status of the former non-provided school and which involved financial liability) or voluntary controlled status (which gave the Church reduced rights but involved no financial liability). In addition a category of voluntary special agreement secondary schools was established to give effect to the provisions of the Education Act of 1936 which had been frustrated by the war. These were important developments, as they placed the Dual System on a surer basis. Briefly, the characteristics of the three types of voluntary school are as follows:

Voluntary Aided School   Two-thirds of the managers are appointed

[1] Cruickshank, op. cit., p. 152.

by the Church and one-third by the L.E.A. Religious instruction and worship is fully denominational. The church authorities, with the aid of a government grant, are responsible for:

(*a*) necessary improvements to existing school buildings;
(*b*) the provision of new school buildings, and in some cases the site;
(*c*) external repairs to school buildings.

The L.E.A. is responsible for all other running costs of the school.

Voluntary Controlled School Two-thirds of the managers are appointed by the L.E.A. and one-third by the Church. The daily act of worship may be denominational. Religious instruction is according to the agreed syllabus, but parents may ask for some denominational instruction. Finance is the entire responsibility of the L.E.A.

Voluntary Special Agreement School The school is established pursuant to an agreement between the Church and the L.E.A. Management is as for an aided school, and the provisions for religious instruction and worship are similar. The financial provisions for paying the cost of running the school are the same as for an aided school.

24 The place of religious education in the county schools was also strengthened by Sections 25 and 26 of the Act, which made school worship and religious instruction in accordance with an agreed syllabus obligatory in all county schools, subject to the Cowper-Temple clause. Conscience clauses remained to protect the rights of teachers who did not wish to participate. Parents also continued to receive the right to withdraw their children from all religious instruction and school worship if they so wished. Their right to withdraw their children for denominational instruction was also protected. The Act further specified the procedure to be followed for the drawing up and adoption of an agreed syllabus by an L.E.A.

25 The 1944 settlement thus continued the Dual System and gave statutory support to religious education in the county schools. The need for compromise over the voluntary schools issue has already been discussed. The wider issues which were influential in the negotiations can now be examined.

26 The background to the whole period was, of course, the Second World War. It was believed that this was being fought to preserve

2

freedom, democracy, and all that was precious in the Western
Christian tradition. Religious education in schools was seen as an
important factor in rebuilding our British civilization on its historic
foundations. A study of the parliamentary debates leading up to the
passing of the 1944 Act makes it clear that this consideration influenced the thoughts and attitudes of many M.P.s. As Lord Butler
stated in a debate on religious education in the House of Lords
on 15 November 1967: "I shall listen with respect to those who
have doubts about religious instruction being compulsory, but I am
convinced of the principle which animated us in the flush of wartime—because, my Lords, this was put through while we were living
in Church House, with the bombs actually raining at the time, and
the sentiments and the emotion of the day must not be forgotten
now that we are in more peaceful but yet quite difficult times."[1]
This was, further, an age in which religious education was seen as
the basis of moral education—recognized as a vital need in the
post-war world. No system of moral instruction for schools based on
rationalist ethics had yet been successfully devised in England, and
the work of Mrs Margaret Knight and her followers lay in the
future.[2]

27 Religious education was, as has been seen above, already well
established on the curriculum of English schools. Lord Butler has
pointed out that when it was made a statutory requirement the only
serious objections raised were by those who questioned if it was
necessary to make compulsory what was in most schools already the
accepted practice.[3] As has been seen, representatives of the Churches
were in close contact with Butler and Chuter Ede over the future of
voluntary schools. They had also very positive views about religious
education in the county schools. As early as 1941, the Archbishops
of Canterbury, York, and Wales had presented their "Five Points"
on this subject. These were that:

(a) religious instruction should be given in schools to all children,
    subject to a conscience clause;
(b) the school day should begin with a collective act of worship;
(c) religious instruction should not be confined to particular periods
    of the school day;

[1] Hansard, vol. 286, no. 8, para. 713.
[2] *Morals Without Religion* (Dobson 1955).
[3] As quoted by Professor W. R. Niblett in *Religious Education 1944–1984*
ed. A. G. Wedderspoon (Allen & Unwin 1966), p. 16.

(*d*) agreed syllabus instruction should be open to inspection;
(*e*) religious knowledge should be included as a subject for the Teacher's Certificate.[1]

Thus, the church representatives had no doubt about the importance of religious education in the county schools. They were concerned to ensure that religious education would be taken seriously in the post-war years and were realists enough to appreciate that conditions would be extremely difficult. They supported the "compulsory" element in religious education as a means of ensuring that the subject would be taken seriously in the schools at a vital but confused time in the nation's history. These men saw the "compulsory" element in the Act as providing some support for the subject in the difficult years ahead. They realized that religious education in schools would not have the support afforded by the examination system and by vocational demand to the teaching of other subjects, e.g. English, history, mathematics, and science. Later developments in religious education suggest that their standpoint was not without its shrewdness.

28 Whereas the Churches were active in making representations about religious education, the secularist organizations were not. Secularist opinion had been opposed to religious education ever since the days of Charles Bradlaugh (1833–1891), but in the wartime period it was insufficiently organized to make any effective impact on the negotiations. The confident optimism of the nineteenth-century rationalists had, moreover, suffered an eclipse since the events of 1914 and 1939. The perfectibility of man through science and reason did not appear to most people to be a very credible notion in the days of Buchenwald and Belsen.

29 Last but not least among the factors in this settlement must be included the personalities of Butler and Temple. Butler understood the importance of the religious issue and had been at pains to give it careful and sympathetic study. Temple was held in immense public esteem, as a distinguished theologian, moralist, and educationist, and as a social thinker of great insight and compassion. These two men knew, liked, and respected one another and both understood to the full the gravity of the issue they discussed. The contribution made by Chuter Ede should also be recognized, as should the spirit

[1] Ibid.

of co-operation shown by the Roman Catholic and Free Church representatives.

30 Criticisms can be raised against the 1944 settlement. It is one thing to pass an Act of Parliament; it is quite another to ensure that the conditions exist whereby the Act can be made educationally effective. Many of the specifically educational problems which have loomed large in religious education since 1944 seem not to have been actively considered, e.g. the staffing problem. Nevertheless it remains a fact that the religious settlement made by the Act has worked for over twenty years, and it would be unrealistic to look for detailed, long-term planning in the confused conditions of the wartime period.

Developments since 1944

31 Religious education was given a fresh impetus by the 1944 Act. In the primary schools the subject was almost invariably taught by the class teacher, and usually at the beginning of the school day. In the secondary schools a few specialist teachers were available, but most of the teaching lay in the hands of non-specialist staff who, not infrequently, were sincere Christians who taught the subject willingly and with conviction. Time was to show that sincerity and conviction, however desirable, are not substitutes for professional competence. Textbooks, visual aids, sometimes even Bibles were in short supply. In the county schools the teaching was in accordance with whatever agreed syllabus had been adopted by the L.E.A. Some had been recently revised, other survived from the pre-war period. The content of most of them was a solid course of biblical study and church history. Professor D. E. Nineham has suggested that what lay behind the agreed syllabuses of the period was the university theology courses of the period, with their strong emphasis on biblical, textual, and historical studies.[1] A safe generalization about most of the syllabuses would be that they tended to be more subject-centred than pupil-related, drawn up more to satisfy scholars and churchmen than to meet the needs of the pupils. More has since been learnt about the religious psychology of childhood, and the needs and interests of young people. In the church voluntary aided schools the teaching was in accordance with the diocesan syllabus— a scheme of denominational teaching drawn up by a diocesan advisory committee.

[1] *Religious Education 1944-1984*, pp. 145-8.

32 Much valuable work was done during this period by the Institute of Christian Education (since merged with the S.C.M. in Schools to form the Christian Education Movement). The I.C.E. assisted teachers of religious education with advice about textbooks, etc.; frequent courses were organized both locally and centrally. In 1954 the I.C.E. conducted a useful piece of research to assess religious education under the 1944 Act after ten years.[1] Three main features were revealed:

(a) The majority of L.E.A.s preferred to make use of an agreed syllabus drawn up by some other L.E.A. rather than produce their own. Five agreed syllabuses were in use between 80 L.E.A.s.[2]

(b) The number of pupils taking examinations in religious knowledge was still comparatively small.[3]

(c) Most alarming of all was what the report revealed about the shortage of trained teachers. It was shown that out of 674 grammar schools in the survey, 312 had no qualified religious education teacher.[4]

In the Birmingham L.E.A., the overall figure showed that 88% of the secondary schools had no qualified religious education teachers and that the lack was most serious in the secondary modern schools.[5]

33 The 1954 I.C.E. report thus made very plain what has been one of the most serious hindrances to the teaching of the subject—a persistent shortfall of qualified teachers. It was thus no great surprise when a research project conducted in 1961 by the University of Sheffield Institute of Education into religious education in secondary schools revealed that the pupils did not remember much of what they had been taught. The Sheffield report was bluntly clear.

The standard of religious knowledge in the schools today, in so far as it has been revealed by the pupils who were tested in the University of Sheffield area, is clearly very poor. . . . It is believed . . . that the results obtained are fairly representative of the state of affairs throughout the country. Happy indeed are those who can declare that the results of this present research bear no resemblance to the conditions obtaining in their own schools.[6]

[1] Institute of Christian Education, *Religious Education in Schools* (N.S.: S.P.C.K. 1954).
[2] Ibid., App. 1.   [3] Ibid., p. 71.
[4] Ibid., p. 56.   [5] Ibid., p. 58.
[6] University of Sheffield Institute of Education, *Religious Education in Secondary Schools* (Nelson 1961), p. 44.

A piece of research by J. W. Packer had shown that the teachers of history were no more successful than teachers of religious education in this respect.[1] But learning and attitude are closely connected in education; the Sheffield report's findings could not be easily discounted. The Report went far to show what was becoming increasingly apparent to the Inspectorate, heads of schools, and all professionally concerned with religious education—that all was not well. Eighteen years after the passing of the 1944 Act there were still too few qualified teachers; too many agreed syllabuses reflected the theological thought and educational practice of an earlier age; no L.E.A. had appointed an adviser in religious education; too many teachers were confused in their aims and their methods.

34 Since the early 1960s we believe it is no exaggeration to say that a minor revolution has taken place in religious education. It has been influenced by three main factors: cultural, theological, and educational.

35 The religious education clauses of the Act passed into law at a time of high national purpose and idealism. Great Britain was still recognized as a major world power, and Winston Churchill as a world statesman. It was the time of the great crusade for the liberation of Europe—a time of planning and hope. Since 1945 much of this hope has faded. World power has passed to the American continent and to the Communist bloc; Great Britain's voice, although influential, is no longer so decisive in the councils of the world. For the first time the British people experienced the bitterness of a decline from greatness. Even in the years of disillusionment after the First World War there was still the Empire with its responsibilities and opportunities. After the Second World War, in Dean Acheson's penetrating phrase, "England has lost an Empire and not yet found a role". This, then, appeared to be the acid fruit of the war years. Over all lay the shadow of the Bomb—the possibility of nuclear annihilation. The result was an increasing sense of purposelessness and cynicism. Yesterday we knew war and economic crises and tomorrow we may indeed all die; concentrate therefore on the satisfactions we know, and let others strive, plan, care, and worry. If the

---

[1] J. W. Packer, Report presented to University of Leeds Institute of Education, 1951, "Enquiry into the amount of religious learning and history possessed by pupils of 16 and 18".

parents had eaten sour grapes, small wonder that their children's teeth should be set on edge.

36 English society was also becoming increasingly urban, dominated at every point by the achievements and assumptions of science and technology. Prestige lay no longer with the statesman and the soldier, but with the physicist, the aerospace engineer, and the surgeon. It was a society which was becoming increasingly depersonalized. A nation of shopkeepers had become a nation of employees in fewer and larger organizations. Birth and death were no longer the common experiences of everyday life, they were screened away in the privacies of the maternity unit and the geriatric ward. So the analysis could continue; it is a well-worn theme. Not all of this is loss, by any means. The growth of great cities and large-scale industrial organizations has enabled many people to enjoy higher living standards, more adequate accommodation, and greater economic security. No one would wish for a return to gunboat diplomacy, the slums of the nineteenth century, or the unemployment of the 1930s.

37 The point being emphasized is that teachers of religious education in the schools found themselves in the early 1960s trying to teach young people who were profoundly influenced by the drag of contemporary cynicism and the materialist assumptions of a culture dominated by science and technology. Religion was seen as neither true nor false but merely irrelevant. Methods of teaching evolved in an earlier age became more and more impracticable.

38 Nor were theological studies unaffected.[1] In 1962 the theological upheaval which had been very long preparing finally burst upon the public. First came the publication by a group of Cambridge theologians of *Soundings*—a collection of essays which expressed very plainly some of the questionings apparent in Christian doctrine, New Testament studies, Christian ethics, and the philosophy of religion.[2] This was followed in 1963, as is well known, by *Honest to God* in which Bishop John Robinson appeared to call in question many accepted beliefs.[3] His book was an attempt to encourage responsible adults in the twentieth century to think about Christian beliefs in a responsible, adult, and contemporary way. It encouraged some, but

---

1 See further paras. 81–109.
2 C.U.P. 1962. 3 S.C.M. 1963.

disconcerted many more. The publicity which this book received resulted in a flood of other books and pamphlets, including *Image Old and New* by the Archbishop of Canterbury, and *Four Anchors from the Stern* by Professor Alan Richardson and others. An even more radical assault on traditional Christian orthodoxies came in Dr P. van Buren's *The Secular Meaning of the Gospel*, which provoked a stern reply from Professor E. L. Mascall, *The Secularisation of Christianity*. What was new about this theological debate was that it was carried on not only in academic circles but also in front of the television cameras. Questions which scholars had discussed for years, even for centuries, were disconcertingly new to many church-goers and non-churchgoers alike, who sat round their television sets in growing bewilderment. The outcome of all this unaccustomed theological upheaval was an unhappy ambivalence. Theologians certainly seemed to be grappling with the sort of questions people wanted to ask. If medieval theologians had been accused—though hardly with justice—of wasting their energies discussing how many angels could dance on the head of a pin, this accusation could not be levelled against their twentieth-century counterparts. But, on the other hand, it seemed that the theologians knew the questions better than the answers and many found this a disconcerting reversal. In 1944 the image of the theologian was for most people Archbishop William Temple; for most in 1964 it was Bishop John Robinson.

39 With the "New Theology" came to be associated the "New Morality". Carefully constructed and responsible works such as *Towards a Quaker View of Sex*[1] and Canon D. Rhymes's *No New Morality*[2] received inordinate and often misunderstood publicity through being published about the time of the Profumo affair. The impression created was that not only Christian doctrines but also Christian ethics were in the melting pot.

40 All this could not but affect the teacher of religious education. Too many pupils (and their parents) gathered just enough from television and the press about the New Theology and the New Morality to misunderstand both. Frustrated in their efforts to follow the complexities of the theological debate, many teachers took refuge in biblical fundamentalism or reluctant agnosticism. Many young teachers, sympathetic to religious education, found it increasingly difficult to take part in what seemed to them an impossible task. It

[1] Friends Home Service 1963.   [2] Constable 1964.

is no surprise to find much evidence of questioning and re-examination within the field of religious education itself during this period.

41 In 1961 Harold Loukes had published *Teenage Religion*. In this book he examined the particular problems of religious education of the 15-year old school leaver. He found much ignorance, and confusion of thought, but great interest. Pupils did not wish to abolish religious education but to improve it. In place of the existing Bible-centred approach Loukes advocated the "problem-centred approach", i.e. the discussion of a wide range of personal, political, and moral problems in the light of Christian insight and experience. He made it very clear that this discussion method was, in the fullest sense of the term, a method of teaching, not merely an opportunity for an "exchange of mutual mystification" between teacher and class. Loukes' book gave rise to a great deal of experimental work in the schools, not only in religious education classes for the middle-school leaver, but also in the sixth forms.[1]

42 In his book *We Teach Them Wrong*, published in 1963, Richard Acland discussed the influence of our contemporary culture on the thought and attitudes of young people. He asserted that we are confronted with a "different kind of animal . . . not one whose basic culture is settled, local, and agricultural, but one whose basic culture is technological, urban, and scientific". He, too, stressed the need for new methods of religious education and supported the approach advocated by Loukes.[2]

43 In 1964 R. J. Goldman published the conclusions of his research into religious thinking from childhood to adolescence.[3] Goldman's main conclusions were (*a*) that up to about the mental age of thirteen, children think in a concrete way and are not capable of that abstract thought which is necessary if theological concepts are to be understood; (*b*) that much traditional religious education in the primary school is an attempt to teach too much too soon. In his later work *Readiness for Religion* Goldman suggested that ". . . it is an impossible task to teach the Bible as such, to children before adolescence".[4] Religious education in the primary schools should therefore be designed to make the child ready for the teaching he would receive in the secondary school. Goldman's work provoked a prolonged and

[1] S.C.M. 1961.   [2] Gollancz 1963.
[3] *Religious Thinking from Childhood to Adolescence* (Routledge 1964).
[4] (Routledge 1965), p. 8.
   2*

stormy controversy. His thesis was criticized on educational,[1] psychological,[2] and theological[3] grounds. Nevertheless, his ideas encouraged a great deal of experimental work in the primary schools and went far to show how little was still known about the religious psychology of younger children. There is no doubt that his research has greatly influenced the approach to the religious education of younger children both in Britain and in North America.

44 Other books stressed the need for new methods, and expressed the concern felt by all at work in the field. In 1965 D. S. Hubery, in his book *Teaching the Christian Faith Today*, supported an experiential approach to religious education. This was published shortly after Diana Dewar's book *Backward Christian Soldiers*, a journalistic survey, which suggested a gloomy picture of almost total failure in the schools.

45 In 1965 the Hibbert Trustees, mindful of the unease felt by many about religious education in schools, devoted the Hibbert Lectures to an examination of the place of "Christianity in Education". In the first two lectures F. H. Hilliard gave a clear and unequivocal statement of the educational justification for religious education in the county schools. These lectures went far to steady the ranks at a time of much pessimism and confusion of thought.[4]

46 Three major reports published by the Central Advisory Council for Education (England) in the period since 1944 made it plain that the "official view" on religious education remained positive. In 1959 the *Crowther Committee* reported on the education of pupils aged 15 to 18. The report is quite explicit on the importance of religious education. On p. 44 it states that: "Teenagers . . . need, perhaps before all else to find a faith to live by. They will not all find precisely the same faith and some will not find any. Education can and should play some part in their search. It can assure them that there is something to search for and it can show them where to look and what other men have found."

[1] F. H. Hilliard, "Children's Religious Thinking", *Learning for Living*, Nov. 1965.
[2] C. M. Fleming, "Research Evidence and Christian Education", *Learning for Living*, Sept. 1966.
[3] K. G. Howkins, *Religious Thinking and Religious Education* (Tyndale Press 1966).
[4] F. H. Hilliard, *Christianity in Education* (Allen & Unwin 1966), Lectures 1 and 2.

47 In 1963 the *Newsom Committee* reported on the education of pupils aged 13 to 16 of average and less than average ability, a report significantly titled *Half Our Future*. Ch. 7 of the report was devoted to "Spiritual and moral development". In this chapter the Newsom Committee stressed the importance of religious instruction and school worship and made a number of suggestions for their improvement. This is emphasized later in the report, in para. 349: "We have already made clear the importance which we attach to . . . that part of religious upbringing which falls to the schools."

48 In 1967 the *Plowden Committee* reported on the education of children up to the age of 12. Whereas the Crowther and Newsom Committees had both stressed the importance of religious education in clear and unambiguous terms, the same cannot be so clearly said for the Plowden Committee. Ch. 17 of the report was devoted to an examination of the place of religious education on the primary school curriculum. Much positive information was expressed in a strangely negative way. In para. 563, for example, the significant fact emerges that the lowest proportion of primary school teachers who would be likely to volunteer to give religious education in the primary schools had been assessed by H.M. Inspectors at 70%. Thus, the report continues, "if religious education in the primary schools were to be staffed only by volunteers, there would be no difficulty in staffing over-all". The chapter assumes the continuance of religious education on the curriculum of the primary school, and makes suggestions about changes in content and method. Nevertheless, perhaps because the Plowden Committee fully realized the size of the problems they might open up, particularly in the primary schools, religious education was not subjected to the thorough examination which, in our view, it needs. A minority report was also included opposing the religious education of young children mainly on the grounds of the inherent unsuitability of the material.

49 Much of the writing about religious education since the early 1960s has tended to be negative and critical, concentrating more on failure than on success. It is important to avoid distortion of view. A distinction has to be observed between that which is true and that which receives publicity. Behind the confusing facade of public debate much competent and faithful teaching has gone on in the schools. Recent research in religious education gives some pointers to the element of success which can be claimed.

50 In 1965 Harold Loukes published *New Ground in Christian Education*.[1] A list of 500 schools had been drawn up in which the religious education had been classified as "successful" by bodies such as the local education authority or university department of education. Loukes was concerned to examine the nature of this "success", and the educational factors which went to produce it. He remained pessimistic about the pupils' retention of religious knowledge and continued to be critical of existing methods. His main conclusion was that "successful" religious education resulted chiefly in the pupils coming through to a shrewd understanding of what is meant by Christian character, Christian personality; "the means are on the whole mistaken, but even these means have proved a vehicle of communication for an ill-defined but moving ideal of human personality". A rather different estimation of "success" emerged from an important research project carried out by Colin Alves, under the auspices of the British Council of Churches, and financed by the Gulbenkian Foundation. This extensive inquiry into religious education in county secondary schools was started in 1964, and the report was published in 1968.[2]

51 Loukes had asserted that the retention of biblical knowledge in the schools in his survey was poor, and summed up his findings with the statement that pupils left school barely knowing the first thing about the Bible. The Alves report produced evidence to suggest that this was too sweeping a generalization. Even so, it did not see "success" in terms of knowledge of the Bible and commitment to a biblical point of view, but more in terms of the degree of importance attributed to religious questions, however answered. It also drew attention to the continuing short supply of teachers in the subject, though pointing to a notable increase since 1954. Perhaps the best commentary on the evidence revealed by this very significant report is that provided by a statement made in the introduction and signed by over thirty representatives of the British Council of Churches:

We find enough encouraging features to justify a New Deal: enough discouragement to show how urgent is the need for it.

As members of this Commission we think that this perceptive generalization remains applicable to religious education at the present time.

[1] S.C.M. 1965.
[2] C. Alves, *Religion and the Secondary School* (SCM 1968).

RELIGIOUS EDUCATION IN WALES

From the earliest times to 1870

Although the early religious history of Wales is different, the close interrelation of educational and religious history from the beginnings until modern times is as true for Wales as it is for England. Since Wales was under the ecclesiastical jurisdiction of Canterbury from Norman times, much of the development was parallel. With the absorption of Wales into the English political system after the 1536 Act of Union similarity of development was still more inevitable. Much of the account already given for England need not therefore be repeated, but certain important differences should be noted.

In the medieval period the monastic schools provided the only available education in a wholly religious context, but with the significant difference for the future that Welsh as an already established literary language held a higher position than did English in the monastic schools of England. Centuries later, however, when the grammar schools eventually threw off the total domination of Latin, the means of communication in the grammar schools of Wales became English, not Welsh. The "first provision for education ever made by the State"[1] in England and Wales was in Wales during the Commonwealth when in the years after 1650, under the Act for the Propagation of the Gospel in Wales, sixty schools were set up and their puritan schoolmasters paid £40 per annum out of the sequestered revenues of clergy ejected from their livings. These schools soon disappeared, but the memory of them prompted another brief experiment in the Restoration period. In an age of bitter intolerance and persecution moderate Puritans and Anglicans with a common concern for the moral condition of Wales co-operated under Thomas Gouge to establish some three hundred Welsh Trust schools in the decade before Gouge's death in 1681.

When the S.P.C.K.—with an important Welsh element among its early members—began to found its charity schools, it was conscious, as one of the Society's early historians stated, of the continuity of this new and more closely Anglican venture with Gouge's work undertaken "divers years ago in north and south Wales".[2] The ninety-six

[1] D. Williams, *A History of Modern Wales* (1950), p. 116.
[2] J. Stowe, ed. J. Strype, *Survey of London . . . from 1633 to the present time* (1720) v, 20.

charity schools, together with 600 others privately endowed, in Wales were more exclusively religious and less industrial in purpose than their English counterparts. When this activity declined in the early 1730s, they were superseded by the circulating schools organized by Griffith Jones. Acting on a similar method used by S.P.C.K. in the north of Scotland, and depending largely on supplies of Welsh Bibles and catechisms from S.P.C.K., Jones organized a system of itinerant schools teaching only reading and the catechism, "for these alone were thought necessary for salvation"[1] to young and old alike. A school would function for about three months in any one place in the parish church vestry or a hired room and the teachers then moved on elsewhere. In twenty-four years until Jones' death in 1761, 3495 classes were held and 158,237 pupils were registered at day-time sessions in addition to adults who came to evening classes. "He helped to make Wales a literate nation" and his schools "were the most important experiment in religious education in the eighteenth century not only in Wales but in Britain and all the British dominions".[2]

Twenty-five years later Thomas Charles, the organizer of Methodism in North Wales, tried to revive the circulating schools, but, following Raikes' success, he soon replaced them with Sunday schools. Catering for all ages and more specifically religious in aim than its English model, the medium of instruction in the Welsh Sunday school was almost exclusively the Welsh language. The importance of the Sunday school as the formative influence in religious education for both young and old, particularly in nonconformist Churches in Wales, until comparatively recent times can hardly be overestimated.

The British and Foreign School Society and the National Society were slow in making headway in Wales until the 1840s, but a National Society report in 1845 criticizing the inadequacy of Welsh educational provision led to the setting up of a Government Commission. The unsympathetic conclusion of the Commissioners that ignorance of English lay at the root of Welsh moral and educational deficiencies provoked strong reaction from Anglicans as well as Nonconformists. "The Treachery of the Blue Books," as the Report was styled, embittered the educational situation in Wales at the very time when the first training colleges were being founded, and for decades afterwards.

[1] D. Williams, op. cit., p. 146.
[2] D. Williams, op. cit., p. 147.

1870–1944

The rapidly growing sectarian bitterness, together with the development of the movement for the disestablishment of the Anglican Church in Wales after 1870, ensured that church schools and religious education remained at the very centre of political controversy for the next three decades and more. The network of national schools with the consequent outcry against "single-school areas", and the continued adherence of most Welsh nonconformists to the principle that religious education should be left to the Churches and their Sunday schools, ensured that a greater proportion of the School Boards in Wales than in England should be secular, especially in the South. (In 1899 out of 320 School Boards in Wales 62 provided no religious instruction.) Similarly, the "rigid undenominationalism"[1] of the county schools established under the Intermediate Education Act of 1889 caused them to become increasingly secular in ethos. Just after the turn of the century some 840 voluntary schools in Wales had an average total attendance of 96,000 while 821 Board schools had an attendance of 171,500, and proportions progressively favoured the latter. Nevertheless, the provisions of the Education Act of 1902 provoked the bitterest controversy in Wales. The "Welsh revolt" of local authorities who refused to administer the Act in so far as it affected the voluntary or "non-provided" schools continued to embarrass the Government until the end of 1905. Nonconformist opinion was, however, by no means uniform, and this fierce struggle over denominational schools in the old pattern was the final stand of "a tradition of political dissent that was weakening fast".[2] The disestablishment of the Church in Wales in 1920 took much of the residual heat out of the debate although the sense of nonconformist grievance and local bitterness remained.

Religious Education and the 1944 Education Act

The Archbishop of Wales was associated with the Archbishops of Canterbury and York in drawing up the "Five Points" in 1941, and in the conversations leading up to the 1944 Education Act Archbishop Temple was speaking for all three Anglican provinces. The Act of 1944 applied to Wales as well as to England, but under its

[1] A. G. Edwards, *Memories*, p. 178.
[2] K. O. Morgan, *Wales in British Politics* (University of Wales Press 1963), p. 198.

provisions the diocesan education committees in the disestablished Welsh province found themselves in a difficult and anomalous position. Nevertheless, the Church in Wales and the main Nonconformist Churches played their part with the Welsh Society of the Institute of Christian Education in drawing up a common Agreed Syllabus of Religious Instruction for the schools of Wales, which was adopted by almost all the local authorities in the Principality.

Developments since 1944

Most Welsh dioceses were unable to retain many of their schools as aided schools, and the policy of rural reorganization has progressively reduced the number of voluntary controlled schools. In the light of the experience and new educational insights of the first twelve years a revision of the Welsh Agreed Syllabus was begun in 1957 and completed five years later, with full co-operation from the Churches and from representatives of the teachers. Although it was compiled before the conclusions of recent research were available, this syllabus is an improvement on its predecessor and embodies the findings of recent educational thought. The Gittins Report, *Primary Education in Wales* (1967), recommended a relaxing of the statutory position relating to religious education. The report suggested that arrangements for corporate worship should be left to the individual head teacher and his staff. Many have regarded this as being too ingenuous to be satisfactory. The Report also called for a handbook of suggestions for teachers to help them use the Revised Welsh Syllabus to best advantage in the light of the latest research. A Joint Policy Committee of the Churches has been in existence for some years in Wales to ensure understanding and common action on problems of religious education.

In the preparation of this special note the Commission acknowledges the assistance of the Reverend Canon D. G. Childs, Principal of Trinity College of Education, Carmarthen, and a member of the Commission.

2

Theology and Education

The Theological Revolution, 1860–1960

52 The revolution in theological thought which has taken place over the past hundred years has profound implications for religious education in schools. In this chapter an attempt will be made to outline some of the main features of this revolution. The importance of such considerations cannot be exaggerated. Changes in the content of any subject are bound to influence the teaching of that subject, whether it be biology, or history, or theology. Too many people have assumed too hastily that the process of theological restatement is to be equated with the growth of disbelief.

53 For centuries theology occupied an honoured place among the disciplines of study. Indeed in the Middle Ages it had been acclaimed as the queen of the sciences, "the architectonic science", as Hastings Rashdall wrote, "whose office was to receive the results of all other sciences and combine them in organic whole".[1] But by the mid-nineteenth century such a conception was threatened both by the growing prestige of the natural sciences and by new methods of historical research. How was the study of theology to relate itself to the new knowledge which was claiming man's attention? The work of F. C. Baur (1792–1860) and the Tübingen school of theologians in Germany marked the start of a radically critical approach to the Bible and to Christian doctrine. In Britain, after some initial inclinations to welcome these new developments, the general reaction was defensive. It was then thought that the special status of theology must be upheld at all costs. Whether viewed from the standpoint of its primacy within the life of the Church or its intimate relation to the Bible, theology was regarded as a subject of unique

---

1 *Mediaeval Universities*, ed. F. M. Powicke and A. B. Emden (Oxford 1936) vol. iii, p. 440.

character and significance. When in 1868 the Honour School of Theology was duly established in Oxford, Dr E. B. Pusey could feel that the setting up of this separate honour school safeguarded the uniqueness of theology within the university system. "Theology", he declared, "is a subject quite apart . . . in it the question is not one of mere knowledge of facts, or of opinions, or of philosophies, or of philosophical theories, but of a revelation of God for the salvation of men."[1] The bearing of such a conception on religious education is obvious. The teaching of "scripture", or "religious knowledge" had to be given a place of primacy in the educational system. Whatever other subjects might be taught, nothing must prevent religious teaching from occupying the place which was due to it within a culture which called itself Christian. In the mid-nineteenth century, "religious education" practised against this background was usually conceived as the authoritarian transference of dogmatic certainties. This was without doubt one important reason for the early development of voluntary schools by religious bodies.

54 The theological developments in the second half of the nineteenth century can now be examined more closely. However differently the task may actually have been carried out, the task of the Christian theologian was essentially conceived (as it always had been) as the interpretation of the whole of reality.

In practice, two particular areas were important—the natural order and the Bible. Such a conception of the theological task can be illustrated by reference to the 19th Psalm, whose author rejoiced in the revelation of the divine glory which he found both in the regularities of the heavens above and in the regularities of the written law below. The works of God evident in the order of nature, the works of God declared on parchments and scrolls through the agency of faithful witnesses—these have been the "documents" which successive generations of theologians have examined, compared, pondered, and sought to interpret for the world of their own time.

55 How was this task being carried out in the mid-nineteenth century? So far as the interpretation of the Bible was concerned, most scholars were still prepared to accept this book as a direct revelation of divine truth. Its text was to be taken at its face value, as literally accurate, a factual description of events. The primary task of theolo-

[1] Quoted by I. T. Ramsey in an article in *Theology*, Dec. 1964.

gians was to master the original languages in which the text had been written; to give as exact a rendering as possible of the author's meaning and so to provide the foundation on which systems of moral and spiritual teaching could be built. The flood of new light which the historical investigations of the nineteenth century had thrown on the characteristics of the age in which the Bible took shape enabled scholars to interpret obscure words or allusions to events in ways which had never before been possible. The Bible was accepted as the vehicle of a direct divine revelation. It was the task of the interpreter to establish the true text, to translate it accurately, and to hand over to the theologians the materials for building Christian doctrine. Thus, if a doctrine could be supported by reference to Scripture that was in principle to establish its truth. Yet it had long been recognized that many of the biblical records needed reconciling and that many of its injunctions appeared irrelevant or unedifying. As a response to these difficulties the method of allegory had come to be widely employed. It was often the mark of a skilled interpreter that he could draw out moral and spiritual truths from seemingly unpromising biblical passages. There could be almost unlimited applications so long as there were no deviations from the integrity of the text in its given literalness.

56 Nevertheless, the serious questionings and criticisms which were already arising in France and Germany became increasingly heard in England. Sooner or later the obvious discrepancies between the biblical account of certain events in past history and that of other historical, literary, and archaeological sources had to be tackled. In 1860 seven authors published a collection of papers entitled *Essays and Reviews* in an attempt to encourage a spirit of free inquiry in religious matters.[1] As a protest against the liberalizing tone of the volume 11,000 of the clergy declared their belief in the inspiration of the Scriptures and the work was synodically condemned in 1864. Theology still rested on what was assumed to be unshaken biblical truth.

57 As late as 1891 Robert Gregory, Dean of St Paul's, could join with seven other deans in issuing a statement on the "Truth of the Holy Scriptures" in which they stated their belief that the Holy Scriptures "are inspired by the Holy Ghost: that they are what they

[1] The seven authors were Frederick Temple, Rowland Williams, Baden Powell, H. Bristow Wilson, Charles Goodwin, Mark Pattison, Benjamin Jowett, described by Dean Burgon as "septem contra Christum".

profess to be: that they mean what they say: and that they declare incontrovertibly the actual historical truth in all records both of past events and of the delivery of predictions to be thereafter fulfilled."[1]

58 So far as the interpretation of the universe was concerned, revolutionary ideas were being propagated by British scientists. From the start of the nineteenth century concepts of progress and evolution had been gaining ever wider acceptance, but it was not until the publication of Darwin's *On the Origin of Species* in 1859 that these concepts seemed to be confirmed as belonging to the very structure of the universe itself. Their implications for the accepted Christian beliefs about creation, providence, and the nature and destiny of man soon became evident. In his interpretation of the world, the Christian theologian had hitherto largely taken for granted the idea of a series of special creations reaching their culmination in the creation of man. Further, while recognizing the existence of evil and suffering in the world, he had assumed that these factors were under the control of a gracious providence through whose direction they were being transmuted into ultimate value within the divine purpose. But what if Darwin was right? Such concepts as the survival of the fittest and the never ceasing conflict within nature itself receive vivid expression in Tennyson's poem *In Memoriam*. "Nature red in tooth and claw" was problem enough, but still more disturbing was the idea that man shared a common biological inheritance with the apes. This seemed to impair his own distinctive nature, to question his origin and threaten his destiny. Most theological students of this period had been reared on William Paley's *View of the Evidences of Christianity*. As the years passed, scientific discoveries and Paley's arguments appeared increasingly irreconcilable.

59 Spencer Leeson provided a moving insight into the intellectual dilemmas of this period when, in the fourth of his 1944 Bampton Lectures on Christian Education, he reflected on his father's gradual loss of faith. His father was a distinguished doctor and public servant who had been brought up in a conventionally religious home in the mid-1850s.

One day a friend put *The Origin of Species* into his hands. This wrecked his faith; chiefly because it was not reconcilable with the biblical account of creation, and as the biblical revelation hung together and was all of one piece, if part of it fell out, the rest would fall out too. If Adam never existed,

[1] W. H. Hutton, *Robert Gregory* (Longmans 1912), p. 296. (It is significant that Dean Gregory was for many years Treasurer of the National Society.)

he did not sin; if he did not sin, man was not fallen; there was therefore
no need for Christ to come. If the Bible was wrong in science, how could
we be sure it was right in theology? We fail in justice and in sympathy if
we make light of the real agony of mind through which he and many of
his contemporaries passed.[1]

60 It is not easy to determine how widespread were the doubts and
uncertainties aroused in Christian circles by the scientific hypotheses
of the late nineteenth century, but it was obviously imperative that
Christian theologians should examine these matters seriously.
Essays and Reviews had made a tentative response, but it was
possible to regard this book as expressing only the questionable
views of an academic minority. It was the publication of *Lux Mundi*
in 1889 which marked in England the beginning of a new era in the
interpretation both of the Bible and of the universe in Christian
theology. This book was a series of essays by a group of theologians
holding responsible academic positions. The editor was Charles
Gore, the contributors included Scott Holland, Edward Talbot, and
Francis Paget. These were able and influential men and their views
had to be taken with great seriousness.

61 *Lux Mundi* was subtitled "A series of studies in the religion of the
Incarnation". This title, with its emphasis on incarnation, proved to
be an apt description of the way in which Anglican theology was to
develop in the next forty years. Churchmen sought to promote
forms of worship which would maintain continuity with the glories
of the Christian tradition and at the same time be truly incarnational
by being related to contemporary movements in art, music, and
society. This was seen as a task of major importance at the beginning
of the twentieth century, when emphasis was laid as much on worship
as on intellectual restatement.

62 If the incarnation was to be taken with full seriousness, what
were its consequences for the interpretation of the Bible and the
universe? If Jesus was a real historic person, how could he have been
all-knowing while he was living as a man of this world? Might Jesus
as a man have shared the limitations of his own contemporaries in
their knowledge of past history and future world developments?
The way was opened for a cautious reconsideration of certain difficult
biblical texts which seemed to contain discrepancies even in statements attributed to Jesus himself. Theologians sought to restate the
Christian belief in the Christ who was both human and divine.

[1] S. Leeson, *Christian Education* (Longmans 1947), pp. 97–8.

Charles Gore was one of many theologians who argued that Christ in his earthly life had "emptied himself" of the attributes of Deity, such as being all-knowing and all-powerful. But what was meant by these terms? Was Christ subject to limitations of a physical and intellectual kind and without flaw only in the perfection of his moral behaviour and filial obedience?

63 The nature of Jesus' humanity became a major subject of theological debate. Some of the greatest works of biblical interpretation around the turn of the century were governed by the conception of the Old Testament as recording the unique preparation for the incarnation and the New Testament as recording the actualization and extension of the incarnation. Through the experience of the people of God under the Old Covenant, the nature of ideal humanity had been partially, even progressively, realized. In the life and career of Jesus this ideal humanity gained full realization so far as limitations of space and time allowed. It was argued that through the ongoing experience of the Christian Church a universal humanity is coming into being, shaped according to the pattern revealed once for all in Jesus the Christ.

64 With the theology of the incarnation as their governing principle, biblical expositors were now able to use an approach to their particular documents and traditions comparable to that employed by secular historians in other fields. They did not abandon their conviction that the whole Bible bore witness to a unique series of divine operations within the history of mankind. At the same time, they recognized that the biblical writers were men exposed to the conditioning factors of their own environments and that to know as much as possible about social structures and changes within these environments was now an indispensable preparation for evaluating and interpreting the documents correctly.

65 In 1884 Charles Gore was appointed Principal of Pusey House, Oxford: in 1942 William Temple became Archbishop of Canterbury. The period which may be termed "From Gore to Temple" was characterized by immense industry along these general lines.[1] No effort was spared to date the documents, to discover the varying literary strands out of which they had been constructed, to expose parallels within other literatures and to gain as clear a picture of

[1] See A. M. Ramsey, *From Gore to Temple* (Longmans 1960).

the Israel of history, the Jesus of history, and the Church of history as was possible. Results were undoubtedly impressive. Many passages of Scripture gained altogether new illumination in the light of archaeological and documentary research. It began to appear that within the grand sweep of secular history a particular redemptive purpose could be shown forth in ever sharpening outline. The Bible and the records of the Christian tradition could be interpreted as revealing a single providential process by which man, who had fallen from his original ideal state, had been apprehended, disciplined, and prepared for the coming of the Christ, had further been instructed, challenged, and inspired by the life and teaching of the Son of God when he came among men, and finally had been progressively redeemed and sanctified by the Spirit of the Risen Lord continuing his work within the Church which he had created.

66 So far as the interpretation of the world was concerned, concepts such as "evolution" and "progress" enjoyed wide acceptance by the end of the nineteenth century. Theologians, as we have already noticed, were at first hesitant to accept any full evolutionary doctrine, though with the increasing interest in history the idea of development had in many ways proved congenial. By the time of *Lux Mundi*, however, a more positive attitude prevailed. J. R. Illingworth, one of the contributors, could affirm that the incarnation may be said to have introduced a new species into the world, a divine man transcending past humanity, as humanity transcended the rest of the animal creation, and communicating his vital energy to subsequent generations of men. The use of the word "transcendent" is significant, for the whole emphasis of the book was towards a more "immanent" approach—i.e. one which stressed the presence of God within his universe. In the eighteenth and nineteenth centuries Christian apologists had relied heavily on the appeal to miracles— dramatic interventions of a divine overlord within the regular operations of his universe. Such an emphasis became increasingly problematic when seen against a background of scientific determinism. It became imperative to bear witness to God's work in the regular and continuous as well as in the exceptional and extraordinary. Yet there was always the danger of falling into pantheism and so equating God with the universe.[1] Theologians continued to

---

[1] Hence J. R. Illingworth's realization that he must follow his book on *Divine Immanence* (1898) by *Divine Transcendence* (1911).

acknowledge the transcendence of God even when, in their interpretation of the world, the categories of immanence seemed often
more congenial and meaningful, and when the concept of miracle as
a divine intervention breaking scientific laws was increasingly problematic.

67 The fact was that they felt obliged to accept an evolutionary
theory of some kind but at the same time they could not allow that
the evolutionary process had been merely accidental and fortuitous.
Why could it not be affirmed that this was the particular method by
which God had created and sustained his universe? If the French
philosopher Bergson could speak in terms of an all pervasive life
force, why could not the Christian theologian use the time-honoured
language of the creative spirit of God? Spirit was thus conceived as
working through the hierarchy of matter, life, and mind, but as for
ever transcending this hierarchy and directing it towards its ultimate
fulfilment. Thus we find William Temple in 1924 claiming that there
are many grades of Reality and that the highest category known in
human experience—Spirit—is only explainable in terms of transcendent Purpose and Will which, operating through it upon all
lower grades, is directing the universe towards its true destiny.

68 There were many variations of this constructive attempt to
reinterpret Christian doctrine within the terms of emergent evolution. God was conceived as neither a remote machine operator nor
as an occasional dramatic intervenor. Rather was he seen as Majestic
Will working in all and through all to accomplish his purpose to bring
all things to their fulfilment within the pattern revealed in his in-
carnate Son. Evolution, development, progress, the life-force were
all notions apparently validated by historical investigations and
scientific discoveries. Theology could not neglect them. Its task was
to reconcile them with its own doctrinal and symbolic heritage, and
particularly with its claim for the uniqueness and finality of Christ.

69 The theological developments of the pre-1914 period impinged
comparatively slightly on religious education in schools. The educational methods and presuppositions of the time gave little scope
for open and free discussion of religious issues. In church schools
the religious teaching was still strictly based on Bible, Prayer Book,
and Catechism and was often delivered in firmly authoritarian fashion. In board schools the curriculum was non-denominational Bible
teaching with a strong historical and ethical emphasis.

70 That a significant change began to take place in western thought in the first quarter of the twentieth century seems now to be obvious. Yet precisely how and when and why this change took place appears almost impossible to determine. Quite clearly the 1914–1918 war was a world-shaking event, particularly in its effect upon Europe. The Christian¦ cause was not helped by the spectacle of Christian armies engaged in their mutual slaughter, using weapons blessed by Christian ministers. Many ordinary folk found it difficult to believe in a God whose purposes seemed to permit such prolonged and senseless carnage. "From the trenches, the prisoners' camp, the hospital and the home the question has been put in the stark brevity of mortal anguish: is there now a God?"; so declared a tract written in 1918.[1] It is not surprising that a book entitled *The Decline of the West* achieved prominence soon after the war ended. Yet even before the war, Post-Impressionist painting, Freudian psychology, Frazer's anthropology, and the works of Dostoievsky were exposing the darker sides of human nature—the fragmented, the subconscious, and the non-rational. It was by no means obvious that liberty and progress were forever assured and that evolution was inevitably upward. The theological climate in England showed little signs of change in the 1920s, though there had emerged a strong strand of liberal theology (represented by such as Hastings Rashdall, F. C. Burkitt, J. F. Bethune-Baker, and C. E. Raven), concerned to look at both the Bible and Christian doctrine through scientific eyes and with an approach and attitude characteristic of the physical and biological sciences.

71 Not until the 1930s did the impact of three important European theologians—Karl Barth, Emil Brunner, and Rudolf Bultmann—begin to be seriously felt. The rise of Nazi power; economic crises in America and Europe; post-war cynicism and disillusionment; the growing awareness of the importance of existentialism—all these factors combined to produce a concern for a basic gospel by which man might renew his courage and order his life. In Germany the Confessional Church, resisting the growth of Nazi power, desperately needed a rallying point. A society which seemed to be disintegrating needed a steadying power. Anxious individuals needed words of strong consolation.

[1] As quoted in A. Marwick, *Britain in the Century of Total War* (Bodley Head 1968), p. 112.

72 Karl Barth and his followers sought to recall their fellow Christians to the distinctiveness of the Christian message and to an approach to the Bible which seemed for many a "strange new world". Man could know God only in so far as God chose to reveal himself. God's sole revelation is in Jesus Christ and the Word of God is his one and only means of communication with man.

The Bible tells us not how we should talk with God but what he says to us; not how we find the way to him, but how he has sought and found the way to us; not the right relation in which we must place ourselves to him, but the covenant which he has made with all who are Abraham's spiritual children and which he has sealed once and for all in Jesus Christ. It is this which is within the Bible. The word of God is within the Bible.[1]

Man's duty is, therefore, that of obedience to the Word. Barth proclaimed this doctrine with passionate fervour and gained an immense following. Emil Brunner was one of Barth's foremost supporters, though he differed from Barth in allowing at least some place to philosophical reasoning and natural theology. Barth was emphatic that man could know God *only* through God's initiative in self-revelation. Brunner held that man could at least go part of the way through his own thought and reflection.

73 Rudolf Bultmann approached the problem differently. The Bible had itself come to birth amidst the clash of nations, and within the precarious existence of the people of God. But the religious experiences and insights contained in the Bible were expressed in the language and thought forms of first-century Palestine. Thus the gospel required to be demythologized—i.e. restated in language and concepts meaningful to twentieth-century Europeans. When this is done, the Gospel of life out of death, which was the message of the Bible, would speak with new clarity to man's death-in-life.

74 Both these viewpoints could well be summarized in an epigram which came out of the Oxford Conference on Life and Work in 1937. When men are saying, "We don't know what the world is coming to", the Christian replies in faith, "I know what has come to the world".[2]

75 All this meant that the emphasis on the interpretation of the

[1] Karl Barth, *The Word of God and the Word of Man* (Harper Torchbook 1957), p. 43 (but first published in a German edition in 1928).

[2] Recalled by Dr F. W. Dillistone who was in Oxford at the time of the conference.

Bible in terms of progressive revelation culminating in a unique
incarnation began, at first almost imperceptibly, to change. The task
of setting out the documents in their chronological order continued:
the attention to texts and correct translations and parallel cultures
and archaeological discoveries was still actively promoted. But there
began to be a renewed concern for the theology of the Bible, for its
witness to the critical acts of God in the history of his people and in
the redemption of mankind. What were the essential elements in the
Gospel proclaimed by the early Church? How far could these be
regarded as answering to age-long yearnings of the Jewish nation
and to the universal needs of mankind? Was perhaps the key to the
interpretation of the Bible not progress but redemption, not incarnation but atonement? Was the alienation of man, in all aspects of his
life in society, of such a kind that nothing less than a message of
total reconciliation could meet his situation?

76 Certainly in the 1930s and 1940s, through the threat and upheaval of war, this new emphasis gained increasing representation
amongst biblical interpreters. What after all had the writers of the
Old Testament been primarily concerned to do? Was it not to bear
witness to the distinctive acts and purposes of the living God,
however the nations might rage and whatever futile devices might
be imagined by the peoples? What again had been the central aim
of the New Testament writers? Was it not to gather together the
testimonies of those who had companied with Jesus of Nazareth or
had received the revelation of the risen Christ, and to transmit the
message of God's saving acts in and through him to men threatened
and anxious within a hostile world? Was it not then the major task
of the interpreter of Scripture to discern the striking parallels between the ancient world and his own time and to apply the message
of salvation, which had brought hope to men in a world which had
once lost its nerve, to the remarkably comparable situation of the
mid-twentieth century?

77 Looking back on the period since 1930 we gain the impression of
a Church under threat from outside and therefore compelled to
redefine its purpose and restructure its organization. Not only behind
the Iron Curtain was the Church an object of persecution, not only
in Nazi Germany had it been exploited. Elsewhere in the world it
was as often as not regarded as a mere irrelevance. Almost inevitably
there was a disposition to close the ranks, to rediscover the secret

of a common life within the Body of Christians. Attempts were made to draw the laity into a further participation in the common life through such experiments as the house church, the Parish and People movement, and by lay training. The ecumenical movement grew in strength and direction as the Churches co-operated more closely. Fresh attempts were made to translate the Bible into twentieth-century English. Schemes for pastoral reorganization were planned in an attempt to grapple with some of the more blatant absurdities in the Church's institutional structure. Confronted by individuals facing a new and unfamiliar world, often lonely and emotionally disturbed, the Church sought ways of reaffirming a gospel of healing and assurance by returning to the apostolic preaching of the New Testament and to the atmosphere of the close-knit apostolic fellowship. But although the Christian sought to derive strength by a return to the good news of God's activity in a critical period of history long ago, this very backward look tended to broaden the gulf between himself and the contemporary world, whose vision was increasingly focused on the shape of things to come.

78 The demands of a second world war had speeded up scientific investigations, with both tragic and constructive possibilities. A new era had been introduced first by the discovery of nuclear fission but more obviously by the exploding of an atomic bomb at Hiroshima. Nuclear power, computers, space travel have followed one another in quick succession and all have affected man's life in society. Even those who sought to retreat within Gothic walls and console themselves with the securities of a bygone age have found it increasingly difficult to do so. Whether they like it or not, Christians and non-Christians alike are caught up into the one communications system, the one economic system, the one world-system of power politics, the one technological system by which the world's resources are organized and employed.

79 Between 1935 and 1960 attempts were made by some Christian theologians to grapple with the theological problems posed by the developing world situation. New theological categories were sought which could more adequately interpret the structures and processes of the world as scientists described them. Far more attention was, however, given to the development of biblical theology. To deal creatively with the issues either of political organization or of scientific investigation seemed to demand specialized knowledge and experience such as few theologians possessed. The Church sought to establish its identity as distinct from the world; theology defined itself largely as the servant of the Church, nourishing its life by elucidating the treasures contained in Holy Scripture. The task of the Christian ministry was seen in terms partly of making better use of the existing structures of the Church and partly of drawing persons into the Church and away from a world which had become increasingly insensitive to the life of the Spirit.

80 This prevailing concern with biblical studies is reflected in the content of many agreed syllabuses in use during this period. The 1949 Cambridgeshire syllabus (used by many other education authorities) prescribed either the study of the Bible or teaching based on the Bible for all pupils aged 5 to 15. The only suggested variation was the study of great Christian personalities, past and present, e.g. St Francis and Albert Schweitzer. Only in the sixth form was the syllabus broadened to include a study of Christian doctrine. The 1947 Surrey syllabus was also used by many other education authorities. The 1963 revision of this syllabus still followed the pattern of biblical study laid down in 1947, although a foretaste of things to come can be seen in the section which deals with the religious education of pupils aged 14 to 16. Here, under the title "The Christian in the Modern World", opportunity is given for a series of lessons on the Christian attitude to work, wealth, power, human relationships, and contemporary science.

Contemporary Theology

81 It is clear that the period we have just surveyed saw new and significant developments in man's idea of the status and function of theology. When the period began theology, with important exceptions such as can be found in the work of Thomas Arnold and F. D. Maurice, was regarded as a subject apart, giving a once-for-all blueprint of the universe, controlling and often prescribing the conclusions in other subjects, while itself being unaffected by discoveries about the world. While it could pronounce on the world around, it remained itself determinative of all other knowledge, a purveyor of truths about nature and human nature into whose framework all other subjects must fit. At its simplest, this theological attitude was expressed in terms of views borrowed somewhat selectively from the Bible as it was then understood—views, for example, about the age of the earth. Even at its most complex, it was still expressed in views borrowed selectively from the Bible—views which were articulated, for example, in doctrines of human nature whose definitive notion was the fall of man and which considered that a sense of deep guilt was an essential preliminary to an acknowledgement of the Christian gospel. Nor should it be forgotten that such doctrines gained popular currency through many hymns which are still in use. To be a Christian was to have this particular theological attitude, and the function of religious education was to impart it.

82 But, as the period wore on, tensions began to develop between theology and man's knowledge of nature, human nature, and history. On the one hand there was the theological view that God controlled the events of nature—rain or sunshine. Natural calamities were viewed as punishment, national prosperity as reward. God was directly involved alike in man's prosperity as in his failure. Further, it was God who gave men the victory in battles between nations. Yet for some four hundred years men had been developing very different interpretations of nature, human nature, and history. It was not until about the middle of the nineteenth century, however, that it was grasped that these different interpretations could neither be ignored nor dismissed. The new ways of talking about the world, about human nature, about history, not only seemed never to need the concept of God, but often seemed to be in head-on collision with all the ways of talking traditional to the theologian. Even today the older ways of talking characterize many of our prayers and much of our popular thinking. With the passage of the years the tensions have increased rather than decreased.

83 What we have noticed, however, is that there were theologians who, during that period, risked unpopularity by taking a lively interest in the world, and by being prepared to take a different view altogether of the relationship between theology and other knowledge. Their significance was twofold. First, it was increasingly realized that the Bible was not something to be taken at its face value, still less to be treated uncritically or selectively. So there arose a desire not to segregate the Bible but to bring to its better understanding all the knowledge and learning that men could supply. There was thus a deep concern to see the books of the Bible in their historical, social, and cultural settings, and to bring to its texts the methods of textual analysis and study that had enabled headway

to be made in such secular disciplines as history and literature. Secondly, there also arose a determination to bring into a single focus the two visions of science and religion and in particular to effect some kind of coherence between the Bible and the natural and behavioural sciences. The world of nature was God's world and these theologians were concerned to forge links between our knowledge of the world and our knowledge of God, and the growing interest we have noticed in the incarnation gave special impetus to this concern.

84 It is against this background, set out in the previous paragraphs of this chapter, that we can best assess the contemporary situation. The theological interest in the world is now even more emphatic and widespread than it was earlier, while at the same time our knowledge of the world, of nature and human nature has increased with unbelievable speed over the last two or three decades. This means that the kind of questions which now haunt Christian believers are radical and far-reaching: Is our secular knowledge of the world, the knowledge supplied by the natural and behavioural sciences, self-sufficient? Is God active in the world at all? On what grounds and in what ways can we be convincingly articulate about the activity of God in the world around us? Such questions as these have also arisen in the context of recent empirical philosophy which has compelled us to ask what our belief in God and in Jesus Christ adds up to, and not least our belief in God's activity in the world.

85 It will be apparent from our survey of recent developments in theology that, like other disciplines, it undergoes fluctuations and is subject to lively controversy. The theologian like other thinkers is assailed by two temptations: that of clinging to an outmoded position when it ought to be given up, and that of embracing contemporary fashions when they ought to be resisted. The question which confronts the Christian today is: How does theology now speak of nature and human nature in the light of all that other disciplines tell us about the world and ourselves? This question arises particularly with regard to the natural and behavioural sciences. The question is all the more pressing, and the matter in many ways made the more difficult by the realization that everything must be grist to the theological mill. For there can be no part of the world with which God has no concern, whether as creator or redeemer. So there arises another version of the question, How can the old doctrines be

expressed in terms of contemporary knowledge? The new version
is: How can there arise around the knowledge of our own day a
theological understanding that can express coherently and with
integrity that "faith to live by" which in an earlier day was provided by earlier stylings of the Christian faith? To answer this
question the theologian must obviously know the vehicles of vision
of former days. In this sense the Christian basically relies, and always
will rely, on the specialist knowledge, the scholarship, and learning
that characterize theology as one academic discipline amongst
others. In reaching his basic theological understanding in this way
he will naturally and inevitably have to come to understand the
secular situations and contexts in which these earlier expressions
emerged. For they will always embody contextual evidence of their
origin. Theological assertions set in this way in their appropriate contexts will then be brought alongside the problems that emerge in
our own day with the hope that around the new pattern of secular
knowledge surrounding the problem there may be rediscovered the
vision and the insight that earlier expressions were meant to preserve.

86 It is plain even from this outline that the task facing theology is
very complex. Christian education as distinct from specialist theological scholarship will be more concerned at present to train people
in an approach, in a "mood and a method", than to impart theological information or even to transmit particular developments in
theological studies. This approach is one which, taking whatever
theological scholarship supplies by way of biblical and doctrinal
understanding, then endeavours to develop links between distinctively theological assertions on the one hand and contemporary
understandings of the world on the other. To say all this is only to
recognize that the prospect facing theology is as novel and far-
reaching as it is difficult. It is a task appropriate to another Renaissance. It has sometimes been thought to call for a new Reformation.
But in the broadest of terms it certainly implies that Christian education takes place in a theological context radically different from that in
which Christian education took place in the period we surveyed in
the first part of this chapter.

87 This broad concept of the task which confronts the Christian
thinker today means that he is inevitably interested in and concerned
with various factors in our contemporary secular world. But this

is not to imply that the Christian thinker accepts uncritically all that the secular world offers him, still less that he restricts himself to this world and this world's knowledge. His aim is to set "the things which are seen" in the context of "the things which are not seen", and there are nowadays, as there always have been, some Christian thinkers who see it as their duty, in pointing to the transcendent dimension, to protest against the commonly accepted values of secular society. This protest has been traditionally exemplified in the Christian tradition by the existence of the religious orders. In any event, the Christian thinker sees this world and this world's knowledge as set within the perspectives of eternity. Thus he will always have both a basis for appreciating this world and also a stimulus for reforming it.

88 (*a*) It is with this approach that the theologian must obviously be aware of and, as far as possible, familiarize himself with the developments that take place in the emergence of a predominantly urban society, a society which is dominated by the achievements and assumptions of science and technology. He will be alive to the possibility that such phenomena as space travel, lunar exploration, and transplant surgery are all developments which may have important, and recognizable benefits. Many new developments in human existence are now possible. There can, in principle, be vast improvements in health and in conditions of work and living. It is our argument that the theologian will recognize that these developments are not without their theological significance and will seek to discover it. Many, for example Harvey Cox,[1] have faced these developments and suggested new theological interpretations. Again, some[2] have noted that the rapid developments in science and technology have presented us with a question than which none could have greater or more far-reaching importance—the very possibility of there being a future to the human race. In this connection we see the possibility of a new significance in, and new understandings of, such concepts as eternal life or the futility of an earthly Utopia.

89 (*b*) Next, the theologian is very conscious of the philosophical revolution which has occurred in Britian over the last thirty years. For many Christians this revolution has been profoundly disturbing. They look back to the day of the absolute idealists when it could

[1] *The Secular City* (S.C.M. 1965; Penguin 1969).
[2] E.g. Hugh Montefiore, *The Question Mark* (Collins 1969).

3

be said, for example, as by the Oxford philosopher William Wallace in a book still being published in 1931, that "religion and philosophy coincide". Or they may recall William Temple's remark in 1924 "that, philosophically, everything was ready for theism and that the construction of a Christocentric metaphysic was now a real possibility".[1] But then there came the logical positivists, and in particular A. J. Ayer's *Language, Truth and Logic* (1935). According to Ayer's Verification Principle a proposition had meaning if, and only if, it could be verified by sense experience or (a weaker form) sense experience was relevant to it. In its stronger form the Principle placed a veto on metaphysics and denied any meaning to theological assertions in so far as they claimed to talk of what was not restricted to sense experience. In its weaker form, it challenged the Christian to give empirical criteria by which his assertions could be checked. In this way the empirical concerns of contemporary philosophy have raised for the Christian believer the question of what kind of situation it is in which his language is grounded.

More generally, recent empiricism has encouraged the secularization of philosophy. Further, while the philosophical interest in language has greatly broadened and mellowed since the restrictive days of the logical positivists' veto, the Christian believer has still to state a case for, and to explicate, the logic of the language he uses. In brief, over a span of about fifty years philosophy in Great Britain has ceased to be a natural ally of the Christian faith and now seems to many Christians to have become an enemy. But it would be rash to suppose, and ill-judged to conclude, that this is the whole story.[2] For on the other side it needs to be said that the very need to explicate the logic of religious language has encouraged some Christian philosophers to search for and to discover logical parallels to religious language in the language of other areas of human discourse and so lead to new ideas of the reasonableness of Christian belief. For example, it appears that the element of self-involvement and commitment, characteristic of religious assertions, is a far more

---

[1] This view he later modified, though not under philosophical pressure. By 1937 he had begun to have "doubts as to the possibility of a Christocentric metaphysic and suggested the necessity of moving in the direction of a theology of redemption which admits that much in the world is irrational and unintelligible." And in 1939 he expressed his conviction "of the impossibility of a Christian metaphysic which embraces all experience in a coherent and comprehensive scheme". The quotations are from Owen C. Thomas, *William Temple's Philosophy of Religion* (S.P.C.K. 1961), p. 12.

[2] I. T. Ramsey, *Religious Studies*, vol. I, no. 1.

ubiquitous feature of language than was once supposed. Further when attention has been focused on the situation in which religious language is grounded, there has been a significant similarity between the different phrases used to speak of it. The characteristic feature of these situations has been described in terms, for example, of "depth", "a new dimension", "disclosure", "vision", phrases which emphasize that such a situation has a basis in sense-experience while also going beyond it.

90 (*c*) In his concern to appreciate contemporary understandings of the world around him, the theologian is also conscious of the development of the psychological sciences. He does, of course, recognize that many psychologists, especially the post-Freudians, are, on the whole, unsympathetic to religious claims, and that a good many of the recent developments along statistical and experimental lines appear to do little justice to the distinctive features of human personality. On the other hand, the theologian is well aware that over this whole field is to be found a new range of insights into man's nature and abilities, and that here are vast areas deserving joint inquiries by psychology and theology alike.

91 (*d*) The theologian also takes note of important developments in sociology, and the influence in particular of Durkheim may be noted. Religion is now studied as a social phenomenon, and there can be no doubt that such studies are mutually enlightening as far as they go. For better or worse, theological beliefs do affect social development and at the same time social structures and social dynamics influence the formulation of theology. Theology will therefore wisely take note of the kind of questions which sociologists are asking and benefit from many sociological conclusions.[1] But beyond this the picture becomes confused. On the one hand, the possibility is aired of the Church as a community needing no more than a secularist understanding, being a social phenomenon somewhat akin to an adult version of a uniformed youth movement. On such a view, the Church would consist of a number of local groups, having some central organization, but for the most part continuing their activities through community singing and morally improving teaching focused

[1] Amongst recent pioneer volumes in this frontier area may be mentioned:
F. Boulard, *Introduction to Religious Sociology* (1954, translated and introduced by M. J. Jackson 1960)
E. R. Wickham, *Church and People in an Industrial City* (Lutterworth 1957)
P. Berger, *The Social Reality of Religion* (Faber 1969).

around an ideal person figure. Such groups, it will be conceded, meet the ritual needs of society through emotionally satisfying ceremonies such as baptism, marriage, burial services, and so on, and the clergy are regarded at best as counsellors and social workers, but no more. We need not deny the truth and importance of such sociological understandings: the controversial question is whether they go far enough. On the other hand, the question can be raised, as by David Martin in his book *A Sociology of English Religion*,[1] as to how far sociology can be value-free, independent of evaluative premises and independent of all presuppositions about man and society. This is a question under debate among many sociologists. In this context, both theology and sociology can share frontier concerns and raise fundamental questions about the presuppositions of human life. Theology may well be able to help itself and also to help the development of sociology by clarifying, through mutual discussion, the place of presuppositions in an intellectual discipline.

92 (*e*) The theologian is also aware of continuing tensions between science and religion, though they have now focused in a different area, the concept of man. Changes both in the Christian's attitude to the Bible and in the scientific attitude to the evolutionary hypothesis, as well as different concepts of scientific method and truth, have led to a greater coherence between science and religion in those fields of physics and biology which placed such strains on the minds and consciences of our nineteenth-century forefathers. But there is at present apparent conflict and serious tension between the scientific and theological understandings of man, not least those scientific understandings which arise out of the work of Francis Crick and James Watson around the D.N.A. molecule, the genetic code, and around developments in molecular biology generally, as well as in the field of endocrinology, with its study of the relations between glandular secretions and human behaviour. The attention of the reader is called to Dr Paul Kent's paper, "The Changing Scene since 1950" (Appendix C).

93 (*f*) Another factor in the contemporary scene with which the theologian needs to reckon is the development of a global awareness due to improved methods of travel and communication. He must recognize that large parts of two continents are now dominated by

[1] S.C.M. 1967.

political systems based on apparently atheistic presuppositions—the U.S.S.R. and China. But even more pertinently he must recognize the fact of the existence of other world religions, sincerely held by reasonable men. That is to say, as he is required to understand, and respond to, the scientific account of the universe, so equally he is required theologically to understand, and respond to, a religious account of the universe as it is particularized in different religions. There have traditionally been two very different Christian attitudes to other religions. For some, as for Tertullian (*c.* 160–220 A.D.) and the Western tradition generally, the exclusiveness of Christianity has often been bought at the cost of denying any significance to other religions. For others, for example Clement of Alexandria (*c.* 150–215 A.D.) and the Eastern tradition, Christianity has been seen as having an inclusive uniqueness which need not deny a significance to other religions, though there has always been the danger that in an extreme form this point of view might suppose that there can be distilled from all religions some common essence which characterizes each of them. These two opposing attitudes have been represented in this century by Hendrik Kraemer[1] and William Hocking[2] respectively. But others, like Max Warren and Ninian Smart, have much more recently, with characteristically different approaches, put forward a view of other religions which neither suggests a segregation which denies significance to all other religions besides Christianity, nor asserts a common essence which takes the distinctiveness from them all. There has thus been a renewed interest in the idea of an inclusive uniqueness.[3] This notion seeks to provide a coherent link between Christian claims for kinship with other religions while preserving that distinctiveness about Christ and the gospel without which there could be no specifically Christian belief. This is a point to which we return later in the chapter.

94 (*g*) The theologian will also recognize that in Britain, and not only in Britain, there is extensive self-criticism of the Church, both of its doctrinal formulation and of its structures. Behind the criticisms of many people, not all of them young, that the Church displays an altogether effete and inflexible character, is something akin to a

[1] *The Christian Message in a Non-Christian World* (Edinburgh House Press 1938).
[2] *Living Religions and a World Faith* (Allen & Unwin 1940).
[3] Cf. the Lambeth Report, 1968.

much more perceptive protest against any harsh, oppressive, or irrelevant authoritarianism. There is a growing recognition that to win anyone's genuine allegiance it is necessary to provide something authoritative in the sense that it wins from people a free response and a spontaneous acknowledgment. This is as true of religious knowledge as of ecclesiastical structures.

95 As the theologian acquaints himself with these various features of contemporary society, its major cultural division becomes the more evident. On the one hand, there remains a broadly Christian outlook which expresses itself in different ways. We shall presently mention some of these. On the other hand, there has been the very significant emergence of a secular humanism which, while also embracing different viewpoints, stands broadly for those whose interpretations of nature, human nature, the world, and history claim to be wholly scientific and empirical. Nor is this merely an intellectual standpoint. Julian Huxley, in *The Humanist Frame*,[1] argues that it may be regarded as a substitute religion. In this setting the work of the British Humanist Association can be seen as meeting many needs beyond those of intellectual satisfaction. Though there are, as we have just granted, differences among humanists themselves, there are certainly some who seek in the context of humanism to have emotionally satisfying ceremonies at times of human crises, e.g. secularist funerals. As is evident from such a book as H. J. Blackham's *Objections to Humanism*[2] this position has an important appeal to many sensitive and critical people and has no little following among intellectuals and academics. Common to all the positions held in this group is the view expounded by such scientists as Julian Huxley and C. H. Waddington and by such anthropologists as Edmund Leach that man is now in a position to control and direct his own future and evolution and to experiment with socially beneficial patterns of living.

96 In responding to such features of the contemporary situation as we have surveyed, theologians have taken up varying positions, some of which will now be mentioned. It must be emphasized that the account which follows concentrates primarily upon the British scene and that the pace of these developments might well be different elsewhere in Europe and in North America.

[1] Allen & Unwin 1961.
[2] Constable 1963.

97 There are some who have been so influenced by secular knowledge that, even though they have set their expositions in some kind of a Christian frame, it is not at all clear whether they are, or would wish to be thought of as being, believers in God in anything like a traditional sense. This is broadly the position of the "Death of God" theologians, such as can be found in books like Thomas Altizer's *The Gospel of Christian Atheism*, William Hamilton's *The New Essence of Christianity*, or *Radical Theology and the Death of God* by Altizer and Hamilton jointly, or Paul van Buren's *The Secular Meaning of the Gospel*. The question is whether their use of terms like God or Jesus Christ differs from the way in which we might refer picturesquely to the gods of Greek mythology. To put the matter in another way, this theological response challenges believers to elucidate their concept of God and Christians in particular to show the kind of situation in which their belief is grounded.

98 There are other theologians who are equally impressed by the need to start with the secular world and to examine the kind of situation in which Christian discourse may be grounded, but, in what appears to be a rather more constructive way, they are concerned to make clear the roots of the Christian religion and to define some of its basic and essential themes. Some try to show how a more systematic theology might be developed from a particular grounding in a significant situation. This kind of response might be exemplified by such books as John Robinson's *Honest to God* and *Exploration into God* and R. Gregor Smith's *The New Man* and *Secular Christianity*. A more systematic discussion might be found in such books as Paul Tillich's *Systematic Theology* and *Ultimate Concern* and John Macquarrie's *Principles of Christian Theology* and *God-Talk*. It is convenient also to mention here those who are distinguishable from more extreme radical theologians and to some extent critical of them, whose training has been in the British empiricist tradition, and who have been positively influenced by it, but who have been much concerned to specify the empirical conditions which must be satisfied— whether logical or material— if theological statements are to be claimed as knowledge. Ian Ramsey's *Religious Language* and *Christian Discourse*, John Hick's *Faith and Knowledge*, Hugh Parry Owen's *Christian Knowledge of God*, and Donald McKinnon's *Borderlands of Theology*, together with related essays in *Prospect for Theology*, edited by F. G. Healey, may be cited as instances of this concern. In differing ways, but all influenced by a contemporary empirical approach, they attempt to elucidate the meaning of the perennial themes of Christian belief.

99 Besides these varied theological responses there are also religious thinkers who would call themselves "process" theologians. Amongst representatives of this approach we note Charles Hartshorne's *The Divine Relativity*, John Cobb's *A Christian Natural Theology*, Norman Pittenger's *The Christian Situation Today*, and Schubert Ogden's *The Reality of God and Other Essays*. These theologians are concerned to search for a new synthesis of knowledge. Influenced by A. N. Whitehead they seek a world view that takes *process* as its key concept and stresses *becoming* rather than being. In this way they avoid what they consider to be some of the metaphysical difficulties of the past, and here they are one with many empirical philosophers. They would see it as an additional merit that, by taking the concept of process as fundamental, they have a world view which readily accepts other concepts such as evolution and human development.

100 At this point reference should also be made to Teilhard de Chardin. While, as we have seen, there are in some areas continuing tensions between science and religion, Teilhard de Chardin, for example in *The Phenomenon of Man*, represents an attempt to engage in large-scale thinking and to produce an overall synthesis in the realms of evolutionary science and religion. Though he has been criticized for moving too easily between logically diverse areas and, in relation to some of his concepts, for being technical without being precise, he points us to a broad perspective on the universe in a way which has earned for him the title of "scientist and seer".[1]

101 We must also note the contribution made by Eric Mascall in his books *He Who Is* and *Existence and Analogy* and the late Austin Farrer in *Finite and Infinite*. These theologians are concerned to take the kind of philosophical understanding of God and the universe which is presented by St Thomas Aquinas and to set it in the context of an intuition, or insight. For this reason they are normally thought of as being existentialist in their approach to St Thomas, rather than

---

[1] See the book by C. E. Raven on Teilhard de Chardin (Collins 1962) which has this as its subtitle.

as taking a more traditional approach which would depend on a highly stylized metaphysical context.

102 A different response to the contemporary scene is to be found in a book such as Thomas Torrance's *Theological Science*, which, with a background of extensive learning, endeavours to provide a contemporary restatement of Christian theology in the Protestant Reformed tradition. On the other hand, Francis Schaeffer's *Escape from Reason* attempts a critique of modern culture in the light of a sixteenth-century view of the authority and function of Holy Scripture.

103 Finally, mention may be made of those who, in the light of recent discussions, would remind Christians of a theme that has belonged to Christian theology from the start and indeed goes back to the Old Testament itself: an awareness that all our talk about God will inevitably be inadequate, that when we have done our best we shall never have produced an entirely satisfactory understanding of God and the world. This position, which may be called Christian agnosticism, is expressed, for example, in Nathaniel Micklem's *A Religion for Agnostics* and Leslie Weatherhead's *The Christian Agnostic*.

104 If there is any common feature between these diverse positions, it would seem to lie in a determination to contend with the practical and intellectual challenge of contemporary secularization and to relate this to developments within theology itself. There is also the desire to examine and to clarify the situation in which religious language is grounded and a desire to talk more reliably of what is at the heart of all religious belief. These are, broadly speaking, some of the main characteristics of the contemporary theological quest.

105 A particular focusing of contemporary problems has occurred around the person of Christ himself. John Robinson, for example, concluded *Honest to God* with a quotation from Herbert Butterfield: "Hold to Christ and for the rest be totally uncommitted."[1] For many this seemed to be a clear and attractive solution and a way out of the present turmoils. But who is the Christ to whom Christians are to hold? How far in "holding to Christ" can they sit loose to other theological claims that would traditionally have been considered to originate from this Christ-commitment? To examine these

[1] *Honest to God*, p. 140.

3*

questions is to come face to face with those New Testament theologians standing in the tradition of Bultmann, who would question how much can be known of Christ and his teaching, and who make no attempt to minimize the complexity of the inquiry. Before we can "hold to Christ" the complex question posed by Leonard Hodgson needs to be faced: "What must the truth have been if it appeared like this to men who thought and spoke like that?"[1] We then add: and how do we articulate it today?

106 It has already been made clear that a condition of grappling with the contemporary intellectual challenge to belief, a task in which the theologians named above have been variously engaged, is that there should be an ongoing concern with what might be called domestic tasks within theology itself. In other words, an adequate response to the contemporary intellectual challenge demands a greater and not a less acquaintance with the body of theological learning and scholarship which has evolved over the centuries. In this way those specific academic disciplines of biblical studies, ecclesiastical history, biblical, historical, and systematic theology, philosophy of religion, Christian doctrine, Christian ethics, and the comparative study of religions remain essential to the kind of task we have been discussing above.

107 At the same time, our own particular concern with religious education in schools will not for the most part be with these disciplines, as such. There will obviously be occasions in secondary schools when, as part of religious education, a kind of theology can be taught, which is related to these academic disciplines as the science and history and English taught in schools are related to those same subjects studied at universities. But religious education in a wider sense is concerned with aiding pupils towards discovering a "faith to live by" and with helping them to think out an overall attitude to the world and its problems. It will therefore be the more closely related to the task we have been describing above, and will be concerned with relating religious knowledge to other understandings of the world so as to constitute something of an overall view. It was a weakness of the minority report of the Plowden Committee that it did not distinguish between these two concepts of, and ingredients in, the teaching element in religious education. Meanwhile, the difficulties of the present position are evident enough. But they are

[1] *For Faith and Freedom* (S.C.M. edn 1968), p. 88.

only matched by the educational worth, as well as the far-reaching value and importance, of what can be properly called religious education.

108 Nowhere are the complexities and difficulties more evident than in the field of Christian ethics. Christians complain of the confusion and diversity of view on fundamental questions about morality. There remains an expectation that somehow Christian ethics will be "derived from" Christian theology in some straightforward fashion and that for Christian morality all we need do is to "apply" Christian doctrines. But, as will be evident, this attitude to Christian ethics is a legacy from that view of theology which is almost a century out of date. Christian ethics is an area in which, for significant assertions to be made, there must be that marriage between theology and the world which we have been discussing above. The confusion and diversity that at present exists in this field is but an indication of the difficulties there are in making an appraisal of traditional theology on the one hand, an assessment of the empirical situation on the other, and then effecting a genuine marriage leading to a creative decision. Thus understood, Christian ethics will be the name given to a method and an approach rather than primarily to a certain group of conclusions. But this is not to deny that there remain certain basic rules or principles expressive of Christian commitment, though not exclusively so, and essential to any ordered society. The theologian increasingly finds himself grappling with commonly acknowledged contemporary problems in company with others who contribute to these problems all that their professional knowledge and expertise can bring. Working with representatives of such disciplines as psychiatry, law, medicine, and social studies and with such professionally trained people as doctors, lawyers, teachers, and social workers, the theologian will bring to the discussion his own theological expertise. For he believes that, if only he will grapple genuinely and with integrity with the problems common to those whose concern he shares, there will emerge from the common discussion a creative insight which he, at any rate, may wish to interpret as the inspiration of God, and from which may well be born new concepts for the better understanding and articulation of his theology.

109 This picture of the contemporary concerns of theology, intricately varied and complex though it is, does not of course deny but rather implies that in the Christian faith there is something "given", something to be taken as a base, which all these different views variously articulate. At the same time we recognize that in their desire to be creative by abandoning some traditional images, or to open up discussion by pointing to the limitations of any language which seeks to express the mystery and infinitude of God, and in their desire to show integrity in their handling of current biblical scholarship, even Christian writers have sometimes given the impression that Christian language talks about nothing in particular. It is therefore important to recall that the different strands of Christian doctrine and differing Christian moral judgements arise around, are ultimately derived from, and point back to God's activity in Christ, what can be spoken of as "the grace of the Lord Jesus Christ, the love of God, and the fellowship of the Holy Spirit". It is to this givenness about the Christian faith which lies behind all its articulation that we must point if we would respond on the one hand to the critic who asserts that the multiple strands of theology talk about nothing, and on the other hand to the teacher who is baffled and even dispirited by the bewilderingly intricate variety which the theological scene presents to him.

Implications for Religious Education

110 If the preceding sections have given us a broad outline of the present preoccupations of Christian theology, what are the implications for a theory and practice of education? What, in this sense, is the "theology of education" which lies behind our report? What is quite clear, of course, is that the institutional direction of a century ago has disappeared with the passing of the theological outlook on which it was based. A century ago university education and secondary education were, for the most part, carried on in institutions with strong ecclesiastical connections, all held together by a fairly coherent theology. The Church of England, the universities of Oxford, Cambridge, and Durham, King's College London, the public schools, and many of the older grammar schools had a broad homogeneity about them. Before the passing of the 1870 Act, elementary education was available in schools almost all of which were founded and maintained by the Churches. It would be naive and false to assert that educational thought was always placed within a coherent theological context and to suppose that the homogeneity of structure was supported by an homogeneity of opinion. But it would be safe enough to say that the status and function of theology as a unique subject among all others, the broad institutional homogeneity of church and school, and the strong political involvement of the Church in education were mutually supporting and powerful in their result.

111 That the situation today is radically different, whether in theology or social structure, is so obvious as scarcely to need emphasis. Education is now carried on in institutions for the most part provided, controlled, and administered by public authorities. Further, the maintained system of education in England and Wales is based on a jealously guarded principle of the distribution of power. Administration is shared jointly between the Department of Education and Science and numerous local education authorities. Policy and curricula are not dictated from some central bureau, but are rather the outcome of a continuing dialogue between those who are partners to a system of multiple influence. In this exercise all may have their say, and the theologian is as free as anyone else to take his place. But he shares a place with the psychologist, economist, sociologist, historian, politician, parent, teacher, educationist, journalist, and others; the theologian will certainly be granted no place of privilege. Unlike a century ago, the theologian cannot expect to construct an educational system whose purpose it is to inculcate certain doctrines, nor would he wish to. This should not be seen as only a political and social change. As we have tried to show,[1] behind this lies a changing attitude to theology and its relation with other areas of human knowledge. Against that general background, what then do we suggest are the implications for religious education of these developments in the theological scene?

(1) *The exploratory nature of Religious Education:*
Religious Education commended for its educational significance

112 It is quite impossible in Christian thought for theology to be a purely speculative discipline; for, in the person of Christ, God and the world meet in a perceptible event, amenable to historical study. In the long run, therefore, Christianity is committed to the recognition of what actually is the case. Research into antiquity, discoveries in natural science, and the advances of reasoned thought are all relevant to a faith which claims not merely to contain true

[1] Paras. 84–109.

statements but to be the truth. The Christian unequivocally accepts the necessity of reasoning, even if he takes the liberty of doubting its ultimate sufficiency. His attitude to education as a whole is a thoroughly positive one.

113 What is the case, then, with *religious* education? The answer does not require prolonged or refined argument. He already accepts that what may be demonstrated rationally to be the case is of relevance to the structure of his belief. His proposals for religious education will therefore emphasize the exploratory aspects of a discipline whose task of interpretation is never complete nor rounded off in a neat system. It must be stressed that this is a consequence of the Christian's particular attitude to the world, and may not necessarily characterize that of any other faith. The argument for religious education depends heavily upon the fact that it can be fashioned upon the open basis of the Christian's contemporary theological commitments. Whether such an exploratory approach can be advanced upon the basis of, for example, contemporary Islamic theology would be open to question.

114 Religious education seeks to make pupils familiar with the framework of Christian concepts and beliefs, and it will best do this by exploring the relationship between the distinctive vocabularies of faith and those of many modern disciplines which relate to man and his environment. This gives religious education a basis on which it can operate and material from which it can draw. As an act of exploration it closely resembles the exploratory nature of much educational activity. It seeks neither to impose nor to indoctrinate. Indeed, in the exploration of beliefs, it must endeavour to provide for the possibility of a built-in self-criticism so as to anticipate from the start the possibility of reasoned choice. But reasoned choice presupposes some substantial grounding in the knowledge on which decision may be based.

115 Let it be granted that there are those who assert that such phrases as "a sense of the infinite" are empty, that religious claims are bogus, and that all religious people, not only Christians, are utterly mistaken and self-deluded. But there would plainly at present be no case for developing a national educational policy for the whole country on this assumption. Religious education as we conceive it is not the inculcation of a system of beliefs which pupils are required to accept. The question is no longer one of handing out doctrinaire blueprints. It is one of commending religious education as something of educational value to those who are concerned to secure for the pupil the maximum enrichment of his or her personality. In other words, religious education has a place in the educational scene on educational grounds, where education is understood as the enriching of a pupil's experience, the opening up of a pupil to all the influences which have coloured his or her environment, and all this sensitively and critically with an endeavour to be as comprehensive and wide-ranging as possible.

116 It is plainly impossible for any theologian or educationist to suppose that all religious education in county schools in England and Wales at the present time can be placed within one specific Christian theological system, such as the closely knit system of religious teaching once sponsored by the Jesuits on the basis of medieval Catholic theology. Nor can the theologian insist on one particular approach to the Bible or one system of biblical interpretation. It is assumed that religious education will include a wide spectrum of Christian belief, and there will be some attempt at understanding the positions of different Christian and quasi-Christian groups in the serious and sympathetic way in which they are studied in Horton Davies's *Christian Deviations: The Challenge of the Sects*.[1] On all these issues a particular teacher can and must make clear the different possibilities, without having that lack of integrity which prevents him from commending his own option. But, throughout, the teaching given in religious education must be based on sound scholarship, intellectual integrity, and a concern for the enrichment of experience. This is not to deny that there may be some schools to which parents send their children with the express desire that, in the context of an exploratory approach of an educational character, they should be given a fuller understanding of, for instance, the particular tenets of the Jewish faith or the ingredients of the Anglican tradition. Further, it would be educationally desirable— we shall argue the general point below—that such an understanding of religion should be associated with some awareness of the worship in which particular religious beliefs and attitudes find their fulfilment, so that in this case one could picture home and school and synagogue or church as forming a compact unity. Nothing that we

[1] Second revised edn (S.C.M. 1965).

have said denies the value of this rather more specific purpose within the whole area of religious education. For, from first to last, it will display scholarship, integrity, and a concern for the enrichment of experience, and while it develops religious education in relation to particular presuppositions and attitudes it will take care to ensure that there is the possibility of built-in self-criticism. This possibility of setting religious education in the widest possible background of school, home, and church, where religious education is set in the context of specific presuppositions and attitudes, and where commitment is married to openness, provides the basis of a case for the voluntary aided school.

(2) *The Significance of Worship*

117 It is plain from what we have said that religious education would be inadequate and unbalanced if it separated itself from worship and moral conduct. The question of morality we take up later. For the moment our point is that some experience of worship is essential on educational grounds if justice is to be done to the content of religious education. This is a point which can be generally recognized, all controversy and special pleading apart. Professor Ninian Smart, discussing the matter in *Reasons and Faiths*, remarks that it is by an understanding of situations in which a sentence might be used that we come to appreciate the "logical style". He continues:

These remarks apply with even greater force than usual to the investigation of spiritual language. There is little hope indeed, for example, of comprehending the point of many utterances by mystics unless we pay attention to the context of behaviour and experience of those who make utterances. Again, to gain an inkling of the nature of the concept of God it is surely requisite to look to the worshipping activities that surround, so to speak, belief in the divine. So it would be distressingly mistaken to regard the propositions of a doctrinal scheme in unnatural loneliness; their spirit becomes manifest only in the company of the peripheral utterances and activities.[1]

Thus it is that religious education would be inadequate, if it does not also have some occasions on which a pattern of rite and ceremony can be experienced. For some this may be a curious and baffling occasion; for others it may cohere with what they already participate in outside the school; for yet others it may be their first occasion of genuine worship. But for all it should lead to a broadening of knowledge and experience. Here is worship legitimately

[1] *Reasons and Faiths*, p. 14.

demanded on educational grounds. While the analogies are not wholly exact, religious education without worship is like geography without field studies, the learning of a language without trips abroad, science without its experiments, the theory of music without singing or playing an instrument, learning to swim without entering the water, and studying literature without reading books.

(3) *The Study of Other Religions*

118 Our argument in ch. 4 will be that, on educational grounds, religious education must set out from some base and that in the schools of England and Wales that base will normally be Christianity. We shall also argue that, where appropriate, opportunities should be provided for the study of other religions.

119 But the question then arises: what in fact is the attitude of the Christian faith to other religions, and can that attitude form the basis for consideration being given to them in religious education at some appropriate stage? For it would be from every point of view undesirable if other religions were introduced only to show how wrong and odd they were in comparison with Christianity. On the face of it the Christian faith makes rather narrow and exclusive claims for itself. It states that God is known sufficiently and finally through his self-revelation in Christ. It has been frequently taught on this basis, that God is known *solely* in Christ; and that all other religions are at the level of heathendom.

> The heathen in his blindness
> Bows down to wood and stone.
>
> Can we, whose souls are lighted
> With wisdom from on high,
> Can we to men benighted
> The lamp of life deny?[1]

This is neither a reliable account of the empirical facts, a sound statement of Christian teaching, nor an adequate understanding of other religions.

120 It would clearly be a mistake to regard the study of any religion as consisting simply of the study of abstracted creeds and rituals. This is obvious in the case of Christianity when we recognize the position of Jesus within the context of the complex religious culture of Judaism. But the same is true of all religions, for they build on,

---

[1] Bishop R. Heber (1783–1826), *English Hymnal* 547, *A & M Revised* 265.

and develop within, a particular civilization with which there is inevitably a two-way relationship. It follows that any study of other religions, whether for their own sake or in their relationship to Christianity, necessarily involves study of the relevant cultural contexts. How far this kind of study of other religions is possible in the school situation is no easy question. We think, therefore, that there is an urgent need, if other religions are to be responsibly and adequately studied, for some careful inquiry to be made into appropriate methods of teaching.

121 It is our view that indifferentist and essentialist standpoints are not only oversimplifications of the facts but are on other grounds untenable from the Christian position. The indifferentist view asserts that no prophet or religious teacher is necessarily of greater value than any other: the essentialist claims that there lies behind all religions an essential truth, to know which is the best and purest religious knowledge one can attain to. To reject these views, however, is not at all to deny that other religions represent ways of accounting for, and unifying, the totality of human experience and of representing that experience to individuals in coherent terms; still less is it to deny that other religions are ways of exploring the furthest reaches of human nature and capacity, and that these may sometimes require to be described in terms of a divine human relationship. But still this does not alter what the Christian would claim to be the distinct nature of Christianity among other religions, for the Christian derives his faith from a unique event.

122 The traditional theological defence of claiming distinctiveness for Christianity, while at the same time granting a significance to other religions, has been in terms of a *logos* theology which considered there to be a "light which lighteneth every man that cometh into the world"; a bond between the Creator and all his creatures—a *lumen naturale*. So, for instance, the early Christian Fathers could speak of "Christians before Christ" and regard Greek philosophy as sharing with Judaism in the preparation for the gospel. Further, it would be claimed that the distinctiveness of Christianity rests not in an exclusive uniqueness but in an inclusive uniqueness—a theme which has been argued by theologians such as C. E. Raven and which was also elaborated in papers preparatory for the 1968 Lambeth Conference. In these ways there is abundant theological justification for a religious education which seeks to embrace other religions besides the Christian faith, and, whatever other defences might be given of the exercise, what is quite clear is that Christians can have their own particular defence of it as well.

123 Thus to take Christianity as a base for religious education does not at all preclude the pupils learning something of the beliefs and sharing in some of the occasions of worship of other religions. The most that the Christian would ask is that as part of the study of other religions there should be a willingness to explore the reasons why Christian claims and beliefs are considered to be distinctive, though naturally this exploration will take place against a recognition that perhaps in the final analysis an individual may decide against the claims of the Christian faith as he has understood them.

(4) *The Moral Strand in Religious Education*

124 It will be readily admitted that within the Christian faith, as in most religions, there will always be a moral strand. Religion as we envisage it implies the acknowledgement of a claim—the vision of an ideal—which is expressed in terms of parables, injunctions arising out of particular situations, maxims, and aphorisms. While it hardly seems possible to have religious education without moral education this does not in any way need to compromise what is traditionally called "the autonomy of morals". This is discussed further in ch. 3, "Religious Education and Moral Education". Moreover, it is logically possible to have moral education without there being explicit religious education. But in this connection it should be recognized that even the teaching of the techniques of moral decision presumably demand specimens of moral decision, and this would presumably imply the acknowledgement of some moral claim to which the moral decision is a response. Such a claim receives a broader interpretation when set within a theological context, though the justification for this will obviously depend on the reliability of the theological context.[1]

125 Further, it is significant that with moral education the problems typical of religious education recur. For if moral education is given, it must enshrine possibilities for built-in criticism and fulfil the very kind of conditions which we have seen must belong to religious

[1] On these points see I. T. Ramsey (ed.) *Christian Ethics and Contemporary Philosophy* (S.C.M. 1966), ch. 2 and Part III.

education as well. Otherwise moral education would be no more than training in social conventions. It could even be authoritarian in the worst sense, and the teaching of morals could be mere conditioning.

(5) *The Status of Religious Knowledge*

126 More requires to be said at this point about the influence of philosophy, as studied in British and American universities, on the manner in which theological questions are now approached. By examining with care and precision the very different uses to which language can be put and the varied types of reasoning appropriate to different disciplines, philosophers have helped to clarify the problems that arise in relating one discipline to another. An initial tendency to reject any claim to meaningfulness, let alone knowledge, which did not satisfy some simple empirical criteria has given way, as we have said earlier in this chapter, to a growing recognition of the variety and complexity of the possible types of human inquiry and their associated languages. Where the issues are inevitably controversial, as in the case of religion and ethics, philosophers would, for the most part, be chary of claiming that they could be settled by philosophical reasoning alone. The effect of philosophical discussion has been rather to bring fundamental questions into clearer focus and to discourage simple solutions. Such developments in philosophy have, for example, encouraged an interest in the contexts and situations in which religious utterances emerge, though it has come to be realized by Christian thinkers that it is as difficult as it is necessary to safeguard an element of transcendence if justice is to be done to the assertions of religion. By showing the self-involving character of religious language, developments in philosophy have stressed the notion of commitment while emphasizing the need to distinguish this from a mere attitude to the world. They have also sought to illuminate religious language by drawing suggestive parallels from elsewhere, for example poetry, though then there is the need to guard against over-easy assimilation. In this way, by showing an interest in situational involvement and illustrative parallels, philosophical reflection matches educational practice and the kind of approach to be found in the teaching of pupils of all age groups. An interest in the different types of meaningful language, and the notion of suggestive parallels in particular, brings the language of religion out of its isolation to set it alongside other languages as a means towards a better understanding of its character. This interest in relating different languages, with the consequential idea that an adequate understanding of a situation brings together different disciplines, encourages a thematic approach in which religious assertions have their own distinctive place. The interest in context and situations points to an experience-centred religious education, as it points also to a teaching method which begins with problems in an endeavour to think through them and to see the points at which theology illustrates them.

127 To seek to exclude religious education from the school curriculum, as some do, on the grounds that "religious knowledge" is "poorly founded as an academic discipline" is to ignore not only the existence of a serious body of responsible scholarship, but to ignore those elements in the intellectual and educational scene with which we have dealt earlier in this chapter.[1] Theology may have itself in part to blame for the misunderstanding of its content and method which its detractors show. But it can hardly be blamed for the ignorance of the contemporary scene which many of its critics display. Such critics also ignore in a conservative and obscurantist way developments over the last decade and more not only in theology but also in philosophy.

(6) *Theology in Higher Education*

128 We think there is great value in closer association between faculties of theology in universities and colleges of education. In so far as it is helped by a development such as the B.Ed. degree, this is to be welcomed. Such closer association is both made possible, and becomes desirable, for two reasons. In the first place there is the obvious fact that professional preparation for the ordained ministry is no longer the prime concern of a university course in theology. Secondly, whether in the university context or in the context of religious education in general, the point which we have been making earlier in this chapter is that theology will always have a special need to relate itself to other disciplines apart from having, as a

[1] Mr David Tribe, for instance, in his pamphlet on "secular education" published by the National Secular Society, states that "Christian theological ideas are suppositions which lack independent verification, and so properly come into the same category as astrology, spiritualism, and demonology, which are excluded (*sic*) from the school curricula. . . . Any act of worship or R.I. syllabus based on them is clearly without acceptable intellectual credentials and should be eliminated from all county schools."

necessary and important basis of that relationship, its own distinctive character as a group of professional disciplines. This wider task of theology in the university was expressed by the then Professor Ian Ramsey in the following terms when preaching before the University of Oxford in 1964 on "the new prospect for theological studies":

This prospect no longer regards theology as a subject "quite apart". On the contrary it sees theology as engaging in dialogue with other disciplines and making possible their cross-fertilization, and all that by bringing them to bear, with itself, on teasing and stubborn problems of contemporary thought and behaviour. At one time, of course, it might have been supposed, and no doubt was supposed, that theology knew already all the answers to all the problems that could arise for man's thinking or action. On this view, it was only a matter of learning what these answers were, in order to be fitted out for all eventualities. That is no longer a credible view. It is not so much that theology does not know the answers, as that there are no answers to be known in that way. Problems of recent thought and behaviour are complex to a degree; and on each problem many disciplines have something to say which needs to be heard. Further, it is now a mark of immaturity for any discipline to think it has ready-made, copy-book answers—whether that discipline is psychology or economics or sociology or philosophy or theology. At the same time, simply because of its past, there is some theological comment available on virtually every problem that can raise its head. With every problem relating to man and his place in the Universe are associated some religious thinking, behaviour and attitudes. But such thinking, behaviour and attitudes interlock for the most part with only out-of-date "secular" thinking about the particular problems. That is the difficulty—and the opportunity. The new prospect for theology arises as and when theology expresses its continuing concern with problems which are of significance to everyone—believer and unbeliever alike; when it arranges for such dialogue between the different disciplines as can provide helpful and informative inroads into a particular problem; and when, as it listens rather than speaks, and learns rather than teaches, it starts to construct theological discourse with a new relevance.

Within a college of education developments in teaching method such as the thematic approach and the integrated day all provide occasions for relating theological studies to other disciplines in the context of common themes or common problems.

(7) *Perspectives on humanity in contemporary educational thought*

129 Against the broad background of the theological considerations we have given comes a possible contribution to educational thought which may be otherwise neglected. Much contemporary educational thought gives the appearance of being dominated by a standpoint which sees human life and existence wholly within a framework supplied by the concepts and beliefs of the natural and behavioural sciences and also by the assumption that "honest doubt" is somehow more honest than "honest faith". It is often a presupposition of educational thinking that the contemporary intellectual debate, so far as religious belief is concerned, has been settled once and for all in a secularist way. Against such a restricted view of human existence, a religious education faithful to the theological perspectives which lie behind it will be constantly endeavouring to do justice to a wider perspective on human nature, a broader and less restrictive humanism. It will therefore seek to preserve in educational discussion, as well as in the practice of teaching, some awareness of a broader area to human nature, of the dimension of "mystery", "depth", "transcendence", of a sense of the unconditioned in human experience.

130 It is in this same context that, presented with certain events and tendencies within education that focus attention on human beings and their relationships, the theologian might be expected to have something valuable to say. Much is said by politicians, sociologists, and others on such movements as student protest, student representation, and so on. But the theologian can certainly have something to contribute to a situation to whose understanding concepts such as human nature, community, reconciliation, are of central importance.

131 Broadening these considerations, it should be clear that the theologian has insights to contribute to educational discussion about the nature of man. One of the basic educational questions is plainly "What kind of being is this whom we seek to educate?" Are human beings no more—though no less—than a combined topic of the natural and behavioural sciences? Do we differ as socially acceptable citizens at all significantly from house-trained dogs? Or are human beings anything more than extremely elaborate computers whose major distinction is that they are comparatively cheap to come by? If this is our view of the nature of man, then the educational process need plainly be no more than a process of individual and social conditioning. For what is quite clear is that what we do in education depends quite basically on our understanding of what it is to be human.

132 When every allowance has been made for differences of emphasis and interpretation, there is a distinctively Christian doctrine of man whose influence has been so pervasive in our own culture that it is easily taken for granted. We believe in the intrinsic worth of each individual, not only as a member of some group, nor only as an exemplar of some virtue, but as the one particular person he is, whether bright or stupid, beautiful or ugly, good or bad. It would be difficult to maintain that this belief is self-evident, indeed it is doubtful if it has arisen spontaneously in cultures unaffected by Judaism and Christianity. We have seen it distorted or denied in our own day. For Christians it derives from a certain conception of man as created in the image of God, redeemed by Jesus Christ, and destined for eternal life. One cannot think of man in this way without also believing that men are to be regarded as God regards them. Beliefs operate at varying levels of profundity and there are many in whom this belief fails to express itself in action—and there are others who share the attitude while rejecting Christian belief. Nevertheless this Christian conception of man and this conviction of the regard due to individual men forms part of a total vision in terms of which it becomes intelligible why a person should care for the interests of those in whom he has otherwise no interest.

133 It is, of course, arguable that there are other ways of thinking of the whole context of human life which provide as ample a justification for this kind of regard, or, indeed, that no justification of any sort is needed. It is up to those who think so to urge their opinion. The challenge to show how Christian attitudes can be defended from other standpoints than Christian belief is becoming more urgent, for two reasons in particular. The *first* is that there are conceptions of man on offer which, taken by themselves, are incompatible with his having the sort of irreducible value which most humanists as well as Christians accord him. Freudian, Marxist, behaviourist, and even some existentialist theories about human nature, however illuminating as contributions to our understanding of man, are of this kind if they are taken as the whole truth. The *second* is that we shall before very long be in a position, as a result of advances in biological science, to modify human nature to an extent hitherto unthought of. It is on the whole the scientists themselves who are most keenly aware of the grave responsibilities with which we shall be inescapably faced, and are looking for the co-operation of all those whose concern is with "the whole man". This means that, even if we should prefer to do so, it is not going to be possible to disengage ourselves from such fundamental questions as what it is, and ought to be, to be a man. If these questions are controversial, as to an increasing extent they obviously are, then we must be prepared to engage in controversy.

134 It is a platitude to say that education is concerned with "the whole man", but it is a platitude that is true and important. It warns us against two dangers. One is that of neglecting the findings of empirical science. If man is not just a "naked ape" he is at least that. The other is that of taking too limiting a view of human potentialities and one that is too narrowly circumscribed by contemporary fashion. There is a constant temptation to avoid one of these dangers merely by embracing the other. As R. S. Peters has wisely remarked, "The time has passed when philosophers could, with a clear conscience, spin theories of human nature out of their own observation and introspection." And the same applies to theologians. It is necessary, as Peters urges, "to get down to work in the philosophy of mind with psychologists, social scientists, historians and men of wide practical experience and shrewd judgment".[1]

135 This is a programme for research and its importance is undeniable. But there is little reason to suppose that we shall soon, if ever, find definitive answers to these fundamental questions about man—what is it to be a man?—which will once and for all satisfy every reasonable man. There will always be need for judgement and decision on the part of individuals and on the part of societies. If it is to some extent a controversial question what goes to make up "the whole man", we can either drop "the whole man" as an educational ideal and accept the risk of impoverishment which that entails, or we can make one or other of the competing concepts at least the model by reference to which we proceed. Thus we have to assume initially either that the child does or that he does not have spiritual needs and a capacity for religious awareness, and that it does or does not matter in relation to the rest of his activities whether these needs are met or these capacities developed.

[1] R. S. Peters, *Ethics and Education*, p. 234.

136 The issue can be put quite plainly. We can make the Christian conception of man our model or we can choose not to do so. What is involved in the former alternative is very broadly set out in this chapter. As we show throughout the Report, the adoption of a starting point does not in any way preclude subjecting it at every stage to criticism and open inquiry. If, however, we choose not to accept the Christian concept of man then two further alternatives meet us: either we accept some other model, or we consciously refuse to accept any model at all. The former of these alternatives is a clear possibility—behaviourist and Marxist models exist, to mention but two. But they can scarcely be said to have been either scientifically demonstrated or universally accepted as a basis for interpreting human life. There remains, then, the possibility of leaving the matter open, and of arguing that it is not the function of the modern secular State in any way to appear to sponsor a model of "the whole man", even as a starting point. This point of view is argued, by Alasdair MacIntyre in his Riddell Lectures *Secularisation and Moral Change*.[1]

137 This latter position could be conscientiously held by many people, not only by agnostics but also by those of deep religious or atheist convictions. So strongly might they feel it to be a prerogative of parental upbringing that a child should receive its first understandings of the meaning of human life from its parents, that they would oppose any invasion of the State into this realm. In theory this is a position of considerable attractiveness. That the secular State should not adopt a standpoint appears to be open, liberal, and tolerant. In practice, however, it is open to at least as many objections as the alternative of choosing a model. From the standpoint of person or state, neutrality is virtually unachievable. In every educational discipline to do with man, evaluative elements appear which are often the more insidious for being unexamined. Among experts this is readily recognized, and techniques are developed, e.g. for enabling the careful reader to allow for the personal standpoint of the author. But we are now considering not merely academic conventions but a nationwide system of education. Our claim is that the explicit recognition of the spiritual needs and capacities of children is a far more desirable position for our modern State to adopt than either an explicit denial of such needs or a refusal to cater for

1 (O.U.P. 1967), esp. Lecture 2.

them in the context of state education. The validity of this claim will naturally be variously estimated.

138 If there is one word which characterizes the Christian gospel it is *agape*, love, and the Christian theologian will seek to examine the significance of Christian love for the whole of the educational process. This love he will want to express, not merely as parent or as teacher, but in all his relationships as an adult with children and young people. It scarcely needs saying that in this attempt he exposes himself to mistakes and misunderstandings. For his own understanding of love he relies deeply upon his own early experiences of it, however much later reflection or experiences as a mature Christian may have modified it. He may make the mistake of being condescending or sentimental, or he may be misunderstood as being so. The love he is trying to reflect needs to be disciplined by the realization both that he stands in need of it himself and that it is given to all as they are. The Christian certainly ought not to be surprised that man at any stage of supposed civilization is deeply prone to what he terms sin. Thus there will be a strong vein of realism running through all that he wants to say about love, either of God, or between man. The activities of the children in William Golding's *Lord of the Flies* do not astonish him. Realism about children is undoubtedly necessary; but all that needs to be said about training or discipline can be included under love for children. The one-sided interpretations of discipline which led to violent physical repression and a joyless upbringing have been rightly abandoned. It has to be acknowledged that the doctrine of original sin, in the understanding of some theologians, often led to the imposition of a violently repressive form of discipline upon children.[1] Both research and experience have helped modern educators to reject this as a distorted understanding of upbringing, and the Christian will want to re-emphasize that only with security and loving care does the child make progress through the critical points in his development. Christian faith cannot claim to have discovered this independently of research or experience; but it can, with full justice, point to its coherence with the teaching about God and to the life of Christ in the gospels. What motivates the Christian in all his various relationships with children, parental, professional, or merely accidental, is a love which reaches out to

---

[1] For a wise interpretation of this much disputed doctrine see Austin Farrer, *Love Almighty and Ills Unlimited* (London 1962) pp. 150ff.

them in their own condition, and which seeks by force of example
to bring home to them a sense of the love of God for them.

139 Each individual as an object of the love of God has therefore
a unique value. Against tendencies to depersonalize and to de-
humanize which are prevalent in society the Christian will want
constantly to emphasize the importance of personal relationships.
The highest analogy he can offer for understanding the being of God
is that of the person. The development of the person in all his aspects,
religious and moral, as well as physical and mental, is therefore a
matter of the deepest importance to him.

140 The love we have spoken of contains and expresses a particular
hope for a child. Without such hope it would be, as so much mere
benevolence in fact is, formless and ultimately valueless. What a
Christian hopes for a child is maturity; but this word itself needs
careful explanation. Maturity is commonly understood negatively,
as a state in which one is no longer moved by the moods and passions
which characterize adolescence. Erik Erikson has helpfully called
the major crisis of adolescence the identity crisis, out of which the
adolescent emerges to some unified understanding of his identity
and roles in the world. For the Christian this forming of a central
perspective takes place around the person of Christ. A "full" or
"abundant" life is a life lived in the body of Christ, the community
of those who are trying to know and to obey God's will for them.
Maturity in this sense is not therefore a merely individual self-
realization. It is the individual discovering his value in a community,
and living out his value to it.

141 Although we have devoted much care and thought to this
chapter of the Report over the past two years, we are well aware
that we have not said the last word on the relationship between
theology and education or on the theological basis for religious
education in schools. We offer these reflections, however, in the hope
that others will devote continuing further study to the important,
complex, and wide-ranging issues which we have raised.

142 The Christian contribution to modern education is an account
of the individual and his potentialities which, as we have sought to
argue, is more true to life than its alternatives, and offers society a
more satisfactory basis from which its educational procedures can
set out. Its special advantage is that it offers for each pupil's considera-

tion criteria by which a critical assessment of his own role in society and the world at large can be made, and by which he may be able to stand over against this society, if need be. It points to an education leading to personal fulfilment and characterized by a critical freedom. Some might say, however, that even if this ideal be acknowledged the result in practice may fall far short of it. Our reply would be that the practical recommendations we make later in this Report are meant to ensure that the gap between ideal and practice is as narrow as possible.

3
Religious Education and Moral Education

Education, Religion, and Morality

143 Whether education is thought of as a process of initiation into the traditions of a society, or as helping the pupil to grow into a responsible adult, or even as training him for a job, morality must have an important place in it. No one engaged in education would deny this, and there can be no doubt that much effective moral education goes on in schools. Yet there has been comparatively little explicit study of the problems involved. Hence the work of the Farmington Trust,[1] set up specifically for research into moral education, is of particular interest.

144 But moral education cannot easily be thought of as a particular "subject" on the time-table. As John Wilson, director of the research unit, says in his *Introduction to Moral Education*, "Any educational process can count as moral education if it is a deliberate process and directed towards producing (or perhaps just produces) the skills or characteristics of a morally educated person."[2] Hence the study of literature or of biology might, and should, contribute to moral education. So, even more importantly, should the entire ethos of the school. Religious education, however, is commonly thought to have a special contribution to make.

145 There are, however, two different standpoints from which its relevance is questioned:

[1] The Farmington Trust set up in 1965 a research unit in Oxford consisting of philosophers, psychologists, and sociologists, to inquire into moral education from a neutral standpoint and eventually to make recommendations to schools and other institutions. The work of the unit will continue for at least ten years and probably longer.

[2] Wilson, Williams, and Sugarman, *Introduction to Moral Education* (Penguin 1967), p. 140.

(1) That of the convinced secularist who holds that the effect on morality of associating it with religion is positively harmful.[1] Not only, as he believes, does it base morality on a false conception of human life, but it tends to invest it with an authoritarian character which militates against its proper development. This has the unwelcome consequence, it is further argued, that those whose morality is based upon religious authority will abandon their morality if they give up their religion.[2]

(2) That of those (whether Christian or non-Christian) who take their stand upon the autonomy of morals and hold that men can discern what is right and wrong independently of their fundamental beliefs about man and the universe.[3]

146 Those who believe that religious education has a special part to play in moral education are also divided. Some hold that morality is so closely bound up with religion as to be unintelligible without it, others that morality without religion, although possible, is bound to be more or less defective. The possibility of these opposing standpoints compels us to consider what *is* the relation between religion and morality, a question that is both difficult and controversial and one which cannot be fully examined in a single chapter.

147 John Wilson argues persuasively the case against regarding morality as entirely dependent on religion. The religious believer is prepared to use moral arguments in defence of his religious beliefs; he can and does enter into significant discussion of moral questions with those who do not share his beliefs; and some at least of the moral principles which he accepts are shared with others, because their acceptance is a necessary condition of the continuance of human society. Thus no one seriously doubts that it is wrong to tell lies, break promises, inflict wanton injury, cheat or steal—it is not surprising that these things are forbidden by the moral codes of virtually all societies. They are not controversial in our own (though the scope and manner of their application sometimes is).

148 These considerations suffice to show that it is possible to have morality, of a sort, without religion. As has been urged by writers

[1] E.g. Margaret Knight, *Morals Without Religion* (Dobson 1955).
[2] See, E. G., W. G. Maclagan *The Theological Frontier of Ethics* (Allen & Unwin 1961), Ch. 7, ESP. pp. 186–8.
[3] For a brief statement, see P. Hirst, "Morals, Religion and the Maintained School", *British Journal of Educational Studies*, Nov. 1965, vol. 14, no. 1.

as different as H. L. A. Hart[1] and C. S. Lewis,[2] we can discern a basic social morality which commands the allegiance of men everywhere. It does not, of course, follow that religion makes no difference to morality, if only because such basic morality is so basic that there is no society whose entire morality is confined to it. There are, moreover, marked differences between societies in the way they interpret its requirements and in the relative importance they attach to different parts of it. Such a basic morality provides little or no guidance about racial discrimination, cruelty to animals, sexual behaviour, attitudes to parents and children, drug addiction, punishment, to name only some of the moral problems of our own contemporary society. Moreover, this basic morality, consisting as it does of prohibitions whose justification is the need to preserve society, depends for its effectiveness upon the individual's having an interest in the preservation of the society to which he belongs, and this he is unlikely to have unless it offers him a meaningful existence and provides some focus for his aspirations.

149 Unless moral education is to be confined to those areas of basic morality which are common to any conceivable moral system— and the inadequacy of this is apparent—it will have to venture into realms in which moral differences reflect differences in ultimate convictions. The point is well made in The British Council of Churches' report *Religion and the Secondary School* which refers to a recently produced humanist scheme of moral education. This scheme outlines the first two main areas of moral education as: "(1) experiences leading to a right evaluation of oneself and one's relationship with others; (2) experiences leading to a valid perspective on man and the universe". On this point the report comments: "These two areas are in fact areas of *religious* education, and the document was right to recognize that they are areas essential to any scheme of moral education."[3] What the report *Religion and the Secondary School* means by calling them "areas of religious education" is that they are areas within which the sort of questions arise with which religion is characteristically concerned, in questions about the nature of man and his place in the universe. Such questions could of course be dealt with, as in a Marxist society, without any reference to religion as such, and religion is more than "a perspective on man and the

[1] *The Concept of Law* (O.U.P. 1961), pp. 189–95.
[2] See *The Abolition of Man* (Bles 1943).
[3] C. Alves, *Religion and the Secondary School* (S.C.M. 1968), p. 149.

universe". But the point intended is a valid one, that moral education must remain inadequate and incomplete if it tries to avoid all reference to basic questions of meaning, purpose, and value.

150 It would be surprising if any more or less comprehensive "philosophy of life", whether religious or not, were entirely without ethical implications, and, in practice, Christians and humanists tend to differ about certain moral issues. It would be both dishonest and ineffective to pretend that these differences do not exist, as it would also be to pretend that there are not important differences about them among Christians and among humanists. Clearly there is everything to be said for stressing the considerations which both Christians and non-Christians regard as important, so long as this is honestly done, but to regard these as the only considerations that matter would be simply to beg some fundamental questions.

151 What has so far been suggested is that a programme of moral education confined to a "basic morality recognized by all civilized people" is of limited practicability. In so far as such a morality can be discovered, it is so general as to be capable of many divergent interpretations and its basis in the preservation of society, although sound as far as it goes, lacks the power to inspire. If we look instead for a national consensus, which makes no claim to universality, we run the risk of seeking to perpetuate whatever happens to be the conventional wisdom of our own time and place as well as blurring fundamental differences which ought to be recognized.

152 We have spoken of the "content" of moral education. To some this may appear to be a wrong approach since it would be to assume that the aim of moral education is to inculcate a certain sort of morality. If this is so, then indeed it becomes important to decide what morality this should be. But should this be the aim? Instead of trying to produce pupils with particular views, ought we not to be attempting simply to produce pupils who are rational, that is, who have the abilities and skills, to consider and assess all these views for themselves? This constitutes a powerful plea against any attempt at moral indoctrination [1] and in favour of what elsewhere in this Report has been called an "open" approach. But it is not clear that it relieves the educator of concern with the content of morality, for the following reasons:

---

[1] See Appendix on "Indoctrination" by Professor B. G. Mitchell.

4

153 1. It is open to question how far it is possible to provide a satisfactory account of morality which is purely formal, i.e. which makes
no reference to the kinds of actions which are from a moral point of
view right or wrong in themselves. It is conceivable, some would
argue, that a man should conform to such formal requirements for
being "morally educated" as consistency, impartiality, and autonomy and yet behave in ways which we should rightly regard as
morally abhorrent. He may be "rational" in this sense and yet
wrong; or he may have good principles but fail to live up to them.

2. Even if we can form a conception of the "morally educated man"
without reference to what such a man would actually think or do,
it seems a very tall order that each child should by the end of his
school career arrive at an entirely "rational" morality from scratch.
There can be few adults, if any, who have achieved it. We can and
certainly should try to develop in ourselves and in our children the
ability to understand and to assess; to recognize our own limitations
as well as not to accept authority uncritically. But we are surely de-
luding ourselves if we think that we or they are going to emerge as
persons whose moral assumptions have purely rational grounds.

3. Even if children are able eventually to leave school as wholly
autonomous "morally educated men", they cannot start so. In the
early stages they will need to learn certain commonly held conclusions
and practices (as they do in history or science). Thus Wilson writes:

> It is no doubt highly desirable that children should be initiated (by imi-
> tation, the force of example, compulsory rules and other methods) into
> a particular moral code or tradition, parts of which they may later fully
> appropriate for themselves or reject. It would be dishonest and grotesque,
> as well as inefficient, for teachers to pretend that they themselves do not
> have such a code, or to be over-hesitant in telling children what it is; and
> for this reason alone it is obviously important that teachers and other
> educators should attempt to make their own beliefs as rational as possible.
> Getting children to "go through the motions" of a moral code, the point
> of which they may come later to see for themselves, is not the whole of
> moral education, but it is no doubt an essential part.[1]

154 There are, as we have seen, some moral rules which are accepted
because they are necessary to the maintenance of any civilized society,
and that children should "go through the motions" as far as these
are concerned is not likely to be contested. The child will come to

---

[1] Wilson, Williams, and Sugarman, op. cit., p. 151.

see in due course why he should tell the truth, keep his promise, help others and not injure them, and so forth. That he should behave in these ways, even if the reasons are not yet fully understood, is indeed necessary to the functioning of the school community itself. The importance of these very basic moral principles is such that it could well be argued that it is in the interests of society that people should get used to observing them even if this means that their motives are not the highest possible. The liberal is inclined to be so impressed with the importance of moral choice that he underestimates the value of a habitual pattern of good behaviour which is by no means just unthinking, but which is not fully reflective. Such is the morality of most ordinary people most of the time. It is not to be despised. It seems, therefore, that we cannot entirely avoid the problem of content by adopting as our aim the production of "morally educated men". We shall need in practice, and perhaps also in theory, some conception of what a good man is like. If so, the question arises, and must be faced, whether the educator can have such a conception and yet be genuinely "open" in his approach.

155 It is important to realize that "openness" is not simply a function of doubt. If it were, many "conclusions" in science, mathematics, and history would have to be taught for the most part in an authoritarian fashion. As it is, in these subjects as in any other, the teacher has a number of procedures of varying merit open to him. He can, if he so wishes, give no other reason than "because I say so" or "because the textbook says so". Or he can indicate how the conclusions are arrived at—at least in principle he can, though in practice he would be limited by the children's capacity to understand (and sometimes his own) and by the shortage of time. He might attempt to illustrate the methods of reasoning involved in relation to a particular example, and ask his pupils to accept his own authority for the possibility of the same being done in other cases. This is, after all, how he himself stands in relation to the subject. He simply is not in a position to check the authorities he accepts to any but a minimal extent, but neither does he swallow what they say uncritically.

156 In morality the situation is very often the same. We are as sure as we possibly can be that it is wrong to kill people for fun, or to lie whenever it pleases us. It would be absurd to pretend otherwise, and dangerous to let children behave in this way if they choose to.

But the teacher is not therefore precluded from helping them to understand for themselves why it would be wrong to do these things. These considerations may help us to construct a bridge between two parts of the educational process which tend to be disjoined in the literature, namely education as "induction" into a tradition and as the development of human potentialities.

157 Whether induction into a tradition can form part of an "open" educational process depends, obviously, on how reasonable the tradition is. A moral tradition expressed in a set of inflexible taboos could scarcely be incorporated into a genuinely liberal education, because, when an explanation was asked for, there would *ex hypothesi* be none available. Where the tradition is a reasonable one, as in the case of natural science and academic history, an explanation could in principle be provided. But, as our discussion has indicated, only in principle. To produce a complete rational justification is in practice impossible. The student of religion or morality, the student of science or history, needs to be inducted into the tradition of these disciplines, a process which involves both learning how to think in the appropriate ways and accepting a good deal on authority. An education in any of these fields would be a failure if it produced people who were subservient and uncritical; it would also be a failure if it produced people who supposed that they could themselves rewrite the entire subject from scratch.

158 Hence "openness" does not require us to proceed as if we were operating in a cultural vacuum—it cannot mean "not having any presuppositions, not accepting anything which one cannot here and now justify to any reasonable man, not being prepared to accept anything on authority". It must mean "not being doctrinaire, encouraging people to think for themselves, being ready to consider arguments against one's own position". As such it is compatible with having and with communicating a definite position which one is prepared to defend.

159 If "openness" is thought of in this way, it makes possible, if not a complete reconciliation of the attitudes of radicals and conservatives, at least a fruitful tension between them. An extreme liberal educational theory would allow no role to conservatives at all; they could only be attacked as enemies to progress. Their desire to ensure that the best of our cultural inheritance is preserved and handed on to the young could only be stigmatized as unthinking obscurantism.

It is generally understood that an educated man is not one who totally rejects tradition and starts afresh, nor even one who accepts tradition only so far as he is able to justify it in terms of some clearly articulated principles, but rather one who has been initiated into a tradition which he to a greater or lesser extent respects, and to a greater or lesser extent criticizes. There is room for considerable difference of emphasis. Both the radical and the conservative will have legitimate educational roles, the former testing the tradition and seeking to discover and reform its inadequacies, the latter seeking to ensure that what is of permanent value is not thoughtlessly discarded.

160 A case in which the nature of the educational problem can be clearly seen is that of sexual morality. It is no use here appealing to a "basic morality", because it is not possible to discover a consensus on all points between all societies. The only common factor is that all societies require some form of institution of marriage, with its associated responsibilities. Our own traditional code has been based on the Christian principle that sexual intercourse shall be exclusively heterosexual and confined to marriage. There is not on this matter an absolutely clear line to be drawn between Christians and humanists, since some Christians favour a "new morality" and some humanists accept the traditional ethic, but it is probable that there is still an overall majority in favour of the traditional view.

161 In so far as moral education includes sexual morality—and it is difficult to see how it could be excluded—it enters an area in which religion makes a difference both theoretically and in practice. Even if the ideal is to produce "the morally educated man" and not to induce particular moral virtues, it would seem necessary that pupils should have some understanding of the Christian principles underlying the traditional sexual ethic. Moreover, since they will have in due course to decide where they themselves stand, they will need to become acquainted with the whole scheme of ideas from which it derives. Not only will they require some religious education, but they will need to be able to grasp its moral implications. This conclusion could be resisted only if it were to be accepted that there are no good grounds in Christian belief for a particular sexual ethic; that chastity as traditionally conceived is either not a virtue or not a Christian virtue. If chastity is not a virtue then Christians are simply mistaken if they think that it is and their opinions do not merit serious consideration. If it is not a Christian virtue, that is, if there are no specifically Christian reasons for supposing it to be one, then there is no need to bring Christianity into the discussion.

162 Now these are all controversial questions and it is no part of our intention to try to settle them in this Report. But in the end they cannot be avoided. We can neither neglect the case for a more permissive morality, nor assume without argument that the traditional ethic is obsolete. Since Christianity has been largely influential in forming the educational practices and institutions whose retention, abolition, or reformation is under review, it is central to the debate. It would appear that, so far as sexual morality is concerned, moral education, if taken seriously, would involve consideration of the sort of issues which are the characteristic concern of religious education. And this becomes clearer still if the question is not only how we should live, but why we should pay any attention to morality at all. Thoughtful adolescents are increasingly unimpressed with appeals to social necessity unless they can see that the social institutions themselves make possible a life that is worthy of human beings. The claims that society makes upon them must be seen in relation to the claims of other people, and their estimate of the nature and authority of these claims is bound in the end to be affected by their understanding of what it is to be a man.

163 So far as the "humanistic" function of education is concerned, the foregoing discussion raises no serious problems. An open moral education should fit quite easily with an open religious education. The difficulty arises with the "inducting" function, which is concerned with initiating the young into the customs of adult society. It is true that by the time questions of sexual morality become pressing pupils have reached an age at which they can to some extent understand and judge the issues for themselves, but it is also an age at which they are particularly susceptible to the appeal of pop culture and emotions are difficult to cope with. And however "open" the school may wish to be, it still has to make its own rules of behaviour. On the face of it there would seem to be three possible approaches:

(*a*) To avoid treating it as a moral issue and concentrate on prudential considerations, such as avoidance of pregnancy, keeping

clear of the law, not getting involved in relationships whose un-
foreseen emotional demands one is unable to cope with, and so
on. There is a lot that can usefully be said along these lines.

(*b*) Making clear what we believe to be right, while being prepared
to defend it and conceding that it is not universally accepted.
That is what many Christian parents do with their own children.

(*c*) Acquainting the children with the whole range of possible attitudes, both moral and prudential, and leaving them to decide
for themselves.

If (*a*) alone is adopted, some of the pupils are likely to ask whether
moral questions are not also involved, and their questions will have
either to be answered or evaded. If all reference to morality is successfully kept out, pupils may well draw the inference that the moral
questions do not arise or are not important. If, on the other hand,
(*c*) is adopted, the pupils will surely want to know where the teacher
himself stands, and this means what ground, religious or other, he
takes his stand upon.

164 Bearing in mind the need for a stable framework it would seem
that, at the earliest age at which discussion of these issues needs to
take place, it is not enough to give prudential advice alone, or to
leave pupils to make up their own minds. Neither of these (nor the
two together), gives them enough security. Teachers must be prepared to adopt a definite approach. If so, a decision is required as
to what approach is to be taken.

165 This excursion into the problem of sex education has been
undertaken because this is one of the more important areas in which
moral questions are controversial and in which religious principles
play a specific role. In the light of it, it certainly appears unreasonable
to keep religious and moral education entirely separate. Religious
education would be incomplete if its moral implications were unexplored: moral education would be equally incomplete if it attempted
to evade the fundamental questions about human life with which
Christianity is concerned. How these questions are answered, indeed
whether they are raised at all, has importance not only for the individual's beliefs about what is right and wrong, but also for his understanding of the basis of morality in the needs and claims of other
people.

166 It remains to ask whether the case for religious education depends on the nature of the contribution it can make to moral education. If there is anything in what we have been saying, religious education is an end in itself and not just a means to moral education. However important morality may be in the Christian or any other life, it is not the whole of it; and it is arguable that to teach religion for the sake of morality is to reverse the proper priorities. Whether this is so or not, it would be unwise to beg the question at the start. The case for religious education which has been developed in the Report stands on its own feet.

Moral Education and the School

167 In considering the relation between religion and morality, we have tried to take into account recent changes in our society, particularly in its attitudes to moral principle and practice. These changes in society have affected the concept of moral education in at least three important respects:

(a) *Its Purpose* Today's approach is less authoritarian and more individualistic. Moral education must therefore seek to inform, to provoke what has been well described as "compassionate reasoning", and to encourage personal responsibility, rather than to inculcate unthinking acceptance and submission.

(b) *Its Content* Since the content of moral education is bound to change as society's convictions about moral virtues and duties alter, it must today take account not only of generally agreed views of morality but also of significant differences about moral principle and/or practice which exist within our complex society.

(c) *Its Method* Today the "induction" of young children into moral practice must, as we have already argued, be such as can be rationally examined and justified during adolescence. The moral education of adolescents must therefore actually provide for and encourage rational discussion and personal decision.

168 When the Education Act of 1944 was framed, it was assumed that, though acceptance of Christianity would plainly not be universal in our society, it would at any rate be sufficiently typical of the majority to allow Christianity to be the main basis of moral education. Thus the White Paper which H.M. Government issued as a preliminary to the publication of the Education Bill declared:

There has been a very general wish, not confined to representatives of the

Churches, that religious education should be given a more defined place in the life and work of the schools, *springing from the desire to revive the spiritual and personal values in our society and in our national traditions.* The Church, the family, the local community and the teacher all have their part to play in imparting religious instruction to the young.[1]

169 This attitude continued to be reflected in certain official Government publications as late as 1959. In that year appeared a Ministry of Education publication called *Citizens Growing Up*, which referred at some length to the need for a religious faith if personal and social values were to be effective in the education of the young. This assumption is no longer one which can be safely or easily made. In the complex society in which our children are now growing up moral education certainly continues for some people to be intimately associated with their Christian or other organized religious beliefs and practices, but for others it is rooted in a variety of more vaguely religious, or in humanistic, convictions.

170 It is for this reason that some have argued, as we have already remarked, that to base moral education in schools almost entirely upon religious beliefs and practices might be to run the risk that those young people who eventually reject organized religion may in the process also reject the moral principles and standards which have been intimately associated with it. Though we have no evidence which would substantiate this contention, we accept the principle that the nature of our society by its very complexity makes it advisable that moral education in schools should proceed in a manner which establishes its significance and its claims equally for the person with religious, as for the person who holds to other, convictions, about the meaning and purpose of human life.

171 This does not, however, imply that religious and moral education could or should proceed entirely independently of one another. We have already argued that religious education would be incomplete if its moral implications were unexplored, and that moral education would be inadequate if it attempted to evade the fundamental questions about human life with which Christianity is concerned. For this reason, and because Christianity has played an important part in the moral as well as in the religious life of our society, it is clear that religious education must continue to make an important contribution to the moral education of pupils in the schools. It is

[1] Cmd 6458, para. 36: our italics.

4*

equally clear that other aspects of the life and work of the school in which moral principles or practices are concerned must be expected sometimes to involve the consideration of issues which are essentially religious in character.

172 Any attempt to define the contribution which religious education can make to the moral education of children and young people must depend upon the answer given to a preliminary question, namely: What part does the school in general play in the process? Behind this question, of course, lurks yet another: What is the part played by heredity and what is the part played by environment? Briefly the answer to this latter question seems to be that both play a part, and an interactive part, though of the two "nurture" appears to play a somewhat stronger role than "nature". To consider the "nurture" aspect first.

173 School is one of three main environmental agencies involved in the total process of moral development, the other two being the home (including here any associations home may have with a church) and the wider society with which children come increasingly into contact outside both home and school. It has usually been believed that potentially the home is the most influential of these three agencies and the little research that has so far been undertaken seems to bear this out, though it has to be remembered that it is impossible to generalize about "the home". There is some evidence to suggest that children from "higher status" homes are better prepared than children from "lower status" homes to adjust themselves to the demands of society in and beyond the school. This seems to be the result of different attitudes on the part of parents as to the methods by which to develop desired behaviour in their children.[1]

174 The influence of the wider society beyond school and home becomes increasingly significant with the development of the adolescent stage. In recent years parents, teachers, and others have become increasingly aware of the force of a youth or teenage culture which stands in certain respects in contrast to the main types of adult culture. One aspect of the existence of a youth culture is to be seen in the influence which, in certain cities, gangs exert upon the attitudes and behaviour of individual teenagers; another is to be

[1] Some evidence relating to home influence is summarized in ch. 8 of Wilson, Williams, and Sugarman, op. cit.

seen in the attraction of the less aggressive types of teenage interests and activities. In the latter, distinctive forms of dress, dance, and music are probably less significant than the accompanying codes of behaviour which are often openly at variance with those characteristic of adult society as a whole.

175 The school is in an intermediate situation between those other two main agencies—home and the wider society. For the infant, school becomes a gentle first move from the shelter of home towards wider society. The infant teacher stands to some extent in the place of the mother, but being a teacher has more opportunity to set going the process of the child's introduction to a wider society. This process is carried to further stages in the junior and secondary school as the role of the teacher changes and a gradually increasing formality in the atmosphere of the school is experienced. The function of the school here is to help the child to move with growing confidence in a gradually widening society by encouraging him to face it realistically and critically and eventually to come to terms with it for himself.

176 To the adolescent, teachers, even where they encourage him to look critically at adult society, are nevertheless part of adult society, and school life as a whole with its routine of required work, with its more formal personal relations between the pupil and his peers on the one hand and the staff on the other, with its rules and conventions, is seen by the adolescent as a means of initiating him into adult society. The plan of the Newsom Report was that the secondary school should relate its activities even more closely to adult society in educating those adolescents who would soon be leaving school to work and generally to begin to take their place in an adult society. The fact is, however, that the adolescent in school now finds himself confronted not with one but with two main patterns of interests, attitudes, and behaviour. On the one hand, he feels the attraction of the "youth" culture which is backed by the appeal of his peer group, and, on the other, he is aware of the "culture" of adult society. This and the further fact that adult "culture" is itself diversified would suggest that the school's task in moral education is one of considerable complexity, calling for a good deal of insight, sensitivity, and sympathy on the part of teachers.

177 Our knowledge of the part played by "nature" is likewise very incomplete. It would probably be generally agreed that since moral development is intimately linked with the whole development of personality, the insights which the research and theories of Freud, Adler, Jung, and their successors have provided into the importance of subconscious factors in the growth of personality cannot be ignored. At least parents, teachers, and others concerned with the moral training and education of the young will nowadays beware of regarding all irregular or anti-social behaviour as necessarily the result of conscious ill will and will seek to use these occurrences creatively for educational purposes.

178 Of more immediate significance perhaps has been the kind of research fostered by J. Piaget, P. Bovet, L. Kohlberg, and others concerned to discover whether moral growth passes through any regular stages. Though this type of research has focused upon the attitudes and behaviour of individual children, it must be recognized that it examines features of moral development which are the product not only of "natural" individual development but also of social influence. In the last resort it is impossible to distinguish the two. There is a substantial body of research on the subject of mental health, all of which underlines the important part played by social factors in children's moral development.[1] Bearing this caveat in mind, it may be said that there is some evidence to suggest that stages may well be characteristic of the process and that three in particular may be marked (though attempts are being made to distinguish further sub-divisions).

Infancy A pre-moral stage at which children learn to obey in order to avoid punishment or to obtain rewards. The foundations of satisfactory moral growth are dependent upon the parents, especially the mother, providing the kind of environment in which both a sense of acceptance, and an encouragement to begin first explorations, of the real world are present.

Preadolescence The child begins through school in particular to move out into a wider society. He accepts authority and has a tendency to conform to parents, teachers, and school rules in order to avoid disapproval; his morality is largely "heteronomous" in character. The child from a "higher-status" home may be assisted at this stage by having the sort of parents who attempt to explain why certain kinds of behaviour are required.

[1] See the extensive literature published under the auspices of the world Federation for Mental Health.

Adolescence This is the stage at which the "autonomous" phase in moral growth should begin to predominate. The development of the capacity to think in abstract terms makes possible the consideration of moral principles. Increased awareness of "self" and the appeal of moral ideals ("ego-ideals") can lead to the acceptance of personal values and a code of behaviour. The "heteronomous" element (pressures of convention, rules, laws) can now be incorporated to a greater or lesser degree in the individual's own consciously accepted personal "code". Today this process is probably more complex as a result of conflict, even if temporary, between the kinds of values and behaviour inherent in the various aspects of "youth" and "adult" culture.[1]

179 If the moral development of the young may normally be expected to pass through such stages as these, then it is clear that the precise way in which the school plays its part will vary with the home and the wider society. In playing this role an important part of the school's function, in moral education in particular, is, as has already been said, to encourage the pupil to come to terms with society in a critical and not in a purely passive spirit.

180 There is a broad area of school life in which the task of moral education should be seen as a responsibility shared by all members of the school staff, namely, in the effort to maintain and develop a sound "ethos" of the school. The moral values and practices which characterize a school society and which manifest themselves in every aspect of its life and work, though they must be subject to regular scrutiny and criticism, need to be upheld and, when occasion arises, explained and defended. This explanation and defence may sometimes involve the discussion of fundamental issues, including religious beliefs and practices. If a member of the staff feels reluctant or un-qualified to discuss the religious aspect of such matters, the respon-sibility for this part of the discussion can and should be handed over

[1] An important comment has recently been made on the relation between the "heteronomous" and "autonomous" elements within a person's individual code of behaviour. It has often been assumed in the past that the former was associated with an authoritarian approach to morality which fell away when the "autono-mous" stage was reached. Norman Williams of the Farmington Trust Research Unit has suggested that this is to oversimplify and has put forward an alternative scheme of analysis, namely the four modes of "self-considering", "other-considering", "self-obeying", and "other-obeying", both the last two being basically authoritarian. He makes the further point that only rarely will an individual's responses fall consistently within one of these categories alone; most people's behaviour is made up of actions in at least three of these modes.

to a colleague who is able and willing to accept it. Failure to explore fully with pupils fundamental questions which arise directly out of the actual moral demands made upon them by the school community as a whole must be regarded as a weakness in moral education. Moral education in schools has too often suffered from the naive assumptions that it is mainly concerned with talk rather than with practice, and that most of the talking is the responsibility of the "R.E. specialist". The main difference between the primary and the secondary school here will be that in the former the "heteronomous" morality of the child implies that explanation and certainly discussion will need to play a less prominent part than in the latter.

181 In arguing that the "ethos" of a school must be subject to regular scrutiny and criticism we have been concerned to guard against the danger that individual teachers may feel inhibited from giving honest expression to their own convictions on certain moral issues. Not only must they be free to do so but the effectiveness and realism of the school's "ethos" will depend upon their doing so. The proper place for them to do this, however, is in staff meetings in which the general pattern of the life and work of the school can be determined by discussion and agreement on the part of the whole staff.

182 We welcome two developments in particular which in recent years have done much, in schools where they have been fostered, to emphasize that moral education is concerned with practice as well as with talk. The first is the involvement of the pupils in certain responsibilities for behaviour and discipline, through such institutions as staff/pupils' committees or councils. The second is the growth of community-service projects which are designed to involve pupils in a variety of services to people in the community around the school. With careful planning and the necessary safeguards it is clear that both kinds of activity are of considerable value in moral education.

183 Within the staff of a school as a whole a greater responsibility for moral education must inevitably fall upon those members whose work involves them in learning situations in which human behaviour, attitudes, and ideals are brought explicitly into view. History, geography, literature, and religion are the main, though certainly not the only, areas of the curriculum where this occurs. No doubt many teachers already recognize the importance of allowing, and indeed of encouraging, the consideration by their pupils of the moral aspects of the characters, behaviour, and events which form an essential part of these aspects of their learning. We would stress the fact that it is a responsibility which must be accepted by all who engage in this work, and that here again appropriate action must be taken, at secondary school level in particular, to ensure that pupils explore for themselves those fundamental questions which are raised in these areas of the curriculum.

The Contribution of Religious Education

184 The teacher responsible for religious education will, in our view, continue to have a significant contribution to make to the moral education of the pupils in a school. His task is that of presenting to his pupils examples of Christian attitudes and behaviour, and at the secondary stage of exploring with them the nature and grounds of the moral implications of Christian and other convictions and attitudes and their application to a wide range of personal, social, and international issues. He will, however, at the same time be careful to emphasize that the Christian has no monopoly of concern for such matters. It is essential to the proper consideration of moral issues that the teacher of religious education should be scrupulously honest, from the infant school right up to the sixth form, in making it plain when he is presenting the religious view of the good life. Agreed syllabuses have too often tended to imply that all good people have been and are Christians; there are, however, welcome signs that some recent versions of these syllabuses adopt a more realistic standpoint.

185 There is some evidence to suggest that the notion of "readiness" needs to be applied to moral education as it is already being applied to the planning of other aspects of the curriculum.[1] Thus, up to mental age 13 or so, it will be rare for the religious education lesson to include any discussion of Christian morality in abstract terms. The teacher's work up to this stage will, in order to present the moral challenge, concentrate upon actual examples of men and women, Christians and non-Christians, who have tried or are trying to live the good life in the circumstances of their time and situation. In doing so he will need to look somewhat critically at the failure of the older agreed syllabuses to distinguish between the historical or

[1] W. Kay, *Moral Development* (Allen & Unwin 1968), pp. 249–53.

theological *motif* which led to the inclusion of certain traditions in
the Old Testament (and occasionally also in the New Testament)
Canon, and the level of morality reflected in such traditions. The
lives of certain of the "heroes", for example Jacob, Samson, Jeph-
thah, who figure in such traditions, viewed at this distance, can only
be described as immoral. Unless the teacher is careful to distinguish
between historical or theological reasons which led to the inclusion
of such traditions in the Old Testament and the sub-morality inherent
in them, religious education here could well inhibit rather than foster
moral education.

186 From mental age 13 onwards the emphasis will be increasingly
upon discussion of moral issues with the aim of uncovering the nature
of, and the reasons for, Christian and other attitudes and/or practice.
Recent investigations have revealed the extent to which both the
more and the less able adolescents are interested to find out what
religion has to say about moral issues of which they are beginning
to become conscious in their own experience. The best starting-point
for such discussion is often to be found in the actual experience of
adolescents themselves rather than in the apparently remote biblical
or later historical material which used to be regarded as the normal
starting-point.

187 It will be open to the teacher to decide, in the light of the circumstances in which he is working and in consultation with the head,
to what extent it is desirable to enlist the co-operation of other
members of the school staff, or of suitable persons from outside the
school, to discuss some of these moral issues from standpoints other
than the Christian, as part of the religious education course itself.
Whether or not this is done—and we recognize that the time available
for religious education in some school time-tables may militate
against such a procedure—it is plainly important that room for some
contribution to the discussion of moral principle and practice, from
members of the school staff and from others who do not start from
a Christian standpoint, should be found at some point in the time-
table.

188 At this stage, however, it must be recognized that the task of
the teacher of religious education becomes more difficult. There is
considerable diversity among Christians themselves on specific
moral issues such as premarital sexual relations, homosexuality, the

nature of marriage, divorce, the use of drugs, race-relations, war, and "the bomb". Behind this diversity, and to some extent accounting for it, lies the further difficulty that Christian attitudes to, and thinking about, moral principle and practice reflect disagreement and even hesitation. The traditional view that for the Christian morality means "doing the will of God" or "following the example of our Lord", as revealed in the Bible and interpreted in succeeding generations by the Church, seems to some Christians no longer adequate either in theory or in practice. For them one or other form of what has come to be called "agapism",[1] namely, the application to particular moral problems or situations of the general principle of "the law of love (*agape*)", "love" of God and of one's "neighbour", seems at once more informative and more effective. Thus in the realm of Christian Ethics a transitional and at present somewhat confused situation obtains, which is not dissimilar from, and in some respects is directly related to, the state of contemporary Christian Theology. But it is a mistake to regard this situation as sinister. It is one in which teachers and learners are co-operating in a spirit of search and exploration.

[1] W. Lillie, "Is there a tenable Religious Theory of Ethics?", *Religious Studies* 3, No. 1 (March 1967), pp. 313–21 and P. Ramsey, "Deeds and Rules in Christian Ethics", *Scottish Journal of Theology*, Occasional Paper no. 11 (1965) (Oliver & Boyd).

4

Religious Education in Schools with special reference to County Schools

Aims

189 It is our purpose in this chapter to examine and discuss some basic issues of policy and principle affecting religious education. We do not intend to embark on a prolonged examination of the many detailed practical problems connected with the actual teaching of the subject in the school situation. We have, however, provided an extensive bibliography to which reference may be made. In our examination of this subject we have taken account of certain research projects which have been completed in recent years.[1] We find that, apart from these, there is at present a paucity of reliable research material relating to religious education in general and in particular to the religious education of (*a*) junior children and (*b*) less able children at both junior and secondary level. We are in this chapter principally concerned with religious education in county schools. We are not concerned in the same way with the specific problems of religious education in Church of England voluntary schools or in independent or direct grant schools, although many of the issues discussed will be highly relevant to them. In any case, certain aspects of religious education in independent and direct grant schools and in Church of England voluntary schools are discussed further in chs. 5 and 7.

[1] E.g.: H. Loukes, *New Ground in Christian Education* (S.C.M. 1965).
　　　R. J. Goldman, *Religious Thinking from Childhood to Adolescence* (Routledge & Kegan Paul 1964).
　　　E. Cox, *Sixth Form Religion* (S.C.M. 1967).
　　　R. J. Rees, *Background and Belief* (S.C.M. 1967).
　　　C. Alves, *Religion and the Secondary School* (S.C.M. 1968).
　　　C. C. M. Jones, *Worship in the Secondary School* (S.C.M. 1969).
　　　K. E. Hyde, *Religion and Slow Learners* (S.C.M. 1969).

190 *We wish to emphasize that we are not a Research Unit and have had neither the time nor the financial resources to embark on formal research projects on our own account.* We believe, however, that a careful examination of fundamental policy and principle is both necessary and timely. In the past "policy", if such it can be called, relating to religious education has been more the outcome of an amalgam of ecclesiastical, social, and political pressures, educational custom, and adult nostalgia, than the result of carefully examined theological, philosophical, and educational considerations.

191 We recognize that "religious education" in the schools of England and Wales has two essential components:

1. Religious Teaching, i.e. what pupils learn about the subject through curricular and extra-curricular study and activity.
2. Worship, i.e. what pupils experience through participation in acts of worship in school. We recognize that the many complex problems connected with school worship require separate treatment.[1]

Some Previous Arguments

192 We begin by examining some arguments which have been used in the past to justify or to support the inclusion of religious education on the school curriculum. These arguments are certainly not wholly to be discounted. They are still relevant to any discussion of the subject. But we believe that they should be regarded as of supportive value rather than of primary significance.

The Nature of Society and Public Opinion

193 At the time of the passing of the 1944 Education Act, there were many who held that England was a Christian country, that Christian teachers in Christian schools should do their duty to Christian parents by teaching their children the Christian faith. This is the background of public opinion to the White Paper which was published as a prelude to the 1944 Act.

There has been a very general wish, not confined to representatives of the Churches, that religious education should be given a more defined place in the life and work of the schools, springing from the desire to revive the spiritual and personal values in our society and in our national tradition.

[1] See paras. 284–320 below.

The Church, the family, the local community and the teacher—all have their part to play in imparting religious instruction to the young. In order to emphasize the importance of the subject, provision will be made for the school day in all primary and secondary schools to begin with a corporate act of worship, except where this is impracticable owing to the nature of the school premises, and for religious instruction to be given. At present this is the practice in the great majority of schools and this practice will receive statutory sanction and be universal.[1]

194 There are some who argue that Britain is still a Christian country and that public opinion has not substantially altered since 1944. Mr P. R. May and Mr O. R. Johnston in *Religion in our Schools* point out that the Churches are large and significant social groups; that the Christian faith is the state religion and receives official recognition at events such as Coronations and Assize services; that the main-stream Christian Churches are given time on TV and radio; that opinion polls show that the vast majority of English people describe themselves as "Christian" and are in favour of religious education. Their position may be summarized by the quotation they provide from T. S. Eliot: "A society has not ceased to be Christian until it has become positively something else."[2]

195 Others such as Mr H. L. Elvin have argued that England is now a religiously "pluralistic" or "open" or "multi-belief" society;[3] that, whereas a minority of committed and practising Christians still exist, the majority of English people tend to indifference and reveal varying degrees of thinking or unthinking agnosticism. The existence of an articulate body of secularist opinion should also be recognized, together with the existence of other sizeable religious groups such as Jews and, in areas with a recent immigrant population, Moslems, Sikhs, and Hindus. Others have sought to argue that England is now for all practical purposes a secularist society, that the religious groupings are dwindling into insignificance and that such public religious observances as remain represent little more than custom and sentiment, nostalgic survivals of an irrelevant medievalism.[4]

196 Recent sociological research[5] suggests that this is a subject

[1] White Paper, *Educational Reconstruction*, Cmd 6458, para. 36.
[2] P. R. May and O. R. Johnston, *Religion in our Schools* (Hodder 1968), p. 32.
[3] E.g. in Ch. 10 of *Religious Education 1944–1984*, ed. A. G. Wedderspoon (Allen & Unwin 1966).
[4] E.g. H. J. Blackham, *Religion in a Modern Society* (Constable 1966).
[5] E.g. D. Martin, *A Sociology of English Religion* (S.C.M. 1967).

which does not lend itself to sweeping or facile generalizations. It might seem difficult to argue that England is still a Christian society when only about 10% of the population are committed and practising members of the Christian Church. But it seems equally difficult to argue that ours is an avowedly "pluralistic" or "secularist" society when 80% to 90% identify themselves with Christianity. It is not evident how far the sociologists of religion can clarify this problem. Meanwhile, the fact remains that the Christian faith has long been interwoven with the institutions of English public life, and on the question of providing religious education in schools the weight of public opinion is quite clearly favourable.[1]

197 These are important and relevant factors. The schools of England and Wales are the schools of a democratic society and it is axiomatic that public opinion must be fully taken into account when educational problems are being considered. Nevertheless, arguments from public opinion and the nature of society, however important, cannot be by themselves wholly definitive. Well organized pressure groups could create a public opinion to support the teaching of a particular subject to school pupils, but this would be inconclusive unless it could be shown that the subject in question was a sufficiently acceptable educational discipline to justify its inclusion in the curriculum. Likewise, religious education cannot rest its case solely on the pressure of public opinion, however positive. It must be shown to have an important contribution to make to general education if its place is to be secured. What applies to other subjects and disciplines must equally apply to religious education.

The Cultural Argument

198 This asserts that religious education is essential because we in England are heirs to the cultural tradition of the West; the Christian faith is so interwoven with our history, art, music, and literature that it would not be possible to teach these subjects in schools without some teaching about the Christian religion. The argument that, for example, the history of England in the sixteenth and seventeenth centuries would be incomprehensible without some understanding

---

[1] E.g. N.O.P. *New Society*, May 1965.
   P. R. May and O. R. Johnston, *Durham Research Review*, April 1967.
   Gallup Poll on *T.V. and Religion* (A.B.C. Television 1964).
   N.O.P., March 1969.

of the Bible and the Christian faith is, of course, irrefutable. But this could adequately be done within the history course itself, as could the Aztec religion be taught in the course of studying the conquest of Mexico. Even the National Secular Society recognizes that religion may be studied within the context of history or literature. But this is certainly not religious education as we understand it, and as we shall describe it in this chapter.

Religion and Morality

199 In the nineteenth century religious education was seen by most as the essential basis of moral education and its place on the school curriculum was frequently argued for this instrumental reason. This subject has been discussed in more detail in ch. 3. Moral education is now seen to be a many-sided process in which a wide variety of different agencies make their influence felt. Home, school, neighbourhood, peer groups, mass media communication, are only some among many sources of moral education. Within the school itself it is a complex process and certainly cannot be limited to the teaching of any one subject on the curriculum. The relations between religion and morality are such that religious education will have a valuable part to play in the wider task of moral education, but its place on the curriculum cannot be justified solely by an argument of this kind.

Tradition

200 It is sometimes said to be unthinkable that religion should not be taught in schools because of its long history—it is an essential part of the tradition of English education. But educational problems cannot be solved only by appeal to past traditions, or the school curriculum would still be based on classics and the cane.

The Educational Argument

201 All major educational reports in recent years have made it plain that the principal argument for religious education in county schools is that it is a subject with its own inherent educational value and must have its place on the curriculum for educational reasons. We entirely agree.

202 As has already been stated in ch. 1, this view found expression in the Spens Report of 1938 on Secondary Education, where the affirmation was made that "no boy or girl can be counted as properly educated unless he or she has been made aware of the fact of the existence of a religious interpretation of life". This essentially educational approach is developed by the Crowther and Newsom Reports.

The teenagers with whom we are concerned need, perhaps before all else, to find a faith to live by. They will not all find precisely the same faith and some will not find any. Education can and should play some part in their search. It can assure them that there is something to search for and it can show them where to look and what other men have found (Crowther, p. 44).

The best schools give their pupils something which they do not get elsewhere, something which they know they need when they receive it, though they had not realised the lack before. We believe that this can be, and usually is, given in a way which does justice to the mixed society in which we live, recognising the range and degrees of religious belief and practice to be found in it, and respecting the right of the individual conscience to be provided with the material on which freely to decide its path (Newsom, pp. 55–6).

203 Very broadly, what lies behind these statements are certain assumptions about the nature of man, about religion, and about the educational process. In former ages man was thought of as body and soul. Nowadays it is a good deal more difficult to find a generally acceptable formula. To the behaviourist, man is a complicated piece of social patterning; others see him as a piece of mobile biochemistry, wholly part of the natural order and subject to control by external stimuli. Very many people, and all Christians, would see this as inadequate, untrue to the richness and depth of human experience. Man is a phenomenon, a complex structure of physical, emotional, and psychical characteristics and there are aspects of his being which are not adequately explained by any reductionist theories,[1] whether in science or psychology.[2]

204 Man is a creature who finds himself perplexed with the mystery of his existence. He knows that he is, and ponders why he is, what

[1] Reductionist Theories: attempts to "reduce" the complexity of problems so as to explain them within the context of some particular set of scientific or psychological presuppositions. Reductionism is thus based on the view that there is one particular area of discourse to which all other types of language must be reduced. It would, for example, be reductionism to assert that man was "nothing but" a naked ape and that his behavioural problems could be satisfactorily explained by the zoologist alone.
[2] See further, ch. 2, paras. 131–137 above.

he is, and what he is for. From the start of recorded history he has
sought to find answers to the enigma of his origin and destiny, he
has puzzled about the meaning and purpose of his life. He has sought
explanations for his pain, his suffering, and the fact of his finitude.
He has sought value systems to provide dignity and direction to his
life. The great religions of the world find their frame of reference
within these ultimate questions which man has asked and continues
to ask—questions which are part of the human condition.

205 The existence of a religious interpretation of life is a fact of
history and of present human experience. There are many millions
of men and women throughout the world who find through their
religious beliefs a deep meaning and purpose for their lives and a
system of values by which their lives can be lived. There appears to
be a "spiritual dimension" in man's nature which requires to be
expressed by "religion" of one kind or another. By religion we mean
some pattern of belief and behaviour related to the questions of
man's ultimate concern. For some, it is an Eastern religion; for some it
is Christianity; for others it is one of the secular creeds of the West,
for example Marxism; for others it is agnostic humanism; for many
it may be little more than moral stoicism. Man seems to have to find
"a faith to live by", however noble, or simple, or debased. Young
people share in the human condition. They should have some opportunity to learn that religion is a feature of this condition, and
for some men a deeply significant area of human knowledge and
experience.

206 But is it right that this opportunity should be provided within
the processes of formal education? Should this not be wholly the
responsibility of the religious organizations and the home? One of
the more obvious truisms to be culled from the writings of the educational philosophers is that a distinction has to be observed between
training and education. An "educated" person is one who has
achieved something more than mastery of a craft or skill, or the
assimilation of a body of knowledge. In recent years many descriptions of the purposes of education in western society have been
advanced. "The education of the whole man", "education for
growth", "education for self-fulfilment", and so on. It would be
possible to embark on extended arguments to show that the teaching
of religion could be given a place in the educational processes envisaged by these descriptions. But it would be more profitable to

limit the discussion to a concept of education which is influential at the present time.

207 By reaction from philosophies of education which were influenced by metaphysical thinking, a recent description of the educational process sees education as initiation. It is the task of the teacher to initiate the young into bodies of knowledge, activities, modes of thought and conduct, which are believed by society to have "worthwhileness". "Education implies standards, not necessarily aims . . . it consists of initiating others into activities, modes of conduct and thought which have standards written into them by reference to which it is possible to act, think and feel with varying degrees of skill, reverence and taste."[1]

208 If education is to be conceived in this way—as initiation into public traditions—it can be reasonably argued that public religious traditions are candidates for inclusion if such religious traditions are thought by society to possess the required criteria of "worthwhileness". This process will involve rigorous thought and study, for the only way of mastering the "language" of any form of thought or activity is by being first initiated into its "literature". Thus the development of religious appreciation and understanding will involve the close study of texts and beliefs, forms of worship, social and ethical teaching.

209 R. S. Peters has suggested that "to be educated is not to have arrived at a destination: it is to travel with a different view".[2] We think that an understanding of the religious interpretation of life should be a feature of this view.

210 The argument so far has been that the nature of man, the fact of the existence of a religious interpretation of life, and the nature and purpose of the educational process, point to the need for some form of religious education. The term "religious education" has been given, so far, very wide and general meaning. Does it follow from this that religious education should take the form it does in schools in England and Wales at present? The argument thus far might be taken to imply that, while religious education should take place, it

[1] R. S. Peters in *Philosophical Analysis and Education*, ed. R. D. Archambault (Routledge & Kegan Paul 1965), p. 107.
[2] Op. cit., p. 110.

should be a generalized study of all world religions and belief systems. In short, why should it take place in schools, and why should it be mainly the study of Christianity?

211 Religious education has its place on the school curriculum because it draws attention to a significant area of human thought and activity. A curriculum which excluded religion would seem to proclaim that religion has not been as real in men's lives as science, or politics, or economics. By omission it would appear to deny that religion has been and still is important in man's history. To the question, would something be lost if religious education were excluded from the school curriculum, we must answer, definitely yes.

212 If then religious education should continue to have its place on the curricula of English schools because a curriculum without it would be seriously deficient, why should it remain as specifically Christian? The comparative study of religions and other belief systems will certainly have an important place in the religious education of many pupils. More will be said of this later, when the content of the religious education curriculum is being examined. Nevertheless, it must be recognized that the kind of understanding which is involved in religious education, as we shall later show, can be achieved only if pupils study the religious tradition or traditions of their own particular culture. For the great majority of pupils in England and Wales this is the Christian faith.[1]

213 The claims of religions differ profoundly in certain respects and so do the cultures which they have influenced. All serious religious thought and experience has arisen within a tradition and cannot be understood apart from it. Hence there cannot be a religious education which is concerned simply with religion as such. It would be educationally unrealistic to propose that all pupils in the schools of England and Wales should study the Bible and, *as well*, the *Qur'ān*, the *Bhagavadgītā*, the *Upaniṣads*, and the Buddhist scriptures. This would inevitably lead to extreme superficiality, even if there were enough teachers possessing the relevant qualifications. Religious education, to be of any value, must involve the thorough study of some particular religion. In the final analysis, the decision as to

[1] We fully recognize that Jewish parents will wish their children to be educated in the Jewish faith. We further recognize that the parents of some immigrant children will wish them to be taught their particular faith.

which particular religion will be studied will depend not only on what religion is prevalent in the culture, but on the extent to which that religion is believed to be true.

214 The argument has thus been that religious education, in one form or another, contributes something of value to the education of children and young persons and that the content of the curriculum in this country should consist mainly of the exploration of the literature and beliefs of the Christian faith. This, in the very broadest terms, is the educational argument for religious education which finds expression in the various official reports of recent years. What has been said so far in this chapter is only the barest outline of an argument which could be given a great deal of detailed expansion.

215 If religious education is placed in this general educational context, what should be its aim? The aim of religious education should be to explore the place and significance of religion in human life and so to make a distinctive contribution to each pupil's search for a faith by which to live.[1]

216 To achieve this aim, the teacher will seek to introduce most pupils to that biblical, historical, and theological knowledge which forms the cognitive basis of the Christian faith. This will be done with careful reference to the ages, interests, and degrees of comprehension of the pupils. The teacher will also seek to show his pupils the insights provided by Christian faith and experience into a wide range of personal, social, and ethical problems. Moreover, he will seek to discuss with his pupils the various answers and approaches provided by this faith to those basic questions of life and existence which perplex all thoughtful men. Where appropriate, he will also study other religions and belief systems. The teacher is thus seeking rather to initiate his pupils into knowledge which he encourages them to explore and appreciate, than into a system of belief which he requires them to accept.

217 To press for acceptance of a particular faith or belief system is the duty and privilege of the Churches and other similar religious bodies. It is certainly not the task of a teacher in a county school. If the teacher is to press for any conversion, it is conversion from a shallow and unreflective attitude to life. If he is to press for commitment, it is commitment to the religious quest, to that search for

[1] Cf. Crowther Report para. 66, p. 44 (as quoted in para. 202 above).

meaning, purpose, and value which is open to all men. We fully accept that the teacher's own personal presuppositions, enthusiasms, and prejudices are likely to show themselves at every stage, and must be frankly recognized by him and by his pupils. This will, of course, apply no less, for example, to the teacher of history, literature, art, or music. We are certainly not advocating deliberate prejudice in the teaching of any subject but merely stating a fact of educational activity.

218 This chapter has emphasized so far the importance of religious education in the general education of all pupils. The question now arises, what of the conscience clauses for teachers and the withdrawal rights possessed by parents? Given so clear an educational emphasis, will any teacher or parent think it necessary to exercise these rights? Despite the educational argument which has been put forward we think that the conscience clauses and the withdrawal rights should be retained. Experience suggests that there will be parents who, for atheistic or for sectarian reasons, will not wish their children to receive formal religious teaching of any kind. There will be teachers of similar persuasion. Their conscientious scruples should be respected. It is our hope, however, that teachers and parents will in future think it less necessary to exercise their legal rights as this clearly stated educational emphasis becomes more widely understood.[1]

Content and Method

219 In this part of the chapter we attempt to show how the principles enunciated in paras. 201–218 above could be worked out in schools. We are certainly not attempting to draw up some ideal syllabus for use in all the schools of England and Wales.This leads us first to consider agreed syllabuses, which are principally the concern of county and non-denominational voluntary schools. We do not think that the existing complicated legal machinery for drawing up, adopting, or varying an agreed syllabus should be retained. This is a

---

[1] We recognize that this presents an anomalous position. If religious education is to take its place on the school curriculum for educational reasons, then why should it be the one subject from which pupils may legally be withdrawn? A secular humanist teacher may intrude his own personal presuppositions into the teaching of, say, science or history. A parent with strong religious beliefs may protest that his child is subjected to teaching of this kind, but he possesses no right of withdrawal. Thus the problem of "withdrawal rights" raises broader issues and the teaching of other subjects could sometimes be such as to justify parental request for withdrawal. Nevertheless, we recognize that the issue is a particularly sensitive one where the teaching of religion is concerned.

relic of the ecclesiastical era in religious education, when the content of the curriculum had to be "agreed" between representatives of the Church of England, other Churches in the area which had a claim to be heard, the local education authority, and teachers. We are aware that much creative work was done, and some impressive syllabuses have emerged from it; but we believe this legal machinery to be no longer relevant. Moreover, we see no reason why, in religious education any more than in any other subject, one particular syllabus should be imposed by any local education authority.

220 We seek for religious education the same freedom which is enjoyed by every other subject. This does not mean, of course, that every teacher of every subject is simply left to his own resources. There is an increasing range of conferences, courses, discussions in teachers' centres, and professional subject associations, as well as a constant flow of books and advisory literature. There are specialist H.M.I.s, and local education authorities employ advisers for many subjects of the curriculum; at present far too few, in our judgement, employ one for religious education. What we are stressing is that the normal arrangements for curriculum development should apply to religious education as to every other subject. Handbooks of suggestions, in one form or another, are published both by the Department of Education and Science and by individual local education authorities and deal with various subjects. Each local education authority should ensure that a handbook of suggestions is available for the teachers of religious education in their area. Some local education authorities will wish to draw up their own handbooks and so will call on theologians, educationists, and teachers with the relevant knowledge and experience. It is important that such handbooks should be regularly revised.

The Religious Education of Children and Pre-adolescents 5 to 13+

221 Educational reorganization makes it difficult to speak of infant, junior, and secondary schools, as in the recent past. Meanwhile, no single new pattern of schooling has yet emerged. Under these circumstances, we will focus our discussion on the pupil's stages of development rather than on the type of school. The developmental stages recognized by teachers in other subjects are no less important for religious education. The intuitive thought of the very young child progresses to the slightly more concrete and factual approach of the

7 to 9 year old. By the mental age of 9, the child will be forming attitudes to ideas and institutions which, while still in concrete terms, are preparing him for future learning. From mental age 9 to 13+ pupils become gradually more able to think in abstract and symbolic terms. It is significant that recent educational research has gone far to support the experience of many teachers that round about the mental age of 13+ the pupil reaches an important developmental threshold in religious education. It is usually at this stage that the pupil becomes capable of beginning that abstract conceptual thought which is necessary for any deep religious understanding and insight. If this is true (and the basic principle enjoys a wide degree of acceptance among educators even if its implications are disputed), then it follows that the curriculum must be planned accordingly.

222 It must not, however, be forgotten that religious education has other dimensions than those of conceptual thought. Many children will be slow to reach the developmental stages indicated above. But religious sensitivity does not wait upon religious thinking. It depends on satisfying experiences of human relationship, on attitudes communicated through adult companionship, and on the exploration of everyday experience at more than superficial levels. These aspects of religious development must also find a place in religious education in the classroom.

PUPILS OF MENTAL AGE 5 to 7

223 In considering the religious education of children from mental age 5 to 7 we stress that it is the attitudes formed in home and community in the pre-school years which provide the foundation on which the school must build. These will vary from district to district, from school to school, and sometimes even from year to year in the same school. There are many homes where spiritual values are respected: there are many others in which not even lip-service is paid to any consideration but self-interest. It follows, therefore, that children begin their formal education with very various physical, psychological, sociological, and economic advantages and disadvantages. Some children—and not by any means necessarily from the economically poorest homes—are emotionally deprived. Others may have had no play experience. In any group the quality of religious education possible at this stage will depend on what the children bring with them and on the level at which their needs can be met. For all, it will be necessary to offer experience of security, affection, and reassurance. For some this is all that can be achieved at this stage, but for others, with a richer linguistic background and a greater degree of emotional security, much more will be possible. The presence of either in a group will have inevitable repercussions on what is possible for the group as a whole.

224 We stress the importance in this respect of adequate pre-school facilities in play groups or nursery classes—a theme well developed by the Plowden Committee in their report. Of crucial importance for religious education at this stage is the quality of the general education available to the child. This is true for all aspects of work with very young children, but it is no less important for religious education. There are still schools where harassed teachers struggle with over-crowded classes in unsatisfactory buildings.

225 In the past, religious education at the 5 to 7 stage often consisted mainly of Bible stories read or told to the class. Most teachers would now reject the view that the mere transmission of information is a major part of education at this stage. A great deal of experiment is being undertaken to meet a new understanding of the religious needs of very young children. Few teachers would claim that any certainty of approach has as yet been achieved. We are agreed that a diet of Bible stories, however carefully selected and sincerely delivered, will be of limited educational value at this stage.

226 The young child arrives in school with a miscellaneous set of impressions derived from his environment. He may have been told that God made him, that God made the flowers, and that Grandma has died and gone to be with God in heaven. He will know that some importance is attached by adults to the Christian year, even if this is only in terms of Christmas presents, hot cross buns, Easter eggs, and new clothes at Whitsun. The religious educator is faced with the question: "How can these vague and confused intimations from the culture be made meaningful to the child so that, as he matures, he may recognize that they come from ideas sincerely held by thinking people and are not just quaint irrelevancies from a bygone age?"

227 The modern infant teacher recognizes that children of this age group learn most through activity and experience. This has long been accepted in the teaching of other subjects. We wish to emphasize that it should be equally accepted in religious education. The infant teacher may wish to show the relationship between these events of the Christian year and the life of Jesus, and she may wish to do this by the use of carefully selected Bible stories, model-making, painting and drawing, music and play. These are well-tried methods and they still have their value. Nevertheless, it must be recognized that very little of an infant child's experience will be directly mirrored in biblical material and that careful selection is essential. Teachers will vary in the extent to which they find selected biblical material relevant to shared experience in the classroom. We do not think that, at this stage, the Bible can be used as a textbook, or as material taught for its own sake.

228 The work of the infant and lower junior teacher in religious education is not only to meet the needs of the young child but also to prepare the child to be able to comprehend and assess religious concepts at the appropriate time. Discussion at the secondary stage of "God the Creator" may have little signficance unless the pupil carries within himself satisfying experiences of creativity and knows that to create is to care, even to love. Talk about the concept of God as love will be so many empty words unless pupils carry within themselves the experience of a loving relationship. For most pupils this comes from home and parents, but not for all. As we have stressed, a great part of an infant teacher's work will be ministering security, assuring of significance, building community in all sorts of ways not necessarily connected with religious education "lessons". This is highly relevant to the development of later religious understanding, for it will provide the experiential basis without which the religious concept will be devoid of inner meaning. Likewise, the value and effectiveness of later discussion about beauty, truth, and goodness depend much on the young child's experience of discrimination between beauty and ugliness, truth and falsehood, good and evil.

229 The young child has a natural sense of wonder at the world around him and a curiosity to explore within it. The whole curriculum of an infant school may foster the development of this sense of wonder; it is highly relevant to the later development of religious understanding and cannot be confined to the religious education "lessons". In art, music, story, and drama, teachers and pupils will explore together a wide variety of human experience, at the level of their own group or class, which will help them later on to understand the interpretative language of the Bible. The experiential foundations will thus be laid for later understanding of the symbolic language of religion. For infant children to have experienced love, security, and joy; to have learned to use their bodies and the resources of language to express themselves and their responses to the world around them, is to make possible later religious development far more adequately than by giving them a religious vocabulary and a repertoire of biblical anecdotes. Throughout, the teacher will be leading the pupils not from one dogmatic certainty to another, but from one occasion of wonder to another.

230 More and more teachers of young children are finding that thematic teaching provides the most helpful approach. Not only does this enable them to pay due regard to the developmental needs of the child, but it provides a framework in which emotion can be nurtured, apprehension widened, sensitivity deepened, perception stimulated, and relationships built. In thematic exploration the Bible will not be absent, but it will be used where it is relevant to the experience being explored. Where it is a book of personal importance to the teacher the children should be aware of this. If we want them to give the Bible adequate attention in their secondary years, they must learn in their earlier years that it is a book for adults. For the teacher herself it is the best of source books, in which life-themes are worked out at adult level. Thematic teaching is no soft option. It is very demanding, and many teachers would welcome in-service training in which they can explore its possibilities with their colleagues and discover why the Bible holds the place it does for Christian people. Most teachers were themselves victims of "too much too soon".

231 The infant teacher stands at the beginning of a long process of growth to maturity. But we wish to stress that religious education in the infant school has a place, significance, and value of its own; it is not simply the development of readiness for later religious understanding, important though that is.

PUPILS OF MENTAL AGE 7 TO 13+

232 The need for deepening the foundation laid down in the early years continues throughout the educational process. This means that teachers can never be concerned merely with the words they speak, but must give full attention to the formation of relationships, the encouragement of positive attitudes, and the stimulation of interest. Much of this will be done through the diffused operation of the

5

moment by moment give and take of the classroom, but, as the child grows older, more deliberate and concentrated activity will centre round life-themes. Ideas such as courage, forgiveness, wonder, power, and friendship may be introduced, though in factual and imaginative rather than in theoretical terms. (For examples of thematic material see Bibliography).

233 With classes in the "middle childhood" range (i.e. mental age 7 to 9 years old approximately) the treatment will differ from that of younger children more in the intensity and complexity with which such themes can be pursued than in any basic change of approach. Themes can take longer to work through, and can cover much more widely ranging material. But it still remains true that all the activity and discussion centring on these themes should be related at every point to the experience, abilities, needs, and interests of the pupils, and that maximum scope and stimulus should be given for each pupil's individual inquiry. We wish to emphasize most strongly that fully effective implementation of this method requires ample provision of books and materials and a suitable school environment.

234 The child growing out of infancy is not only capable of exploring more complex and interrelated areas of experience, but also becomes eagerly fascinated by the amassing of factual information about the whole environment in which his life is set. Although this stage does not reach its climax until about mental age 9 or 10, or even later, nevertheless "the need for facts" must be progressively catered for throughout the 7+ period. This may lead some teachers to set the study of life-themes within a whole series of factual inquiry projects or environmental studies. We recognize that there are many experienced teachers of junior children who believe that this growing concern with factual information enables the average child of mental age 9 or so upwards to enjoy, and benefit from, a more direct and traditional approach to religious education. Simple study of "the social background to the life of Jesus", or of "the local church as a building and as a community", or of "the compiling and transmission of the Bible", all now become possible, as well as rather more connected and extended use of biographical material than has previously been used in the context of thematic work.

235 It is particularly important at this stage to keep the developing pattern of a child's religious education firmly in view. In examining possible ways of teaching, it must be recognized that blue-prints are impossible and that in the last resort the individual teacher has to choose the approach best suited to the needs and interests of each particular class and to his own personal abilities. There is no one approach valid for all teachers in all schools at all times. Nevertheless, there is need for each teacher to ensure that his overall approach is a balanced one, one which attempts to meet all the needs of his pupils, and not one which merely gives his (or their) particular hobby-horses free and monopolistic rein. There is value in having one member of staff to act as co-ordinator to ensure that the religious education follows some coherent pattern, particularly in a school where some teachers favour thematic teaching and others favour a more traditionalist approach.

236 If a teacher feels himself to be most effective handling traditional biblical material, he should make sure that he treats the material in such a way that it provides maximum scope and stimulus for each pupil's individual exploration, not merely of the factual content, but also of areas of the pupil's own experience which may be illuminated by the biblical material. He should also make sure that his Bible teaching is not something quite divorced from the rest of the curriculum in the eyes of the children.

crucial

237 When an integrated-day or free-day is in operation, we think that religious education should be fully integrated, and that a thematic approach is the most suitable method. We further recognize that this could raise problems with regard to the strict exercise of "withdrawal rights" under the 1944 Act, but trust that when the educational purpose of religious education (particularly when fully integrated) becomes generally understood, any need for "withdrawal" will be seen to diminish.

238 We also recognize that there are many experienced teachers of junior children who think that very little biblical material can be seen by their pupils to be illuminating at this stage and that fear of teaching "too much too soon" may cause them to drop using the Bible altogether. We think that such teachers should recognize that from about the mental age of 8 right up to the edge of adolescence is an "acquisitive" age when the foundations of religious knowledge including knowledge about the Bible can be laid, and that this operation is just as much a part of religious education as is the

development of religious insight and the cultivation of the ability
to handle theological thought-forms.

239 Just as with the young child the two elements to keep in balance
are the general enrichment of experience and the development of an
awareness of the religious associations of certain cultural phenomena,
so, as the child moves into the next stage, a balance must be preserved
between the exploration of relationships and emotions, and the
gradual acquisition of new factual information about the phenomenon of Christianity, or of whatever religious system is being studied.
With Christianity, this factual information should eventually cover
not only the visible phenomenon of the present-day Church, but
also its origins in the life and ministry of Jesus Christ. This will include not merely a study of events from Jesus' life, but also an attempt
to gain further insight into his teaching, through an exploration of
certain biblical themes and symbols (e.g. Light, Water, King, Father)
building on work started right back in the infant stage. It will also
include the study of some examples of Christianity in action as seen
in the lives and activities of certain memorable individuals.

240 As the pupil moves into the final stage before adolescence, attention must be given to a new aspect of his development. As we have
already said, from about the mental age of 13+ the pupil becomes
able to think in more abstract terms. It is important that this development should be prepared for, and indeed fostered, by ample
opportunity for what is best described as ordered conversation at
the pre-adolescent stage. ("Discussion" is a term more appropriate
to adolescents and adults.) A real feeling of freedom to ask questions,
make comments, and to question the answers given, should be a
feature of any religious education in the late childhood or pre-adolescent age range. Besides this need to use language about religion
at this stage, however inadequately, there is also need to begin a
conscious exploration of the use of symbols, and a reasonably simple
categorization of biblical and other literature into, for example
"story", "history", "law", "poetry", and "science". This should
have been embarked on before the time when the adolescent starts
to try to make such distinctions for himself.

241 As suggested above, before adolescence the child is limited in
his ability to handle theological language with understanding, though
certain preliminary steps can be taken towards this. However, the

essential task of the teacher in these pre-adolescent years is to broaden and deepen the pupil's areas of experience, especially those areas affecting relationships and self-evaluation, and to build up his interest in religion as a phenomenon in his environment and his concern with the questions to which "religious" answers are given. At this stage the teacher cannot ask for "commitment to the religious quest", but he can seek to arouse in his pupils both an awareness of the existence of this quest as part of human experience, and also an awakening sense of its importance. The aim in the teaching of religion to the pre-adolescent should always be seen in relation to the aim of religious education in general—namely to explore the place and significance of religion in human life and so to make a distinctive contribution to each pupil's search for a faith by which to live.

242 We wish again to emphasize at this point that the pupil in school is also a member of the small community which is his home and that large community which is society. Some will also be members of "Sunday schools" connected with various Churches and denominations. Others will also belong to voluntary organizations with some religious orientation (e.g. Scouts and Guides). All will be looking forward to a freer and fuller participation in "teenage" culture and their standards of value and judgement will already be forming under the influence of that culture. In this Report we are studying religious education in schools, but we fully recognize that the religious influences of home and society are profoundly important and have to be considered when the pupil's overall religious development is being considered. Research projects both in the U.S.A. and in this country show that home influence is the factor of prime importance and that the pupil's religious development in the school environment is related to it.[1] It is important that teachers of religious education should be aware of the various environmental influences which affect the religious development of their pupils, particularly the various aims and methods adopted by Sunday schools and other agencies of voluntary religious education which their pupils may attend.

[1] Greeley and Rossi, *The Educat on of Catholic Americans* (Aldine 1967).
 A. E. C. W. Spencer's article in *Religious Education Today*, ed. Dom P. Jebb (Darton, Longman and Todd 1968).

The Religious Education of Adolescents 13+ to 18

THE CHARACTERISTICS OF PUPILS AGE 13+ TO 16

243 It is unwise to generalize about young people at any age, but it becomes doubly hazardous when considering adolescents. Nevertheless, some tentative outline of the characteristics of adolescents ought to be attempted, if religious education is to shape itself to meet their particular needs. First, and most obviously, they often have greater capacity for religious understanding and insight. Discussion of basic questions of meaning and belief in a more abstract way becomes increasingly possible, even though large areas of ignorance and misconception remain to be clarified. This is not to gloss over the problems raised by low ability groups, who find the greatest difficulty in comprehending anything about adult religious belief. The onset of puberty is reflected both in increased consciousness of self and awareness of the sexual element in human life. Adolescents tend to behave in ways which are intense, personal, and emotional. This will often show itself in a freshness of outlook and an openness to different viewpoints. It is tacitly assumed, for example, that it is worth while to look for meaning in life and that the questions raised by the search are real and important. Yet the age group is temperamentally variable and subject to extremes of mood. There can be few teachers who have not found themselves baffled when confronted by a class which would be one day responsive and interested and the next bored and lifeless.

244 The combined pressures of developing independence and of the attitudes of contemporary society may also result in hostility and criticism. What may seem to be (or may, in fact, be) unwarranted dogmatism on the part of religious people goes far to account for this reaction. In religious as in other matters there is a natural resistance on the part of adolescents to being "told" what to believe, even though in another mood they may openly seek for guidance. Precisely because adolescents are in process of growing up, they are reaching out for adult status and for assurance of their independence and freedom from control. It is salutary to remember that schools and teachers often seem remote from the real concerns of adolescents. It is especially true of pupils high in what has been called "teenager-commitment" that the sense of belonging to an identifiable group is strong—a group which is set over against the values and attitudes

of older people, including teachers and the Church. The influence
of this factor has been discussed at greater length in ch. 3.

PRINCIPLES UNDERLYING RELIGIOUS EDUCATION AT THIS STAGE

245 Religious education for these young people should take account
of the above-mentioned aspects of the adolescent personality.
Attempts to do this have led in recent years to the use of certain
terms—notably "child-centred", "relevant", and "open-ended"—
which are currently in vogue, and to some of which reference has
already been made. It is necessary to examine them more fully.
"Child-centred" religious education is commonly set against
"Bible-centred"; "relevant" against "historical" or "factual";
"open-ended" against "authoritarian" or "dogmatic". All reflect
important changes in principle yet all need some definition lest they
become mere slogans.

246 Child-centred.   In one sense "child-centred" religious education is as meaningless as man-centred theology. We suggest that it
should be replaced by the more coherent term "pupil-related". In
this form it is a term with implications for method and content. It
suggests the selection of material appropriate to the pupil's developing needs and capacities, and methods which call into play his interest
and personal activity. It means that we begin, in our educational
thinking, with the pupil. It ought not to mean that we distort the
subject matter to suit his whims or deficiencies.

247 Relevant.   The antithesis between "relevant" and "historical"
or "factual" is a false one. Material which may seem irrelevant can,
by suitable teaching, become highly relevant, and to omit what is
historical or factual, on those grounds alone, would make teaching
about most major religions impossible. What is being emphasized
here is that the material selected must be studied in such a way that
what it has to say about the lives, problems, and concerns of young
people living in today's world can be clearly appreciated. The Bible
in this respect is far from being an irrelevant book.

248 Open-ended.   This should not be taken to imply an orgy of
relativism where the teacher pretends that any opinion is as good as
any other. Discussion will be as intelligent, rigorous, and informed
as possible. Nor does it mean that the teacher is fearful of disclosing
what others have concluded about the topic or what convictions he
himself holds. It does mean that religious education is conducted in

the form of an exploration, that no one viewpoint is considered automatically or regarded as invariably correct, and that pupils' opinions, sincerely held, are treated with the utmost seriousness. A further aspect of this subject is examined more fully in the appendix on "Indoctrination" contributed by Professor B. G. Mitchell.[1]

THE CONTENT OF THE CURRICULUM 13+ TO 16

249 This section is concerned with the needs of pupils in the middle and upper ability range of the secondary school in the 13+ to 16 age group. The particular problems of the religious education of slow-learning pupils are briefly considered in a separate section. (see paras. 279–283 below).

250 This is the stage at which the necessary foundation of religious knowledge should be laid as soundly as possible. Free and open discussion will, as we stress below, have a necessary part in this process and will serve to assist understanding and to stimulate interest. Nevertheless, as with other subjects on the school curriculum, there is a content of fact and information which has to be rigorously studied if this subject is to have any educational value. Furthermore, the critical and wide-ranging exploration of beliefs and ethical problems later in the sixth form will depend to no small extent on the religious information acquired at this earlier stage. In outlining certain particular areas of study, we take for granted the teacher's freedom to select and present material as he thinks fit, having in mind the criteria of pupil-relatedness, relevance, and open-endedness discussed above. The teacher will make use of all sound teaching methods, including project work, personal and group research, educational visits, films, film-strips, music, art, dance, mime, creative writing—indeed, any method that will improve comprehension, open up experience, encourage discovery, and stimulate awareness. Nor do we wish to deny a continuing place to a responsible use of "chalk and talk".

251 For the majority of pupils religious education will involve the exploration of the Christian tradition. It is evident that in this context there are certain areas of study which are of prime importance and which could scarcely be omitted without involving a greater or lesser degree of educational deficiency. The study of the life, teaching, and ministry of Jesus Christ, with particular reference to the New

[1] Appendix B.

Testament, is obviously of central importance. This should be supplemented by study of the main stages in the later development of the Christian Church, with particular reference to the work and influence of significant and creative personalities from St Paul to the present day. The study of the Old Testament must have its necessary place, though we should be opposed to an approach which involved detailed historical study of it. We think it more important that pupils in this age group should have sufficient understanding of the historical background to be able to appreciate the main passages of literary or religious significance and its main personalities and religious ideas. Some attempt should also be made to provide pupils with a brief introduction to the main world religions, their places of origin, areas where they are most prevalent, the number of their adherents, and their central beliefs. Many teachers will wish to make use of the G.C.E. O level examination courses or the more flexible courses provided by the C.S.E. examination. We recognize that some teachers consider that public examinations in religious education are undesirable, on the grounds that they have a restrictive effect. This is not a view which we share.[1]

252 In stressing the cognitive element in religious education with pupils in this age group, we are not unaware that they may also gain much through participation in activities such as voluntary service to the local community which play an important part in religious education in many schools. We see study and service as complementary to one another rather than as alternatives.

THE CENTRALITY OF DISCUSSION

253 The list of methods and techniques suggested in the preceding section shows the range and variety of approaches which can and should be used with this age group. However, no other method holds quite so important a place, or is more appropriate at this stage, than discussion. Rightly used, this approach is personal, systematic, demanding, and open. It implies the to and fro of intelligent adult conversation. It is, however, a method of teaching like any other and cannot be attempted without thought, care, and preparation. Inconclusive discussions may well evoke the valid criticism: "We don't do anything in religious education; we just discuss." If in-

---

[1] We recognize that this section relates to the education of pupils who are studying the Christian religious tradition and that the study of other religious traditions will be appropriate to the needs of pupils of other religious faiths.

5*

adequately prepared, they may well grind to a halt or become dominated by the teacher or by pupils whose powers of expression may
be out of proportion to their powers of thought.[1]

RELIGIOUS EDUCATION IN INTEGRATED STUDIES

254 We recognize that there is considerable diversity of opinion on
this subject amongst practising teachers. Much research and experiment remains to be done. We believe, however, that the following
considerations are relevant to a responsible discussion of the place
of religious education in integrated studies.

255 Theological considerations provide some degree of support for
this development. Religion in general and Christianity in particular
are essentially concerned with the whole of life. Integrated studies
are a means by which religion can be seen as influencing and being
influenced by wider movements in society. As has been made clear
in our chapter on Theology and Education, it is not only those who
work in schools who need to relate their religious studies to broader
patterns of interdisciplinary inquiry. Yet over against this we have
to recognize that the Christian faith has a distinctive body of biblical
and doctrinal teaching which has to be understood in its own terms
as well as being studied in its inter-disciplinary relatedness.

256 Educationally considered, the inclusion of religious education in
integrated studies has much to commend it. The ways in which
religion affects daily life, or how beliefs about the nature of the world
affect behaviour in it, are more readily appreciated when the tendency
towards fragmentation of knowledge has been resisted and when the
pupil is allowed to perceive something of its unity. It is worth pointing out here that while religious education combines fairly obviously
with literature, geography, and history, it is by no means irrelevant
to biology and physics.

257 Many of the schemes which have been proposed for integrated
studies would be seriously deficient if in their study of human nature
and institutions, they omitted the religious dimension. Topics like
"The Family", "Man in Community", "Prejudice", cannot be

[1] Course books using the discussion method are numerous and vary much in
quality. For a useful and detailed account of the technique, the reader is referred
to H. Loukes, *Teenage Religion* (S.C.M. 1961), pp. 106–15 and to his later work,
New Ground in Christian Education (S.C.M. 1965). See also *Humanities and the
Young School Leaver: an Approach through R.E.*, published by the Schools
Council (1969).

studied adequately without consideration of the particular viewpoint of religious faith.

258 Two caveats should, however, be entered:

The first is that integrated studies lose their value if the programme of work consists merely of a collection of half-related topics from different subjects, with only a superficial unity. To be successful, they call for careful selection and planning and competent teaching by all involved. This is an important point to which we return later in this chapter. The second is that the religious education teacher may in certain circumstances lose a measure of freedom. A project on the local community may allow him full freedom to undertake a survey of religion in the locality, involving visits to places of worship, interviews with local clergy and ministers, the study of architecture, organization, beliefs, and attitudes, and some account of the positive contribution of religious bodies to the community in social service or youth groups. But, equally, he may well find another project more restricting. It is possible to exaggerate the force of these two objections. What is important at this exploratory stage is that teachers of religious education should be prepared to participate fully in research and experiment.

THE SCHOOL LEAVER AT 15 TO 16

259 All that has been said of adolescents in general applies with particular force to school leavers since they are looking forward to taking their places as adults within the community. Some of their most significant characteristics are those which they share with all adults. They want to be treated seriously, to be valued as persons, to have a contribution to make to society, to understand themselves and their relation to the world at large.

260 Yet the end of school life is particularly significant since a feeling of finality broods over the leaving year. It is the teacher's last opportunity to lead his pupils to deeper understanding and more mature judgement. It will be for many pupils the last chance to discuss intelligently and systematically the special insights of the Christian faith. At this stage too, the adolescent's desire to reach out for adult status often becomes pressingly urgent. It is not uncommon for him to fret under the restrictions of school organization and, when future employment has been settled, to view education as a tiresome irrelevance. It is also a time when personal relationships, particularly those associated with parental authority and the opposite sex, raise serious questions of attitude and behaviour. Many are also under a different kind of pressure. For possibly the first time in their lives they see that the decisions they have to make are ones which may be vital to their own future. Some face the problem of finding a job, others are aware that their future will depend on their examination results. As has been said, their entry into the adult world is very close and many of them sense that the values the school has supported, with varying degrees of success, may shortly be challenged and may sometimes be replaced by others. Idealism is often an early casualty. "His first reaction may well be disgust . . . with the cynicism of the world. What will his second be? It is likely to be to fall into line."[1]

261 Syllabus construction at this stage must always take account of the hopes, difficulties, anxieties, attitudes, and interests of the young people themselves. The quality of teaching should be authoritative, but not authoritarian. From the material set out in his handbook of suggestions it would seem sound policy for the teacher to select those topics which allow exploration, in ways appropriate to the school leaver's needs and concerns, of the two important areas of behaviour and belief. The teacher should seek to give positive help and encourage thoughtful and responsible decision making.

262 Questions of Behaviour.   The study made by Mr H. Loukes[2] of a number of psychological investigations showed a measure of agreement about those topics of concern to the young which were also of undeniable intrinsic importance. Many, if not most, of these were problems of behaviour. This part of the final year's work should be prepared to consider such subjects as:

Advertising and its pressures
"Snobbery" and social divisions
Race relations
Family relationships and responsibilities
Marriage preparation and sex relationships
Choice of work
The creative use of leisure
Problems of elderly people
Human suffering
War and peace in a nuclear age
Drug addiction

[1] Crowther Report (268).   [2] *Teenage Religion*, ch. 3.

This list will both indicate the scope of the inquiry and suggest other subjects. Fortunately, a variety of course books to assist the teacher is now available and the choice appears to be increasing at an encouraging rate.

263 Questions of Belief. The division here is arbitrary, as belief and behaviour are interrelated, but the particular stress in this half of the course is on basic questions of belief—about God, Christ, the world, the nature of man, and the fact of death. It will give opportunity, where relevant and practicable, to consider the answers given to these questions, not only by Christianity, but also by other religions and philosophies. The constant appeal for teaching about other religions is a genuine one and should be heeded, but with a clear appreciation both of the reasons for, and also of the difficulties in, embarking on this type of teaching. It is important that in a world which is steadily "shrinking" as a result of increasingly rapid communications, pupils should not leave school ignorant of the existence of the other great living religions of the world and of at least some of the basic facts about them.

264 It would be idle to pretend that, even if time allowed, teachers and pupils brought up in a Judaeo-Christian religious environment could expect to aim at or attain a depth of insight into the attitudes, beliefs, and religious experiences which lie behind the religions of the Middle and Far East comparable to that which they could hope to reach from the study of the Christian religion. Even so, acquaintance with some basic facts about other men's religions and the social and cultural contexts within which they find expression can itself broaden not only the pupils' religious but also their international understanding.

265 The interest of the younger school leaver in the type of religious education to which we are here alluding can in many cases be heightened by linking it with the examinations for the Certificate of Secondary Education. Syllabuses devised by Regional Examining Boards for the Mode 1 type of examination frequently encourage pupils to reflect upon the application of Christian beliefs and practices to various aspects of contemporary life. Where schools opt to enter candidates for the Mode 2 or, still more, Mode 3 examinations, they can enjoy greater liberty in adapting the examination requirements to the type of religious education developed in the school itself.

RELIGIOUS EDUCATION IN THE SIXTH FORM

266 We are convinced that this can be one of the most interesting and rewarding areas of religious education. We do not deny the existence of problems but believe that these are far outweighed by the very positive response which pupils may give to teaching of the right kind.

267 When so much sixth form work is concerned with academic achievement, religious education may share in the lack of esteem accorded to other subjects which are given only "minority time". The teacher may often be confronted with a great deal of ignorance and false assumption on the part of the pupils, and much criticism of the apparent irrelevance of organized religion, the pettiness of denominational differences, and the more absurd manifestations of religious dogmatism. Yet research evidence makes it quite clear that sixth-formers are often greatly interested in religious issues.[1] The experience of many teachers bears witness to the depth and reality of this interest and to the liveliness and honesty of the pupils' approach at this stage. There is often a renewed willingness to discuss and to argue, to learn and to participate.

268 The need to work out a personal philosophy of life and a responsible ethical code is widely realized among sixth-formers. Their willingness to become involved, whether locally or internationally, shows itself in many ways. Whether it takes the form of sharing responsibility for school worship, helping with immigrant or handicapped children, with the rehabilitation of ex-prisoners, with the care of the elderly or in association with organizations and causes such as V.S.O., C.S.V.,[2] and Shelter, or in growing commitment to a career or profession, this in turn leads to the recognition of further need for study and guidance of the right kind. Here more than ever an authoritarian approach is completely unacceptable to them. The teacher best suited to work at this level is one whose scholarship and personality command respect and who is at the same time prepared to listen and to learn. "I think the personality of the teacher

[1] E. Cox, *Sixth Form Religion* (S.C.M. 1967).
   C. Alves, *Religion and the Secondary School* (S.C.M. 1968).
[2] Voluntary Service Overseas; Community Service Volunteers.

(in sixth form R.K.) matters very much; dogma and pomposity go down very badly",[1] wrote an undergraduate.

269 Religious education in the sixth form must make the same intellectual demands as other subjects and the pupil has a right to expect his teachers to be theologically competent. "My sixth form course in R.E. was a good one, including a good deal of difficult theology",[2] writes a woman undergraduate. "The teaching was intelligent; answers to doubts and criticisms were not automatic or even dogmatic." Sixth-formers are often astonished to discover the competence and scope of biblical and theological scholarship. As Professor D. E. Nineham has said:

... no schoolboy who knew anything about the work of a Bultmann, a Tillich, a de Chardin or a Marcel could suppose that their minds were appreciably less able or their methods less intellectually respectable than those, let us say, of a Russell, a Sartre, a Hoyle or an A. J. P. Taylor.[3]

270 We have some sympathy with the sixth-former who wrote, with obvious feeling, "God is above examinations", but remain of the opinion that G.C.E. advanced level examination courses can prove very valuable, not necessarily only for pupils who may be considering further studies in theology at a university or college of education. Nor is the G.C.E. ordinary level examination course without some value at this stage. Syllabuses, it is true, have too often tended to be unnecessarily overweighted with detailed biblical material and could with advantage be modified to include more study of recent historical and theological developments. Nevertheless, such courses can be the means of laying the foundations of a fuller knowledge of the Christian tradition and of acquiring some of the tools which are essential to the further study of theology. We are glad to note that some examining bodies have already revised their O and A level examination syllabuses.

271 The numbers of pupils in school taking advanced level examinations in religious knowledge, though still small in comparison with entries for most other subjects, have noticeably increased proportionately in recent years. Nor must it be forgotten that the value of such serious academic study is not confined to those following the

[1] R. J. Rees, *Background and Belief* (S.C.M. 1967).
[2] Op cit., p. 100.
[3] *Religious Education 1944–1984*, ed. A. G. Wedderspoon (Allen & Unwin 1966), p. 155.

examination course. The presence of such a group within the sixth form may act as a stimulus to the rest. Indeed, there is something to be said for the kind of examination course which is aimed at a somewhat lower standard than the advanced level being made more widely available in the sixth form so that those with the necessary time and inclination may take advantage of this kind of study in greater maturity and outside the pressures of the O level year. At the same time it is desirable that examination candidates should be given the opportunity to take part in general sixth form lessons with their wider opportunities for discussion and exploration.

272 While it is clearly important to provide effective religious education for the proportion of sixth-formers (approximately 40%) who are preparing for university and college entrance, the needs of the 60% for whom a somewhat less academic approach may be appropriate must also be most carefully considered. To a large extent the needs of the two groups are the same: all sixth-formers have the same need to be treated as persons, to be taken seriously as individuals, and to meet adults on as equal a footing as possible. It is important that this need is met in religious education where the value of every person's point of view should be seen to be recognized and where serious discussion can take place in a more relaxed atmosphere than is possible where the scene is dominated by the demands of examination courses. It is also desirable that there should be some freedom of choice at this stage—of subjects within one course, or, better still, between courses and teachers.

273 We recognize that there are a number of different possibilities and many practical difficulties in the sixth form situation. There is, for example, the development of integrated "general studies" courses whereby religious education stakes its claim along with other subjects for minority time. Advocates of integration argue that it becomes possible to study the subject more deeply than can be managed in the one period a week generally available for sixth form religious education. Further, this joint work alongside other subjects may help to demonstrate the wider relevance of religion and may perhaps go some way to remove the still prevalent idea that certain authorities—such as scientists and theologians—have nothing to say to one another. On the other hand, as has been suggested earlier in this chapter, what is gained in breadth may here be lost in depth. The demands in terms of careful planning, willingness to co-operate,

and general academic competence are very considerable. "Integration" is no easy way out. It may well happen that no subject is studied in a reputable way and religious education may well emerge as the least well served.

274 A recommendation for more generous time-tabling as a first requirement for a serious treatment of the subject is made by R. J. Rees in his book *Background and Belief*.[1] He notes that 17% of his sample of third-year students had received no religious instruction in the sixth form and only 25% had received more than one period a week. He continues: "How to achieve this is a question to which few head teachers in an examination-crazed world know the answer." A teacher in a London grammar school, writing of his decision to "go into partnership with the General Studies Department",[2] gave as his reason "the difficulties involved in claiming the interest of sixth-formers for a subject that received one period a week against the six, seven, or eight periods allotted to the A level courses". Adequate treatment of the subject presupposes smaller groups as well as more time, especially since the weight of sixth-formers' approval lies on the discussion method and "problem-centred" teaching.[3] Lack of time is probably the reason for the poverty of sixth form reading about religion also noted by Rees.[4] "There is no escaping from the conclusion that most sixth-formers form their religious attitudes in a haze of ignorance about current religious thought." Yet, as we have suggested, increase of time may not by itself lead in practice to the advancement of this or any other "integrated" subject.

275 It is common for the first year sixth-former in particular to become aware of the enormous gaps in the framework of his knowledge of religion and to be ready for a review and reassessment of ideas already acquired. There are misconceptions to be corrected and gaps to be filled and the whole to be integrated into a more mature body of knowledge. This is a good time for further work on the study of world religions, as it is also for a review of the main doctrines of the Christian faith. This can be done by making use of a separate allocation of time. Alternatively, it may be useful to explore a broad theme such as the nature and destiny of man, drawing

[1] Pp. 110–11.
[2] C.E.M. booklet *Religious Education in the Sixth Form*, February 1966.
[3] Rees, op. cit., p. 112.
[4] Op. cit., p. 113.

upon works of philosophy, science, and literature as well as the Bible. It is well to remember that such inter-disciplinary study demands not less but greater specialization, not lowering but raising of standards, for this in the end must be the result of working on common problems which constantly push back the frontiers of separate disciplines. We realize these are issues ranging well beyond the sixth form, but it is important to see sixth form developments against their wider context.

276 The second year is the ideal stage for the discussion of the wide range of religious, philosophical, and moral problems which are especially absorbing to the young adult. Newspaper and other articles, books, TV and radio broadcasts may be used as a starting-point for the exploration of such subjects as the ethics of chemical and biological warfare, organ transplants, euthanasia, contraception, apartheid, and censorship.[1] Issues of a similar kind are sometimes specifically dealt with in B.B.C. broadcasts for sixth forms. The availability of inexpensive paperbacked books of good quality has greatly extended the possibilities for further study and research. It is possible also to make good use of a critical study of current plays, films, and novels and to discuss the religious and philosophical ideas which arise in the context of history, literature, and many other subjects. Many modern novels—for example, *Lord of the Flies*—deal with important religious issues, even if they would not be classified as "religious" books. Indeed, it is important to make use of any opportunity to discover what concerns and interests the sixth-former, the more especially since the limited time available for religious education makes it the more difficult for teacher and pupil alike to know and be known.

277 But it must be realized that there may be some pupils for whom an approach of this kind is lacking in meaning or interest. The language of music or the visual arts may speak more to them, and at greater depth. The study of religion through music and art can be of great value and interest. A pupil with artistic talents may well have his interest stimulated by a study of religious themes in western art

[1] In the C.E.M. booklet, *Religious Education in the Sixth Form* (February 1966) reference is made to the individual pursuit within one group of the following list of themes: Islam, capital punishment, medieval morality plays, the Book of Genesis, Calvin, Mormons, Teilhard de Chardin, mysticism, Roman Catholicism, and the problem of innocent suffering.

and so wish to go on to study their theological context and significance. Likewise a pupil with musical talents may find the exploration of religious themes in music more meaningful in the light of his or her particular interests.

278 The sixth-former is also, of course, a school leaver. Whether the pupil leaves at 15/16 or at 18/19, it is important that he or she should have had opportunity to discuss the sort of problems of personal behaviour and belief to which reference was made in a previous section. These pupils are right to expect that their religious education should be of help to them in making responsible choices over a wide range of personal, social, and moral issues.

THE RELIGIOUS EDUCATION OF SLOW-LEARNING ADOLESCENTS [1]

279 Slow-learning pupils present a wide variety of problems which vary considerably from child to child and between schools in one district and another. Slow-learning children have a limited vocabulary, poor reading ability, and limited powers of written expression; some of them may be quite illiterate. There are some who are retarded only in reading skills, but are normal in other areas of learning. More serious are the added problems of those children who are drawn from socially deprived areas, with backgrounds of bad housing and insecure home life. They may show by their behaviour that their basic needs for acceptance, love, and significance are not satisfied, and schools by their demands and standards may frustrate rather than satisfy these needs.

280 A great deal of research remains to be done on this subject, but such work as has been done shows that many slow-learning pupils never advance beyond the level of religious understanding normally achieved by 9 year old juniors, and some do not reach even this level. Recently conducted research suggests that religious thinking remains concrete and pictorial, devoid of abstractions, for nearly a quarter of the pupils in fully comprehensive schools. This means that they can express ideas of God only in rather crude anthropomorphic ways, with little or no understanding of the ideas of God conceived in abstract terms. Even a simple study of the life of Christ can only be attempted in the last two years before school-leaving with any certainty that most will learn something, and with the realization

[1] On this subject, further reference may be made to K. E. Hyde, *Religion and Slow Learners* (S.C.M. 1969).

that a few may only achieve the level of knowledge and insight commonly found amongst junior pupils of average ability. The relevance of these findings for religious education cannot be over-emphasized.

281 The more serious the lack of verbal ability, the greater the difficulty of presenting the traditional biblical content of religious education so that it can be understood and be seen to be meaningful for present-day life. All research studies in religious education that have attempted to isolate the responses of slow-learning pupils point to their extreme difficulty in comprehending the traditional language of religion. Such a problem is not restricted to religious education, but affects all topics dependent on verbal learning. Since the publication of the Newsom Report *Half our Future*, there is a growing realization that it is not adequate for slow learners merely to be given work that is only a simplification of traditional methods of study. Many schools are able to make specific provision for these pupils by "streaming" or "setting". It has been strongly argued that much more practical work is needed, and that it should be based on a range of interdisciplinary inquiries related to a specific topic and so allow the slow-learner to work within his own limits. Wide areas of moral inquiry can be dealt with by this technique, but the task of helping these pupils to understand Christian doctrine at even a simple level is much more difficult because of the limited mental ability of pupils to deal with any but concrete ideas; the current reassessment of the nature of religious language makes the problem even greater.

282 But though these slow-learning adolescents are markedly lacking in mental ability, they may not be so in feeling and sensitivity. Despite an inability to cope mentally, the slow-learning adolescent is maturing physically and emotionally. He needs help, therefore, in articulating the thoughts and questions he is beginning to feel about himself—his hopes, fears, strengths, and weaknesses, loves and hates. This is where the adaptation of various creative media which allow self-expression such as film, drama, movement and creative art are of value in religious education in that they develop the basic self-awareness, including emotional awareness, which is an essential prerequisite of religious awareness. A young person who has begun to find himself through such media is already on the way to asking religious questions. It is only when he recognizes the validity of the questions for himself that he will listen to some of the answers. Such answers have to be expressed in exceedingly simple terms.

283 Slow-learning pupils also respond with interest to talks from visiting speakers who speak from personal experience of faith leading to practical action. They may also learn much from participation in projects of community and social service and an exchange of the thoughts and feelings they have experienced in carrying it out. Deep human problems and needs may in this way be identified from their own experience. Some of the disadvantages which some schools suffer in the way of staffing and accommodation aggravate the problem of giving a fair deal to slow-learning pupils. We lay strong emphasis on the need for further research into this whole subject.

Worship in the County Schools

284 It must be emphasized that the subject under examination in this section of the chapter is worship in the county schools. We are not here concerned with the specific problems of worship in voluntary schools, or in independent or direct grant schools, although many of the issues discussed will be relevant to them. In many church voluntary schools, the form of worship may be regulated in accordance with the requirements of a Trust Deed. Worship in independent schools is not subject to statutory regulation: in direct grant schools it is. Certain aspects of worship in independent schools and voluntary schools are discussed further in chs. 5 and 7.

285 School worship, like religious instruction, is an obligation laid on every county school by the 1944 Education Act. "The school day in every county school and in every voluntary school shall begin with collective worship on the part of all pupils in attendance at the school" (Section 25 (i)). This worship shall not, in county schools, be distinctive of any particular denomination. The Act also makes legal provision for parents who wish to withdraw their children from both worship and religious instruction. The freedom of the teacher is similarly protected by clauses which state that no teacher shall be compelled to attend the daily act of worship and none shall "receive any less emolument, or be deprived of, or disqualified for, any promotion" by reason of such abstention.

286 The 1944 Act merely gave statutory support to what was already recognized procedure in most schools. The practice of beginning and sometimes ending the school day with prayers had long been customary and went back to the years before 1870 when public education was almost entirely provided by voluntary schools. In most inde-

pendent schools, likewise, daily chapel was a well-established tradition by the late nineteenth century. An interesting glimpse of the
situation between the wars can be obtained from the *Regulations
for and Syllabus of Religious Instruction in County Schools*, issued
by the Surrey Education Committee in 1925 (revised edition). These
regulations laid down that "the school session shall each day begin
with prayers, including a hymn, and the afternoon session shall close
with prayers and a hymn. The Lord's Prayer shall be said daily."
We have already discussed, in ch. 1, the various factors which influenced the religious settlement made in 1944. Worship received
statutory support as part of the general restructuring of religious
education and the dual system. Nevertheless, a study of the debates
leading up to the passing of the 1944 Act make clear that the "compulsory" element in school worship was much debated at the time and
there were not a few who doubted the wisdom of such a requirement.

287 Although the 1944 Act uses the term "corporate worship",
schools very often use the term Morning Assembly. Generalizations
are perilous on this subject, but in many primary and secondary
schools Assembly consists of a hymn; a reading from the Bible, or
from some inspirational literature; prayers and the Lord's Prayer.
It will usually be conducted by the head teacher and will take place
in the school hall at the beginning of each day. The Assembly will
frequently conclude with a variety of notices, or other instructions
and exhortations from the head teacher or staff. Exceptions to this
pattern can readily be found and there may be considerable variations
as between primary and secondary schools. In primary schools, for
example, Assembly may be a more informal proceeding than would
be customary or possible in a large secondary school. In some schools
experiments are taking place to discover new and more meaningful
patterns of worship. In many schools Assembly is conducted with
care and dignity and with staff and pupil participation in both the
planning and conduct of worship. In some others it is a perfunctory
non-event, neglected by the staff and regarded by the pupils with
contempt. The evidence presented to the Commission contained no
lack of horror stories on this subject.

288 School worship is a subject on which the Commission received a
substantial body of evidence. Many shades of opinion were represented, from the frankly ecclesiastical to the extreme secularist. The
main weight of evidence was in favour of the continued provision

of some form of regular worship in schools. But the evidence also revealed much division of opinion about the desirability of a daily act of corporate worship continuing to be a statutory obligation on all types of primary and secondary schools.

289 We have studied this evidence and now set out the arguments for and against, as they appear to us, in the light of our study and discussion. We distinguish between arguments for and against school worship as such and arguments for and against the existing statutory requirements. We emphasize that we are categorizing arguments presented to us.

School Worship

290 Arguments for:

(a) Worship in its various forms is an essential feature of all religions. Thus, if religious education is to continue in schools, some initiation into the experience of worship must necessarily be provided as part of that education. This is most conveniently done on the school premises and within the school community.

(b) Such attempts as have been made to discover public opinion on this subject reveal general support for school worship. The main weight of evidence presented to us was clearly positive.

(c) Human beings both young and old have certain deep personal and emotional needs which are met through participation in religious or quasi-religious ritual. Men require occasions for celebration and reflection. In the school situation worship provides an opportunity whereby these needs may be met.

(d) It also provides an opportunity for:
(1) Staff and pupils who are practising Christians to dedicate themselves and their work to God and seek his guidance and support.
(2) Staff and pupils who are not committed Christians to reaffirm their personal ideals and values.

(e) Many important English public events, for example Coronations, Assizes, Remembrance Day, etc., are associated with religious services. There is much popular churchgoing at Christmas and Easter. A very substantial proportion of people are married in church or chapel and have their children baptized. All but a fractional minority are buried or cremated with religious ritual, and the practice of holding memorial services for local and national figures is widespread. There is still a loosely defined but clearly observable tradition of worship in English life, and school worship provides some initiation into this tradition.

291 Arguments against:

(*a*) School worship presupposes the truth of Christian theological propositions and assumes the validity of the practices of Christian prayer. Whereas it is reasonable that Christian staff and pupils may voluntarily assemble for this purpose out of school hours and may invite others to join them, it is intolerable that this should be regarded as a formal activity in the publicly provided schools of a society which evinces a relatively small degree of religious commitment. A twentieth-century State should preserve strict neutrality on religious questions, which are matters for private decision, not public control.

(*b*) The nature of the worship situation makes discussion, question, and argument impossible, thus laying itself open to the charge of "indoctrination" in a way that classroom teaching does not.

(*c*) School worship is, in practice, often so badly done as to be counter-productive. Pupils receive an unpleasant inoculation which deters them from participation in the worship of the Church in later adult life.

The Existing Statutory Requirements relating to the Daily Act of morning Assembly

292 Arguments for:

(*a*) This is a well-accepted practice in English schools; there is no need to change for the sake of change.

(*b*) Daily Assembly fulfils a valuable function within the school community. It expresses the corporate life of the school, serves as a useful agency for transmitting school values, and provides a mood-setting formality for the start of the day.

(*c*) If the statutory requirements were removed, Assembly might wither away through hostility, timidity, or sloth on the part of some staff and pupils.

(*d*) One of the functions of the law is to protect. Just as compulsory education protects children from not being educated, so a statutory obligation to provide school worship protects pupils from the aridity of never experiencing worship at all. It also serves to protect the head teacher. Complete removal of statutory control might expose many head teachers to strong local pressures from sectarian and from secularist groups.

(*e*) If the statutory requirements were removed, society would receive the impression that Parliament did not think school worship important and had capitulated to secularist pressures.

293 Arguments against:

(*a*) Worship is an interior state, an attitude of the whole person. The most that can be compelled by legislative decree is the provision of an act of worship, not worship itself.

(*b*) The present statutory requirements engender a variety of attitudes including boredom, apathy, unease, and even resentment and hostility.

(*c*) Some teachers, and particularly some humanist teachers, feel they have to pretend to religious belief and conceal their own views if they are not to be branded as uncooperative. The situation may be particularly difficult for humanist head teachers who feel they can only conduct a daily act of worship by compromise of conscience.

(*d*) A compulsory daily act of school worship may easily degenerate into a mindless routine, leading to formalism and indifferentism.

(*e*) In many schools the exact requirements of the Act are unworkable through inadequate or unsuitable accommodation.

(*f*) The whole political, social, educational, ecclesiastical, and theological climate has changed so far since 1944 as to render the statutory regulations no longer appropriate.

294 Even this brief survey of the arguments will serve to illustrate the conflict of views which exists on this subject. The most obvious confusion is that between school assembly and school worship. These are not synonymous, they have only become so through use and custom. It would be quite possible for the school assembly to be a wholly secular ceremony, somewhat akin to the "opening exercises" in the schools of the U.S.A. Such a ceremony could be an expression of the school's corporate life, an agency for transmitting ideals, and a valuable mood-setting formality. It could provide a forum for the giving of notices and exhortations by the head teacher. But this would not be an act of worship. We fully recognize that the question of school worship is not wholly distinct from that of school assembly since an assembly is the most obvious place for collective worship to take place. Nevertheless, discussion about this problem will be more coherent if we concentrate on defining the meaning and purpose of school worship on its own account. The question is, therefore, not so much: Should there be school assemblies? but rather: Should there be assemblies for school worship? To this question of the provision of worship in the formal life of the school we now turn.

Christian Worship

295 Christian worship in its normal usage refers to the offering in corporate gatherings of prayer and praise to God through Christ. From the earliest times Christians have gathered, whether in churches or in improvised surroundings, to worship God in this way. Worship may be offered formally, in fixed rites, or it may be offered without set forms, or even in corporate silence as in the Quaker tradition. However diverse may be the forms which Christian worship may take, the common purpose is to respond appropriately to the love and grace of God as seen in Jesus Christ, and to make the divine power a reality in the lives of the worshippers. Forms of worship designed for special occasions—for example baptism, marriage, burial —are to be found in all denominations. Likewise, forms of worship are frequently devised for national or local occasions such as Remembrance Day or Mayor's Sunday. Theologians have stressed the priority of worship over doctrinal formulation. The earliest Christians, for example, found themselves worshipping Christ before they reached any formal theological definitions of his person and nature. The point has often been made that *lex adorandi est lex credendi*: we believe according as we worship. Theological statements may often seem incredible when worship is neglected; on the other hand, theology must constantly bring worship under the critique of rational judgement and articulate its essential meaning so that those who worship with their emotions may also worship with their understanding.

296 The above paragraph represents a very brief, traditional description of the nature and purpose of Christian worship. But it is our view that an act of worship cannot solely be defined as a religious ritual whereby believers respond to the God in whom they believe. This is to adopt too restrictive a definition and one which fails to take account of worship's diverse origins and the diversity of human reactions. An act of worship has in practice many facets and evokes various levels of response; it does not lend itself to narrow, rigid, or exclusive definitions. For one person, attendance at an act of worship may be expressive of deep religious faith; for another, it may be an expression of humility and awe before the mystery of Being; for another it may be only an expression of world-weariness and fear, of a desire to rest in the eternal changelessness. Each of these, so long as it is sincere, has genuine value. Attendance at an act of worship does not necessarily imply or presuppose total personal commitment to the object of worship.

Worship and Religious Education

297 Worship is a significant feature of all major world religions. It has certainly been so in the Christian tradition. A course of study designed to explore the place and significance of religion in human life necessarily implies some exploration of the meaning of worship. We have argued earlier in this chapter that the religion to be studied by most pupils in English schools should be the Christian faith. It clearly follows that experience of Christian worship is an essential part of religious education, as we have defined it. Failure to provide pupils with regular opportunities to experience worship would mean that an essential dimension in their religious education would be lacking. The exploration of religious beliefs through classroom study and discussion requires to be complemented by that exploration of religious practice which the experience of worship provides. Straightforward considerations of time and motion clearly imply that, for most pupils, their regular experience of school worship will be that which is provided on the school premises. We nevertheless recognize the value of occasional educational visits to the religious worship of various Churches and denominations so long as such visits are carefully prepared for and tactfully conducted. This is, in our view, the one most cogent reason why school worship must remain in English schools, although we recognize that its form and frequency may in some schools be very different from what at present prevails.

298 At this point the question may be asked: "How can an act of worship simply be an educational experience? Is this not to rob it of some much deeper meaning and significance?" Such a question mistakes the direction of the argument. We are maintaining that,

just as artistic capacities cannot be developed without being exercised, by painting pictures or making music, so religious understanding cannot be developed without experience of worship. This does
not imply that worship is to be regarded as no more than a means to
the pupils' religious development. It can only be worship if it is
indeed the appropriate response of creature to creator and, as such,
an activity to be undertaken for its own sake. To regard it in this way
is admittedly, and as the secularist maintains, to assume the truth
of certain Christian doctrines. But, as we have argued elsewhere, it
is unavoidably necessary to start from some basic assumptions[1] and
this does not imply lack of integrity or openness.

299 An act of worship has two main elements: the expressive and
the didactic. The significance of these must be considered. An act
of worship provides a means whereby the worshipper can express
his response to God, through joining in ritual acts. He may be expressing adoration, penitence, thanksgiving, and petition. But he
may well not—he may come to worship with nothing more than his
own needs and fears. As has been already made clear, the nature and
quality of response will vary greatly between individuals. For some
it will be an expression of faith; for others it will be an expression of
a desire for faith; for others all that may be expressed is interest, desire
for expansion of experience, and an awareness of the religious quest.

300 An act of worship also has a didactic element. Through joining
in the ritual, the participant is instructed by readings, by the words of
hymns and psalms, by addresses, and to some extent by symbolic
acts and movements. Thus, the worship situation is also to some considerable extent a teaching situation. This is particularly marked in
the worship of an historical religion such as Christianity. A teaching
element has been inherent in Christian worship since its very beginning. In the overwhelming majority of English schools there will
be found some proportion of practising Christian staff and pupils,
or pupils from practising Christian homes who desire their children
to attend school worship. For such staff and pupils school worship
may be both an expressive and a didactic experience. We have already
stressed that the response expressed will vary greatly between individuals, but for members of this group the response will be some
form of expression of faith, consecration, and dedication. For pupils
who are not practising Christians, and who may not come from homes

[1] See ch. 2, paras. 136 and 137 above.

which respect any spiritual values, school worship may have a lesser degree of expressive significance, but it will certainly have as great a didactic importance. Hymns, prayers, and readings and occasional addresses will, together with the whole experience of worship, provide an essential supplement to classroom study.

Worship and the School Community

301 A school is an educational community, it is not just a set of buildings in which a group of teachers happen to teach and a variety of pupils happen to learn. Much of the educational worth of a school depends on the quality of its community life, on its "tone", "atmosphere", or "ethos". Community cohesion depends on such factors as common interests and values, common premises, accepted leaders, and the regular performance of community acts or rituals. Where much depends on close community cohesion, for example, in naval and military forces, great significance will be attached to acts and rituals which serve to develop community spirit. In the school situation, the creation of community cohesion is the outcome of many different factors, but the school Assembly must be accorded a place of particular significance. The type and quality of this particular act will be an important influence in creating the "ethos" of the school community.

302 In England, for very many years, the quality of the school Assembly has been felt to derive from the act of Christian worship with which it has been traditionally associated. In school Assembly, however, staff and pupils form a microcosm of that larger society of which the school is a part. It has long been recognized, therefore, that the act of worship in a school has been in some ways similar to, yet in other ways dissimilar from, the act of worship of a committed Christian congregation. It is quite unrealistic to suppose that the school community is the same as the church community, and school worship cannot be placed in the same category as, for example, High Mass or Sung Eucharist. Services of this kind are acts of worship of committed Christian congregations. School worship is in one aspect to be seen as more clearly associated with those acts of worship for specific occasions which are a feature of our national life. Events such as assize services, public memorial services, and days of remembrance are religious services in which the community comes before God in a corporate act. Such services do not presuppose the individual commitment of all those who attend them; they have a symbolic significance, representing society's disposition towards religion. They also meet society's ritual needs and point to that dimension of mystery and the unconditioned in the context of which human life has to be lived.

303 Let us suppose, for the sake of our discussion, that school assemblies continue to be a regular feature of school life, but that acts of worship are completely forbidden. What would take their place? We have discussed this question with much interest and recognize a number of possible substitutes:

304 (*a*) A nationalist ceremony, somewhat similar to the "opening exercises" of the state schools in the U.S.A. The purpose of this would be to express a shared nationality and the ceremony might consist of the singing of the National Anthem, the presentation of the Union Jack, and selected readings from the writings of great Englishmen. While in no way wishing to deny the richness of our national heritage, we find it difficult to imagine anything less inherently desirable or more irrelevant to the needs of young people in this country in the latter part of the twentieth century.

305 (*b*) Some form of ceremony expressing shared values within each individual school community, as interpreted by the staff and pupils of each school. We view this proposal with unease. Some schools would tackle this problem with great imagination, energy, and intelligence, but we fear that many schools would not. Merely to hand over the problem to the individual schools would be an evasion of the issue and would lead to much grave confusion, even banality. The nature of the school's community act is a matter of public concern and one which has public significance.

306 (*c*) A secularist ceremony, designed to express the values of a shared humanity and consisting of selections from great music and readings from great literature. We recognize that this is a more realistic possibility, but we cannot recommend that a daily school assembly should be a secularist ceremony of this kind, for that would have very clear irreligious implications. A ceremony designed solely to express "the values of shared humanity" and studiously excluding all "religious" material would assert that the contemporary debate between the religious and secularist interpretations of life had been settled. This is very far from the truth. We agree that school assemblies should sometimes be secular (not secularist) assemblies and should consist of selections from great music and literature. But a ceremony which expresses "the values of a shared humanity" must at least sometimes recognize that religious values are a feature of this humanity.

307 In this section we have argued that school Assembly is an educationally and culturally significant event, expressive of society's values and (when properly conducted) influential in the creation of the atmosphere of the school community. The question is, therefore: What system of values does society wish to see respected and expressed in its publicly provided schools? But behind this lies another and more crucial question: What is the belief-system of the English people? For values and beliefs are essentially interconnected. This is an issue which we have discussed earlier in this chapter. We reject the view that England is a post-Christian, religiously neutral society. We believe it to be more accurate to describe England as a post-ecclesiastical society, evincing varying degrees of Christian commitment and association. It is certainly quite false to describe present-day England as a secularist society, consciously and positively committed to a secular humanist interpretation of life. All the evidence presented to us, together with our own study and discussion of the question, leads us to the conclusion that, at present, society in England is positively rather than negatively disposed to religion and to an acceptance of Christian personal, spiritual, and moral values. We judge that society wishes to see these values respected and expressed in schools. One of the means by which this has been achieved in the past is by the preservation of collective worship as a regular feature of school Assembly. We do not think that this tradition should be lightly abandoned.

308 We conclude that regular opportunities for school worship should continue to be provided for two principal reasons:

(a) The experience of worship is a necessary part of religious education.

(b) School worship is expressive of society's positive disposition towards religion and contributes to the preservation within the the school community of those spiritual, personal, and moral values which derive from the Christian tradition.

The Future Pattern of School Worship

309 Regular acts of worship should continue, and should be attended by all pupils except those withdrawn by their parents. Schools should be left free to make their own arrangements with regard to the fulfilling of this requirement. Some schools may continue to have daily acts of worship, others may choose to have, say, two or three acts of worship each week, attended by different age or house groups. A greater element of flexibility should be allowed to schools than is permitted by existing legislation.

310 We emphasize that school worship does require some degree of statutory regulation. If full responsibility for policy decisions on this subject were to be transferred entirely to the local education authorities or to the school governors or managers, or to the head teachers and staff, then policies might change as personnel changed. It hardly needs to be stressed that this would be educationally undesirable. We are also agreed that responsibility cannot simply be left to the individual head teacher. The evidence presented to us makes very clear that heads have no wish to be subjected to the possibility of conflicting demands by local pressure groups.

311 Whereas the general oversight of the arrangements for school worship must be the ultimate responsibility of the head teacher, the actual planning and conduct of the worship may fittingly be delegated to, or shared with, staff and pupils. We expect that the religious education staff will wish to participate fully in this, but that other members of staff will also wish to do so.

312 We think that many schools will wish to have some assemblies at which worship does not take place. On these occasions there may be addresses on matters of public concern by the head teacher, or a member of staff, or a visiting speaker. Or there may be selections from great music and literature. We recognize the educational value of assemblies of this kind.

313 Given the approach to religious education discussed earlier in this chapter, it follows that the worship in most county schools will continue to be placed within the Christian tradition, but not distinctive of any one particular denomination.

314 County schools with a large proportion of Jewish pupils present a special problem. In such schools it should be recognized that two religious traditions exist side by side, and the religious education given in these schools must be allowed to cater for both.

315 We find it impossible to generalize about worship in schools situated in areas with a substantial immigrant population. We recognize not only a number of theological and educational problems, but also many potentially grave social problems connected with this issue. How may religious freedom, educational opportunity, and racial harmony be preserved? We believe that this is a situation which calls for *ad hoc* arrangements, made in the light of the local situation and of some broad general principles. The duty of regulating the pattern of school worship in schools of this kind could well lie with the governors or managers of each school, in consultation with the staff of the school concerned, the local education authority, and H.M.I. Throughout, the wishes of the parents should be respected and positive efforts made to discover what those wishes are. We realize that this proposal will require most careful statutory clarification, and that much further study of this whole problem is required.

316 We do not recommend the regular adoption of acts of worship supposedly designed to meet the needs of those of all faiths and of none. Services consisting of hymns of nature, prayers of universal appeal, together with readings from all the religions and philosophies of the world are not, in our view, desirable as regular acts of school worship. Nevertheless, we recognize the value of occasional experimental services, carefully designed to incorporate many of the significant similarities which exist between the main world religions. We stress the need for careful, intelligent, and informed preparation of such services.

317 We are certain that the "conscience" clauses for teachers which are already a feature of the existing legislation should be retained. We also hope that the more flexible approach to school worship which we are proposing will prove a considerable easement of conscience to those agnostic teachers who find the present arrangements offensive. But we also think that the well-known statement by Archbishop William Temple on this subject remains relevant: "I think teachers are a little liable to ignore the fact that while it is objectionable to force the teachers to conduct prayers against their consciences, it is also objectionable to force children to omit prayers for the sake of the teachers' consciences."

6

318 The principle of withdrawal from religious teaching and school worship is well established and clearly stated in the existing legislation. All parents have the right to withdraw their children from school worship if they wish to do so. We are emphatic that these rights should be preserved, but we are concerned that they should be exercised in a more educationally creative way. At present parents have merely to state their wishes and the pupil is withdrawn. We think it desirable that:

1. Pupils, other than those attending sixth form courses, may be withdrawn by their parents, after discussion between parents and head teacher. Such discussion might serve to clear up misunderstandings about school worship and to consider its significance within the pupil's total education.

2. Sixth form pupils may be withdrawn by their parents after discussion between parents, head teacher, and pupil. We recognize that pupils of sixth form age may have sincere conscientious scruples about attending school worship, and it is our view that they should be provided with a forum in which these scruples can be sympathetically heard and intelligently discussed. We stress that an absolute legal right of withdrawal rests in both instances with the parents, but it would be desirable that this withdrawal should be exercised only after responsible discussion, and that pupils of sixth form age should be partners to the discussion.[1]

These recommendations are made in the light of the situation existing at present in the schools. We fully realize that the raising of the school leaving age and the possible development of a system of tertiary education will present a different situation and will involve a full reconsideration of the whole question of worship in tertiary colleges.

319 We have already referred to the value of educational visits to places of worship and the need for such visits to be carefully prepared for and prearranged. We also stress the value of occasional school services in local places of public worship. It is already a growing custom for schools to hold services at the beginning and end of term and at Christmas in local churches or chapels. We regard this as a desirable development and one which is entirely reasonable in the light of recent ecumenical developments. Where the local church

---

[1] We recognize that reconsideration of the legal position will be necessary in view of the lowering of the age of majority.

is a building of particular historic importance, or architectural beauty, then we would regard this development as particularly desirable. A sacred building, used as such for many centuries, has its own expressive and didactic significance; pupils should not be denied the experience of worship within it.

320 As throughout this Report, so in this section, we are mainly concerned to clarify principle and policy rather than to make detailed suggestions about method. We recognize that methods of conducting school worship will vary between primary and secondary schools and between age groups within those schools. There are, however, a substantial number of books on this subject and we are confident that teachers seeking advice on how best to conduct school worship in the varying age groups will be able to find much useful material. A selection from the books at present available is provided in the bibliography.

The Supply and Training of Teachers

321 Both the Newsom and Plowden Reports refer to the demands upon the modern teacher as "frighteningly high", and speak of the teacher as "the key figure" upon whom the future of education depends. What is happening therefore in the supply and training of teachers is of the utmost importance for the consideration of any facet of education, and religious education (whether in voluntary or county schools) is no exception.

322 Teacher shortage, economic pressure, insufficient places for training, growing demands for a larger national teaching force, all mean that the setting in which we are to look at the particular problems of religious education is one of urgency. The demand for teachers is subject to short-term fluctuation. There is, however, an overall shortage of teachers in general and the particular problems of the supply of teachers of religious education have to be seen within this wider context. It must also be remembered that the demand for specialist teachers of religious education increased steadily in the years following 1944.[1] The clauses on religious education in the

---

[1] We recognize that some teachers have undertaken the work of R.E. specialists who would claim to possess no academic or professional qualifications for so doing. Nevertheless, we share the view frequently expressed from the Spens Report onwards that it is highly desirable that teachers who "specialize" in religious education should, wherever possible, possess or acquire one of the recognized specialist qualifications in Theology or Religious Education.

1944 Act created an immediate demand for teachers in all kinds of schools, which in turn necessitated the establishment of religious education departments[1] in most colleges of education, and the appointment of specialists in religious education on the staffs of some university education departments. Twenty-five years is not long for such development, especially when we remember the post-war difficulties in this country. A great deal has been done, and in the colleges of education the introduction of the three-year course in 1960, the rapid expansion of the colleges, and more recently the introduction of B.Ed. courses, have ensured better equipped religious education departments both in staffing and in courses. Moreover, these developments have opened up another possible career to those reading for degrees in theology. Even so, much remains to be done. With these two points in mind we now turn to the two main sources of teacher supply and look at the particular questions of the supply of religious education teachers and their preparation for teaching.

Colleges of Education

323 There are at present 160 colleges of education in England and Wales offering courses in initial teacher training. 53 of these are voluntary colleges; 27 colleges are Anglican foundations (25 Church of England and 2 Church in Wales); 17 are Roman Catholic colleges; 2 are Methodist; 1 is styled Free Church; and 6 are undenominational. The large majority of students entering colleges of education take the three-year course leading to the award of the Certificate in Education of the University School or Institute of Education to which the college belongs. For the most part the colleges at present supply teachers for primary and secondary schools, though grammar schools almost entirely and comprehensive schools very largely look to the universities for their teachers. Since the colleges provide the only source of primary teachers, the emphasis is upon the infant and junior age-ranges, and, in order to ensure a balance of training in favour of primary work, severe restrictions are placed upon entry to secondary courses, both in numbers and in the choice of subjects which can be offered to secondary students. The primary age-range has

[1] Various titles are given by colleges of education to the department responsible for the training of teachers of religious education. "Divinity", "Religious Studies", "Religious Education", "Theology", are all in use. We select the title "Religious Education Department" as most nearly describing the department's function.

traditionally been one attracting women rather than men, but efforts are now being made to attract more men into the primary schools. More than two-thirds of the entry are women, and while the expansion of the colleges has shown some increase in the recruitment of men, this has not kept pace with the increase in the number of women.

324 Those responsible for the admission of students need to be satisfied that the candidate possesses the personal qualities necessary for teaching and the academic potential for undertaking the course. The minimum academic qualifications currently laid down by the Department of Education and Science are five O level passes in the General Certificate of Education examination, but the standard of entry is usually a good deal higher than this minimum suggests. The number of students entering colleges of education with an A level pass in religious knowledge is substantial and does not compare too unfavourably with some other subjects, although the figures give no ground for complacency.

All courses in 1969 entry	*Men*	*Women*
A level passes in:		
Religious Knowledge	204	1,808
English Literature	1,753	8,465
History	1,682	3,986
Geography	1,765	3,211
French	436	2,349
Art	654	2,331
Biology	281	1,203
Music	94	405
Mathematics	676	908
Physics	371	260
Chemistry	297	317

325 In the Certificate courses provided by most colleges every student is required to specialize for the full length of the course in one or two main subjects. In a college where only one main subject is offered this means a student will spend approximately one-third of his time in the study of his chosen subject, and therefore a study in some depth is required. In colleges where two main subjects are offered the same amount of time is spent in varying proportions between the two subjects. A few University Schools or Institutes of Education (which control academic requirements for the various courses) rule that a main subject syllabus must contain a teaching component (some study of the teaching of the subject), but the courses are primarily academic subjects studied at the students' level, and the syllabus will, within the limitations imposed by the general course, reflect a university approach. Time is the perennial problem, and it must be remembered that a professional training is being combined with academic work. With the limited staffing resources of a religious education department, it is an even bigger problem to cater for a wide ability range. There are criteria other than the strictly academic in judging the fitness of a candidate to enter the college course, and the academic standard of those students in a particular subject department can be very uneven. For the abler student something like a general degree standard can be achieved in the three-year course, but the needs of the academically less able have to be catered for as well. This is a situation perhaps better known in religious education departments than in most. There are a number of students expressing a desire to take religious education who have had no opportunity for serious study of the subject in school. Other students who may have studied it to O and A level in accordance with a predominantly biblical approach may expect a similar approach in college and may be disconcerted by a college syllabus which is likely to include such subjects as Church History, Philosophy of Religion, the study of world religions, the psychology of religion, and the principles of education in relation to the teaching of religion. In addition there are always a few students who choose the subject for pietistic reasons, perhaps with narrow sectarian backgrounds, who are disturbed by modern approaches to theological scholarship and religious education. For these reasons it is quite common to find that religious education departments do not demand previous qualifications in religious knowledge, as other departments usually do in their subjects. Good qualifications in English, history, or languages are of obvious importance in religious education.

326 Religious education syllabuses vary considerably and are at present undergoing alterations, in some cases quite radical, so that it would be unwise to make any generalizations about them. The inauguration of four-year courses leading to the Bachelor of Education degree has given increased scope for academic work in the colleges. In most schemes the fourth year is spent entirely in the study of education (philosophy, history, sociology, and psychology in relation to education) and the specialist subject the student has

offered for the Certificate examination. In most institutes Theology
is accepted for such courses. About 10% of the students in colleges
of education offer religious education as a main (i.e. specialist)
subject (in Church of England colleges the proportion is marginally
higher—12½%), and it is from these students that specialist teachers
are mainly drawn. Main subject work in colleges of education rests
upon the conviction that study in depth is essential for the making
of a good teacher. The immediate relevance of the subject to teaching
at a particular level is not the primary consideration. Nevertheless,
all study takes place in the context of teacher education, and professional needs must always be considered. For those preparing to
teach in secondary schools the main subject will, of course, be their
teaching subject. For the rest (the majority) the immediate relevance
of some aspects of the religious education syllabus to the teaching
of, say, five year olds, may be difficult to state, but the importance
for the future of religious education of having theologically competent teachers at every stage of educational development cannot be
exaggerated.

327 In addition to the main subject courses, all colleges offer what
are variously known as basic or curriculum or professional courses
which are designed to give attention to the teaching needs of various
aspects of the school curriculum. Except for those who have conscientious objection to attending such courses, the majority of students still give some consideration to the religious needs of children
and the ways of meeting those needs in the age-groups they are preparing to teach. In both length and content these courses vary considerably and are at present being subjected to a good deal of questioning. Some courses are strictly confined to methods of teaching.
Others are concerned with the religious development of children.
A third type consists of extending the student's knowledge of the
Bible and of Christian doctrine. Quite apart from the severe difficulties presented within many colleges by the limitations of staffing
and time, and the very mixed background of the students, the problems are made worse by the ignorance, misinformation, and general
perplexity in all matters of belief which is characteristic of the age
we live in. The real problem in these courses is not just remedial,
making up gaps in knowledge and removing misconceptions; it lies
in the emotional attitudes which young people bring to the subject
of religion. To be successful the basic course must have its roots in

the students' own limited experience, in the needs of the children they are preparing to teach, and in the subject matter of religious belief and experience.

328 The vast majority of the students attending these courses will later teach the subject as class teachers in primary schools. Recent sociological research has illustrated the importance of their task and the need for more adequate preparation. Dr David Martin has suggested that, in England "the central figure for teaching Christianity is a lady in a primary school".[1] With the development of middle schools there is a growing need for an increase in the number of teachers with more adequate professional and academic equipment. For this purpose, the basic course cannot be regarded as adequate.

329 This is not the place to enter into a prolonged discussion of possible developments. We recognize that much experimentation is going on. Interdisciplinary projects often provide a new setting for religious teaching. Some colleges are experimenting with courses in combined or integrated studies, in which the student examines the relationship between theology and other disciplines, and studies the influence that religion has had, and still does have, on political and social developments. Closer integration with the work of the education department and teaching in small groups appear to be desirable developments. Also some attention to the recent researches into the religious education of children often provides a new starting-point for fruitful discussion, and is essential for an approach to modern teaching. In some ways the confusion over basic courses reflects the present confusion in schools over the aims of religious education.

The University Departments of Education

330 The university departments of education are mainly responsible for the provision of one-year courses of professional education for graduates, though such courses are now available in some colleges of education. Students entering these courses have already spent three years in academic study, usually specializing in a subject which now becomes a teaching subject. The one-year course therefore concentrates mainly upon the study of the principles and methods of education, with, on average, ten weeks of this academic year spent on teaching practice in schools. In recent years the Education Studies

[1] D. Martin, *A Sociology of English Religion* (S.C.M. 1967), p. 89.

syllabus has been broken down into a study of the contribution made by the component disciplines to educational thinking and practice, namely, psychology, sociology, philosophy, and history. In addition, the method of teaching the student's main subject is studied, together with that of a subsidiary subject. Courses in audio-visual aids, physical education, art, music, drama, and other subjects are also usually available. Some university departments include religious education as a subsidiary subject.

331 In the sphere of religious education, therefore, the university theology faculties or schools together with the university education departments are responsible, in the main, for the supply of specialist teachers in our grammar and comprehensive schools. What are the needs of these schools and how are the universities meeting them?

332 This question was examined in 1964/65. It was found that "about 170/180 specialist teachers become available to the schools each year".[1] Under the heading of "specialist teachers" were included (*a*) teachers with theology degrees, or general degrees including theology; (*b*) teachers completing the full-time course for the Diploma in Religious Education; (*c*) those taking part-time and external degrees in theology. The inquiry concluded that ". . . the total of specialist teachers in the schools needs to be nearly doubled in the next ten years, and that the output of new specialist teachers from university departments and institutes of education needs to be trebled, if we are to hope for any solid improvement in the quality of the religious education to be given to our abler pupils".[2]

333 In a later report, *Religion and the Secondary School* (S.C.M. 1968), a chapter was devoted to a study of the teachers of religious education. Although the report indicated certain signs that the staffing situation had improved over the past 15 to 20 years the conclusion was that "we are still far from having a teaching force for religious education which is fully qualified either by reason of training or of length of experience" (p. 90).

Prospect

334 This is an area of teacher supply and demand in which statistics are difficult to obtain. We welcome the setting up of an inquiry by

[1] F. H. Hilliard in *Religious Education 1944–1984* (Allen & Unwin 1966), p. 99.
[2] Ibid., p. 102.

6*

the Education Department of the British Council of Churches into the problem of the supply and training of teachers of religious education. Because of this inquiry we have deliberately limited the range and extent of our own comments on this subject. We hope that this inquiry may encourage those responsible for theological education in universities to bear in mind the needs of teachers of religious education when the structure of degree courses is being revised.

335 When we try to take stock of the teacher supply situation for religious education, we are impressed by how much has been done in a relatively short time. But we are even more impressed by how inadequate it all is. It is important, however, to emphasize that the problem is not just one of quantity. It depends upon many other factors. In the past religious education was hindered by denominational strife. Nowadays many prospective teachers are inhibited by the force of contemporary secularization and the apparent confusion of the contemporary theological and ethical debate. They may also fear that the prolonged debate about the place of religion in education has cast a shadow of uncertainty on the whole subject.

336 All this means that the quality of teachers is of paramount importance, and indeed more important than their number. It is not often appreciated how difficult it is to produce teachers of religious education. This is the age when young people ought to be grappling with their own beliefs and are often at the point of maximum uncertainty and confusion. The increasing number of older students in training, therefore, could be significant for religious education. With their greater maturity, and often with the experience of bringing up their own children, "mature" students could provide a considerable strengthening to the teaching of religion. Some of the best teachers of religious education are those who have come to it in middle life and who bring a depth and a purpose which is the fruit of their own life experience.

337 The Plowden Report has drawn attention to three other considerations.

It seems reasonable to expect that some voluntary colleges should be a major source of teachers able to act as advisers to their colleagues in primary schools, who are willing to give religious education but aware of their limitations. If practising teachers are to be brought up to date in the knowledge required to give religious education satisfactorily, and if they are to become familiar with modern methods of teaching the subject, systematic provision of in-service training should be made. Another important way of raising the standard of religious education should be the appointment of advisers in this subject by local authorities.

There is no reason to believe that the voluntary colleges are unaware of their responsibilities in supplying teachers of religious education, and much will depend on them maintaining and indeed increasing the number of such teachers. The Plowden Report's suggestion, however, is far-reaching since it envisages a possible form of consultative specialization[1] in the primary school while still relying on the general responsibilities of the class teacher. It is clear that specialization in the traditional sense is undesirable. It is equally clear that a good deal of the junior curriculum will demand specialist knowledge, and this includes religious education. Junior staffing may well mean more team teaching and the implications such a development has for training may well be something the voluntary colleges could investigate together.

338 In-service training is another aspect of teacher education which deserves much greater attention. At the time of writing there are still five colleges of education providing one-year supplementary courses in religious education for teachers who have proved their worth, providing, as they do, a valuable opportunity for experienced teachers to engage in deeper theological study, and it would be a pity if the tradition died as the supply of two-year trained students diminished. Four colleges offer one-term courses, all of which are designed to bring serving teachers up to date in biblical and educational studies. Three universities, Leeds, London, and Nottingham, offer one-year diploma courses in religious education, consisting of theological studies and a study of the practical problems of religious education. These courses are for serving teachers, but in addition to these courses some local education authorities provide short courses on a number of subjects in school holidays, in evening classes, or at weekends. The possibility of B.Ed. courses for serving teachers has now been opened up. Such courses will provide further opportunities for the advanced study of religious education both on a part-time basis and on full secondment. Religious education has now been officially recognized as a shortage subject, and it is to be hoped

[1] A member of staff who will study the particular methods and problems of religious education and will be made available to his colleagues for consultation and advice.

that every encouragement will be given officially to meet the shortage of teachers by mounting more short courses, and by seeing the subject figures predominantly in the expanding volume of in-service training. Teachers' centres have also a significant local role in this process. We also recognize that a large number of useful and relevant courses are provided by the university extra-mural departments and by voluntary bodies such as the Christian Education Movement, and by some diocesan education committees.

339 The third suggestion made in the paragraph quoted from the Plowden Report is to extend the appointment of advisers in religious education by local education authorities. It is disappointing that so few authorities have so far made appointments of this kind. It is obvious that such appointments could do much to raise the standard of religious education within schools. Such an officer would advise the authority on provisions for religious education in the schools, and the staff on religious teaching. Another aspect of his work might well be the care of probationary teachers. The difficulties experienced by young teachers in their first posts leads in too many cases to a loss of enthusiasm and interest. Some available help and encouragement from an adviser could do a great deal to keep alive a sense of the importance of religious education and to stimulate further endeavour.

340 In this part of the chapter we have done little more than present facts. There are so many new factors in the present situation, so many new developments in religious and educational studies, in school reorganization and planning, so much that is new in attitudes to religion in young and old; a more detailed examination of all problems involved is quite beyond our immediate brief. We conclude by stressing the importance of the vocation to teaching, having particularly in mind the needs of religious education both in church and county schools. Educational improvements essentially depend on the quantity and quality of teachers: this is true for religious education as it is for every other subject.

5

Certain Considerations Relating to Religious Education in Independent and Direct Grant Schools

341 The proportion of pupils attending independent and direct grant schools in England and Wales (6·8%) is exceedingly small by comparison with the 93·2% who are receiving their education in schools maintained by local authorities. Throughout this Report we have concentrated our discussion on religious education within the maintained system and we do not make any attempt in this chapter to present a survey of religious education in independent and direct grant schools at the present time. The category of "independent schools", in particular, covers a bewildering variety of educational institutions. We could not make any responsible analysis of the situation in these schools in one chapter, and, even if we wished to, no research evidence exists upon which we might base our judgements. We thus confine ourselves to "certain considerations relating to religious education in independent and direct grant schools" and stress that the comments which follow are not to be taken as referring necessarily to any and every independent and direct grant school. As we stated at the beginning of the previous chapter, we are not a research unit. We did, however, conduct some inquiries of our own among the independent and direct grant schools. These enquiries illustrated the extraordinary range of the work being done in the schools—examples were found of both the best and the worst religious education. But they illustrated most clearly of all the urgent need for extensive research into this whole field. "Public school religion" inspires passionate loyalty and also excites passionate hostility. It is surprising that no person or organization appears yet to have attempted to discover the facts. There is an urgent need for more research in this whole field, and in this context we welcome the setting up in 1969 of a research project, under the auspices of the Head-masters' Conference, into religious education in boys' boarding schools. We hope that this will represent only the first of many en-quiries into different aspects of religious and moral education in independent and direct grant schools of all types.

Introduction

342 Before considering the particular areas where the independent schools might be thought to have a contribution to make to develop-ments in religious education, we must note certain points about their past history and present status. The independent schools have, in general, deliberately attempted to provide a Christian education. We need not look further back than the reforming movement which began in the second quarter of the nineteenth century and which is traditionally associated with the name of Thomas Arnold. We have already seen in ch. 1 that Arnold stated that the priorities of educa-tion should be, in order, Christian growth, gentlemanly conduct, and intellectual development. He was not, of course, without predecessors in, for instance, his development of the prefectorial system, but as Dr E. B. Castle says, "He was the first to use his school chapel in any real sense as a growing point of adolescent religion".[1] The most notable features of the Arnold tradition "are still the ones which characterize public school religion today, though it is important to remember that the independent schools do not conform and never have conformed to a homogeneous pattern . . . it would be nearer the truth to maintain that no two public schools are alike."[2] Gradu-ally, during the nineteenth century, the old religious institutions in many existing schools were given new life, and the new schools that were founded in the nineteenth and twentieth centuries all tended to conform to the new ideal of "godliness and all good learning". Nathaniel Woodard in particular intended his schools to be a "mission to the middle classes",[3] and to be closely associated with the life of the Church. Many girls' schools have been similarly

[1] E. B. Castle, *Moral Education in Christian Times* (Allen & Unwin 1958), p. 288.
[2] S. J. Curtis, *Education in Britain since 1900* (Dakers 1952), p. 160.
[3] B. Heeney, *Mission to the Middle Classes* (S.P.C.K. 1969).

orientated,[1] and most preparatory schools have sought to extend the process to earlier years. Parents have certainly patronized independent schools at least partly in order that their children should receive a Christian education, as we were reminded in the evidence to the Commission from the Association of Headmistresses of Preparatory Schools. A recent book on the preparatory schools, written from inside the system, includes these words: "It is not surprising to find that these schools place religion in its broadest sense in the forefront of their priorities, and it is evident that they remain little bastions of Christian faith in a world grown largely materialistic."[2] Although this precise claim might be disputed, the general intention is accepted. At an important conference held at Bloxham School in 1967, attended by over twenty headmasters and over seventy chaplains, a strong general conviction was expressed that there could still be a "Christian school", despite the great uncertainty shown about all the main areas of school religion.

343 We also note that many independent and direct grant schools have some Church of England foundation or affiliation. A survey of independent school constitutions undertaken on behalf of the Church of England Board of Education in 1964–5 found that 105 or 106 boys' independent and direct grant schools and 64, possibly 73, girls' independent and direct grant schools, a total of 179 out of 205 investigated, had connections with the Church of England. The strict legal status varies: some schools are Church of England educational foundations, some are Church of England schools "by usage", and some are Christian Faith schools which have "adhered to" the Church of England. In 1969 we conducted a short inquiry among schools on "List 70" (independent schools recognized as efficient by the Department of Education and Science). We deliberately excluded those schools whose constitutions had been examined in the Board of Education survey quoted above, i.e. schools which were members of the Headmasters' Conference and the Governing Bodies of Girls' Schools Association. We also, obviously, excluded Roman Catholic independent schools. We found a similarly high incidence of affiliation to the Church of England among the remaining schools sur-

[1] "To secure the cordial adherence and co-operation of all members of the Church of England who acknowledge the duty of giving definite religious instruction as an essential part of education"—from the *Manifesto of the Church Schools Company* 1833, quoted in E. Moberly Bell, *History of the Church Schools Company 1883–1958* (S.P.C.K. 1958), p. 10.

[2] P. L. Masters, *Preparatory Schools Today* (Black 1966), p. 81.

veyed. With many of the independent and direct grant schools the Anglican connection is very close; the ancient cathedral schools, the choir schools, the Woodard schools, and the schools run by Anglican religious orders, to name only the most obvious. There were at the end of 1963 no less than 338 churches, chapels, and places of Anglican worship in schools of all kinds in England.[1]

344 In view of these facts it is not surprising that, for better or for worse, the independent and direct grant schools have occupied a quasi-formal position in the general life of the Church of England. The 1944 Report of the Committee on the Public Schools stated plainly that, after the passing of the Endowed Schools Act of 1869, "the larger and better known Public Schools gained for themselves an even more widely recognized . . . status in the Church of England"[2] In the nineteenth century many distinguished churchmen, such as A. C. Benson and Frederick Temple, served as headmasters of public schools; in more recent times both Archbishop William Temple and his successor, Archbishop Geoffrey Fisher, had previously been headmasters of Repton. Furthermore, the independent and direct grant schools have in general—though with important and often overlooked exceptions—tended to draw most of their pupils from middle- and upper-class homes. Thus, the Church of England and the independent and direct grant schools have, for many years, found their most active supporters from among the same social group. At present, most diocesan bishops are prepared to devote some proportion of their time to visiting, preaching, or confirming in the independent schools in their dioceses. A bishop, currently the Bishop of Horsham, is nominated by the Archbishop of Canterbury to be pastorally concerned with school chaplains and to try to act as a contact between headmasters and clergy seeking appointments as school chaplains.

345 Unlike the vast majority of maintained schools, the independent schools have, by long tradition, appointed ordained men to their staffs to serve as school chaplains. In the 1968 *Public Schools Year Book* 228 clergymen are listed as holding appointments in 145 public schools. We have found that chaplains are to be found in the ratio of approximately one to every 200 or 300 pupils in the majority of

[1] *Facts and Figures about the Church of England* (C.I.O. 1965).
[2] *The Public Schools and the General Educational System* (H.M.S.O. 1944), p. 42.

Headmasters' Conference schools, and in a significant number of girls' schools, preparatory schools, and other independent schools on List 70.[1] There has been for over thirty years an annual conference and retreat for chaplains and schoolmasters in holy orders. This conference is not limited to those from independent schools, but in practice draws most of its members from this group. The presence of these chaplains partly accounts for the continued practice of school confirmation, particularly in boarding schools. The proportion of pupils confirmed varies from an overwhelming majority of those who pass through these schools to an insignificant minority.

346 Another important feature of the independent schools, with considerable repercussions for their religious education, is that they include a large proportion of boarding schools.[2] We have noted above that the practice of school confirmation is particularly to be found in boarding schools. A boarding school housemaster, housemistress, or tutor inevitably plays a pastoral role more continuously than any day school master or mistress. The 1944 Report said: "The continuity of boarding school life naturally opens special opportunities."[3] The majority of boarding schools seem still to have house prayers, and some have introduced house celebrations of Holy Communion. In a significant number of boarding schools there are weekday celebrations in the chapel, and weekday voluntary services in the evening, particularly during Lent.

347 But the most significant single feature of these schools is that, unlike maintained and direct grant schools, they are independent, deriving their freedom from the absence of public financial support. They are of course subject to the same educational pressures, often initiated by the State, as any other schools. But in the last resort these schools enjoy a very large measure of freedom so long as certain very basic medical and legal requirements are met. Furthermore, the independent schools are not subject to the religious clauses of the 1944 Education Act. This means that as regards classroom work they do not have to follow any syllabus drawn up by an outside authority, nor do they necessarily have to have one or more periods of religious education in every class at every level of the school. Nor are they

[1] We consider that, despite the increasing number of ordained men working in maintained schools, the independent schools have still too generous a proportion of the total number of ordained men working in schools.
[2] This is not true of the direct grant schools, which are mainly day schools.
[3] Op. cit., p. 49.

bound to have a daily act of worship, still less to start the day with
an act of worship except in so far as their trust deeds may specify.
On the other hand, they are the only sort of school where there is
no statutory right of withdrawal at parents' request from religious
teaching or from worship. This is, of course, because parents have
voluntarily contracted into the school and accept the religious education as part of the general education provided. Despite what is often
alleged, there appears to be little pressure for change on headmasters
and headmistresses from parents, old boys, or governing bodies,
concerning the religious provisions in these schools. Where pressure
for change exists, it usually originates with younger staff and pupils.

*Areas where independent schools might make a particular contribution
to the development of Religious Education*

(1) *Teaching*

348 The first relevant feature here is the independence from outside
control, but such evidence as we have acquired shows very little of
significance accruing from this independence. Syllabuses vary widely,
and not all schools have a syllabus to follow. If it is possible to
generalize, they tend to progress from work centred on the Bible and
worship to the study of broader questions related to Christianity in
the modern world, ethics, and the study of world religions. In this
respect, the pattern of work is very broadly similar to that in most
maintained schools. We note, however, that the preparatory schools
have hitherto concentrated very largely on "Scripture". Only one
of 34 schools which answered a questionnaire we sent out was prepared to acknowledge some experimental teaching, where Goldman's
thematic approach was being tried with 8-year olds. In general evidence submitted to the Commission by the Association of Headmistresses of Preparatory Schools we were told: "None of the heads
who have replied in detail . . . makes any reference to Goldman or
Loukes. . . . It seems unlikely that (the influence of Goldman) will
bring about any radical change in the preparatory girls' schools."
In evidence presented to us from some public schools we found much
dissatisfaction with the Bible-centred teaching in preparatory schools.
This to some extent stems from the fact that the boys' preparatory
schools are not without external pressures with regard to the content
of their teaching. They exist chiefly to get pupils through Common
Entrance, and the traditional syllabus for this is largely Bible-based.

Now that Scripture is no longer required as a pass subject, and now that there is an alternative paper which is far less Bible-based, some degree of experimental teaching should be possible.[1] In the public schools, such aspects as the number of periods allotted to the subject, and the number of pupils taking O and A level examinations, vary as widely as in maintained schools, though it is probable that more independent schools find a place in their time-tables for two, or, if there are public examinations, more periods a week. Proportionately more O and A level work is done in the girls' schools. We made an inquiry into the attitudes to religious education of approximately 400 sixth-formers in six girls' and six boys' independent schools. Nearly twice as many regarded the religious education they had received as "useful" or "valuable" than as "not particularly useful". The highest value was put on discussion work; evidence presented to us also showed that an increasing number of schools were using group techniques and discussion methods with upper forms.[2]

349 The second relevant feature of religious education in the independent schools is the presence of chaplains, who have at least the theological qualifications required for ordination; many also have degrees in theology. This is not to say that all the teaching of "divinity" is in the hands of ordained men. We have found that the proportion of lay staff involved in religious education varied from none to half the total staff. Very few independent boys' schools have laymen primarily engaged to teach divinity or with special qualifications to do so. But many girls' schools have women religious education specialists, often with impressive theological qualifications. The advantages of having ordained men to teach religious education seem, however, to be somewhat offset by the fact that perhaps only 10%[3] of these men have formal teaching qualifications, apart from their degrees and ordination training. This is at present only to be expected, since the independent schools have a long tradition of teachers qualified only by their university degrees. But they are now increasingly expecting professional teaching qualifications for teachers of all other subjects. It may, of course, be true that as the community life of a school has an important influence on religious educa-

[1] A recent I.A.P.S. handbook (*Prospect* 1965) points the way forward to some "modern approaches".
[2] This is broadly in line with the findings of E. Cox, *Sixth Form Religion* (S.C.M. 1967).
[3] This was the proportion in 46 boys' schools which answered a questionnaire sent out by the Commission.

tion, the general standing of an individual in the community and his witness as a Christian are as important as formal qualifications. But the school that made this point to us added that the most respected teachers of religious education are those capable of teaching some other subject professionally as well. We believe that the majority of chaplains would benefit from some degree of professional teacher training. Many could with advantage make use of such facilities for in-service training as may be available in their area. Teachers of religious education in girls' schools have expressed the need for some kind of professional association somewhat akin to the annual conference for chaplains and schoolmasters in holy orders, to which reference has already been made. Such an association could well be organized by the teachers themselves: in the interim they might gain much through joining in meetings and study courses arranged for teachers in maintained schools, including those organized locally in teachers' centres.

(2) *School Worship*

350 The independence from statutory control enjoyed by independent school chapels is, as we have noted, balanced in many cases by the provisions of trust deeds. The precise nature of the services that may be performed in school chapels and the limits of the bishop's jurisdiction are, we have found, matters of very great legal complexity.[1] We find that the majority of boys' public schools are experimenting to some degree with school worship.[2] An example may be given: one school began experimenting in 1968 with a Saturday evening prayer session.

About 30/40 come and after . . . some quiet devotional music, they relax their bodies and achieve some element of silent meditation. The atmosphere is as informal as the school chapel will permit. . . . They stay, although allowed to leave earlier, for the full half hour and discussion about techniques of prayer is carried on in the corridor afterwards.[3]

Other examples could be cited of the use of contemporary music, dance, and drama, in addition to examples of the wide range of liturgical experiment currently proceeding throughout the rest of the

[1] See appendix D (legal note relating to public school chapels), prepared by B. Ludlow Thorne.
[2] This was the situation in 39 of the 46 schools mentioned in the previous footnote.
[3] School Chaplains' Encyclical No. 13.

Church of England. As with teaching, we found less tendency to experiment in the boys' preparatory schools, though *Prospect* and its predecessor *Foundations* (1959) made helpful suggestions about suitable forms of worship for younger pupils. One school sent us a long account of what seemed an intelligent attempt "to involve the children, getting them enthusiastic and willing to contribute". On the whole we do not think that the independent status of the schools has had any significant influence on attempts to produce appropriate forms of worship. An equally wide range of experiment is noticeable in school assemblies in maintained schools.

351 The existence of school chapels is, however, a significant factor. A great church, or even a small one, has a different effect on the worshippers and on the type of service from that which will be possible in a multi-purpose school hall. On the debit side, the architecture, setting, organ and choir can make a wide variety of services seem similar, and many chapels are ill-adapted for modern liturgical experiments. Yet a liturgical service, conducted with all the resources on which a large school can draw, congregational and choral singing of all kinds, and often organ music of a high quality, may still give to some pupils a vision of what church worship at its best can be. The tension over compulsory worship, which seems almost universal, is exacerbated when the worship is, or seems to the pupils to be, both formal and tedious. Dr R. Lambert writes: "(Another) cause of discontent with religion is the nature of the services. For large numbers of boys and girls the content is monotonous (this we heard many hundreds of times), or cold and remote, something lacking spontaneity or giving no opportunity of participation to the pupils themselves."[1] The liturgical approach that is to some extent dictated by the chapels and by the boarding feature of Sunday worship at school gives some positive opportunities for pupils to grow as practising members of the Church. They can accept responsibility for duties connected with the school chapel; as servers, offertory bearers, choristers, chapel wardens, sacristans, members of a chapel committee with advisory duties. In some schools chaplains have been able to arrange that these duties have been linked to a pastoral concern for other pupils, such as confirmation candidates. The chapel at a boarding school also makes possible the provision of services for

[1] Royston Lambert, *The Hothouse Society* (Weidenfeld & Nicholson 1968), p. 103. This book is compiled from the writings of 10,080 pupils in 66 boarding schools and the author's evaluation of these.

special occasions which have more the "feel" of the parish festivals which the pupils are missing than could be so without a chapel: Harvest festival and Christmas carol services are obvious examples. It also provides a most suitable setting for the performance of the great classics of choral religious music.

352 We have noted above certain consequences for school worship if the school is entirely or partly boarding. Worship in boarding houses, as anywhere else, can degenerate into a perfunctory routine; but at its best it can provide a profound experience of the religious dimension within what for many pupils is the main focus of their school life. Especially notable is the value assigned by many school chaplains to the house Communion, particularly when given as informal a setting as possible. It is emphasized that it must not be imposed on the house from without, or done as a stunt, but must express the sense of Christian fellowship already existing in the house. It is most fully meaningful when it involves not only the pupils but masters, tutors, matrons, and domestic staff. A boarding school pupil is likely to find it difficult to make any very effective contact with his own parish church, if he is away from it for weeks on end. Boarding schools have, we believe, made important efforts to compensate for this and to link worship to service by forming connections with the religious or welfare life of the community where they are placed, particularly through community service groups. These are tending to replace the old public school missions in distant downtown areas.

353 The presence of a chaplain on the staff of an independent school will make eucharistic worship possible. This should be the central feature of the religious life of a school associated with the Church of England. School chaplains should also be more abreast than lay teachers are likely to be of both traditional and experimental liturgical approaches. The annual conference mentioned above and the "School Chaplains' Encyclicals"[1] make for an interchange of information about liturgical as well as academic and pastoral matters.

354 We recognize very frankly that this whole subject is vexed by varying degrees of compulsion and the resentment it causes amongst many pupils at the present time. This is evident in the quotation from

[1] Brief papers that have appeared three times a year since 1964, edited by a public school chaplain and dealing with topics of common concern.

Dr R. Lambert given above. There seems little doubt that the traditional surfeit of weekday and Sunday services does not necessarily make for a substantial body of convinced worshippers. A number of schools are experimenting with voluntary daily services.[1] The headmaster of one boarding school, where since 1963 the only compulsory element has been a Sunday Eucharist, an address without a service on a weekday evening, and house prayers once a week, writes to us: "It is interesting that this degree of voluntary attendance helps to remove the anti-Chapel feeling, including (resentment against) the compulsory services themselves." He adds that this is a small school with a Woodard tradition, and doubts "whether one would get the same sort of reaction in a large school without a very sound and long Chapel tradition". At this school in the first experimental year practically all boys ceased to attend voluntary services, but in the next three years the average number of voluntary services attended per boy per week rose to about two. This highlights the importance of allowing several years to elapse before the worth of such experiments is definitely assessed. We believe that there is potentially much of value to all schools in such experiments. They are certainly growing in number in the independent schools. It would be possible to put up a case for making certain services or, as in the school mentioned above, addresses on a religious subject divorced from a service, compulsory only for sixth-formers. But it is very important that the misconception that worship is only for juniors and can be abandoned after a certain age should be seen for the fallacy which it is. In the independent schools this misconception has actually been stimulated by a not uncommon practice of making an extra Sunday service compulsory for juniors, and even, paradoxically, by the practice of school confirmation. All too often—as in a parish—this marks an end, a passing out from the Church rather than an entry into its adult life.

(3) *The Creation of a Christian Community*

355 One of the traditional features of the independent schools, as we have seen at the outset of this chapter, is that they have attempted to create a self-contained Christian community, co-extensive with the school. The education, it has been assumed, was being given for

[1] Most if not all boarding schools now only have one compulsory Sunday service.

future service as members of an assured élite within a stable and stratified society. This type of education demanded a somewhat authoritarian and conformist approach. It is obvious that the ethos of modern society is working against these traditions. It is well known that the very existence of the independent schools in their present form is questioned. This has led to something of a crisis of confidence within the independent schools, however much it is concealed behind an air of assurance. This is bound to be reflected in the religious life of the school, particularly as there exists a more general loss of nerve throughout the Church. Again, the independent schools are increasingly having to work with a system of education based on as little compulsory direction as possible. The social divisions of an earlier age are fast crumbling. In so far as pupils see themselves as members of a future élite, it is an élite of successful technocrats or tycoons, rather than as public servants. They are very conscious of the "rat-race" necessary to achieve élite status, symbolized in schools by G.C.E. O and A level results and university entries.   The tendency is no longer for the pupil to concentrate his interests on the small world of the school, let alone the even smaller one of the house. Pupils in independent schools feel the influence of the contemporary teenage culture just as powerfully as pupils in maintained and direct grant schools, and the restrictions inevitable in any school, especially a boarding school, are felt by many as irksome features of a disliked "establishment". Sir Desmond Lee quoted in his Hibbert Lecture from the report on a questionnaire given to boys at Winchester in 1964: "It is at present somewhat unfashionable to be appreciative of the 'establishment', and Chapel remains basically—if regrettably —'establishment'." He asks: "Do we continue to assume that the school community and the Christian community are the same?" [1] The question, as he says, is not easy: but he is probably right in saying that the answer is no. But because of the continuing traditions of school chapel, chaplains, confirmation, house prayers, it is probable that Christianity is generally considered to give its approval to whatever the school seems to stand for much more than is the case with the maintained schools. The current tendencies towards rejection by some pupils of the traditional ethos of the school have obvious implications for their religious attitudes. But what do these continuing religious traditions amount to? A school chaplain has

---

[1] *Christianity in Education* (Allen & Unwin 1966), pp. 57, 56.

recently asked in the magazine published by the Headmasters' Conference:

How far are the organisation of worship, religious education, and preparation for confirmation governed by the dictates of a higher secular convenience? How far do chapel and Christianity survive almost accidentally because of their niche in tradition? How often is chapel supported by "authority" primarily because it is supposed to make a useful contribution to the creation of a community consciousness, and to fulfil a valuable disciplinary function?[1]

This echoes a phrase from Mr J. Wilson's *Public Schools and Private Practice*: "Religion is used by most schools, if only unconsciously, as a social reinforcement for the disciplinary and moral system as a whole".[2] These remarks are pertinent and serve to illustrate the contemporary questioning of the traditional conception of the Christian community of the school.

356 It is obvious that the boarding factor is a vitally important influence in the creation of Christian community within the school. We have noted the degree in which boarding house staff stand *in loco parentis*. This raises the issue of the paternalism inseparable from the house system. Paternalism is not necessarily a dirty word. But it is surely time to ask what the parent–child relationship ought to be, with particular reference to the religious development of children and young people. There have undoubtedly been, and perhaps are, examples of misdirected paternalism on the part of some housemasters and housemistresses. But we believe it to be true that those doing this work today are in the main fulfilling the Christian parental role with insight and dedication.

357 The traditional practice of confirmation in the independent schools has, as we have already suggested, played an ambivalent role in the Christian life of the schools. On the one hand it has been all too often in the past a ceremony undergone by almost all pupils, whatever degree of Christian commitment they have reached— "conformation" rather than confirmation. On the other hand, to quote Sir Desmond Lee, "one should not forget the sincerity of effort

---

[1] *Conference*, March 1966.
[2] (Allen & Unwin 1962). Quoted by J. L. C. Dancy, *The Public Schools and the Future* (Faber 1963), p. 69. Dancy disagrees, asserting that "Religion is no longer treated in the public schools as a supernatural sanction for morality— whether for the accepted standards of adult life or for the code of rules of the school" (op. cit., p. 70).

involved and its importance to the Christian community; absurdities and flaws lie on the surface, but a deeper current often flowed below".[1] It is too often true that confirmation corresponds at the time with a wave of idealism in the candidate, which as often as not subsides, leaving the young person disappointed or openly recalcitrant. While confirmation preparation still continues in the great majority of boarding or mainly boarding schools, actual numbers confirmed have in most cases fallen in recent years. The average proportion of pupils confirmed while at school appears to be now about half the pupils in attendance. We believe that most schools are concerned that this should be a real act of commitment and that the candidates should receive a thorough preparation. In the case of boarding schools, boys and girls may well have to be confirmed at school, either because their families have no settled parish church connections, or because the home parishes cannot arrange confirmations at suitable times in school holidays.[2] We certainly think that this is a feature of the religious life of the independent schools which cannot be widely copied by schools in the maintained system. It depends too much on the boarding situation or, in the independent day schools, on a close-knit school community.

358 It is obvious that the ability and the personality of the chaplain are important factors in the creation of a Christian community within the school. There is no doubt that a school chaplaincy is a crucial appointment, the value of which can bear comparison with that of every other part of the ordained ministry. The comparatively small number of people to whom the chaplain ministers (and to the pupils must be added some degree of responsibility for the teaching staff and for all other school employees) is offset by the closeness of personal contact with these individuals. For the chaplain, this involves an integration with the total life of the school as complete as is necessary for him to fulfil not only a teaching and liturgical but also a pastoral role. In some schools chaplains have responsibilities for some area of the school's life: house tutor, careers master, social service organizer. These can often lead directly to pastoral contacts, even if care is necessary to ensure against a degree of over-involve-

---

[1] Op. cit., p. 53.
[2] Most chaplains normally try to establish contact with parish clergy at this stage, not always with success.

ment in the general life of the school. Dr R. Lambert has a useful warning against this:

In boarding schools religious occasions often have other functions—administrative ones—and chaplains often teach and exercise ordinary disciplinary roles. These mixtures often confuse children and, to their mind, degrade religious occasions or render chaplains hypocrites or baffling and unapproachable.[1]

This is not to gainsay the point we have already made that the chaplain should be a professionally competent teacher, ideally in some other subject as well as religious education. There is a need to explore the relations between school chaplains and local parish clergy, rural deaneries, and diocesan education authorities. Their own pastoral needs should be the concern of their diocesan bishop, and this should certainly involve something more than just a formal licensing. The local diocesan bishop should be more closely involved than he usually is with appointments. It was put to us by some chaplains that the present system whereby one bishop is pastorally responsible for all school chaplains and concerned with appointments is not ideal simply because the work involved demands very much more than the part-time attention which is all that a suffragan bishop can spare. If the recommendations of *Partners in Ministry*[2] are adopted, clergy working in schools will come into the category of those "on the books" of their diocese. This may prove to be a more secure relationship than at present some feel they enjoy, particularly as regards future employment.

359 The whole subject of the creation of a Christian community in the independent schools has been jeopardized by the link between these schools and economic and social "privilege". The schools are sensitive to the charge that the Christian communities that have been created have had an unchristian strain in their very composition. Archbishop William Temple, himself a former public school headmaster, wrote: "That what is generally felt to be the best form of education should be reserved to those whose parents are able to pay expensive fees ... makes a cleavage in the educational and social life of the country as a whole, which is itself destructive of the best fellowship."[3]

[1] Op. cit., p. 102.
[2] The Report of the Commission on the Deployment and Payment of the Clergy (C.I.O. 1967).
[3] *Christianity and Social Order* (Penguin 1943), p. 68.

360 It is certain that the Church of England has never properly come to terms with the facts of exclusiveness and privilege implied by the existence of the independent schools. But it is difficult to know what the Church as a corporate body can do about this as the schools are obviously, and by definition, independent. Certainly it cannot withdraw its traditional interest and involvement in these schools. The schools themselves are all too conscious these days of the contradiction between their professed Christian ideals and their actual social make-up. But they also seem powerless to effect much change, unless they surrender their independence to a greater extent than the vast majority have been willing to do. We have already noticed that independence, *per se*, does not seem to have been responsible in recent years for any very spectacular developments in either the teaching or the worship characteristic of the religious education within the independent schools.

361 We do not wish to end on too negative a note. The independent schools have in the past made a significant contribution to the ideal and practice of Christian education. If they can preserve their virtues while ridding themselves of what distorts them, then their independence may well once more enable them to make a distinctive and positive contribution to religious education. They have much experience and many resources, and the opportunity to remain committed to the Christian faith. They should all, as some are doing, encourage experiment and critical inquiry, welcome dissent, insist on competent teaching, and be ready to explore the implications of the Faith for contemporary life. What they must not do is to remain little "bastions" of an outworn social, educational, and religious order.

6

Religious Education in Other Western Societies

362 A brief examination of the situation relating to religious education in the schools of some other western societies may assist the placing of our own problems in a broader perspective and contribute something towards their solution. An extensive comparative study is neither possible nor desirable in a report of this kind.

363 We focus our attention on the situation at present in the following areas:

(1) Scotland;
(2) Northern Ireland;
(3) The U.S.A.;
(4) The Province of Ontario in Canada;
(5) Certain countries in western Europe.

364 Uninformed discussion about religious education may sometimes give the impression that it is a phenomenon peculiar to England and Wales, but long since abandoned or prohibited by more enlightened and progressive societies. This is not true, as the rest of this chapter will serve to make clear. The limited scope of this Report prevented us from embarking on a worldwide survey; we have therefore concentrated on certain areas of particular importance at the present time.

(1) *Scotland*

365 The different historical and ecclesiastical background has meant that the situation in Scotland does not exactly correspond to that in England. This shows itself in two main areas: the statutory arrangements relating to denominational schools, and the place of religious education in public (i.e. local authority) schools.

Denominational schools

366 Prior to the Education (Scotland) Act of 1872, there was a statutory requirement for the establishment of parochial and burgh schools and for their supervision by the local parish minister. Up till 1861, schoolmasters were required to subscribe to the Confession of Faith of the Church of Scotland. After 1861 this was replaced by a solemn declaration that the teacher undertook never to endeavour to teach or inculcate any opinions opposed to the Divine authority of the Holy Scriptures or to the doctrines of the Shorter Catechism, and that he would not exercise his functions to the prejudice or subversion of the doctrines and privileges of the Church of Scotland. Alongside these statutory schools there were a very considerable number of schools belonging to churches and other bodies or maintained by private enterprise. Unlike the English 1870 Education Act, the Scottish 1872 Act provided for the transfer to the new school boards, not merely of the existing parochial and burgh schools, but also of voluntary schools if their managers so wished. A number of Presbyterian schools were so transferred but only a handful of Episcopalian and Roman Catholic schools. The result of the Act was inevitable, and may be summed up in the words of the report of the Scottish Education Department, 1878–9.

> The mass of the Scotch people are Presbyterians, and for these the national schools may be said to exist, just as the Roman Catholic and Episcopal schools respectively exist for these denominations. The public schools are to all intents and purposes denominational schools. Public and Presbyterian are practically interchangeable terms.

367 By 1918 the growing cost of education made it increasingly difficult for the voluntary schools to maintain their standards or efficiency. The only equitable solution was adopted in the Education (Scotland) Act of that year. This made it possible for voluntary schools to be transferred to the local education authorities on agreed conditions of purchase or lease, and for these schools henceforth to be managed and maintained as public schools, with the provisos that:

(a) teachers appointed must be approved as regards religious belief and character by representatives of the church or denomination concerned;

(b) subject to the conscience clause, time set apart for religious instruction should be not less than was customary before the transfer. The provisions for religious instruction generally made it unnecessary to specify that it was denominational instruction which was to continue: "use and wont" in a denominational school obviously implied denominational teaching.

It was also laid down that if it is agreed by the Scottish Education Department that a new denominational school is required, the education authority may provide such a school and manage it on the same terms as a transferred school. Effectively, therefore denominational schools in Scotland have *mutatis mutandis* the same rights and privileges as voluntary aided schools in England, but with the important difference that they enjoy 100% public financial support. As can be imagined, there has been, and is now, no denominational opposition to this arrangement, and it has not been a matter of friction between the Churches. Discussion of the future continuation of the system is sporadic and somewhat desultory, and based on the desirability or otherwise of denominational segregation of children, particularly in the light of present moves towards comprehensive secondary education.

Religious Instruction in Public Schools

368 Under the 1872 Act, all the parish minister's responsibilities with regard to public schools were transferred to the School Board. The established (Presbyterian) Church therefore ceased to have any control over religious instruction. At the same time, the preamble to the Act declared that it had been the custom to give instruction in religion to children whose parents did not object to such instruction, and that it was expedient that managers of public schools should be at liberty to continue this custom. The right of parents to withdraw their children was protected. The result of this was that religious instruction was continued, in the customary phrase, "according to use and wont". In practice, this meant the teaching of the Bible and the Shorter Catechism. This formal arrangement has been continued down to the present time, except that, apart from a few areas, the use of the Shorter Catechism has been discontinued and most syllabuses commonly in use include a good deal of extra-biblical material of various kinds. The main statutory amendment has been that of the Local Government (Scotland) Act, 1929, which provided *inter alia* that it should not be lawful for a council to discontinue religious instruction unless a duly approved resolution of the council has been submitted to, and passed by a majority in, a special poll of local electors. No such proposals have ever been made or polls held.

369 At the same time it should also be borne in mind that the Presbyterian tradition is opposed to any state control or supervision of religion or religious teaching. As a result, local Authorities and the Scottish Education Department exercise no responsibilities in regard to such teaching. The subject is not inspected by Her Majesty's Inspectors, there are no "agreed syllabuses", and there are no local authority inspectors. In view of the fact that the responsibility of the Church was removed in 1872, this has left a vacuum which shows itself in a number of ways.

370 There is no authority outside the school with any responsibility for ensuring that religious instruction is given or for what is done in time set apart for it. The very nature of the situation makes it impossible to obtain accurate knowledge of what in practice is actually happening in the schools.

371 Until the recent formation of the General Teaching Council for Scotland, recognition of teachers was in the hands of the Scottish Education Department. For secondary school work, they granted recognition in specific subjects, e.g. English, mathematics, or history. It was therefore impossible for a teacher to qualify as a teacher of religious instruction: such a recognition would have implied that his religious qualifications were being tested by a secular body. Any teacher appointed to teach religious subjects had to qualify in some other school subject. Until quite recently, such specialist appointments were almost unknown. They are now more common, and an Association of Teachers of Religious Education in Scottish Secondary Schools has been formed. Nevertheless, the requirements mean that a man or woman wishing to specialize must have a double qualification, i.e. either theology as part of an Ordinary (i.e. General) degree, or a B.D. degree obtained as a post-graduate qualification. The number of those with such B.D. qualifications is confined almost entirely to those trained as ministers. It also means that teachers find that their main specialism tends to have priority in the minds of authorities and head teachers and that promotion prospects in religious education are limited. In this connection it may also be noted that there is no conscience clause for teachers, and although it seems probable that head teachers attempt to respect the views of their teachers, it does mean that problems of staffing the subject (at least in theory) do not arise.

372 Until recently the conduct of secondary school examinations was directly in the hands of the Scottish Education Department, exercised through H.M.I.s. This meant that there were no examinations available in religious education. Pupils wishing to present the subject had to apply for examination to one of the English boards. Responsibility has, however, now been taken by the Examining Board for the Scottish Certificate of Education.

373 Taken together, these various factors have meant in practice that the standard of secondary teaching in the subject has in many cases been low; that the number of pupils coming up to university intending to read theology in order to teach it in school has been small; and that theological education in the universities has been almost entirely directed towards candidates for the ordained ministry —a tendency strengthened by the close association of the university faculties of theology with the church colleges for training ministers. There have been some attempts to improve the situation. There came into existence in the 1920s a joint committee of the Education Institute of Scotland and of representatives of the Churches. Known as the Scottish Joint Committee on Religious Education, this has produced syllabuses for use in schools, and is currently issuing a revised syllabus. These have, for the most part, been much more teachers' guides and handbooks than mere syllabuses, and have helped to give untrained or inexperienced teachers both the guidance of a syllabus and the practical help of what are almost lesson outlines.

374 At the local level there has been considerable co-operation between church and school with the appointment of local ministers as school chaplains. Such chaplains are formally appointed to all schools through the process of joint consultation. Their effectiveness varies but in some places does form the basis of a valuable and fruitful partnership. In the colleges of education, arrangements are made for students intending to teach in primary schools to receive courses in religious education and for intending secondary teachers to have the opportunity to train for the work, either in a general way or through more specialized courses. For this purpose a diploma in

7

religious education is available, requiring both a minimum academic attainment in a university theology course and successful completion of a college course in theory and practice of religious education. The question of recognition and registration of teachers on the basis of qualifications in religious education is currently under discussion by the General Teaching Council. So, too, is the question of an examination in religious studies by the Scottish Certificate of Education Board. It is doubtful, however, if any decision on either of these will be reached until after the publication of the report of the Departmental Committee on Religious Education. This Committee was set up in 1968 under the chairmanship of Professor W. M. Millar to review "within the existing framework of the statutory provisions governing the obligation to continue religious instruction, the responsibility for its content and the question of its inspection ... the current practice of Scottish schools (other than Roman Catholic schools) with regard to moral and religious education". It may be thought that the terms of reference of the committee effectively preclude it from tackling the really urgent problems: whether they do so in fact remains to be seen when their report is eventually published.

375 What are the main tensions apparent at present? First of course, the question of content, of what is to be taught. With this historical and ecclesiastical background, it is inevitable that religious education should have been thought of in terms of Christian nurture, as "Church-based" or "Bible-based". Such a view would still be vigorously propounded by many at the present time. Yet it is clear that many others believe that such a concept of religious education is largely irrelevant to the rapid development of the "open" or "secular" society in the Scottish cities. There are many undertones and overtones to this debate, and it would certainly be wrong to think of it as a conflict between teachers and churchmen. It is complicated also by the very varied social and religious situations in different parts of Scotland. The position in the Highlands and Islands is emphatically not the same as that in Glasgow or Edinburgh, and it is doubtful if one uniform solution will meet the needs of all areas.

376 The question of the relationship between religious education and moral education is also coming to the fore. The humanist and secularist lobbies are not as active in Scotland as in England, but the problems are just as real. Even so, it seems probable that only a

minority would disagree with the view put forward by almost all
those submitting evidence to the Departmental Committee that moral
education must in the Scottish tradition be closely linked with, if not
based on, the Bible and the Christian faith.

377 The place of specialist teachers in schools is, surprisingly enough,
also a matter for debate. Until quite recently, the Educational Institute of Scotland was against such specialist appointments, though
they have now changed their position. There is still, however, no
complete unanimity of view among the various teachers' organizations about the desirability of recognizing religious education as a
school subject; about proper means of qualification; organization
of departments; and promotion prospects. Nor is there at present
any agitation by these organizations for the introduction of a conscience clause for teachers, though there are many teachers, particularly among the younger and more recently qualified, who would
consider this a proper and necessary development.

378 It may be that the Millar report, when it is published, will be
able to do no more than highlight the major problems. It is to be hoped
that the report will be able to suggest some practical measures to be
taken—for example on qualification of teachers and on examinations.
On the really fundamental matters, however, the report must surely
reflect the uncertainty and division of opinion about this whole
subject which is found at present. It will, therefore certainly provoke
a good deal of further debate. This could result in considerable
advance both in understanding and practice. If so, what happens in
Scotland could easily be influential for developments elsewhere.[1]

(2) *Northern Ireland*

379 The development of education in Northern Ireland in the post-
war era has been influenced by the same thinking and research as in
the rest of the United Kingdom. The general pattern of the clauses
of the 1947 Northern Ireland Education Act which relate to worship
in schools and to the giving of religious instruction is similar to the
1944 Education Act for England and Wales. There are, however,
important differences in the detailed provisions whereby the similar

[1] In the preparation of this section the Commission gratefully acknowledges the
assistance of the Rev J. A. Wainwright of Moray House College of Education,
Edinburgh.

intentions of the two Acts are to be carried out. As circumstances and traditions in Northern Ireland are in some ways significantly different this is only to be expected. As well as these natural differences in the practical working-out of the legislation, the most obvious contrast between the two Acts is in what is omitted from the 1947 Act. Instead of the provisions which describe how the preparation and adoption of an agreed syllabus of religious instruction should be carried out, it is laid down that "in any county school . . . the religious instruction given to any pupils in attendance at such a school shall be undenominational religious instruction, that is to say, instruction based upon the Holy Scriptures according to some authoritative version or versions thereof, but excluding instruction as to any tenet which is distinctive of any particular religious denomination". There is also a section entitled "Religious Education not to be inspected by the Ministry of Education" which reads: "It shall be no part of the duties of inspectors or other officers of the Ministry appointed to report for the purposes of this Act as to the efficiency of any school, to inspect or examine the religious education given in the school." This prohibition ties in with the general provision which states that "Ministers of religion and other suitable persons (including teachers of the school) to whom the parents do not object shall be granted reasonable access at convenient times to pupils in any county school or voluntary school for the purpose of giving religious instruction to such pupils, and of inspecting and examining the religious instruction given to such pupils."

380 These various provisions have meant in practice that it has been the responsibility of the clergy and ministers of the three denominations which have had an effective stake in the educational system, to direct, support, and encourage the development of religious education in the schools, whether they are "county" schools or belong to the very small number of "voluntary" schools which have remained under the direct control of either the Church of Ireland, or the Presbyterian Church in Ireland, or the Methodist Church in Ireland. Under the provisions of the 1920 and 1930 Northern Ireland Education Acts the great majority of the voluntary schools which had been established and maintained by these Churches were, over the years, transferred to the local education authorities. In return for this transfer of property, the right to appoint representatives both to the Education Committees and also to the management committees of such schools was recognized. More recently it has been agreed by the local education authorities and the Ministry of Education that new schools built in new development areas should have the same kind of representation from the Churches on their committees of management. This has meant that these three Churches, who by now have transferred almost all their schools, have by virtue of this been seen to have a continuing right to play a part in the development of education in new areas. This fair-minded approach on the part of the Ministry of Education has gone some way to allay the fears of those —members of the Church of Ireland especially—who have felt that in giving up direct control of schools the Church has opted out of any effective voice in education. In the past the normal pattern in the country has been for each parish to have its small school, but, with the development of education and the need for larger and better equipped "central" schools, the Church found itself in a dilemma. Most parishes were too small to undertake the responsibility of a large school, and in any case lay people generally saw no reason for contributing large sums for building schools less than half of whose pupils would be members of their Church. On the other hand the dioceses had never thought of themselves as educational planning units but only as providing the minimum machinery for co-ordinating the educational work of parishes. There are no funds available to a diocese for educational development. Thus, over the years, the institutional involvement of the Church of Ireland in education has come to be much diminished.

Church, School, Community, and Religious Education

381 The Presbyterian Church in Ireland has tended to view its relationships with schools differently from the Church of Ireland, or even from the Church of Scotland with which it has close links. The point at which this difference is most clearly seen is in the attitude to the clause which states that "Ministers of religion and other suitable persons (including teachers of the school) to whom parents do not object shall be granted reasonable access at convenient times to pupils in any county school or voluntary school for the purpose of giving religious instruction". It has been the continuing policy of the Church of Ireland to urge upon its clergy their responsibility to make use of this "right of access" to their children so as to teach the catechism or other church formularies on one day of the week, and so also to have the opportunity of developing a relationship with teachers in the school. Obviously it could be very inconvenient for the school to separate out Church of Ireland children for this purpose unless both Presbyterian and Methodist ministers are prepared to co-operate and come regularly week by week on an agreed day and time to teach their children. The Presbyterian tradition, however, is to emphasize the primary importance of the proclamation of the Word rather than school teaching. In practice many ministers have often felt that they should leave the work of teaching in school to those who are trained for it. Many have also considered that definite "Church-committed" teaching should not be given in the school but in the more sympathetic atmosphere of the home or the Sunday school. Thus, rather than spend time teaching in schools where they may not be professionally competent, many Presbyterian ministers have tended to think that their duty is to ensure that reliable teachers are appointed who will carry out the religious education that the community as a whole wants.

382 Unfortunately the appointment of teachers has until recently been a source of real tension. There was a notorious occasion some years ago when a school management committee dominated by Presbyterian interest appointed only Presbyterians to fill a number of teaching vacancies. The next week in another part of the country only Anglicans were appointed by a school management committee dominated by Church of Ireland interest. This open expression of rivalry brought matters to a head, and a very different atmosphere now prevails. In the circumstances it is not surprising that the Methodist Church, with its much smaller numbers, has sought to press for all teaching appointments to be made by the teaching profession rather than by the representatives of the community. The positive feeling that underlies this rather unpleasant expression of sectarianism is the knowledge that education and religious education cannot in the end be separated, and that the most important factor in conveying understanding is the personality of the teacher. Many clergy and ministers give much time and care to the schools through their membership of school committees and feel themselves to represent, in a true sense, the interests of parents. It is comparatively rare, however, to find effective parent–teacher associations, and there is a need to develop a much more responsible concern for schools amongst all church members, so that all is not left to the clergy.

Inspection

383 Under the 1947 Act the inspection of religious education in county schools has been undertaken by the clergy of the three "interested" denominations, assisted occasionally by a Church Army captain or a Presbyterian woman worker. The phrase "convenient times" has generally been interpreted to mean one particular time each year when, for an hour or so, a group of clerical inspectors visits a school and examines the pupils in the religious education which they have received. Organizing this inspection is a complex operation involving close co-operation between the "chief inspectors", who are clergy or ministers appointed on a part-time basis by dioceses, presbyteries, or circuits. The carrying out of these inspections by clergy or ministers takes up a considerable amount of time and energy. A conscientious man might visit as many as 18 schools between February and May. The inspection is resented by many teachers, especially in secondary schools, who see it as an affront to their professional competence, a hindrance to effective teaching, a waste of time on the part of the clergy, and the best way of promoting "window-dressing" rather than anything that could be called serious religious education. But it should also be recognized that in many schools the inspection, while questionable as an educational activity, has served a variety of purposes whose significance it is not easy to assess in any definite way. In a girls' secondary school, for example, slightly more than half the teachers approved of the "examination" as conducted by fourteen visiting ministers and thought it a good one of its kind. "The children like it and it's an incentive to them" was a comment made by one of the teachers.

384 The Boards of Education of the Churches concerned have recently made efforts to deal with this complex and difficult situation. Two aspects of the matter have to be particularly considered. Some research, the results of which should be published shortly, has been carried out into attitudes to religious education in schools among sixth-formers. One conclusion which seems to be suggested is that while the attitude of parents to religious education in schools is roughly comparable to the figures given for various surveys in England, the attitude of sixth-formers seems appreciably less favourable than their opposite numbers in England. While allowing for the passions which "religion" excites in Northern Ireland, it is only reasonable to suppose that their experience of religious education must be one of the factors contributing to this less favourable attitude. Again, it can hardly be suggested with any degree of confidence that the kind of religious education which the inspection has tended to encourage is such as effectively to promote changes of attitude that will lead to more Christian tolerance and understanding in the community.

385 In 1966 an approach was made to the Local Education Authorities about the appointment of Advisers in Religious Education in the following terms:

The Boards of Education of the Church of Ireland, the Methodist Church and the Presbyterian Church are at present much concerned with the quality of the Religious Education being given in county schools in accordance with the Education Act (Northern Ireland) 1947. Much progress has taken place in the provision of syllabuses and the training of teachers, but the Boards believe that the appointment of an adviser in Religious Education by each L.E.A., similar to the Advisers and Organisers in other subjects, would contribute greatly to the quality of the teaching. Such an appointment would help a local education authority fulfil its duty of contributing "towards the spiritual, moral, mental and physical development of the community . . ."

It is much to be hoped that effective action will be taken by local education authorities on this recommendation. At about the same time the Boards had been encouraging various experiments in new approaches to the inspection in secondary schools. Instead of coming altogether on one day, it was suggested that inspectors should go into their assigned classes at a time during a three-week period when there was a regular religious education lesson. Three or four clergymen were asked to be responsible for a particular school and to go in several times during the year to see teachers and particular classes. The Ministry's report on *The Curriculum of Secondary Schools* published in 1968, while being very critical of the present system of inspection ("This annual visitation wins no real respect amongst the teachers and they have a right to expect that it should be replaced by less formal but more co-operative effort") goes on to commend these experiments which are currently taking place in the Belfast area.

Syllabuses

386 No provision was made in the 1947 Act for the setting up of machinery for the preparation of agreed syllabuses. This meant that the content of the curriculum was largely determined by existing tradition and so basically consisted of the outline of Old Testament history, the four Gospels, the Acts of the Apostles, the Creed, the Lord's Prayer, and the Ten Commandments. In 1943 a committee was established with official representation from the teachers' organizations as well as from the three Churches. It published a programme of "Graded Courses of Bible Instruction for Day Schools" which was approved by the competent authorities of these Churches. Increasing pressure to have the programme radically revised came to a head in 1962, when serious consideration was given to a proposal that material then being developed in Scotland could be used in Northern Ireland. In the end the committee decided to put out its own interim programme, which was basically the old programme with only minor clarifications and additions. This was published in 1966 and was intended to bridge the gap while a thorough investigation of the situation and a full revision could be undertaken. In the same year the important decision was taken to form the Religious Education Council, with equal representation from the Churches and the teachers' organizations. For the first time representation was sought from "other smaller Churches which have an interest in education" and also from each of the eight education authorities. One of the Council's first acts was to negotiate with the L.E.A.s in order to promote a pilot scheme in eighty selected classes in primary schools spread over the North of Ireland. The scheme has been based on the West Riding Agreed Syllabus and is planned to run for three years. The L.E.A.s agreed to provide a total of £1,000 a year for buying extra books and materials and for enabling effective consultation to take place between the teachers involved. Much enthusiasm has been generated in the schools, and in 1969 a large exhibition was held in order to give an opportunity for teachers, clergy, and the public in general to see something of recent developments in religious education.

387 Dissatisfaction with the provision whereby the senior grade of the "Graded Courses of Bible Instruction for Day Schools" was to be used in the Secondary Intermediate schools, led to the setting up of a committee in 1957 with the task of preparing a syllabus in religious education which would meet the needs of what Newsom has called "the average child". It was not until 1962 that the first-year handbook was finally published under the general title *God was in*

7*

Christ. Many teachers were confused by its thematic approach and the way in which it moved from New Testament to Old and back again without regard for historical sequence. Numerous meetings of teachers were held to introduce this new approach. The second-year book was published in 1963 and the third and fourth years together in 1965. The report on *The Curriculum of Secondary Schools* comments that this syllabus is not an easy alternative, and its demands on the teacher are considerable. "What is, in fact, demanded is a specialist approach and the task of guiding religious education must more and more become the province of the specialist teacher."

388 The passing of the 1947 Act was the stimulus which brought about the setting up of a Joint Conference on Religious Instruction in Northern Ireland Grammar Schools. The resulting *Northern Ireland Grammar School Syllabus in Religious Instruction and Handbook for Teachers* was published in 1949 "with the approval of the Joint Board of the Churches and with the assistance of grants from the Northern Ireland Education Authorities". The first printing sold rapidly because of considerable interest shown in England, but also because a fierce local controversy sprang up on the fundamentalist issue. The approval given by the joint board of the Churches came under considerable criticism from members of the boards of education on the grounds that some of the statements and articles were theologically suspect. This syllabus has since been revised and is now used in schools both north and south of the border. The particular interest of this syllabus is the emphasis it gives to sixth form work. The present provision for religious education in secondary schools is for at least three periods a week up to O level. This enables some quite effective work to be done in this subject. It is hoped that papers in religious education will shortly be accepted by the Northern Ireland G.C.E. Committee. A number of schools present pupils for examinations set by other examining boards.

Teachers

389 A survey to collect evidence on the position and teaching of religious education in secondary intermediate and grammar schools attended by children of Protestant parents in the Belfast area was carried out by the teachers' branch of the Christian Education Movement in 1968. The main aim of the survey was to gain some indication of the attitudes of teachers to teaching religious education and also to find out about their professional qualifications. Of the 29 schools which were asked to co-operate, 19 sent in returns, and while the questionnaire used was not designed to give more than a general picture of the situation, the impression given was not encouraging. Over the previous three years 75% of the teachers in secondary (intermediate) schools had been involved in some teaching of religious education. 17% of all teachers in the survey said they were unwilling to teach the subject. Thus in spite of the widespread involvement in teaching the subject the figures suggest that no teacher is being pressed to any intolerable violation of his conscience. On the other hand, 45% said that they were willing to teach religious education only where there was a shortage. When this figure is taken in conjunction with the fact that only 10% of those who teach the subject claimed to have any qualifications for it, there are substantial grounds for the all too common complaints of young people about comparative standards with other subjects. The closer correspondence in the figures in grammar schools between those who teach the subject and those who are unreservedly willing to do so seems due to the fact that these schools have more specialists and also use ministers of religion on a part-time basis.

390 Conscientious teachers have sometimes said that in their experience religious education has been so badly taught that it would be better to omit it altogether from the school curriculum. The sense of frustration here expressed suggests that the main barrier to effective work is not the basic unwillingness of teachers but their unease at being faced with a teaching situation of great importance for which they feel themselves ill-equipped and unsupported by competent help and advice. The religious education department in Stranmillis College of Education, Belfast, was established in 1960 and has provided a four-year course for those who want to become "semi-specialists" and teach religious education in secondary schools. More schools are now anxious to provide posts in religious education and to establish effective departments. This is an indication that the teaching of the subject is being treated with a greater degree of serious and professional responsibility. Degree courses in religious studies are now replacing the four-year course and these are being developed in close co-operation with the two Roman Catholic colleges of education.

Roman Catholic Schools

391 The main impression given by Roman Catholic spokesmen is that the overall pattern which the 1947 Act supplies has given much the same kind of opportunities and has presented much the same kind of difficulties as in the schools attended by the children of Protestant parents. The continuing close link between Roman Catholic school, parish, and church is often physically expressed by the fact that new schools are built in the grounds of churches or as near to them as possible. The parish priest is manager of the school and will expect to visit it regularly, though he would not usually teach a class except for some special reason. In the primary schools the teachers are responsible for teaching religion on the basis of an "integrated" approach developed from a recently revised series of American text-books. This series had grown out of the needs of the American situation where religion often had to be taught by untrained lay people, and some teachers were resentful of its over-elaborate and "un-professional" approach. In the secondary schools the situation is much more fluid. No one syllabus or series of books is used. The majority of teachers take part in teaching religion and the same feelings of uncertainty about the task may lead to the expression of negative attitudes. One large secondary school in the Belfast area has changed over to using specialists for most of the teaching, a trend which will almost certainly be followed by other schools. Each Roman Catholic diocese appoints ecclesiastical inspectors of schools, but these priests now see their work as "advisory" rather than in the traditional sense of "inspecting" schools. They arrange courses of lectures for teachers—often on the best use of the Bible in religious education. Where there is a large secondary school, priests from several parishes may decide to work in the school as a team, each teaching one or two forms. Many have used discussion methods and the response of the pupils has been heartening. Some of the bishops have been asking their priests to recognize the need for them to function as "counsellors" in schools as well as teachers.

Conclusion

392 The religious and political tensions in Northern Ireland continue to give cause for very grave concern. These tensions inevitably mean that the question of maintaining entirely "separate" education for Roman Catholic children cannot be a matter of indifference to the community as a whole. Not long ago two separate schools were established in a country town where previously there had been one of the very few secondary schools in which Protestant and Roman Catholic children had shared a common education. There may have been special considerations in this instance, but it was a great discouragement to those in Northern Ireland and elsewhere who look for signs that the ecumenical advance generated through the Vatican Council is finding effective means of expression.

393 We do not in any way wish to minimize the complexity of the political, social, economic, and religious problems of Northern Ireland at the present time. But we do wish to make clear that one of the consequences of religious education, as we on this Commission understand it, should be growth in sensitivity, tolerance, and mutual understanding. It is our hope that religious education in schools could, over the years, make its own contribution to the development of greater social cohesion, though that will not be the prime reason for its place on the school curriculum. We also hope that all the ecclesiastical authorities in Northern Ireland, including the Roman Catholic Church, will consult together as a matter of extreme seriousness and urgency to examine ways and means whereby denominational schools could contribute to social integration. We recognize that this will present a challenge to ecumenical seriousness and we are too sensitive to the problems to suppose that there will be any quick or easy solution.[1]

(3) *The U.S.A.*

394 The historical and constitutional development of the U.S.A. has been such as to lead to a strict separation between Church and State in all matters concerned with public education. Until comparatively recently the Churches conceived their educational task in almost entirely "domestic" terms. The Roman Catholic Church developed an extensive network of "parochial schools"—day schools wholly financed and administered by the Church and providing a Catholic education for the children of Catholic parents. These schools receive no financial aid from the State, and there has even been opposition to Catholic pupils being accorded transport facilities on school buses

[1] In the preparation of this section the Commission gratefully acknowledges the assistance of the Rev J. R. B. McDonald, of Stranmillis College of Education, Belfast.

financed by public funds. The Protestant Churches have developed a system of Christian education based on "church schools"—large, well-organized Sunday schools associated with individual churches, usually with special buildings and often with full time organizers, paid teachers, and high quality literature. There are also private day and boarding schools maintained by Churches or by other bodies. Until very recently, religious teaching has been strictly excluded from the curriculum of all "public" (i.e. state) schools in the U.S.A.

395 A point of view sometimes heard in discussions about the future of religious education in England is that we should "adopt the American system". Its advocates point to the high level of church-going and religious interest in the U.S.A. and compare this with the very different situation observable in England and Wales. The comparative health of the American churches is, according to this argument, to be attributed—at least in part—to the following two factors:

(*a*) Young people learn their faith within the context of a worshipping and ongoing Christian community—a community with which they may remain associated for the rest of their lives.

(*b*) They are not inoculated against religion by indifferent and undenominational religious teaching in their day schools—teaching which they will be likely to reject as being among other childish things to be abandoned on leaving school.

396 As a Commission we were anxious to examine this argument as closely as possible. In the Spring of 1968 the Secretary made a visit to the U.S.A. to study the situation at first hand and to have discussions with American educators and churchmen. We believe that the standpoint of those who would advocate the adoption of the American system is one which contains many unexamined assumptions. It certainly does not accurately reflect either the reality of the present situation with regard to religious teaching in state schools in the U.S.A., or the questioning currently taking place there about the future of "Christian education" and of the Roman Catholic parochial schools.

397 For many years, the place of religion in the state-supported schools in the United States has been unclear. There has been a variety of practices, depending on a curious maze of state laws and interpretations by state officers. Certainly there has been no national policy, even though the Supreme Court has from time to time made decisions on specific issues. In some states, the schools have been the equivalent of Protestant church schools, having Protestant school worship, teaching the Bible in the King James version, and having Protestant services for school leavers. In four states the teaching of evolution has been banned as "contrary to the Bible". In the newer states in the West, separation of Church and State has been interpreted more strictly, so that worship and instruction in the Bible have been banned although Christmas pageants and school leavers' services have remained. But in recent years even Christmas pageants have been objected to by Jewish and other religious groups. Roman Catholics before Vatican II were sometimes forbidden to attend services for school leavers. So confused a situation obviously required clarification and three factors have made for recent change.

398 The first is the national government's concern with education. This has hitherto been financed and directed on the state and local levels, but federal money has recently poured into many school districts. There has also been concern for private and church-related schools, although no money for their maintenance has been made available chiefly because of the Church–State separation. Secondly, there is the thawing of relations between Catholics and Protestants, due to Vatican II, and also between Christians and Jews, so that dialogue has become possible on a wider basis. Thirdly, there has been a series of Supreme Court decisions which have restricted some practices and enlarged the possibility of others. It is already generally agreed, as a result of a number of decisions by the Supreme Court or interpretations by state officers, that religion may be taught from school on a released time basis. Pupils are released for this instruction during legal school time, provided the religious instruction is given off the school premises but under religious auspices recognized by the school board. Pupils in private or denominational schools may attend state schools on a "shared time" basis for courses that have "no religious significance" (anything from sewing to computer training). Services for school leavers have continued in many communities and have in some schools become ecumenical, with Protestant, Catholic, and Jewish leadership.

399 What has been forbidden has been primarily school prayers, including the use of the Lord's Prayer, and the devotional use of the Bible. The Supreme Court considers these practices to be contrary to those clauses of the Constitution which are concerned with the freedom of religion and the separation of Church and State. Some schools in strongly Protestant districts have ignored these decisions, and as no one in the U.S.A. is likely to be gaoled for praying, it is presumed that the practices will continue in remoter areas. But on the whole, there is no regular school worship or Bible study in the state schools of the U.S.A. But the same Supreme. Court decision that finally forbade these practices made it clear that the state schools have a responsibility for teaching *about* religion on educational grounds.

400 Such practices as "readings from the speeches and messages of great Americans ... or from the documents of our heritage of liberty, daily recitation of the Pledge of Allegiance, or even the observance of a moment of reverent silence at the opening of class" are permissible. Furthermore, Mr Justice Brennan wrote:

The holding of the Court today plainly does not foreclose teaching about the Holy Scriptures or about the differences between religious sects in classes in literature or history. Indeed, whether or not the Bible is involved, it would be impossible to teach meaningfully many subjects in the social sciences or the humanities without some mention of religion. To what extent, and at what points in the curriculum religious materials should be cited, are matters which the courts ought to entrust very largely to the experienced officials who superintend our Nation's public schools. (374 U.S. 203,300.)

It was also made clear that

in addition, it might well be said that one's education is not complete without a study of comparative religion or the history of religion and its relationship to the advancement of civilization.

It certainly may be said that the Bible is worthy of study for its literary and historic qualities. Nothing we have said here indicates that such study of the Bible or of religion, when presented as part of a secular program of education, may not be effected consistent with the First Amendment ... (374 U.S. 203,225.)

Mr Justice Goldberg, in a concurring opinion, joined in by Mr Justice Harlan, wrote:

Neither the state nor this Court can or should ignore the significance of the fact that a vast portion of our people believe in and worship God and that many of our legal, political and personal values derive historically from religious teachings. Government must inevitably take cognizance of the existence of religion and, indeed, under certain circumstances the First Amendment may require that it do so. And it seems clear to me from the opinion in the present and past cases that the Court would recognize the propriety of providing military chaplains and of teaching about religion, as distinguished from the teaching of religion, in the public schools. (374 U.S. 203,306.)

401 These quotations illustrate the standpoint adopted by the U.S. Supreme Court. It is clear that the Court presupposes that the U.S.A. is a nation in which most people have some degree of religious affiliation, that the religious history of the nation contributes to an understanding of its development, and that within a pluralistic society it is possible to come to some understanding of religious teaching without abrogating the separation of Church and State. Indeed, these quotations suggest that, for the sake of education, the law requires that religion shall not be ignored in framing the curriculum.

402 The Department of Justice of the Commonwealth of Pennsylvania, in its interpretation of the Court's decision, recommended the following practices as permissible in the state schools:

(1) daily recitation of the Pledge of Allegiance (which states that the U.S.A. as a nation is "under God")
(2) a period of silent meditation
(3) readings from great literature, messages and speeches of great Americans and from other documents illustrative of the American heritage (at this point excluding the Bible)
(4) presentation of inspirational music, poetry, and art
(5) the objective study about religion as a cultural force, probably within other disciplines
(6) the objective study of comparative religion or the history of religion
(7) Bible study for literary and historic qualities as part of a secular program of education.

On the basis of this interpretation, the Legislature of Pennsylvania moved a mandate to create courses about religion and assigned to the department of religious studies of Pennsylvania State University the task of providing curriculum materials.

403 There are other similar experiments currently taking place, mostly within the restrictions outlined by the Court. Some experiments, however, are related to the development of moral and spiritual values, with implications for discovering the meaning of events from a theological perspective.

404 The present situation (1970) in the U.S.A. may be very briefly summarized as follows:

(1) There is a wide measure of general agreement that the teaching of religion leading to commitment to a particular faith or Church is not only no part of the state school's responsibility, but is also unconstitutional.

(2) A fairly widespread measure of agreement exists amongst churchmen and educators that "teaching about religion" should find a place on the curriculum of secondary schools.

(3) A number of experiments are currently taking place to examine the educational feasibility of such courses.

(4) These developments are also taking place alongside reappraisals by Protestant Church authorities of the traditional structures of church-based "Christian education" in Sunday schools.

(5) There is some evidence of reappraisal by the Roman Catholic Church of its traditional policies with regard to parochial schools.

405 We note these changes with considerable interest and concern. It is evident that the American situation as regards religious education has altered and is still doing so. It certainly provides no clear justification for any substantial change of policy in England and Wales. We think that American educators and churchmen have still much work to do. Their most serious problem would seem to hinge on the distinction between "teaching religion"—which is forbidden —and "teaching about religion"—which is to be encouraged. We think this distinction is more easily made in theory than in practice.[1]

(4) *The Province of Ontario in Canada*

406 In Canada education is a provincial, not a federal, responsibility; there is, therefore, no nation-wide policy with regard to religious education. The necessarily limited scope of this Report makes it quite impossible for us to examine developments in religious education throughout the whole of Canada. There have, for instance, been interesting recent changes in the religious teaching given both in Protestant and in Roman Catholic schools in the Province of Quebec. We focus our attention on the Province of Ontario—a large, rapidly developing province containing the nation's capital, Ottawa, and the

---

[1] In the preparation of this section the Commission gratefully acknowledges the assistance of Professor Randolph Miller, Professor of Christian Education, The Divinity School, Yale University.

extensive metropolitan area of Toronto. Geographically close to the U.S.A., it still retains many cultural links with Europe.

407 In the province of Ontario religious teaching has been a feature of the school curriculum since the mid-nineteenth century. In 1823 the Reverend J. Strachan, President of the Board of Education of Upper Canada, planned a system of education "under the direction of the Church of England ... to combat the rise of dangerous democratic ideas and to strengthen loyalty to Great Britain". This scheme did not materialize, but religious teaching, of sorts, had been taking place in Ontario schools from 1816 onwards. In 1936 the Inter-Church Committee on Religious Education was set up to promote religious education and Bible reading in schools. In 1944 a Conservative government, under the Hon. George Drew as Premier and Minister of Education, introduced legislation making religious education obligatory in all public schools. "It is probably correct to conclude that this ... was due in no small part to Premier Drew's interest in and approval of what was happening in England."[1] Religious education had to be given in accordance with a series of teachers' guides—a series originally drawn up for use in English schools, but later adapted for Canadian use. The 1960 regulations for religious education in Ontario schools provided for: two periods per week, of one half-hour, of religious instruction in accordance with the revised course of study, i.e. the Teachers' Guides, grades 1–8; the Bible, and a book of Bible readings authorized for use in schools. Increasing dissatisfaction with these arrangements led to the setting up in January 1966 of a committee to inquire into religious education in the public schools. This committee was set up by the Provincial Minister of Education, under the chairmanship of the Hon. J. Keiller Mackay, former Justice of the Supreme Court of Ontario and Lieutenant Governor of the Province. Its report was published in February 1969.[2]

408 The report distinguished between religion as a subject for study and religion as a manifestation of faith. As a subject for study the committee accepted that it will be encountered in all areas of the curriculum, but when taught in a period set aside they concluded that

[1] E. R. McLean, *Religion in Ontario Schools* (Ryerson Press, Toronto 1965), p. 22.
[2] *Religious Information and Moral Development*—The Report of the Keiller Mackay Committee: Price $2.00 from: The Publications Office, The Ontario Department of Education, 44 Eglinton Avenue West, Toronto 197, Ontario.

it was "all too likely" to become an exercise in religious commitment. The committee expressed dissatisfaction with the existing series
of teachers' guides: "In our opinion this material is a vehicle leading
to religious commitment rather than to true education." The committee examined the possibility that the existing course should be
improved and developed along the lines of some more recently
revised English agreed syllabuses, but rejected it on the grounds that
any course which could be acceptable to all "would be too bland to
be effective". The recommendation was, therefore, that the existing
scheme of religious education should be discontinued. The report did,
however, recommend that in elementary schools the school day
should begin with "opening exercises" consisting of the National
Anthem and a prayer of universal character or the Lord's Prayer,
led by the class teacher. In secondary schools opening exercises may
be held on special occasions such as award days and school concerts.
The purpose of these opening exercises would be inspirational and
dedicational rather than confessional.

409 The Report also recommended that the provision of information
about the religions of the world is an essential element in the educational process. This religious information should therefore be provided at every stage from the kindergarten to grade 13. "Prosely-
tization" of the pupils should be avoided, and biblical stories should
be presented in the same manner as other works of art and literature.
Optional courses for the study of world religions should also be made
available for the 11th and 12th grades in high schools (i.e. sixth-
formers); such courses should be taught by the staff of the history
department.

410 In addition to these provisions for religious information and
opening exercises, the Mackay report also recommended a programme of moral development, the purpose of which was stated to
be "to stimulate moral reasoning rather than to inculcate moral
absolutes". This definition of moral development would imply a
programme of discussion lessons related to stages of moral growth.
The report recommended that the problems to be discussed should
be of two sorts: (1) those arising out of anecdotal material introduced by the teacher; (2) those arising out of readings, e.g. in history
and literature.

411 Preliminary reaction in Canada to these proposals, perhaps understandably, has been very mixed. The Ontario Inter-Church Committee on Religious Education in Schools has made the following statement:

We . . . concur heartily in the Mackay Committee's recommendation to discontinue the present course. We are considerably less impressed with the alternative proposed. It appears to us gravely superficial and inadequate. The task of conceiving and implementing an adequate contemporary policy on the place of religion in public education has hardly been started.[1]

It is evident that the problems of religious education in the public schools are likely to be debated in the Province of Ontario for some time yet. We think it improbable that the recommendations of the Mackay report will all be accepted in their present form. Here again, the position is one of debate and uncertainty.[2]

(5) *Certain countries in Western Europe*[3]

412 The introduction to the 1966 edition of the World Year Book of Education, *Church and State in Education*, stresses that in making comparisons between one country and another it is important to distinguish not only between countries in which Church and State are formally separated and those in which one particular religion is recognized as that of the State, but also between countries in which one particular denomination predominates and those in which—as in Britain—many denominations are to be found. So far as arrangements for religious education in the public system of education are concerned, there is a good deal of overlap between these broad categories. It must, however, be generally acknowledged that relations between Church and State have been easiest and least complicated in those countries, such as Spain, Sweden, and Austria, in which the large majority of citizens belong, formally at any rate, to one denomination and few of the remainder are actively opposed to that denomination. There may be all sorts of reasons for this;

1 *Teaching Religion in Public Education* (C. A. Russell, 277 3rd Street, Midland, Ontario).

2 In April 1968 the Secretary of the Commission visited the Province of Ontario and was able to meet both the Keiller Mackay Committee and also the Ontario Inter-Church Committee on Religious Education.

3 The situation relating to religious education in schools is set out in the official regulations of the Ministries of Education of various European countries. It can also be found in the more easily obtainable and assimilable *Guide to School Systems* published in 1964 by the Council of Europe (revised 1969). Much factual material is also available in *The World Year Book of Education 1966: Church and State in Education*, ed. G. Z. F. Bereday and J. A. Lauwerys (Evans 1966).

one of the most potent is probably the fact that in such a situation the
Church has rarely found it necessary to identify itself publicly with
any particular political party or ideology. This seems to be equally
true whether the dominant religion is or is not the official "state"
religion and irrespective of the extent to which church schools are
aided from public funds.

413 A very different situation exists in countries where there is a
dominant denomination, but where there is also considerable opposition from those who would describe themselves as humanists,
liberals, agnostics, or atheists. In their very different ways France and
our own country provide examples of this situation. In such countries
opposition to any claims by the dominant Church to have any say,
let alone a controlling say, in the field of public education is widespread and active. It is certainly not confined to the question of
finance. It goes far deeper than this and is concerned above all else
with the preservation, or the establishment, of a State which in all
its fundamentals is secular or at least "neutral" in matters of religious
belief and practice. In this situation schools are inevitably in the forefront of controversy, and it is easy to understand how in some
countries the Church has found it necessary to enter the political
field and to support openly specific requirements and candidates
whose policies are in line with its own objectives. In Belgium, for
example, the present Christian Socialist party was once known as the
Catholic party and came into being in order to campaign for increased grants from public funds for church (i.e. Roman Catholic)
schools: even today it has never formally accepted the principle of
secular schools notwithstanding the fact that it has broadened the
basis of its policies far beyond the comparatively narrow "schools"
issue and no longer receives the automatic support of all "church"
people. Here then, for a variety of historical reasons, the issue of
secularism is "alive" to an extent not hitherto experienced in the
group of countries to which our own country belongs, i.e. those in
which, whether or not there is a state church or a formally secular
State, there is a variety of denominations.

414 So far as Western Europe is concerned this latter group consists
of the United Kingdom and Holland with perhaps one or two other
countries on the fringe. The predominant factors in such countries
might be summarized as follows: (*a*) for all the current outcry in
certain quarters, there exists no real deep-rooted hostility to religious

teaching in the schools; (*b*) the state-maintained school is something quite recognizably different from a secular school in, say, France. If there is very little anticlericalism in such countries, it is partly because the various churches have accepted the principle that to refrain from active proselytizing is only a reasonable response to subventions for church schools from public funds, and partly because the State, being a comparative latecomer in the field of educational provision, inherited a situation in which the Churches were not merely already on the ground but virtually monopolized it, thus saving the State a very considerable capital expenditure. In such circumstances the establishment of some sort of working partnership was an unavoidable and not altogether unwelcome necessity.

We now examine the salient features in a number of countries:

415 In *Spain*, we note the co-existence of state schools with private (almost exclusively church) schools. The right of the Roman Catholic Church to organize and maintain its own schools is written into all current legislation. The teachers in these schools are appointed by the church authorities, although they have to have qualifications similar to those of their colleagues in state schools. Financial responsibility for church schools rests with the church authorities, but the state requirement for a certain number of free places in such schools can, in certain circumstances, be met by a grant from the Ministry of Education. The State also controls the inspection and supervision of teachers and retains oversight of the content of the curriculum. Article 27 of the 1953 Concordat between Spain and the Holy See required the Spanish Government to guarantee the teaching of the Roman Catholic faith as an obligatory subject in all schools, whether State-provided or not. Children of non-Catholic parents may be withdrawn on written application.

416 In *Sweden*, Church and State used to be closely integrated and even now nearly 100% of Swedes still belong, nominally at least, to the national Church. The trend in education in recent years has, however, been towards increasing secularization. The reforms of 1962 (in particular the setting up of the nine years' comprehensive school) and those of 1964 (the extension of the comprehensive system to upper secondary education) did not provoke much hostility between Church and State. But the place of religious instruction was a highly controversial issue. Pressure of public opinion ensured that religious teaching still found a place on the curriculum, but state regulations laid down the amount of time to be given to religious instruction and decreed its purpose to be informative and neutral. The comparative study of religion and social ethics characterize the religious instruction to such an extent that the study of the Christian faith appears to have no particularly significant place, despite the fact that it is the prevalent religion of the culture. In view of the very neutral purpose of this religious instruction, arrangements for withdrawal do not seem to be needed. There are few specially appointed or trained teachers of religion. The Church has now no schools of its own. Denominational instruction is permitted in the few private schools which exist, but such schools can receive state aid only if they fulfil specific needs, e.g. boarding education for pupils whose parents are abroad.

417 The situation in predominantly Lutheran *Denmark* is very different. Religious instruction is a compulsory subject for all children throughout the seven years of obligatory schooling. It must be given in accordance with the teaching of the Evangelical (Lutheran) Church of Denmark. The syllabus, which is drawn up by the Ministry of Education, consists of a study of the Bible ("texts"), Christian faith ("dogma"), church history, and the Danish Hymn Book. The teaching is given by the regular class teacher who may, however, opt out on grounds of conscience, provided that he can make suitable arrangements, including remuneration, for an approved substitute. A teacher who is not a member of the Lutheran Church is not allowed to teach religion, and is obliged to make arrangements for a substitute. Children can be withdrawn by their parents so long as the parents can show that the children will receive religious instruction elsewhere, for example under the auspices of the local church. Parents who do not belong to any Church are required to educate their children in social ethics. If they fail to do so, the State will intervene as a matter of right and of law. Private independent schools also exist, together with denominational (confessional) schools. These schools are free to make their own arrangements for religious education provided that the principle of compulsion is observed. Financial assistance is available for confessional schools on the basis of 85% of the teachers' salaries, plus a capitation grant amounting to 50% of the average cost per place of a pupil in the local public school.

418 Broadly similar arrangements exist in *Norway*, where religious instruction is, again, a compulsory subject in all public schools. Its aim is defined, at the primary stage, as that of affording "a means of contributing towards a child's Christian and moral upbringing" and, at the secondary stage, as "the giving to pupils a wider knowledge and deeper understanding of the Christian faith with a view to intensifying and strengthening their religious and moral life". The syllabus is laid down by the Ministry of Church and Education and is broadly similar in concept to the Danish syllabus, but the subject does not, as in Denmark, form part of the written examination in either of the school-leaving examinations. Another aspect in which Norway differs from Denmark is that at the secondary stage the teaching is given not by the ordinary class teachers but by religious specialists who are clergymen of the Norwegian state Church (Lutheran Evangelical). Pupils may be withdrawn at the request of their parents. Unlike Denmark, no statutory responsibility for the inclusion of religious instruction in the curriculum rests upon private or confessional schools. The question of financial assistance to such schools is under current consideration: hitherto occasional grants have been made to such schools on the basis of an *ad hoc* evaluation of the quality of the education provided.

419 Even so brief a summary as this of the position in three of the Scandinavian countries reveals a marked difference of attitude and of practice. There is an obvious gap between Sweden on the one hand and Denmark and Norway on the other. It may well be that, so far as results are concerned, the difference is more apparent than real, but on paper there emerges a clear-cut distinction between a frankly neutralist and a formally positive approach.

Two other countries with close geographical and economic links again reveal a marked difference of approach and treatment.

420 In *Belgium*, only about 1% of the population is non-Roman Catholic. The position relating to church schools and religious education is very controversial, as it has been for many years. In the immediate post-1945 period, church schools were a shuttlecock in the often bitter strife between the Roman Catholic Church and the political parties. This situation is now much modified as a result of increased cooperation between political parties over educational problems. The so-called "scholastic pact" of 1958 resulted in the subsidizing of church schools, which were still educating approximately 60% of the school population. State schools are required to adhere to the principle of religious neutrality, but religious education

can be given in them, subject to the usual withdrawal rights. A
declaration made in 1963 gives pupils in primary and secondary
schools the statutory right, expressed through parental request, to
attend not only the various religious courses but also the courses in
non-sectarian moral education. The scholastic pact expires in 1970–1,
and the future of church schools and religious education can only be
regarded as a very uncertain issue.

421 *Holland*, on the other hand, offers a picture so different that it
is worth brief study though the solution achieved by Dutch prag-
matism is hardly likely to be applicable elsewhere. In a country in
which those who profess formal allegiance to any church are divided
in almost equal proportions between Roman Catholics and Protestants, a *modus vivendi* between the two main denominations and the
State has long been established on educational issues. Between 70%
and 75% of Dutch children attend "private" schools, of which the
great majority are church schools. There is no distinction in fact or
in law in Holland between public education and private education
whether denominational or non-denominational. Holland long since
abandoned the concept of the "common school" in favour of a
system whereby public and private schools could operate side by
side on equal terms. About 80% of infants' schools, 70% of primary
(junior) schools and 90% of vocational training schools are private
schools: only in the academic secondary school does state provision
predominate. These private schools are subsidized by a scheme known
in Holland as "financial equalization", under which any school with
an approved number of pupils can reclaim from the State all its
current and capital expenditure, whatever its nature may be, and
irrespective of its secular or religious character. This is, perhaps, the
predictable outcome of a situation in which the two main religious
communities are roughly equal in numbers and in which secular
schools, whether public or private, appeal only to a minority of the
citizens. It is also clear that only the smallness of the country makes
such an arrangement, with its inevitable measure of duplicated
provision, financially acceptable. Religion is not a regular subject in
the public schools, but the local churches can demand time and
facilities for the teaching of religion to those pupils whose parents
ask for it. Secular "moral" instruction is given in public schools as a
matter of course. Private schools run by the churches offer not only
biblical and other religious instruction of a denominational character,

but also classroom prayers and even occasional opportunities for school worship. Public opinion would not have it otherwise in a country in which regular church attendance is still probably more widespread than in most other countries of Western Europe.

422 *Switzerland* has no centralized administration in the field of education. Autonomous responsibility rests with each of the twenty-five cantons or half-cantons. There are therefore in Switzerland no fewer than twenty-five educational systems and there is a baffling diversity of structures, teaching methods, and nomenclature. So far as religious instruction is concerned it is possible to identify three main groupings of cantonal arrangements, all of which conform to those articles of the Swiss Federal Constitution which guarantee religious freedom and protect citizens from any form of discrimination on religious grounds. In particular these articles make possible the release of pupils, on grounds of conscience or of parental wishes, from participation in any religious instruction classes. So far as religious education in the state schools is concerned the following are the three main groupings:

423 *Cantons which make no provision for religious instruction in the curriculum.* These are only three in number—Geneva, Neuchatel, and Basle (Ville), all cantons which for geographical and historical reasons have been subject to French influence and, in particular, to French devotion to the concept of the *école laïque*. In Geneva Church and State are formally separated by the cantonal constitution which states categorically (article 137) that "religious education" is separate from all other aspects of education. All three cantons hold to the view that religious education is the concern not of the State but of the different religious communities: Geneva and Basle (Ville), unlike Neuchatel, do what they can to facilitate the work of these communities, for example, by placing school buildings (but not school time) at their disposal for this purpose. Article 18 of the current education law of Geneva states that the time allowed for religious education must not encroach upon the time set aside for ordinary education.

424 *Cantons which include in the curriculum of the "public" schools' Bible study, moral and ethical instruction of a non-denominational character, such lessons being regarded as obligatory and being given, normally, by the ordinary class teacher.* These eight cantons also allow the various religious organizations to give denominational instruction to pupils whose parents ask for it in addition to the obligatory instruction mentioned above. At first sight the official arrangement appears to offer a typical example of Swiss tolerance and neutrality. But many thoughtful Swiss recognize certain inconsistencies. Effective Bible teaching, say these Swiss educators, presupposes at least a basic acceptance of the Christian faith, and many are finding it difficult to reconcile this with the fact that there will be a number of agnostics among class teachers required to give such teaching. On the other hand a certain measure of detachment on the part of the teacher is held to be not without its advantage, provided that it does not result in any undermining of the faith of the pupils. Swiss educators are also unhappy about the situation of the convinced Christians among the ranks of teachers obliged to teach on an undenominational basis. The educational authorities of these eight cantons would at least claim that by their interdenominational regulations they are attempting to give a specifically Christian intention to their school system.

425 *Cantons which include denominational religious instruction as an integral part of the curriculum of "public" schools.* These fourteen cantons (many, but not all, predominantly Roman Catholic) delegate to the appropriate church authorities not only the drawing up of a syllabus and the choice of textbooks but also the instruction itself. Most of them have a clearly defined religious majority; Roman Catholic in, for example, the canton of Uri, but Protestant in Vaud. In others, for example in the canton of St Gallen, the religious communities are so evenly balanced in numbers that separate public schools for each denomination have been established. In all cases the cantonal education laws conform to the religious principles set out in the Federal Constitution, even though they sometimes, as in Uri and Vaud, include a statement as to the religious affiliations of the majority of their citizens. A country of such diverse races, languages, cultures, and faiths as is Switzerland is bound to experience in education, as elsewhere, the constant pull and strain arising from conflicting aspirations and traditions. Religious education can certainly claim no exemption from these tensions and voices are still raised which maintain that by their very nature the denominational public schools belonging to this group of cantons are an infringement of the Federal Constitution with its emphasis on freedom of conscience, neutrality, and absence of religious discrimination. Although it is possible that a majority of all Swiss citizens would feel that the denominational public schools of this group do not provide the right answer to a difficult problem, it seems fairly certain that a majority would agree that in practice their continued existence is unobjectionable and that in their day to day administration they observe both the letter and the spirit of the Federal Constitution. As it is, they remain as a rather remarkable example of co-operation between Church and State, and this is equally true whether the Church concerned is the Roman Catholic Church or the National Evangelical Reformed Church of Switzerland.

426 On private schools in Switzerland all that need be said is that they can be set up at all levels in all cantons (except for one in which private primary schools are not allowed). Church schools are treated on the same basis as any other private schools, but the conditions under which they are supervised by the State vary so much from one canton to another that no overall picture emerges. In some cantons which are predominantly Roman Catholic, secondary education is only available in private denominational schools.

427 So far as *France* is concerned, we are unable to do more than to set the present position in its historical perspective. It is worth noting at the outset that the principle of absolute state control of schools was enunciated as far back as 1763 and that although it was supported by the theorists of the revolution it was never fully implemented by them or their immediate successors. Even the Code Napoléon applied only to the newly established *lycées* and left the general education of the children of the poor at elementary level largely to the churches through the medium of the teaching orders. It was not until 1833 that the State began to accept responsibility at this level, and by then the Church was strong enough to be able to insist upon compulsory religious instruction as part of the curriculum in these schools. From 1850 onwards the Church increasingly broke into the state monopoly of secondary education. The result was a Catholic–Republican struggle of such animosity and bitterness as virtually to dominate the subsequent history of French education right down to the end of the second world war. But the struggle between Church and State had already become less bitter in the years after 1918. Too many people were, as a result of their traumatic war experiences, becoming increasingly indifferent to these old and largely irrelevant quarrels. If there was nothing worthy of the name of a religious revival, there did at least develop a desire for at least some sort of compromise. By 1939 "private" schools (predominantly church schools) were educating something like 15% of the school population at primary level and 47% at secondary level. They operated of course with no financial aid from the State. Various post-war pressures led, however, to the introduction of tentative and strictly controlled forms of financial assistance for private schools. At the secondary stage, these were helped to increased popularity among parents and students by their comparative freedom from the excessive rigidity of the curricula and methods of the state *lycées*. It should be noted that at the elementary level there has been a different historical development. In 1905 the bishops were forced to sanction attendance of children at state schools which were, of course, available in every locality. This was not only a matter of political pressure but a realistic acceptance of the fact that there had never been a widespread parental concern for a full Roman Catholic education at this stage.

428 If, however, the State has, in general, adopted a more conciliatory attitude in recent years it is because it can negotiate from a position of strength. By its absolute control of the system of public examinations the State ultimately controls, in essentials, the conditions under which private schools are allowed to operate. The Church is, also, no longer so aggressively anti-republican as it once was and the State is viewed by many leading churchmen increasingly as a guarantor of the conditions under which alone the Church can best carry out its work.

429 In a country of divided beliefs the formula of the neutral school may be the only workable formula, provided that the school takes care to respect the religious convictions of its pupils and their parents. Many Frenchmen would agree that this is precisely what the state school now does, and they would add that the "neutral" instruction given in such schools is not of a character which does anything to weaken faith or shake firmly held convictions. This is particularly true when account is taken of the optional religious instruction which can be given on the school premises, out of school hours, by school chaplains (*aumoniers*) and parish priests.

430 No account of the situation in France can omit brief reference to the entirely different situation in Alsace-Lorraine. The principle of denominational schools, Catholic and Protestant, with religious instruction paid for by the State as a part of the normal curriculum has long been accepted and is a non-contentious factor in public debate.

431 In the Federal Republic of *West Germany* the position is almost as complicated as in Switzerland. The eleven *Länder* which comprise the Federal Republic are virtually independent states so far as education is concerned. Although some harmonization of policy is achieved through the medium of the Standing Conference of Ministers of Education, this does not in practice amount to much more than ensuring such co-ordination of curricula and examinations as is necessary to facilitate pupil transfer when parents move to take up employment in a different *Land*. It does not cover religious instruction and the question of church schools, a field in which each *Land* makes its own arrangements.

432 In Hamburg, for example (79% Protestant) the law requires the giving of religious instruction in all state schools, with parental rights of withdrawal. The syllabus is Lutheran in character and is drawn up by the church authorities in association with the *Schulbehörde*. The instruction is given by the ordinary members of the teaching staff, who have the right to claim exemption. Church schools receive financial assistance from the *Land* government to the extent of (*a*) 90% of the teachers' salaries and (*b*) 100% of maintenance costs. The exact sums involved are agreed by the parties concerned and are not subject to legislative arrangements; this informal procedure is said to be one of the reasons why in Hamburg there is little, if any, friction between Church and State.

433 The basic requirement whereby religious instruction must be given in state schools is typical of West Germany as a whole. This is laid down in Article 7 of the *Grundgesetz* (basic law) of 1949, which further states that the instruction given must be in accordance with the principles of the various religious communities, but without prejudice to the rights of minorities and to the State's right of supervision. It is of interest to note that the right of withdrawal can in the case of pupils over fourteen in some *Länder* be exercised by the pupils themselves.

434 In Hessen, to take another example (64% Protestant, 32% Roman Catholic), children of all denominations are usually educated together in the state schools and religious instruction is a normal though non-obligatory part of the curriculum. Private schools are relatively few in number; they are only financially aided by the State up to a certain level and on condition that they reach educational standards entitling them to be accepted as substitutes for state institutions.

435 In Nordrhein–Westfalen, where over 50% of the school population belongs to the Roman Catholic Church, denominational schools (Catholic and Protestant) have a formal place in the state provision. They may be established wherever numbers are sufficient to ensure their efficient and economic running, but this requirement appears to be interpreted in such broad terms that even one class and one teacher can qualify as an efficient school. Religious instruction is a normal class subject in all schools, state or private. Curricula and textbooks are subject to the approval of the appropriate church or religious community.[1]

436 From the brief and largely factual survey contained in this chapter certain fundamental points emerge:

(a) Religious education in state and private schools is a feature of the educational systems of many other western societies. It is certainly not peculiar to England and Wales.
(b) The co-existence of state-aided church schools with state schools is also a feature of many other European countries. The Dual System is, in its details, peculiar to England, but the principle of Church/State co-operation over denominational schools is well established elsewhere in Europe.
(c) "Adopting the American system" is no answer to the problems of religious education in this country. The situation in the U.S.A. is in process of change and, if anything, appears to be in many ways moving closer to our own.

We note that the position behind the Iron Curtain may be summarized in one brief statement: religious education in state schools is not permitted in those European countries which are now avowedly Communist states. The significance of this needs no emphasis.

[1] The preparation of section 5 of this chapter owes much to the experience of Mr J. G. M. Allcock, c.b. His work with the Council of Europe in recent years has given him knowledge and understanding of the educational systems of Europe, and we wish to acknowledge our gratitude to him.

7
Church Schools

The Churches' Educational Concern[1]

Christianity is an historical religion, which means, among other things, that it has to do with what is going on in history. And education is now an enormous part of what is going on. If it were only because so many people are so much involved for so large a part of their lives in education now, Christians would have to turn their most critical and constructive attention upon the phenomenon.

But Christian interest in how education happens and concern for what goes on in education far antedates the current educational explosion. In long stretches of history the Church was the major patron of study and sponsor of learning. So even nowadays when central governments pay closer and closer attention to an enterprise which they support and on which they depend, the churches' attention must still be turned toward education. Massively, often unconsciously, almost inescapably, in the various governments' schools personalities are being formed, values and ideals assigned, the whole shape of the future decided. It is a Christian's concern for the wholeness of the human being, for the quality of the common life, for the direction in which man goes that turns him toward education now and sets him inside it and will not let him disengage.

Worshippers of the God of all truth serve him when they search for information, when they are humble before facts and ambitious for their humane use, when they excite and equip others for the same quest. This aspect of the human enterprise, in which Christians have always been deeply involved and for which they have sometimes been principally responsible, has abruptly swelled beyond recognition. Christians must be alert to what is going on in education and thoughtful about its implications. We do not ask for our important old place in the educational system. We do not demand a special new place. We ask how we may best serve these welcome new developments.

437 These extracts are from the first section[2] of the findings of the *Joint Study Commission on Education* whose *Report* was presented to

[1] Church schools in Wales have their own special problems, and neither all the arguments nor all the conclusions contained in this chapter apply to them. See special note, p. 271.
[2] Paras. 19, 26–8, 36–7, 40.

the Fourth Assembly of the World Council of Churches at Uppsala in 1968. The report brought to the attention of the delegates a forceful reminder of the Churches' worldwide concern with educational processes and institutions. It is important to start with such a broad vision of education, set in the context of world development.

438 A similar estimate of the Church of England's concern is to be found in a statement prepared by the Bishop of Hertford, whose ministry is set in the sort of sub-urban area in which pressures towards social and cultural change quickly become apparent:

The Christian must be the first to rejoice in the immense revolution which is going on in the world of education. We are all familiar with the far-reaching plans of educationists which are intended to widen the scope and improve the quality of education in every field, from the nursery school to the university.

In all this the Church is privileged to work in partnership with the State. The significance of the part we have to play is not based on the contribution we have made in this field in the past, great as it was. Nor is it based on our vested interests in existing schools and colleges, nor in any desire to capture the young by indoctrination. We are in, and will remain in, education because that is where we belong. The pursuit of truth and the imparting of it are very much our business, as are the healthy enlargement of men's minds and personalities and the creation of truly human relationships and communities.[1]

439 Both these quotations rightly stress the importance of the Churches' concern with the general education of the whole community. But the Churches frequently express their educational concern also in terms of a specific, domestic, educational task, a task sometimes defined as "Christian nurture", sometimes as "instruction in the faith". Whichever of these terms is used, the basic purpose underlying them both is seen as the equipping of Christian people for their life in the world.

440 There was a time when this twofold concern of the Church with the nation's "general" education and its own "domestic" educational task, was held by many churchmen to be a single undifferentiated concern. Probably from the time of Alfred right up to the Victorian age, the quality of the common life of the country was felt to be at one with the health of the community of God's Church; the healthy enlargement of men's minds and personalities was taken as being

[1] In *Looking Forward to the Seventies*, ed. Peter Bander (Colin Smythe 1968), p. 271.

indistinguishable from their nurture and training within the Christian faith. When the National Society was founded in 1811, its purpose was "to educate the children of the poor in the principles of the Established Church", and, although the existence of Dissenters was acknowledged by the Society, their number within the community was not thought to be sufficient to justify the introduction of "some additional system [of education] which should be more comprehensive of the youthful population at large".[1] This did not mean that the content of education in schools founded by the Churches was restricted to matters of ecclesiastical concern, to Bible knowledge and catechism alone. The rudiments of a general education were felt to be an essential ingredient in the overall process of Christian nurture. That this was acknowledged by the government is shown by the fact that, when in 1870 the system of Board Schools was instituted in order to supplement the work initiated by the Churches and other voluntary agencies, it was not thought to be necessary that children attending church schools should receive any extra general education.

441 It is extremely important to recognize at the outset that the Church of England voluntary school of today is an institution whose roots go back into a past where its role was seen as twofold. It was general, to serve the nation through its children, and domestic, to equip the children of the Church to take their places in the Christian community. The two roles were at that time indistinguishable, for nation and Church were, theoretically, one, and the domestic task was seen as including the general, for members of the theoretically national Christian community would not have been equipped for their role in life if they were uneducated in the most general sense of that word. Recognition of this historical background helps one to see that nineteenth-century Anglican education was not quite as misguided and perverse as it is sometimes represented as being, but it also brings out the significance of the social and ecclesiastical changes which have occurred since those days and the need for changes in educational policy to match these developments.

[1] See p. 69 of the *Report of the Parliamentary Committee on the State of Education 1834* (quoted in *Educational Documents, England & Wales 1816–1967*, by J. Stuart Maclure (Chapman & Hall 1968), p. 35). It should, of course, be recognized that "some additional system" did already exist in the schools established by the British and Foreign School Society (see ch. 1).

442 This double role played by Anglican voluntary schools was an almost exclusively Anglican phenomenon. The primary purpose of most of the other voluntary schools was explicitly domestic. For example, the classic formula for the Roman Catholic system of church schools has been "Every Catholic child from a Catholic home to be taught by Catholic teachers in a Catholic school"; there is here certainly no thought of identifying the Church's children with the nation's children. This formula has recently been challenged by some within the Roman Catholic Church; but this does not affect the fact that it has been central to Roman Catholic educational thinking for many decades past and still remains the Roman Catholic Church's official policy.

443 We recognize that this domestic view of the voluntary school is by no means simply inward-looking and self-centred. In the words of the headmaster of a Jewish aided school:

Jewish schools impregnate Jewish children with the ideals and culture of their religion, in order that they can be better fitted . . . to make a specific and unique contribution to the mosaic of civilisation.[1]

But the point remains that these are schools for Jewish children. Their task is primarily domestic.

444 Nowadays no one would pretend to claim that nation and Church are coextensive; yet no one sensitive to the mission of the Church of England can deny that, as well as the domestic task which Anglican schools still have, they have inherited the general task of making a direct contribution to the education of the nation's children. The question which faces the Church of England on this issue is this: Does the perpetuation of its voluntary schools within the maintained system provide the best means by which it can (*a*) serve the new developments in general education and (*b*) pursue some part of its domestic educational task, supplemented by its own particular educational agencies which operate fully within the context of local church life?

The Years Ahead: Developments in Education

445 Before attempting to answer what we have suggested is the basic question facing the Church of England with regard to its voluntary

[1] Edward Conway in *Looking Forward to the Seventies*, pp. 292–4.

schools, we must try to look into the future. In this section we consider some likely educational developments during the next twenty or thirty years; in the next we look at possible changes within the Church itself. Perhaps a later generation will have cause to smile at our tentative predictions; but at least they will not be able to say we did not try.

446 We stand now almost at the mid-point between the Education Act of 1944 and the end of the twentieth century. One thing can be predicted with complete certainty: the remaining years of the century will see continuous growth in the number of young people. The latest forecast, for maintained primary and secondary schools alone, is that the number of pupils in them, at present just under 8 million, will be 11·1 million in 1990. In 1955 it was 6·5 million. Contributing substantially to this growth is the increasing number of young people aged 16 and over who are expected to remain in school—from 344,000 in 1970 to 1,017,000 in 1990. In a later section of this chapter we attempt to estimate what the growth of the young population could mean for church schools. Because the country's first duty in education is to provide enough teachers and buildings for all children at school, resources will have to be found for that before any can be used for other desirable purposes. The breathless experience of 1945 to 1970 will continue for another thirty years. Nevertheless, there will, we hope, be improved standards—better staffing ratios, smaller classes and groups, better buildings, more books and equipment. More will be done in nursery education and in the provision of special education for the handicapped; in particular, the imminent transfer of junior training centres from the health to the education authorities is bound to bring substantial new developments in this field. Yet even now education is the largest single item in the national and local budgets taken together: annual expenditure is over £2,000 million, and half of this is for primary and secondary education.

447 Whether or not the recommendations of the Redcliffe-Maud Commission are adopted, there are likely to be changes in the organization of local education authorities. Either authorities will become bigger and fewer or there will be a reversion to something like the situation before 1945; certain duties (e.g. to provide further education) falling on one tier of authorities and the rest on a lower tier. Ways will be sought of making the powers of managers and governors more meaningful and, more generally and at all levels, of bringing about a genuine partnership of all concerned in providing education, superseding the present mixture of benevolent paternalism and the master-servant relationship.

448 Even more important, however, for the Church's thinking and planning is the perpetual reorganization which is so prominent a feature of the educational scene. "The completion of reorganization is the most crying need in the field of whole-time education," said the White Paper *Educational Reconstruction* in July 1943: the reorganization it had in mind was the phasing out of the all-age school; yet, in spite of all efforts that have gone towards achieving this, the last all-age school will not disappear until this year (1970). Since 1950 a new kind of reorganization has overlapped the old, as the development of comprehensive education at the secondary as well as the primary stage has gathered pace. Whether it becomes universal or not, it will certainly become far more widespread than it is now; and, whatever authorities' long-term plans may be, it is likely to take as long to bring them properly to fruition as it has taken to reorganize the last all-age school. If so, we are immediately looking to 1995. Moreover, it would be surprising if other kinds of reorganization did not emerge before then. Already larger schools are being created as a result partly of educational, partly of economic trends. Furthermore, not unconnected with these problems, there is the question of the role of the independent and the direct grant school.

449 The comfortable days when there was a change of school for some at seven and for all at eleven have gone. Between five and eighteen there is now no age (except perhaps six) at which children somewhere may not be moving from one school to another. A common pattern will not emerge again (if ever it does) until very many years of the current phase of reorganization have passed. Practically all authorities have one particular problem to solve, and it will not be solved easily: Should education after the age of sixteen continue to take place in school or as part of further education? Where must provision be made for the trebling of numbers in the top age-groups, to which we have already referred? If sixth form colleges have come to stay, will they be schools or establishments of further education? Many people have looked forward to the raising of the school-leaving age to sixteen as the last step but one in raising it to eighteen. Are we now to discover that sixteen is the end and that

all full-time education after that age is to come within further (or
tertiary) education?

450 Obviously this debate is one which is by no means of only
academic interest to the Church. On one side are the problems of
school design and costs; on the other are many questions connected
with the Church's wide educational concerns. The link between the
Church and some of the older universities is strong and obvious; it
can never be as strong with the other universities or with any other
establishments of higher and further education, apart from its own
colleges of education. Has it gone far enough yet in its thinking about
chaplaincy services and its concern for religious education in departments of general studies?

451 Developments in the training of teachers during the last twenty-
five years have been no less marked than those in other fields of
education, and the Churches have been heavily involved through
their own colleges. The normal two-year course has grown to three
years; much critical thinking and many experiments are taking place
as colleges and universities work out a fourth year leading to the
degree of Bachelor of Education. But there are still searching inquiries to be made into the role of colleges of education. Within the
university departments of education there is much to be done in
critical re-examination of the content and aims of the diploma year,
soon to be compulsory for all graduate teachers. An even more
striking recent development in the training of teachers has been the
enormous growth of opportunity for in-service training; yet this
development is only in its infancy. The creation of C.S.E. examining
bodies; the establishment of the Schools Council; the enthusiastic
support of the Department of Education and Science, the Nuffield
Foundation, and other independent bodies for experimental work
in mathematics, science, and languages; all this led to the novel
idea of teachers' centres in a few localities. It was soon realized that
here was an idea for general application. Discussion and practical
work in teachers' centres cover every aspect of the curriculum—
content, aim, and method—and will eventually cover it at all levels.

452 As society becomes more complex, as all aspects of community
life become more and more interdependent, social institutions will be
more inextricably bound up with one another and the school will
be one of the most important social agencies. The old notion of

corporate parish responsibility—public order, social life, church, school, poor relief, reading room, and so forth—is returning fast on the immensely greater scale of the whole Welfare State. The greatest political problem of the remaining years of this century will be how to achieve this efficiently without the loss of all the advantages that human individuality brings to the community and without denying an effective place to the corporate common sense of properly elected local bodies. The integration of an increasing immigrant population, and of their children, will continue to be an urgent problem.

453 Schools, we have suggested, will become one of the most important social agencies. The pattern we are thinking of is not the one which is still familiar to a large number of educated people from middle class homes who keenly seek a good education for their children as their own parents sought one for them. Parents from such homes are still able to provide support and guidance during the first stages of education, though they may be more at a loss when faced with the bewildering world of further education and future careers. At the other extreme are the feckless in every kind of environment, and here for some time the whole educational system has been doing what it can, with all the other social agencies, often (like them) with inadequate resources. Between the two extremes lie many varieties of human need, from the spiritually and culturally barren houses enjoying a considerable degree of material comfort, to homes with a good sense of priorities which they are prevented from achieving because of impoverished surroundings in down-town districts. Within this broad band lie the educational priority areas, recently discerned by the Plowden Committee, where schools, colleges, and every other educational resource (including broadcasting, adult education, arts associations, sports councils, and the youth service as an integral part, not an appendage) must join forces with housing, health, child care, social welfare, police, probation, planning, and many voluntary agencies including the churches. All the experts in each of these areas of concern and care must band together as teams, not as committees, to solve the innumerable practical problems which will present themselves daily. Only if teachers and lecturers show themselves not in the guise of dispensers of something called education but as people jointly involved in the social problems, at their deepest levels, can schools and colleges fulfil their proper function. Equally, the social services must learn to accept that this is how many teachers see themselves and be willing to accord them a place in local teamwork. This is no more than a restatement in particular circumstances of the general principle that a school's first duty is to meet the needs of its own pupils. It is a task which will take us well into the twenty-first century.

The Years Ahead: The Mission of the Church of England

454 Any comment on the Dual System which is to be worth considering must be made not only in the context of likely changes in the educational system of our society, but also (so far as the Church of England is concerned) in the context of changing ideas concerning the pattern of the Church's mission to that society. This is not a propitious time for making general statements about the work and mission of the Church of England. It is now twenty-five years since the publication of the Report, *Towards the Conversion of England*.[1] In those years the Church of England has addressed itself to many other tasks such as intercommunion with other Christian traditions and the reform of its own internal structure, administration, and finance. At certain moments the Church has felt an air of expectancy, as, for example, at the enthronement of Dr A. M. Ramsey as Archbishop of Canterbury, when he took as the text for his sermon the words: "And there went with him a band of men, whose hearts God had touched."[2] But even so, the mood of these moments did not resemble the sense of clear opportunity such as marked the end of the war in 1945. Then, the tasks facing the Church of England seemed more clearly defined: evangelism, in fairly traditional terms, reconstruction of congregational life in the parishes, and a massive restocking of the ordained ministry to make good the loss and delay of the wartime years. With this sense of opportunity, clergy and laity also believed that they would have public support. The task was to reawaken faith, rather than to defend it against radical assault; to repair the traditional structures of the Church, rather than to question them.

455 It would be impossible to define the tasks facing the Church today in such traditionalist terms. The movement towards intercommunion and organic unity amongst Christians of different

[1] *Towards the Conversion of England*. A plan dedicated to the memory of Archbishop William Temple. Report of a commission on evangelism. Press and Publications Board, Church Assembly, 1945.

[2] A. M. Ramsey, *Canterbury Essays and Addresses* (S.P.C.K. 1964), p. 165.

8*

traditions has excited some lay interest in recent times, but, as David Edwards points out, whilst "reunion will often be the spearhead of renewal in the Churches", at the same time "no challenge to entrenched institutionalism is sufficiently powerful except the challenge of a definite plan to unite the existing institutions with each other. Only this apparently dull, administrative proposal brings about the necessary self-examination in churches from top to bottom, as leaders and led alike are driven to ask: what is essential?"[1] The recent history of Anglican–Methodist negotiations illustrates this assertion. In Anglican circles the discussion has sharpened the differences between conservative standpoints (whether Catholic or Evangelical) at the one extreme, the large body of middle opinion, and, at the other extreme, those who viewed the negotiations as a tedious exercise in ecclesiastical sociology. But there is a further divergence of opinion, less easy to measure in terms of numbers, and resulting from the differing answers given to the question, what is essential?

456 In terms of theological belief this divergence can be traced in a comparison between the cautious and undogmatic tone of *Soundings* and the far more confident (though occasionally self-critical) contents of *Keele 67*, the Statement of the National Evangelical Anglican Congress. If the former speaks of having to begin all over again, the latter makes it clear that one wing of the Church of England still finds it possible to affirm its "belief in the historic faith of the Church, in an age in which it has come under attack from both outside and inside the Church". But the *Keele 67* Report is notable also because it confesses, to the shame of those for whom it speaks, "that we have not thought sufficiently deeply or radically about the problems of our society", and resolves that they will "give themselves to more study of these critical issues in future". To this extent the Report reflects the increased social and political awareness of Christians of very different backgrounds, which has encouraged many of them, some systematically, and others more emotionally, to begin at the other end. For some this has brought about a renewal in worship, but for others it has produced the opposite effect, of regarding institutional worship and the organization of the Church as irrelevant to the modern situation.

457 The Church of England is a very loose-knit form of episcopal

[1] D. Edwards, *Religion and Change* (Hodder and Stoughton 1969), p. 277.

congregationalism. It is quite innocent of any coherent system of personnel administration. All shades of theological belief are tolerated, from near traditionalist Roman Catholicism at the one extreme to near secular humanism at the other. It is exceedingly difficult to see how so diverse an organization could have a generally acceptable policy on any topic of major controversy, or how its mission to society could be stated in any simple or direct terms. Its unity lies in its diversity and, in the present theological climate, its strength lies in its refusal to limit itself to any one set of rigid doctrinal formulations. Reform is in the air, but, as David Edwards has said, " Millions of words of modern Christian self-criticism have been spoken or printed, but it is not easy to trace a strong thread running through the details. . . . So much of the prophecy has seemed either vaguely idealistic or cruelly destructive. Conferences have come, and conferences have gone; books have exploded, and books have been forgotten; and the local churches, sullenly resentful or cheerfully ignorant, have remained much as they were before the prophets arose."[1]

458 It is equally difficult to generalize about the relationship between clergy and laity in the Church of England. In some communities the incumbent is still a local leader, with some measure of local prestige and civic recognition. In other places he has become one Christian minister among many, with no particular standing outside his own congregation. In down-town areas of large cities, the clergyman's position as counsellor, welfare worker, club organizer, and general leader has remained and in some places grown, because of the continuing social withdrawal from these districts. But as far as the ministry is concerned, leadership is not a prescriptive right of the Anglican clergy. It can pass to the ministers, of whatever denomination, who show most active concern and practical enterprise on the spot. The *Paul Report*[2] and the *Fenton Morley Report*[3] both look towards the development of a ministry which is determined by the nature of the Church's mission as a whole to twentieth-century England, which, according to the latter "means that the present way of doing things needs radical revision". They look forward to a situation wherein the clergyman will derive his status from his ordination and from being "on the strength" of a diocese rather

[1] Ibid., pp. 270f.
[2] *The Deployment and Payment of the Clergy.* 1964.
[3] *Partners in Ministry.* 1967.

than from his particular appointment. The vision is of specialized ministries alongside the residential pastorate, with a high degree of flexibility and clerical mobility, in accordance with realized needs, seen on a diocesan, or larger, scale.

459 The debate continues on these reports, and, as in the case of movements towards reunion, clear decisions have not yet been made. Discussion about reform and reconstruction in the Church is sometimes conducted against the background of traditional assumptions about the pastoral role both of the ordained ministry and of the Church as a whole in relation to society. But the long-term effects of a predominantly critical education, the emergence of a worldwide culture of youth, the breakdown of customary patterns of authority, and the growth of contemporary secularization, all makes it perilous to predict the patterns of ministry which may have developed a generation from now.

460 A further set of issues, closely related both to the structural reform of the Church of England, as of any church, as well as to the effectiveness of the ministry, has received treatment in an important study by P. F. Rudge, *Ministry and Management*.[1] He examines the root question of the purpose of the Church, and echoes the opinion that "no substitute can be found for the definition of the goal of the Church as the increase among men of the love of God and neighbour". The organization and management of the Church must keep this clearly in focus, and "guard against deflection in the direction of more proximate goals". Whilst no one would be so naive as to imagine that reform of management in the Church of England would by itself offer a cure-all for its present multiple problems, some urgent study of aims and methods is called for in view of the increasing sense of strain and inadequacy which many of the clergy feel when called on to fulfil a modern task with often anachronistic administrative structures, buildings, financial arrangements, and territorial patterns.

461 The various changes in patterns of working, in structures and organization, in attitudes and roles, which are likely to arise from the present process of self-examination being conducted by the Church, will all affect the traditional relationship which has existed between

[1] Tavistock Publications 1968.

the Church of England and the institutions of English society, and are likely to cause even greater changes in the relationship between Church and school, both at national and local level. It is against this background that discussion of the future of church schools must be conducted. Only one point is completely clear: on the subject of church schools the Church of England has never had one generally agreed policy. It certainly has none today.

The Issues Involved

462 The majority of the organizations offering evidence to the Commission were in favour of retaining denominational voluntary schools within the English educational system. Representatives of the teaching profession and of educational administrators offered continuing majority support for the principle lying behind the present Dual System, though with reservations about some of the ways it has worked out in practice. Similarly, majority support for the system was apparent in the evidence presented by diocesan education committees, which have a particular responsibility in maintaining the Anglican Church's contribution to the Dual System. Despite this overall support, however, a number of fundamental questions have been raised concerning the present position, both by teachers and by clergy, quite apart from the condemnation of the system as a whole which has been made by the secular humanist organizations.[1] Debate arises within three main areas which can be classified as (1) theological, (2) educational, and (3) economic. It will be seen that these are by no means watertight classifications, and that there is considerable overlap and interplay between the different arguments set out below. However, we think that some such categorization is of use when we are attempting to survey a very complex field.

(1) *Theological Arguments*

463 *Argument A* The first objection to Anglican participation in the Dual System comes from those who see the relationship between Church and society in terms of the Anglican Establishment. They would point to the fact that the Church of England is the established

---

[1] In their replies to the Commission's questionnaire the British Humanist Association, The Humanist Teachers' Association, the National Secular Society, and the Progressive League all opposed the continuance of the Dual System.

Church, and would say that this means not only that the Anglican Church is in a special relationship to the State, but that the State is in a special relationship to the Anglican Church. This relationship should be worked out in terms of partnership in every area of social activity: schools, hospitals, welfare work, civic ceremonies, and so on. Working from this basis, the upholders of this argument claim that the Church of England should have become fully involved with the work of the county schools, and a real form of partnership should have been developed there.

464 The groundwork for such a partnership was set out in the Report of the Parliamentary Committee of 1818, in which arrangements were suggested by which "the desirable object" of "connecting the educational system with the Church Establishment" might be secured. (Placing the appointment of all schoolmasters in the hands of "the parish vestry, subject to the approbation of the parson and the visitation of the diocesan", was the major arrangement proposed.) The 1818 Committee was, however, also aware of the "injustice to Dissenters" that such a system might involve. When, in 1839, the Committee of Council for Education was set up, the position of the Established Church was regarded more ambivalently. The most that the Home Secretary felt able to say was that "much may be effected by a temperate attention to the fair claims of the Established Church, and the religious freedom sanctioned by the law. On this subject I need only say that it is Her Majesty's wish that the youth of this Kingdom should be religiously brought up, and that the right of conscience should be respected."[1] Already in 1834 Parliamentary Commissioners had used phrases such as "one class for church children and one class for all other denominations", possibly implying that they regarded the Church of England as a denomination rather than as the Established Church, and this tendency reached its climax in the so-called Cowper–Temple clause in the 1870 Elementary Education Act, which stated that "no religious catechism or religious formulary which is distinctive of any particular denomination shall be taught in any school provided by a School Board". This applied to Anglican doctrines as much as to those of any other Church. Yet the 1944 Act in its Fifth Schedule unquestionably recognizes that in England, though not in Wales and Monmouthshire, the Church of England occupies a special position.

---

[1] Letter from Lord John Russell to the Lord President of the Council, 4.2.1839.

465 In considering the implications of this position, so this argument runs, the Church of England should be forced to wake up to the fact that its educational role for over a century has been ambiguous in the extreme. If it is the established Church, then as such it should take steps to fulfil its duties in all maintained schools, and bring to an end its system of "Church" schools which are, on this basis, a totally unnecessary anomaly. This is not a call for the abolition of the entire Dual System, however, only for the disbanding of the Anglican element within it. If the established Church were working in full partnership with the State, then it would be only right and proper that denominational bodies should have the opportunity to opt out of an educational system based on this partnership. Denominational schools would therefore be a very necessary provision alongside the proper functioning of the Church–State system.

466 If, on the other hand, the Church of England is not in an established position *vis à vis* the schools of the nation (and as long ago as 1902 the Prime Minister, Mr A. J. Balfour, stated quite categorically that "we have as a community repudiated responsibility for teaching a particular form of religion",[1]) then, so this argument goes, there should be an end to any pretence that the Anglican Church is anything more than one of the denominations and it should settle down to using its church schools for the benefit of its domestic community with no more delusions about their responsibility towards the community at large, other than that kind of indirect responsibility spoken of by Edward Conway in the quotation earlier in this chapter. It should be noted that Anglican voluntary schools in Wales are already in this non-established position.

467 *Argument B* A differently based objection comes from those who may be described as Christian radicals. In their eyes the Church's task is to permeate society, to be directly involved in society's activities as a leavening influence. For them it is being false to the Church's true role to think in terms of the Church preserving its own system of educational institutions. In earlier centuries it was right for the Church to provide schools, seeing that the State made no such provision. But now that there is a fully established system of publicly maintained schools, Christian involvement in education should take the form of personal service directly within this system. Even if the Church had money enough and to spare for the running of its schools,

[1] See *Hansard*, 24.3.1902.

so this argument goes, it would be theologically at fault to persist with an educational system inherited from the completely different circumstances of the last century. Quite apart from the general principle of service from within, there are certain practical consequences of the Church still maintaining its own schools which the proponents of these arguments regard as objectionable: (*a*) the church school, they claim, may become an inward-looking community, shut off from the secular world; (*b*) it also, by virtue of remaining identifiably different, may act as a distorting magnet within the educational system, attracting to itself the service of Christian teachers who should be spread abroad throughout the system as a whole.[1] Support for this principle of service from within the secular system also comes from some Evangelicals. While they will not share some of the theological premises from which this argument is often derived, they may nevertheless support the general direction of the argument, in so far as they see their task as being basically a missionary one.

468 *Argument C*   A further objection to the Dual System is grounded in the contention that, as the system operates, the church school is prevented from being fully integrated into the institutional life of its parent congregation. Conditions originally laid down in the 1870 Act are reflected in the working of the 1944 Act: "It shall not be required, as a condition of any pupil attending . . . any voluntary school, that he shall attend . . . any Sunday school, or place of religious worship."[2] What is more, under the terms of the 1946 Act it is only "on any special occasion" that an aided school may begin the day with collective worship elsewhere than on the school premises, and the intention of the Act is clear that such special occasions should be very few. For these reasons it becomes in practice extremely difficult for any strong link in worship to be forged between the school and the church building used by the parent congregation. Except under the most liberal interpretation of these regulations, so this argument claims, the Dual System represents not a workable compromise but a complete abandonment of the essential charac-

[1] It is interesting to compare this argument with the comment contained in the evidence submitted by the Headmasters' Association: "The existence of denominational schools can also cause an unhappy limitation of the Christian concern of the Church so that it concentrates too much of its attention and resources on the schools of its own denomination and shows too little concern for the religious education of children in county schools."
[2] See section 25(3) of the 1944 Act.

teristic of a church school, i.e. that it should be closely integrated with the life and work of the local worshipping community.

The Theological Arguments Considered

469 We wish to make it absolutely clear that the Commission has seen its task to be the examination of the Dual System, not by any means necessarily a defence of it. Members came to this task with varying viewpoints and varying opinions. It would certainly not reflect the Commission's approach to the issues if this section of our report simply set out to answer one by one the arguments brought forward in the three areas under consideration. However, it is obviously necessary at this point to examine the theological arguments which have been stated above and to see what may be set forward in counterargument.

470 Argument A (the "Establishment" argument)—clearly the Church of England's role in education is not the only one of its activities to have been complicated by the fact of its being the Established Church. One need only look at the problem surrounding baptism to see its effects there. Because the general community and the Church's domestic community have been identified to some degree with each other for so long, it is not surprising that there is still a general expectation that baptism in the parish church is the birthright of every Englishman, and for the Church of England to make a distinction at this point between its members and the community at large may be regarded as an attempt to evade its national responsibilities. Yet, on the other hand, there are fewer and fewer areas of national life in which the Church of England has special rights as compared with the other Churches. Establishment today has virtually become an arrangement whereby the nation has the expectation of certain rights within the life of the Church of England, but the Church has comparatively few rights within the life of the nation. This is not intended as a complaint, merely as a statement of fact. But if these are indeed the facts, then the two clear alternatives posed by the upholders of Argument A cease to be clear alternatives at all. It is not a simple choice between insisting on "established" rights throughout the nation's schools on the one hand or confining one's attention to a purely domestic community on the other. It is virtually impossible to draw a clear line round the "domestic" community of the Church of England. This still remains one of the features which distinguishes it from the other denominations.[1]

471 However logically (or theologically) untidy it may seem to be, as a result of its historical development the Church of England finds itself today in the position of having educational aims and responsibilities which we have categorized as both general and domestic. Failure to take both these areas of responsibility into account characterizes the other two theological arguments. Argument C, which sees school and Church as inextricably linked, is not giving sufficient weight to the church schools' responsibilities to the local community at large, which may well include a significant number of non-Anglican families. The upholders of Argument B ("service from within") are right to object to ghetto-like huddles and they are also right to call for Christian teachers to work in county schools, but it is not necessary to close down all church schools to achieve these objectives.

(2) *Educational Arguments*

472 *Argument A* The main educational criticism of the whole concept of church schools springs from their identification as "denominational" schools, i.e. schools within which denominational religious instruction can be freely given. Those who put forward this argument point to a whole range of documents and pronouncements from the founding of the National Society right up to 1944 and beyond. The National Society's stated aim, they point out, was "the education of the children of the poor in the principles of the established Church". The fundamental difference between church schools and county schools from 1870 onwards has been that in the latter religious instruction may not include any "religious catechism or religious formulary which is distinctive of any particular denomination" (the Cowper–Temple clause), whereas in the former catechisms have been widely used as a means of religious instruction. They would also point to the fact that in the early 1920s, in response to attempts by the then President of the Board of Education, Mr H. A. L. Fisher, to abolish the Dual System and to "secure by agreement a single national organization of elementary schools", both the Education Committee of the Church Assembly and the National Society

[1] The emergence of synodical government may possibly produce a more precise definition of church membership.

were ready to give up the separate status of church schools in return for a guarantee of conditions permitting denominational teaching in county schools, given as an integral part of the time-table. What seems to have been regarded as central to the continuation of "education in the principles of the established Church" was not the existence of church schools, but the presence of denominational instruction on school time-tables.

473 Denominational instruction, these critics suggest, was still uppermost in the negotiations leading up to the 1944 Act. The 1943 White Paper *Educational Reconstruction* reasserted that "the State, concerned though it is to ensure a sound religious basis for all education, cannot take on itself the full responsibility for fostering the teaching of formularies distinctive of particular denominations designed to attach children to particular worshipping communities" (para. 54). The implication is that this latter aim can be and is the function of church schools, and indeed the summary of advantages of the new proposals included specific reference to the fact that "the voluntary schools retain liberty for the teaching of the tenets of the Church with which they are associated" (para. 59), i.e. "denominational religious instruction will continue to be given" (para. 56B). The critics of denominational schools, however, point to recent research into religious education[1] and claim that it has established that denominational instruction (as opposed to religious education) is educationally quite inappropriate to the primary school, and only rarely acceptable at the secondary level. If, therefore, the Church's justification for having its own schools is that this guarantees that denominational instruction can be given to certain pupils, then, this argument concludes, the Dual System might as well be dismantled forthwith, as it is built on an educational fallacy.

474 *Argument B* The above argument occurs in a more polemical form in the writings of some secular humanists. The National Secular Society, for example, asserts that the "religious training given in Church schools usually takes the form of indoctrination". The British Humanist Association expresses the same criticism more subtly, but none the less forcefully:

Although indoctrination is explicitly and repeatedly disavowed, the Plowden Report on the curriculum explicitly stated that children should

[1] For example, R. J. Goldman, *Religious Thinking from Childhood to Adolescence* (Routledge 1964).
H. Loukes, *New Ground in Christian Education.* (S.C.M. 1965).

be taught to know and love God, and not be confused by being taught to doubt before faith is established. Humanists are totally opposed to indoctrination and the limiting of a child's religious knowledge to almost total emphasis on one faith.[1]

475 *Argument C* Some humanists also claim that the presence of church schools within what is supposed to be a national educational system is a source of divisiveness and as such is intolerable. Other major sources of divisiveness, such as the segregation of pupils at 11+ into separate grammar and modern schools, are being eradicated from the system. Thus it is indefensible, they say, to perpetuate this fundamental duality, particularly as the criterion of division is hardly an educational one at all. In their evidence to the Commission both the British Humanist Association and the National Secular Society were united in this basic criticism of the existing situation—"Humanists regard it as actively harmful that children should be segregated into different religious groupings for their whole school life at large. Under whatever auspices, exclusive experience of a closed school community is a wrong basis for education" (B.H.A.). "We consider that denominational schools are inherently wrong. Children should never be segregated according to their parents' religion" (N.S.S.).[2] The firmness with which they hold to this principle is illustrated by the British Humanist Association's further assertion: "We do not want Humanist Voluntary Aided schools, nor Humanism substituted for R.I. Any sectarian approach is obviously improper today." As for the idea of extending the aided school principle to meet the needs of the newly resident Sikh, Hindu, and Muslim communities (as it has already been extended to the Jewish community), this is abhorrent to the British Humanist Association and National Secular Society as being an extension of the principle of "religious segregation", made in this instance particularly intolerable "as in most cases religious would coincide with racial segregation".

476 *Argument D* In addition to the arguments set out above, "Humanists argue that the State should not be involved in financing the religious teaching of individual Churches or religious bodies.

[1] See further Professor B. G. Mitchell's Appendix on "Indoctrination", pp. 353–7 below.
[2] Cf. the comment from the Free Church Federal Council: "The idea of denominational enclaves is not a good one socially or educationally."

This should be left to the home and the Church, without either support or interference from the state" (Evidence from the B.H.A.). If the continuation even of church aided schools depends, as it seems to, on grants from public funds of 80% towards the cost of buildings, and 100% of the cost of running the schools (including teachers' salaries), then this alone is sufficient to condemn the system in their eyes.

477 *Argument E* On a matter of professional privilege some evidence presented to the Commission claimed that the presence of voluntary schools within the maintained system produces a barrier to promotion which operates against anyone who is not an Anglican or Roman Catholic. Over a third (37%) of all primary schools are aided or controlled schools and so, it is asserted, headships of these schools naturally tend to be given to practising Anglicans or Roman Catholics. This might not matter so much, the argument runs, were it not for the fact that most voluntary schools tend to be among the smaller ones and so have a special position as first rung on the promotion ladder. This, it is claimed, serves to keep many aspiring Humanist and agnostic teachers off the ladder altogether, and provides a clear example of a built-in system of institutional discrimination. (This "strongly felt objection to the dual system" was also noted in the 1943 White Paper *Educational Reconstruction*, para. 53.)

478 *Argument F* Another consequence of the existence of the Dual System which seems to its critics to confer unjustifiable privileges on Church schools is the existence of single-school areas.[1] "What is totally unjustifiable is the continued existence of areas in which the only available school is a Church of England Voluntary Aided or Voluntary Controlled school" (B.H.A.). "We are particularly concerned at the position in single-school areas, and feel that schools in these areas should be transferred to local authority control immediately" (N.S.S.). Concern about single-school areas, moreover, is not confined to the Humanist organizations. Both the Free Church Federal Council and the Methodist Education Committee "would oppose the creation of any new single-school area"; the Christian Education Movement believes that "provision should be made in the state system to preserve the right of parents to send their children to

---

[1] The term refers to those thinly populated areas whose one and only school was originally provided by the National Society or similar voluntary body, and where the numbers of children needing schooling have remained too small to justify the provision of a second school (by a L.E.A.).

non-denominational schools, and this puts a question mark against the continuation of single-school areas"; the Association of Head Mistresses also records concern about this situation, and evidence submitted to the Commission from individual members of the general public frequently complains about the "injustice" inflicted on atheist and agnostic parents in such areas.[1]

The Educational Arguments Considered

479 The last two arguments (E and F) mentioned above are, of course, criticisms of certain details connected with the Dual System as it happens to have developed, rather than criticisms of the system in principle.

480 The problem of denominational appointments (E), as has been said above, was noted in the 1943 White Paper. At that time 50% of the nation's schools were the equivalent of Church of England voluntary aided schools (the category of voluntary controlled not yet having been created). This obviously was a restricting factor of some significance for the agnostic teacher seeking promotion. Today, however, only 12% of the nation's primary schools are Church of England voluntary aided schools.[2] This figure tends to decrease each year as smaller schools are closed or amalgamated. It is difficult to argue with much realism that the presence of this small group within the system offers an unfair advantage to aspiring heads who are members of the Church of England and represents an intolerable barrier to the promotion of secular humanists.

481 Similarly the problem of single-school areas (F) must not be allowed to get out of proportion. The number of such areas is certainly not sufficient by itself to justify the abolition of all voluntary schools, and is part of the much larger problem of parental choice. There are many other restrictions on the free exercise of parental choice which was enunciated as a point of general principle in the 1944 Act. The absence of church school provision from the great majority of educational areas is only one example of such restriction, but an example which more than balances out the supposed privilege enjoyed by the Church of England through the existence of a

[1] See further, House of Commons debate on second reading of 1967 Education Bill.
[2] A further 8% are Roman Catholic aided primary schools.

few single-school areas. Nevertheless, we accept that in some single-school areas cases of real difficulty have arisen, and the implications of this will be considered further in a later section of this chapter. (See para. 525.)

482 The other educational arguments raise more fundamental issues. Most of the arguments spring from the assumption that church schools exist solely, or largely, for the purpose of propagating the specific religious teaching of the Church which sponsors them. In (C) however, the objection is not so much to the religious teaching given in the schools as to the fact that pupils are what the British Humanist Association calls "segregated" into "closed communities". This argument accuses the Churches not merely of wanting to teach their children one particular set of beliefs but also of trying to prevent them from coming into contact with anyone who may hold a different set. Now, if an aided school were in fact intended as a device by which its pupils might be protected from unwelcome ideas current in the world outside, then such a closed community would indeed be educationally limiting, even harmful. But, some would ask, if an aided school does not have this protective role, what justification can there be for it? Is any purpose to be served by bringing together children from a common background of belief unless their thinking is to be confined to an examination of that system of beliefs to the exclusion of all other systems? If the pupils in an aided school are to be free to meet and be influenced by the whole range of ideas current in contemporary society, is there any need to retain a special name and status for such a school?

483 The answer to this fundamental question must be found in a consideration of how a school community's underlying presuppositions are related to its avowed educational aims. It is important to recognize that "openness" does not imply that education shall proceed in a cultural vacuum. Being educationally "open" does not, cannot, mean "not having any presuppositions". Every teacher, every school, works from some presuppositions. The atheist himself does. Openness consists in consciously recognizing the existence of presuppositions, of recognizing their status as presuppositions and not as unchallengeable facts or dogmas, and therefore being ready to consider arguments against them. In this sense openness is compatible with having and with communicating a definite and defensible position, though the possibility of needing to revise this position will never be closed. There are a number of these definite positions in the realm of religious ideas and beliefs represented in this country today, and around each of these different positions clings a whole nexus of educational implications. The communities associated with each position vary considerably in size; but where it becomes an economic possibility for such a community to sponsor a school through which its common presuppositions can be reflected and communicated, then there can be no educational objection to this, provided that the criteria of openness, as defined above, are preserved. The major educational advantage is that the presuppositions underlying both school and home can be the same. The continuation of the Dual System therefore by no means necessarily comes under the criticism that it will encourage the existence of closed school communities.

484 The label "denominational" has been used above as no other single word exists by which the sort of school under discussion can be conveniently identified. However, it is misleading as it seems inevitably to conjure up pictures of authoritarian doctrinal instruction by outdated methods. This is by no means a necessary connotation of the word. It needs to be recognized by all parties in this argument that the Church, in promoting its schools, has not in fact been exclusively concerned with denominational teaching even though an undue emphasis may in the past have been given to such teaching by many churchmen. It must be emphasized yet again that in its concern with the Dual System the Church of England is not seeking special opportunities for denominational instruction, but is affirming the importance of establishing church-related educational communities of a particular quality and character; communities which reflect and exemplify the basic Christian presuppositions about Man and his significance within the universe. It is where the shared assumptions of the members of a school's staff coincide with the assumptions of the parents of the pupils that the educational potential of a church school can become most fully realized. Where a stable context for personal development is provided by a healthy consonance of school and home, each in its turn related to a Church which is itself a positive source of influence in the local community, then the educational processes operating in that situation receive an extra dimension. It is this type of potential which we would claim for the church school, and it is on these grounds that we believe the continued existence of church schools can be justified while meeting the most rigorous educational demands for openness. What goes on in the classrooms of such a school may be indistinguishable from the classroom activities in a county school. But the common, acknowledged background of concern against which such activities are pursued can provide in the church school something of real educational value in pupils' growth towards maturity and fulfilment.

(3) *Economic Arguments*

485 *Argument A* Whatever the outcome of the theological and educational arguments may be, strong opinions have been expressed that the Church can no longer afford financial involvement in the national educational system. The cost to the Church of England of providing new aided school buildings and bringing old ones up to acceptable standards has, so these critics point out, risen steadily over the last decade, despite generous increases in government grants during this period, and the figure was approximately £1¾ million in 1967.[1] As well as money spent on its aided schools, the Church has been committed to heavy expenditure on its colleges of education. Since negotiations began in 1946, the Church has committed itself to finding, both centrally and in other ways, £3½ million to meet the requirements of college expansion programmes. This, of course, is non-repeatable capital expenditure, and no money is required for the net running costs and maintenance of the church colleges. This is provided entirely by public funds. Even so, the college expansion programme has left the Church with an annual debt of £170,000 by way of loan repayment and interest, and it will be a long time before this debt is discharged. This continuing debt, coupled with the rising annual costs on school buildings, has become a burden—so this argument goes—which the Church is simply unable to bear any longer. The proponents of this argument feel their case is made even stronger in the light of current developments in educational planning. Not only will there be the rising costs of keeping the present system adequately served, but there will be the additional massive cost of reorganization on comprehensive lines which will often include changing the role of primary and secondary schools (many of them recently provided with new buildings suitable for their present

[1] This money is raised from various sources, such as endowments, grants from central funds, diocesan funds, and local subscriptions. See the report by Captain H. Lovegrove C.B.E., R.N.(Retd) in the 1969 Report of the Board of Education to the Church Assembly (C.A. 1740).

purpose), and accepting an entirely new commitment—middle schools. Moreover, the changing and expanding pattern of education in the 16–21 age range will almost certainly call for greatly increased expenditure on chaplaincy services to colleges of various types.

486 *Argument B* A further important variation of this argument claims that, although the Church could make the financial effort called for by a continuing involvement at different levels in the Dual System, it should not be asked to do it because it no longer obtains value for its money. As one individual witness to the Commission put it:

If church policy on education since the war has been based on the principle that we need the widest possible dissemination of Christian teaching among the children of this land, then this policy has produced very little result in spite of an expenditure of a very great deal of money. It may be that such a policy underestimated the difficulty of producing Christian formation of character. Unless parents are themselves practising Christians and unless parents and children alike are attached to communities of practising Christians, then the effectiveness of Christian teachers or Christian syllabuses in schools is minimal.

The recognition of the vital contribution of home and Church if school is to be effective as an instrument of Christian nurture is of course no new insight (though it has recently received strong corroborative reinforcement from research like that of Greeley and Rossi among Roman Catholic children in the U.S.A.).[1] What has not been sufficiently recognized, so this argument claims, is the changed social context within which most church schools are now operating. Originally the church school was conceived as having almost an organic unity with the parish church and the local congregation. Even though circumstances had altered to some extent by the time of the 1944 settlement, those responsible for that settlement, so it is claimed, seem to have clung to the traditional conception of the relationship between the church school and the local congregation. But change has accelerated to such an extent over the last quarter of a century that, so it is argued, there are not many

[1] E.g. "The school, it appears, can indeed make a substantial contribution to the development of value-orientated behaviour patterns, but it can do so only when the values of the school are reinforced in the family environment. The school can add an impressive margin to the work of the home, but only when the work of the home has been well done" *The Education of Catholic Americans*, p. 95. Cf. also A. E. C. W. Spencer's article in *Religious Education Today* ed. Dom Philip Jebb (D.L.T. 1968) and *Religion and the Secondary School*, by C. Alves (S.C.M. 1968), pp. 68–70.

places left where the unity of church congregation and church school has been preserved. This is partly due to parochial and educational reorganization. It would be exceptional if the need to close churches or amalgamate parishes coincided with the need to close or amalgamate their schools. It is also partly due to the fact that many parents simply send their children to the nearest school, whatever its official status within the maintained system. In other words, this argument claims, church schools have largely ceased to be church schools in anything other than name. Therefore, the argument runs, the Church should cease pouring £1¾ million each year down this particular drain, and seek to find a more effective instrument of Christian education than the aided school now seems to provide.

487 *Argument C* Arguments very similar to these first two are sometimes brought forward, but in terms of manpower rather than of money. In its more extreme form the argument claims that by dismantling the Dual System, and handing over the administration of church schools to the local education authorities, the Church would relieve itself of an administrative burden, at national, diocesan, and parochial level, and so leave itself free to concentrate on tasks which are more urgent, more the direct concern of the Church, and which are are at the moment being neglected.

488 Another form of this argument claims that there are insufficient practising Anglican teachers to man all the church schools effectively. Unless more teachers can be recruited from the ranks of the Church, thereby diverting a large number of people from potential service to the Church in other equally urgent fields, then, so it is claimed, there is no point in committing the existing Anglican teachers to an enterprise which is only marginally effective.

489 *Argument D* One further variation on this last argument is that the size of the Church's contribution to the national system of education has become so relatively small that it is now insignificant. In the days when (as in 1944) almost half of the schools in the country were Church of England schools, then clearly the Church had a very strong voice in the country's educational counsels. What sort of voice, so the argument runs, is the Church of England likely to have now, when it is financially responsible for only 10% of the schools within the maintained system, when it can provide places in its aided schools for only 5·5% of the pupils of school age, and when it possess only twenty-seven out of one hundred and sixty colleges of education in the country? Is it good stewardship of money, the objectors ask, to pay almost £2 million a year for the privilege of maintaining this toe-hold within the educational system?

The Economic Arguments Considered

490 These arguments must be taken very seriously. There is little point in justifying the continuing participation of the Church of England in the Dual System on theological and educational grounds if it is simply unable to continue to make the necessary financial contribution to the system. One answer to argument A might be to note that none of the diocesan education committees, whose task it is to oversee the details of the Church's major educational expenditure, suggested in their evidence to the Commission that the financial burden involved was beyond the power of the Church to maintain,[1] given the present pattern of priorities within the overall budget at diocesan and central levels, as well as continuing parochial interest in individual local schools.[2]

491 We wish to emphasize that we do not think that a sufficiently overall view of the financial picture has been established by any organization within the Church of England for us to say whether this general picture of optimism is justified. We fully recognize the complexity of educational financing within the Church and we have studied the report presented by Captain H. Lovegrove, deputy secretary of the National Society.[3] We strongly recommend that as a matter of urgency some central body should be charged with the task of collecting detailed information about the Church's educational finance from all relevant sources, so that a full conspectus of the actual situation can be obtained. Only when this is done will the Church be able to make any responsible decisions about any future commitment to the Dual System. Such a body will obviously need to look at the present sources of educational finance, with regard both to present needs and to estimated needs over the next ten to twenty years. It will also have to calculate the cost, over a similar period, of loan repayment on finished projects, of maintenance of

[1] The pessimistic view was in fact recorded as the opinion of a very small minority within one D.E.C. but this was all.
[2] Whether the same response would have been received from diocesan boards of finance is another matter.
[3] Op. cit.

existing plant, and the financing of future projects to which the Church is already committed. But there is an underlying policy question which the Church as a whole must face up to, namely, what rate of development is considered appropriate? This question has, we believe, never been directly faced. Decisions of this kind in the past have usually been dictated by empirical considerations. The Church as a whole has not been exercising responsible steward-ship. The question, therefore, confronting the Church today is not merely "Do we continue to play a part in the Dual System?" but also "If so, how large a part should we play?"

492 As has already been noted, some critics of the present position have claimed (Argument D) that the Church's contribution is already too small to be of significance. Defenders of the situation would probably want to point to recent increases in that contribution as an indication that the Church of England has turned the corner and is on the way towards making a significant contribution again. All that is required, they would say, is a continuation of the present rate of development and the Church will soon become a partner of sub-stance once more. This is, however, a misleading oversimplification.

493 It would be easy for advocates of the Dual System to incline to despair on learning that the number of maintained Church of England schools in England and Wales has decreased from 8422 in 1954 to 6588 in 1969, a net reduction of 1834—an average of 122 a year. Included in this figure is a net reduction of 606 in the number of aided schools—an average of 40 a year.[1] It is not the number of schools, however, but the number of places in schools which is the really significant figure, and unfortunately there is no complete record of this. The best that can be done—and it is a very reasonable basis of calculation—is to use the number of pupils in school. We have chosen 1954 as our starting-point for the simple reason that in that year the number of pupils in maintained Church of England schools in England and Wales amounted to one million. Almost one pupil in every six was in a Church of England school.

494 *Table 1* (p. 236) covers most of the period during which children born in the immediate post-war years (the "bulge") were passing through their primary and secondary schools; this period has also seen

[1] Figures, tables, and charts in this section are based on successive annual volumes of Statistics of Education (H.M.S.O.) and on unpublished figures pro-vided by courtesy of officers of the Department of Education and Science.

the steady trend for more and more young people to stay on at school after reaching school-leaving age; even more importantly, it includes the time of greatest activity in reorganization leading to the abolition of all-age schools (the majority of which were voluntary schools); and, finally, it has felt the beginning of the rapid growth of population in which more children are being born each year than in any year since 1914, except for the years 1920, 1921, and 1947. Table 1 shows that

(a) the decline in the primary school population from 1954 to 1963 and its subsequent growth are common to Church of England schools and to all schools;

(b) there has been a continuous growth in the secondary school population from 1954 to 1969, with only a slight hesitation as the majority of the "bulge" left school; this too is common to Church of England and to all schools;

(c) if primary and secondary schools are taken together, all schools reveal a virtually continuous growth of population; Church of England schools show a fairly sharp decrease to 1963 and thereafter a steady increase.

495 *Chart 1* translates the relationship between the population of Church of England schools and that of all schools into percentages, and at once it can be seen that since 1963 the situation is not as bad as the bare figures of Table 1 might seem to imply. On the other hand, it does not justify any belief that the Church of England, by its considerable expenditure in recent years, is beginning to regain its old position. In primary school population the Church has lost a fair amount of ground; in secondary it has gained a little; altogether it has lost only a little ground. There are now over 900,000 pupils in Church of England schools—more than one child out of every nine at school.

496 These figures might, of course, be fortuitous; they include pupils in controlled schools, where the Church has no financial commitment, and the measure of the Church's ability to prove its concern for its schools is thought by many to be found in what it provides by way of aided and special agreement schools.

497 *Table 2*, which for the sake of brevity omits the years 1955 to 1961, shows similar trends for aided and special agreement schools as Table 1 does for all church schools, and *Chart 2* translates the figures into percentages of pupils in all maintained schools. On this comparison primary schools have lost only a little over half as much ground; secondary schools have gained the same amount; with primary and secondary schools taken together only one-third as much ground has been lost and the position has remained fairly steady since 1963.

498 If we assume that the present level of Church involvement in aided schools—7·6% of the primary school population, 2% of the secondary—is as much as the Church can afford and may be regarded as acceptable, can the Church safely sit back and be sure that, provided its efforts continue unabated as they have since 1963, all will be well? A look into the future shows that it will not and even raises serious doubts whether the present pace can be maintained.

499 The forecast figures in *Table 3* are extracted from the projections in *Statistics of Education* (1968), vol. I, Table 45 (i), published in October 1969. They take into account the increasing number of births expected each year between now and 1985, the raising of the school-leaving age in the educational year 1972–3, and the formidable growth which is forecast in the numbers of pupils staying on after school-leaving age. (Reference was made to this in an earlier section of this chapter, on page 209.) The resultant figures are daunting; and, lest it should be thought that they are too fanciful, it should be remembered that forecast figures in the past have tended to be too conservative, notably those on which the supply of teachers has been calculated from time to time.

500 *Charts 3 A and 3 B* illustrate, for primary and secondary school populations respectively, the number that would be needed in Church of England aided and special agreement schools if 1969 percentages were to be maintained on the forecast figures in Table 3 and the numbers that could be expected if the average annual population increase in aided and special agreement schools during 1963–9 (4800 primary, 1536 secondary) were to be continued from now until 1990.

501 There are two important qualifications to keep in mind as we look at Table 3 and Charts 3 A and 3 B: the first is that the figures assume a continuation of the existing pattern of primary and secondary schools, whereas the period will undoubtedly see the emergence of middle schools containing a very significant proportion of the school population; the second is that they assume that schools will continue to be the institutions in which the great majority of the 16+ population receive their full-time education. As has been noted earlier in this chapter (p. 210–11 above), this is still a matter of debate.

502 With these qualifications in mind, let us examine Charts 3A and 3B. Chart 3A shows that the Church's present rate of investment in aided primary schools, if sustained, will more than match the general increase in school population until about 1986, when it will begin to fall behind; by 1990 it will be 4000 short of the 470,000 needed to maintain the 7·6% relationship.

503 Chart 3B displays a very different picture. During the next two years rising numbers are going to overhaul the present rate of growth in the Church's investment in aided secondary schools, and by a substantial margin. Except for the years around 1985, when the gap

TABLE 1

PUPILS IN MAINTAINED SCHOOLS IN
ENGLAND AND WALES
(January figures: in thousands)

	PRIMARY		SECONDARY		PRIMARY AND SECONDARY	
	C.E.	ALL	C.E.	ALL	C.E.	ALL
1954	933	4,554	67	1,822	1,000	6,376
1955	925	4,601	70	1,915	995	6,516
1956	905	4,592	72	2,057	977	6,649
1957	892	4,590	75	2,186	967	6,777
1958	859	4,508	77	2,331	936	6,839
1959	810	4,308	79	2,593	890	6,901
1960	778	4,201	80	2,723	859	6,924
1961	757	4,133	82	2,829	839	6,962
1962	747	4,130	81	2,836	827	6,965
1963	743	4,145	79	2,781	822	6,925
1964	750	4,204	81	2,830	831	7,034
1965	760	4,273	81	2,819	841	7,092
1966	772	4,366	81	2,817	853	7,183
1967	786	4,495	82	2,833	869	7,328
1968	800	4,647	86	2,895	886	7,542
1969	813	4,789	89*	2,964*	902*	7,753*

* including pupils in middle schools

TABLE 2

PUPILS IN CHURCH OF ENGLAND
AIDED AND SPECIAL AGREEMENT SCHOOLS IN ENGLAND
AND WALES
(January figures: in thousands)

	PRIMARY	SECONDARY	PRIMARY AND SECONDARY
1954	406	40	446
1962	338	52	391
1963	336	51	387
1964	338	54	393
1965	343	54	396
1966	345	55	400
1967	351	55	407
1968	359	58	416
1969	365	60*	425*

* including pupils in the 1 aided middle school

TABLE 3

ESTIMATED NUMBER OF PUPILS
IN ALL MAINTAINED PRIMARY AND SECONDARY SCHOOLS
IN ENGLAND AND WALES
(January figures: in thousands)

	PRIMARY	SECONDARY	PRIMARY AND SECONDARY
1969 (actual)	4,789	2,964*	7,753*
1970	4,920	3,069	7,989
1975	5,125	3,821	8,946
1980	5,404	4,203	9,607
1985	5,800	4,447	10,247
1990	6,183	4,926	11,109

* including pupils in middle schools

9

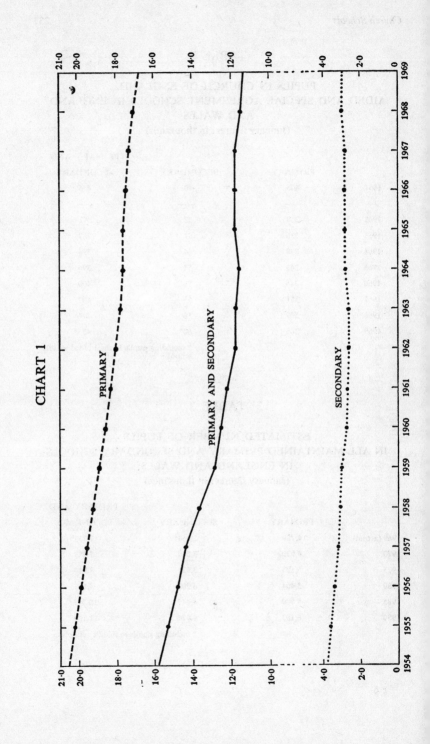

CHART 1

The Durham Report

PUPILS IN MAINTAINED CHURCH OF ENGLAND SCHOOLS AS A PERCENTAGE OF PUPILS IN ALL MAINTAINED SCHOOLS IN ENGLAND AND WALES

(January figures: percentages to one point of decimals)

HORIZONTAL AXIS
years 1954–1969 inclusive

VERTICAL AXIS
2·0   4·0   10·0   12·0   14·0   16·0   18·0   20·0   21·0

PRIMARY POINTS OF INTERSECTION (left to right)
20·5   20·1   19·7   19·4   19·1   18·8   18·5   18·3   18·1   17·9   17·8   17·7   17·5   17·2   17·0

PRIMARY AND SECONDARY POINTS OF INTERSECTION (left to right)
15·7   15·3   14·7   14·3   13·7   12·9   12·4   12·1   11·9   11·9   11·8   11·9   11·9   11·7   11·6

SECONDARY POINTS OF INTERSECTION (left to right)
3·7   3·6   3·5   3·4   3·3   3·1   2·9   2·9   2·8   2·8   2·9   2·9   2·9   3·0   3·0

CHART 2

PUPILS IN CHURCH OF ENGLAND
AIDED AND SPECIAL AGREEMENT SCHOOLS
AS A PERCENTAGE OF PUPILS
IN ALL MAINTAINED SCHOOLS
IN ENGLAND AND WALES
(January figures: percentages to one point of decimals)

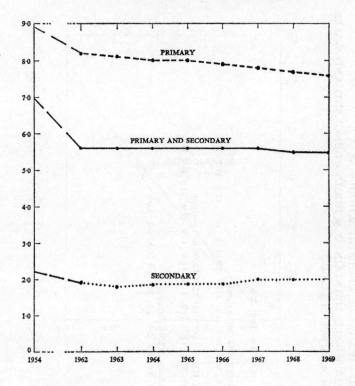

HORIZONTAL AXIS
years 1954 and 1962–1969 inclusive

VERTICAL AXIS
0–9·0 by singles

PRIMARY POINTS OF INTERSECTION (left to right)
8·9 8·2 8·1 8·0 8·0 7·9 7·8 7·7 7·6

PRIMARY AND SECONDARY POINTS OF INTERSECTION (left to right)
7·0 5·6 5·6 5·6 5·6 5·6 5·6 5·5 5·5

SECONDARY POINTS OF INTERSECTION (left to right)
2·2 1·9 1·8 1·9 1·9 1·9 2·0 2·0 2·0

CHART 3A

FORECAST OF NUMBER OF PUPILS
IN CHURCH OF ENGLAND
AIDED AND SPECIAL AGREEMENT SCHOOLS
IN ENGLAND AND WALES
1970–90
PRIMARY
(In thousands)

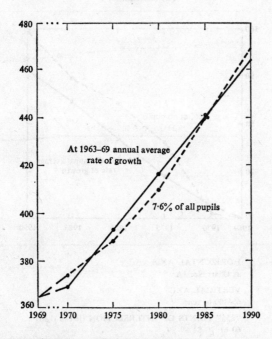

HORIZONTAL AXIS
years 1969, 1970, 1975, 1980, 1985, 1990

VERTICAL AXIS
360–480 by twenties

"7·6%" POINTS OF INTERSECTION (left to right)
365 374 389 411 441 470

"1963–69 AVERAGE" POINTS OF INTERSECTION (left to right)
365 370 394 418 442 466

CHART 3B

FORECAST OF NUMBER OF PUPILS
IN CHURCH OF ENGLAND
AIDED AND SPECIAL AGREEMENT SCHOOLS
IN ENGLAND AND WALES
1970–90

SECONDARY
(In thousands)

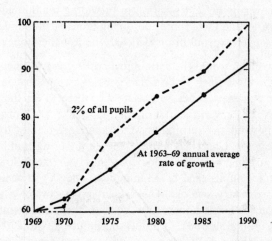

HORIZONTAL AXIS
as Chart No. 3A

VERTICAL AXIS
60–100 by tens

"2%" POINTS OF INTERSECTION (left to right)
60 61 76 84 89 99

"1963–69 AVERAGE" POINTS OF INTERSECTION (left to right)
60 62 69 77 85 92

will be a good deal smaller, the Church will, throughout the whole period, be 7000 short of the number needed to maintain the 2% relationship—7000 short of 99,000 in 1990. Perhaps the most important point to emerge from Chart 3B is that, if this 7000 shortfall is made good by 1975 and the present rate of growth sustained thereafter, the 2% relationship will continue until 1990. Put into more immediately relevant terms this means that the Church will have to make its extra effort during the next five years, while the school-leaving age is in process of being raised. Unless it does so, it may never recover its present position in providing for the older pupils, 16— or 16+; and there is the additional, more earthbound argument that the longer expenditure is delayed, the less the money will buy.

504 How much would the extra effort cost? The two lines on Chart 3A are too close for it to be wise for us to assume that in the early years some primary funds could safely be directed for the benefit of secondary; moreover, the cost of comprehensive reorganization may well swallow up any surplus. It would therefore be best to base our calculations on Chart 3B alone. We cannot bring middle schools into the argument in the hope that they will mean lower costs; provision for pupils aged 11–13 in middle schools will be no cheaper than in secondary schools. The present gross cost of a secondary school place is not less than £500, so that 7000 places would cost at least £3½ million: an 80% grant would reduce this to £700,000—an average of about £140,000 a year for the five years from 1970 to 1975. This figure assumes that building and other costs will not rise above their present level; moreover, it does not include any sum for the purchase of the new sites that will be necessary, the cost of which is difficult to calculate as it varies so much from area to area. We must emphasize again that this £140,000 a year is additional to whatever is needed to maintain growth at its present considerable rate (more than £415,000 a year over the twenty years to 1990); moreover, it does not cover the costs of replacing places lost by the closure of schools, servicing existing loans, improving facilities at existing schools, and carrying on external maintenance, figures for which cannot easily be estimated.

505 We have already recorded our convictions that a central body within the Church should, as a matter of urgency, be charged with the task of working out the Church's educational budget in all its complexity—income as well as expenditure; meanwhile, our calculations and predictions must be regarded as only tentative. On the one side is the fact that the majority of new places provided in the years 1963–9, the period over which present average annual growth has been calculated, had the benefit of only 75% grant, whereas now the rate of grant is 80%. On the other side, much of the money recently used for this purpose has come from the sale of old school sites under section 86 of the 1944 Act, and the indications are that this source of capital is already beginning to dry up. It therefore follows that the £560,000 a year for five years and over £415,000 a year for fifteen years thereafter, which we have tentatively estimated as the cost of the necessary growth, together with the estimated costs of purchasing sites and of the other liabilities listed at the end of the previous paragraph, would have to come directly from Church funds —either from the Church Commissioners, diocesan quotas, or individual parochial contributions. Increased demands will almost certainly be made on these sources for the Church's other urgent needs; and, in the present indefinite state of thinking about its institutional role in education, it is at least questionable whether the Church of England at large will be able to give its schools an even higher financial priority than they already enjoy.

506 To sum up, the economics of the situation seem to indicate that it would be impossible for the Church to improve on its present level of involvement in aided schools in relation to the entire population of maintained schools; indeed, the job of maintaining its present position will perhaps be far greater than it can undertake. It is likely that we shall have to face the prospect that the Church's proportionate contribution to the maintained system will continue to decline, and at a more rapid rate than in the last seven years.

A Basis for Future Thought and Planning

507 Faced with the possible attrition of its aided schools, what should the policy of the Church of England be? There would seem to be three possible courses of action:[1]

(1) The Church could cut its losses and pull out of the Dual System altogether, either gradually or immediately.

[1] The Church could, of course, muddle along making decisions only when forced by circumstances to do so and making them on a purely *ad hoc* basis. This line of action (or inaction) would result in the eventual death of the system from natural causes, and so would have the same ultimate result as (1) above, but it could hardly be described as "policy".

(2) It could decide to stay in, but on a greatly reduced financial basis.

(3) It could attempt to maintain somewhere near its present level of financial involvement in the Dual System, but face up to the fact that even this may mean accepting a quantitatively reduced role.

508 If we were to advocate an immediate withdrawal from the Dual System, this would necessitate the wholesale transfer of the 6700 Church of England schools to the L.E.A.s. How could this be effected? It has been the practice in the few instances since 1944 where a voluntary school has had its status changed and become a county school, that the L.E.A. has agreed to pay an entirely realistic sum in order to purchase the buildings and the site from the trustees. But it would be utterly unrealistic to expect the L.E.A.s, particularly in the present economic situation, to buy out all the Church of England schools in this way. The alternative would be for the Church to seek to give its schools to the L.E.A.s. But any such action would require drastic amendment to the law governing charitable trusts and to the law governing Reverter under the School Sites Act (by which sites which were given for church schools revert to the original donor if the site ceases to be used for the purpose for which it was given). Quite apart from these grave legal complications, there is the additional complication that nearly all the recent building provided for the aided schools has been financed from loans which are still outstanding. L.E.A.s might well look askance at a gift which still needed to be paid for, and the Church would not want to continue paying for something which it had given away. Any attempt by the the Church to withdraw from the Dual System immediately would be fraught with many complex legal, financial, and administrative problems.

509 We now consider the possibility of gradual withdrawal, whereby no new voluntary aided schools are built, no existing ones enlarged, no schools replaced when they are closed or amalgamated. In this way the L.E.A.s would not suddenly have to find large sums of money to buy up the schools wholesale and at once, though they would have, over the years, to make provision in county schools for pupils who might otherwise have had places made available to them in church schools. On the other hand, the Church would immediately be relieved of the burden of finding money for development and im-

9*

provement, and would merely continue to carry minimum maintenance costs (on a decreasing amount of plant) and the repayment
of outstanding loans. When faced with the need for the capital
development of an aided school the managers would make immediate
application for controlled status. Obviously this is at least a practicable suggestion, with certain apparent advantages, and it would be
many years before the last church school had disappeared.

510 The money thus made available to the Church from such endow-
ment trusts as could be used for educational purposes could be used
in a variety of ways. It has for some time been argued by critics of the
present position that the Church could show its educational concern
in a number of other effective ways even if it did put an end to its
financial involvement in aided schools. It could, for example, take
upon itself large-scale responsibilities for research and advisory
services in religious education—work which is still badly needed
throughout most of the country (and which is already being undertaken by a few diocesan education committees). However, consideration of this alternative method of involvement raises the first
of the objections we have to the whole idea of withdrawal from the
Dual System, however gradual, for, if the Church were to abandon
its aided schools, it would abandon its major asset in such research
and advisory work, the very places where its educational experience
has been and must continue to be gained.[1]

511 Other have suggested that the Church could continue to receive
the benefits of such educational experience, but at much less cost to
itself, if it used the money made available by withdrawal from the
Dual System for the setting up of a chain of private fee-paying
schools. This would have the additional advantage, so it is argued, of
removing the curbs which the Dual System has imposed even on
schools with aided status. But the obvious objection to such a suggestion is that any system of fee-paying would inevitably cause these
new-type church schools to become associated with one particular
economic and social grouping and so invalidate any claim the Church

[1] There would, of course, be little point in putting all the Church's resources
into religious educational advisory services for county schools if Religious
Education were in danger of dropping out of the county school curriculum, either
by default or by deliberate decision. Although this is not under present circumstances a foreseeable possibility, it nevertheless must be regarded as a potential
possibility should circumstances change. This is, therefore, another pragmatic
reason why the Church should not abandon the freedom of operation it still has
within its own schools.

might make that it was concerned with the education of the whole nation.

512 A further suggestion is that the Church should use the money now spent on aided schools to improve the standard of her domestic educational provision, by the setting up of a nation-wide system of professional Sunday schools, on the American pattern. But this is to make a double mistake. It not only ignores the Church's concern for the education of the general community of the nation at large (for only a small percentage of children will attend these Sunday schools, however professionally run); it also ignores the Church's concern for the general education of its own community and would only serve to imply a false division between the sacred and the secular.

513 The Commission believes that, unless the Church of England is willing to renounce its traditional responsibilities in the field of general education (and such a renunciation would come at a time when the whole Church throughout the world is being urged to face up to such responsibilities more seriously), then it must find ways of remaining within the partnership which is made possible by the Dual System.

514 With this in mind we now examine the second possibility briefly outlined above, which in the last resort could only be achieved by converting all aided schools into controlled schools. This is quite possible under the law as it now stands. The effect would be to reduce the Church's expenditure virtually to nothing and yet enable it to retain a form of partnership within the Dual System. We find two strong objections to this proposal. The first is that such a proposal looks very much like an attempt to maintain a form of partnership on the cheap. We find this both objectionable and indefensible. It has become increasingly obvious over the past few years that the measure of the Church's commitment to education is seen in terms of the level of financial involvement it is prepared to maintain. But, although it may be legally possible to achieve a wholesale exchange of aided status for controlled status, there would then remain the question of what purpose was being served by continuing the Dual System partnership if it were restricted to controlled schools only. The distinctive contribution which we believe the Church can, and ought, to make to the educational process can be made only where the whole life of a school is based upon those assumptions about Man and his nature which find expression in the Christian gospel. By implication the controlled school gives a more limited opportunity for the Church to express its mission in terms of education than does the aided school. To that extent it is, from the Church's point of view, a second best. That sometimes controlled schools have managed to retain some privileges is not evidence that this is possible but proof that the law has been broken. If the Church of England were to exchange aided status for controlled status throughout all its schools, the only honest and realistic way of looking at this change would be to see it as a legal device for abandoning church schools without actually getting rid of them. This course of action is open to exactly the same objections as were raised against immediate wholesale abandonment a few paragraphs above.

515 We, therefore, conclude that the third possibility is the only one consonant with what we see as the Church's continuing responsibilities in education. The Church should continue to maintain its present financial involvement in aided schools, even though this might mean a quantitatively reduced role. But, as we have seen (Argument D, p. 231), there are those who complain that the Church of England's role within the maintained system is already so far reduced as to be insignificant. This objection must clearly be faced in the process of trying to work out what is the justification for the Church's continuing presence in the Dual System.

516 At the risk of repetition, it might be as well at this point to state once again that the Church of England, by virtue of its special responsibilities within the nation, has long been concerned with the quality of general education available to the community at large. It is also, in common with all other Churches, concerned with the education of its own members, and this means concerned with their general education as well as with their upbringing within a specific religious tradition. It has never been possible for the Church to exercise its general concern for national education by means of complete nation-wide provision of schools. This was obviously the hope of some pioneers at the beginning of the nineteenth century, but it became clear long before 1870 that such a hope could never be achieved. The more realistic hope which has been adopted since then is that the Church would be able to influence what went on in county schools, even if it had no direct control over them. The basis of such influence may at first have been sought simply in its position as the Established Church but, as we have seen, this has long been recognized as in itself an insufficient basis for effective partnership. There are some who have seen the relationship between Church and State within the maintained system as a relationship between business partners, each with a certain measure of bargaining power over the other. Admittedly some measure of negotiation and bargaining has taken place and will continue to take place. Nevertheless, it must be made clear that the Church does not see the partnership in terms of negotiated power; it sees itself more as a working partner, glad to serve within the system and to exercise its influence by example and commendation.

517 It is for this reason that the size of the Church's involvement in the Dual System is not the most crucial factor. What is important is that the involvement shall be of as high a quality and over as wide an educational range as possible, giving the Church both direct experience of the different types and contexts of education and also full opportunity for expressing its beliefs about education in practical terms at all levels. The other point of importance is that the financial involvement of the Church in education needs to be significant in relation to its overall budget. In other words, the seriousness of its contribution should be judged not in proportion to the national outlay but in proportion to its own resources.

518 The basic fallacy of the view that sees the educational partnership between Church and State in terms of economic or political pressures and counterweights lies in its ignoring the fact that the Church's influence operates directly in the classrooms of the nation through the work of individual teachers, advisers, and inspectors; at the level of policy through individual members of education committees, Members of Parliament, and local and central administrators; it also operates at the level of ideas and principles, through the work of individual lecturers in universities, colleges and departments of education, and other institutions of higher and further education. More obviously the Church's influence also operates through those of its officers and members involved in educational administration and planning, whether on school managing bodies, diocesan education committees, or the central committees of the Board of Education. What has sometimes been overlooked in the past is that the Church's official spokesmen may receive little attention if what they say is out of touch with developments within the schools and colleges. There is some danger that the Church's official spokesmen may give the impression that they are only concerned with bricks and mortar, maintenance and expansion, and that they have no real interest in, or knowledge of, educational theory and practice. The world at large could well be forgiven for thinking that the only reason why the Church was allowed to remain as a partner within the national system was because it still had a significant amount of capital investment in it. What is unforgivable is that people within the Church itself should have thought this way. However, the developing financial situation outlined above means that the quality of the Church's contribution may have to continue in future from a smaller institutional presence within the system.

519 We have argued that it is important for the Church of England to remain within the Dual System, even though with a reduced number of schools. Let it be made clear at once, however, that this is not an argument for a simple retention of the existing situation. It is the advocacy of that most difficult of exercises, the retention of certain outward structures from the past coupled with the adoption of certain fundamentally different ways of using and thinking about these structures. Two basic premisses should underline the Church's future thinking and planning: (*a*) church schools are important as providing a means whereby the Church's general presence in education may be realized; (*b*) individual church schools are important because they possess certain educational potentialities not necessarily found in schools of other kinds. The Church obviously needs to speak with authority on educational matters, and the only authority which will be heeded today is the authority which is derived from direct experience, such as can be gained from actual involvement at all levels, theoretical, administrative, practical, in the schools themselves. If the Church ceases to be directly involved in the work of education, then few will listen to any comments it may wish to make on education now or in future. Moreover, if the Church withdraws from the challenge of contemporary education, it will cease to be involved with modern society at one of its most creative points, where the Church can both hope to contribute to the development of society and can learn from society.

520 The other basic premiss we have asserted is that the context of attitudes and values within which education takes place is of fundamental importance, and we have claimed that a church school can become an educational community which brings into explicit focus the shared assumptions of parents and teachers, the link with the Church exemplifying the beliefs about the purpose of education which underlie the school's activities. As we have already argued, real educational benefit can be derived from a situation where the school is able to draw upon influences already at work within the community and bring these to explicit expression. While recognizing that a number of county schools have been able to develop full community links in this way, the church school is in a particularly advantageous position in this respect as a result of the double link with the community which it naturally possesses, through the families of its pupils and also through the members of the church congregation. Moreover, there is a two-way traffic between any school and its community. The concept of the community school envisaged in the Plowden Report (paras. 121–6) is geared as much to the needs of the local community as to the needs of the pupils. The Church, having as it does responsibility for "the creation of truly human relationships and communities", must not neglect any opportunity or channel of community-building. The church school is obviously one such channel, as can be seen in many areas.

521 Some of the Church's critics may be suspicious that by "community-building" here is meant "pew-filling", and that the Church's real interest in maintaining its schools is because they provide fruitful recruiting grounds. Of course the Christian Church believes that a healthy community is one which acknowledges and seeks to live by Christian teaching, but this end is not necessarily achieved simply by persuading as many people as possible to take part in the worshipping life of the Church. The Church's hope and mission within society is more complex and less egocentric than this. Similarly, its understanding of the role of the church school within its surrounding community must be seen as part of this wider, outward-looking mission. It must be admitted that in the past indefensible positions have sometimes been adopted both by some of the Church's educational administrators in their political negotiations, and also in the actual classroom practice of certain clergy and teachers in church schools. But misunderstandings based on such past practice should not be allowed to persist. It needs to be clearly recognized by all parties concerned that the Church of England does not wish to perpetuate the Dual

System for any mere denominational advantage, but because it sees in the Dual System an important opportunity to express in direct service its concern for the general education of the young people of the nation. It also recognizes the importance of a continuing opportunity for community-building in specific local areas by the maintenance of educational communities focused upon the local church. The last few paragraphs have used the term "church school" throughout, but in fact a clear distinction does still need to be made between an aided school and a controlled school. The future of all three types of church school will now be considered in turn.

The Future of the Voluntary Aided School

522 Under present legislation what is currently called an aided school is distinguished by the following main characteristics. Despite the fact that considerable financial aid is received from public funds (covering the full cost of salaries, equipment, and internal maintenance and 80% of the cost of building improvements and external maintenance), the Church retains control within the managerial body, having the right of appointment of two-thirds of the managers, and therefore still carries the ultimate responsibility for:

(a) appointing and employing all the teaching staff, including the head[1] (the L.E.A. fixes the teaching establishment and may have certain powers of veto);

(b) ensuring that religious instruction takes place throughout the school;

(c) maintaining the pattern of worship in the school in accordance with the trust deed—this can be conducted regularly by the incumbent, if so desired;

(d) arranging services for the whole school in the parish church on "special occasions".

523 Clearly these rights and responsibilities must be preserved if a local school is to remain a community which expresses certain common purposes, focused upon the Church. It should perhaps be stressed once again that the common purposes should not be interpreted in any doctrinaire fashion, and that the underlying presuppositions should be subscribed to in a spirit of openness. In

[1] This does not apply to special agreement schools.

carrying out their responsibilities in staff appointments, the managers and governors may properly seek to appoint qualified teachers who are also practising Anglicans, but evidence of sympathy with the ethos and purpose of the school is of more importance than technical ecclesiastical affiliation.

524 Unity of purpose among the staff is, however, not in itself adequate. The general views of the parents and other residents in the area served by the school are also an important factor. Places do exist where, despite over-gloomy overgeneralizations from some ecclesiastical sociologists, the Church does act as a focus for the local community. Where this can be developed into a single focus of Church and aided school the interaction is then doubly beneficial to the community. This does not mean, however, that the provision of an aided school should be dependent on what is sometimes called denominational demand. Quite apart from anything else the phrase "denominational demand" makes little sense when used with reference to the Church of England, which is not a clear-cut community with straightforward criteria of membership. There are various degrees of association ranging from the regular communicant member, duly registered on an electoral roll, to the possibly even unbaptized person who would describe himself on a form as "C. of E." and would be indignant if his right to do so were challenged. But, quite apart from this consideration, we do not believe that the provision of an aided school is only justified where the Church is already the major community focus. In some areas, particularly in some old industrial area parishes, the Church as a worshipping congregation has long ceased to be a major influence, and yet an established aided school in such a place can often itself continue to provide a real focus of community. Similarly, in new areas or in rapidly changing areas, where there is no real community sense at all, an aided school could act as an integrating force, helping parents to discover that there are certain assumptions which they share, rather than building on ones which were already consciously present.

525 Where there is strong local parental antagonism to the Church there would obviously be little point in trying to preserve, or establish, an aided school. For this reason it would seem only proper for the managers of aided schools in single-school areas at least to examine the advisability of exchanging aided status for controlled, provided always that there can be an option for aided status to be restored should parental views change, or should the provision of a new county school make the area no longer single-school.

526 Problems of parental attitudes and parental wishes are by no means confined to single-school areas. In areas which are served by both an aided school and another school, the managers of the aided school always have to decide what criteria for admission shall be agreed. In some places they are largely controlled by L.E.A. zoning policy, having first to accept all pupils who live in a certain area and only then being able to admit children from Anglican families further afield. Often, the greater the freedom from L.E.A. direction, the greater are the problems which arise over admissions. For example, ought preference to be given to children of a family who attend the local parish church somewhat sporadically, or ought it to be given to those from a family who travel weekly to attend another Anglican church (perhaps of a different liturgical tradition) outside the area altogether? This is only one among many situations which at present face aided school managers with difficult decisions term after term. Nearly all of these difficulties come from looking on the aided school as having a primarily domestic responsibility, with the attendant difficulty of defining the precise limits of the relevant domestic community. Many of the difficulties would disappear if the aided school were looked on as a service provided by the Church, rather than something provided for the Church.

527 The admissions policy is settled by the managers in agreement with the L.E.A. and should be on the basis that the first priority is given to children whose homes are in the natural area served by the school. Parents should continue to be informed of their constitutional rights of conscience, but should be urged to consider whether they can accept the general purposes of the school before sending their children to it. At the same time the managers should resist a zoning policy so rigid that parents living outside the natural catchment area are precluded from sending their children to a church school of their choice. It may well be necessary to agree on an *ad hoc* proportion of places available to parents in this position.

528 The Anglican ethos or climate of a church school is engendered partly by the attitudes and loyalties of the staff, but perhaps more obviously by certain other characteristics of the school, some of which were indicated in the list of managers' responsibilities on p. 252 above. The question of religious education in an aided school is too big an issue to deal with at this point in the Report and will be taken up later (pp. 265–7 below). The other characteristics which need mentioning are the place of worship in the life of the school, the role of the local clergy in the life of the school, and the use made of the school buildings in the life of the local community.

529 Two questions regarding worship will have to be answered by a school's managers—the form of worship and, if the law becomes more flexible than it is at present, the regularity of worship. Trust deeds often lay down that the form shall be "according to the practice of the Church of England", but very few schools interpret this as meaning daily matins at school assembly. A number of aided schools have regular celebrations of the Holy Communion on the school premises, to which parents and others are invited. A form appropriate to the age of the pupils in the school will need to be found, and a great deal of what is said in ch. 4 will be applicable in the aided school. However, an aided school might well be distinguishable from a county school in the following ways: (*a*) its "religious" assemblies might be more frequent than in a county school; (*b*) it would continue to worship as a school in the parish church "on special occasions". It is hoped that some of the rather petty regulations which have sprung from the 1946 Act will be modified. It is also to be hoped that the bishops will, in harmony with the recent resolution of Convocation, be ready to extend a welcome to non-Anglican pupils and staff to communicate at an aided school Eucharist. That they were not allowed to do so previously has often been a source of some embarrassment.

530 The role of the local incumbent within the life of the school is of vital importance. He should not be regarded primarily as a teacher. Many incumbents may prefer not to teach at all; some would be well advised not to do so. Perhaps his most important role is the development of effective contact between the life of the school and the life of the local congregation. It is essential that the incumbent should understand and appreciate the educational principles on which the school is operating. This suggests the necessity for special training courses or, at very least, advisory sessions for any clergyman coming to a parish which contains an aided school. There is also the prior necessity for patrons to appoint to such parishes only those clergy who have a real concern for church schools and a real contribution to make to them.

531 Reference to links between the church school and the local community, however, must not be taken to imply that the church school somehow regards itself as outside the community. The foundation managers, who are the representatives of the Church, should use their majority on the managing body to ensure that the facilities of the school premises are made available to the community at large. This is legally permissible under the 1944 Act. It is in this way, as well as through its directly educational activities, that many a church school has come to be regarded as "our school" by the great majority of people living in its vicinity, even though some of them at least would not look upon the parish church or the Church of England as "our church". There are obvious difficulties in the way of care of equipment, cleaning, and general caretaking, but the advantages of allowing the premises to be available in this way seem to make the necessary effort worth while.

532 In some parishes there is a long-standing tradition that the head teacher of a church school has a quasi-official position in the local church life. Many serve as lay readers. We should like to see this tradition strengthened and extended, as evidence of the Church's determination to ensure that its schools are fully part of its total mission in society. Newly appointed heads might, if they so wished, be formally introduced to the local church at one of the regular Sunday services.[1] If the Church is serious in its desire to serve the community through its schools, then opportunity should be given to teachers in those schools to receive a recognized place in its ministry.

533 Much further work remains to be done to set out in detail the characteristics which should distinguish aided schools from county schools in future. We hope that the above paragraphs (coupled with pp, 265–7 below) may go some way towards exemplifying the general principles which the Commission thinks should underlie the concept of the aided school in the future.

The Future of the Voluntary Special Agreement School

534 The special agreement school is something of a halfway house between the aided and the controlled school, though nearer the former than the latter. The Education Act of 1936 was passed at a time when senior schools—the precursors of secondary modern

[1] Cf. "An Office for the Admission of Teachers", in *The Aided Schools Handbook*, by L. Tirrell (N.S.: S.P.C.K. 1969), pp. 36–8.

schools—were being planned by L.E.A.s, and it provided for the raising of the school-leaving age to 15. To induce the Churches to build senior schools and to do away with "senior tops" of all-age schools, the Act allowed them to enter into special agreement with L.E.A.s by which L.E.A.s would make grants of between 50% and 75% towards the capital costs of the new schools. Proposals for 519 agreements were lodged (289 of them by the Roman Catholic Church) but only 37 could be put into effect before war brought school building to a halt.

535 The 1944 Act was obliged to offer the possibility of reviving these proposals, sometimes in modified form, because it made secondary education compulsory for all children and the 1936 terms had been more generous than the 50% maximum grant from the Ministry of Education originally offered under the 1944 Act, and then only under certain conditions, to promoters of new aided secondary schools. But the *quid pro quo* had to be continued; teachers in special agreement schools are employed by the L.E.A.s, not by the governors as in aided schools; moreover, the agreement may set a limit to the number of reserved teachers, i.e. teachers appointed because they are deemed fit and competent to give religious instruction according to the tenets of the Church concerned. Special agreement schools may be converted into aided schools, but only by repayment of the L.E.A.'s grant.

536 The Education Act of 1959 increased the maximum grant payable for aided schools from 50% to 75%, putting them on a par with the most favourable special agreements. The 1967 Education Act increased it further, to 80%. There are 156 special agreement schools in existence, 122 of them Roman Catholic; clearly there will be no more. It would seem sensible to abolish this special category, and it should not be legally or administratively difficult to convert them into aided schools, existing arrangements about sharing their capital costs between the L.E.A.s and the Churches being allowed to continue.

The Future of the Voluntary Controlled School

537 Controlled status was an innovation under the 1944 Act and has, in the event, proved to be only moderately satisfactory. As indicated in ch. 1, an Anglican controlled school is one which was originally

provided by the Church of England, but which subsequent to the 1944 Act passed under the control of a local education authority, and is maintained by the L.E.A. at no cost to the Church. The Church, however, retains some privileges and responsibilities, including the ownership of the site on trust for the maintenance of the Church's work in education. The most significant are:

(a) The right to appoint one-third of the managers of the school.
(b) The right of these foundation managers to be consulted to their satisfaction by the L.E.A. over the appointment of reserved teachers—approximately one-fifth of the staff, who are appointed because they are deemed fit and competent to give religious instruction in accordance with the trust deed.
(c) The right for such teachers (or a clergyman or other person designated by the foundation managers) to give "church teaching" for two periods a week to the children of parents who request it.
(d) The right of maintaining school worship in a form specified by the trust deed, with the possibility of the clergy being occasionally invited to conduct it.
(e) The use of the school premises on Sundays and subject to certain restrictions, at other times.

One consequence of being a controlled school is that the managers might decide to declare, say, Ascension Day as one of the "occasional" holidays allowed by the L.E.A., thus permitting the children who so wish to attend special services in their local churches. If it is an ordinary school day, however, any worship arranged by the school must be on the school premises.

538 It is obvious from this list of "rights" that church privileges in a controlled school are conceived almost entirely in terms of facilities for denominational instruction, terms which are inadequate for achieving the aims set out in paras. 522–33 of this chapter. Moreover, despite the hopes and expectations of a small number submitting evidence to the Commission, we do not think that there is any ground on which the Church would be justified in asking for any basic extension of rights within controlled status—for instance, that the head should be a reserved teacher. Yet, as it stands, controlled status is not merely inadequate but in some circumstances causes active offence. Some educational administrators dislike controlled status because it makes for tedious complications in their work. Some teachers and clergy have adversely commented on an arrangement which seems not merely to encourage the isolation of religious education on the time-table, but actually divides the teaching of the subject into three periods a week of ordinary religious education and two periods of denominational instruction given by a special person (whether lay or ordained).

539 There might well seem to be some grounds for putting an end to what at best appears to be an anomaly. But it must not be forgotten that the Church retains quite genuine responsibilities towards controlled schools as well as somewhat ineffective privileges within them. These responsibilities should not be lightly abandoned. It is suggested, therefore, that controlled status should be retained, but that its basis should in future be seen in terms of a general responsibility, not in terms of an attempt to preserve the relics of a "domestic" task which is no longer appropriate. A controlled school would thus be a school in which the Church was able to give practical expression to its concern with education in general by a careful exercise of its responsibility for choosing one-third of the managers, and by providing support of various sorts to help them carry out their function in the most effective way.

540 If this new understanding of controlled status were to be acceptable two conditions would have to be fulfilled. The first is that the question of managerial responsibility in general should be thoroughly investigated in order to encourage the exercise of real responsibility at this level. The Redcliffe-Maud Commission on Local Government has made recommendations to this effect, as a balancing measure to set against the alleged necessity for having larger units of local government. But whether action is taken or not by the central Government or by the L.E.A.s, it is to be hoped that the Church will find ways of ensuring that managers both know their responsibilities and have proper opportunities to exercise them. Some diocesan education committees already run short training courses and conferences for managers and prospective managers. This service should be extended throughout all dioceses. Diocesan directors of education should also continue to make a special point of urging the managing body of each controlled school in their area to meet regularly, as well as of encouraging the appointment as foundation managers of men and women of the right calibre, having both real concern for the school and insight into its educational problems and potential.

541 The other condition which is necessary to make a new basis for controlled status acceptable is the recognition by everyone concerned that the managers have a general responsibility for the quality of education given in the school. In particular they would assume responsibility for stimulating developments in religious education. It must be stressed that the foundation managers' concern here would be with the quality of the general religious education, and not with any denominational teaching. We hope that this new sense of responsibility for the religious education of the school as a whole would mean that the foundation managers would no longer encourage parents to request denominational instruction for their children. Since not all controlled schools are on a Church of England foundation, it would be improper for us to call for an alteration of the law in this respect. The foundation managers might best exercise their new responsibility by encouraging the training and selection of a new kind of reserved teacher, whose function would be to stimulate and co-ordinate all the work done in religious education.

542 The position of the *ex officio* foundation manager, who is usually the incumbent of the parish in which the school is situated, would be based on a relationship of general service and support to the school, and would not normally include giving denominational religious instruction to children whose parents had requested it. His function would be mainly pastoral. At another level his *ex officio* position would enable him to take the lead in building up good community relations with the school. In controlled schools the *ex officio* foundation manager should come to be regarded much more as a school chaplain than as the guardian of denominational rights. Similarly, the link between the diocese and the classroom would not be in terms of "inspecting denominational religious instruction", as now, but in terms of provision of a diocesan advisory service for the general religious education offered by the school (carried out in close co-operation with the work done by the L.E.A. adviser in religious education, where such an officer existed).

543 These suggestions, if carried out, would bring about a change in the character and practice of a number of controlled schools. It should therefore be made possible by law for controlled status to be changed to aided status where the local community wishes a closer degree of association between Church and school to continue, provided of course that they are willing and able to take on the financial responsibilities which aided status brings with it, including some appropriate reimbursement to L.E.A.s for enlargements, improvements, and maintenance already carried out.

Planning and Administration

544 The new way of looking at church schools that we have tried to present in the last three sections has considerable repercussions not merely for the pattern of work and management in individual schools, but also for diocesan and national planning. Despite some evidence of thought and effort put into policy making by diocesan education committees and the Schools Council of the Board of Education, it is nevertheless difficult to discover any common thread of policy running through individual decisions as to where church schools should be closed down, where new ones should be established, where existing ones should be enlarged. But it must be recalled that the very nature of the Dual System implies that the Churches do not have a free hand in determining policy. The development plan for an area is determined by the L.E.A. and the Department of Education and Science on the basis of purely educational considerations; church authorities have a consultative but not a determining role.

545 Since 1944 some individual members of diocesan education committees have tended to take parental denominational demands as their major criterion in policy-making. Others seem to have wanted to operate on a policy of "preserve as many church schools as possible", with little attention paid to local attitudes towards the Church. Others again have tended to try to seize any new opportunity for expansion which came their way, provided the money could be raised. Yet others have hankered after a policy of continuous local retrenchment, apparently regarding their task as being to save diocesan funds from being encumbered with what seemed to them to be profitless plant. As a result of these conflicting views among their members, diocesan education committees have on occasion presented a picture of indecision and inconsistency. This is said not in a spirit of criticism but in understanding sympathy for those who have to operate a system which is the result of historical accident, and where no generally agreed policies have ever been established. What complicates the situation still further is that, even where a diocesan education committee has established a clear policy, it is sometimes frustrated in its prosecution because of resistance on the part of individual managing bodies.

546 Because the present situation calls for urgent action, the Commission believes that the powers of diocesan education committees should be strengthened to enable them to carry out extensive reorganization and concentration of resources. This would require the active support of both central and local government authorities, since it implies a curtailment of the present legal autonomy of church educational foundations. If Parliament will not grant wider powers to diocesan authorities, then we recognize that a policy of reorganization and redeployment of resources can be carried out only by the good will and co-operation of managers and governors. It is, therefore, all the more important that diocesan education committees should have clear and consistent policies, worked out in close agreement with a central Church co-ordinating body. The reasons lying behind this recommendation are twofold:

547 First, the present distribution of aided schools is largely the result of entirely haphazard historical developments. There are 2711 Church of England aided primary schools scattered at random up and down the country, heavily concentrated in some areas, almost non-existent in others. Different dioceses already have, by choice or economic compulsion, different balances between the numbers of aided and of controlled schools. On the other hand, there are only 146 Church of England aided secondary schools in the whole country. The contrasting position of the Roman Catholic aided schools is very clear from their parallel figures. They have 1908 aided primary schools, and 529 aided secondary schools, a balance resulting from a much more deliberately planned programme of development.

548 Secondly, reorganization of education at secondary level and the development of middle schools create financial problems which may well exacerbate present difficulties unless a policy of rationalization and concentration of resources can be agreed by all concerned at national, diocesan, and school levels. In consultation with L.E.A.s and the Department of Education and Science an attempt must be made to agree on the number and location of aided schools of these types, with a view to concentrating the Church's limited financial resources upon them. We fully realize that this will require much diplomatic and administrative skill. But, unless something along these lines can be achieved, we foresee a decline in the Church's involvement in these areas of education, and further deterioration of the present confused situation. The position is made even more complicated by the differing tempo at which comprehensive school development has taken place in the various dioceses and local authority areas.

549 It was suggested earlier in this chapter that it is important for the Church to have direct experience throughout the whole range of the national educational system. This would imply that there should be aided schools right the way through from nursery schools to sixth form colleges. What is more, wherever participation occurs it should be at as high a level of excellence as can be achieved, and excellence calls for expense. Involvement at secondary level will inevitably be considerably more expensive than at primary level. For these two reasons it will almost certainly be necessary to reduce the number of aided primary schools, thereby releasing money needed for improvement and expansion elsewhere in the system. All this will call not merely for diocesan but for national co-ordination of planning. This will be one of the duties of the appropriate central body. Similarly, there should be a strong planning body at diocesan level in close touch with the central planning agency, and closely related to local managing and governing bodies.

550 The issues discussed above raise further problems over the identification of what is the local community for which the school provides a centre, and more particularly which is the local congregation and who the local incumbent through whom the Church links are specifically maintained. The latter question will prove less of a difficulty if the concept of area team ministries develops throughout the country. There might even be some measure of shared or allotted responsibility amongst the congregations within a deanery for the provision of the necessary parochial links and facilities.

551 There may seem to be an inconsistency between our recognition of the importance of local links and local pastoral responsibility and our recommendations relating to centralization of co-ordinating policy. We see no such inconsistency, though we do see the danger of a certain selfish form of parochialism disclaiming pastoral responsibility if it is to be shorn of ultimate control and financial responsibility. Nevertheless, we believe the need for a co-ordinated policy to be so strong that we would even advocate the re-establishment, wherever possible, of parochial educational trusts on a deanery or diocesan basis and a similar pooling of parochial contributions towards education, so that the rationalization of the aided school system can be made more thoroughgoing than the tying down of funds solely to specific parishes often allows.

Diocesan and Central Support and Advisory Services

552 As has been said above, the sort of help and training already being given by some diocesan authorities to managers of church schools needs to be extended throughout every diocese. Similarly, there needs to be advice available to those clergy who have responsibility for church schools. Some clergy regard teaching as part of their ministry and some (for the most part in secondary schools) get paid for doing so. Each diocese ought to lay down regulations governing the payment of such men, in order to reduce the occasions of complaint sometimes to be met with under the present haphazard arrangements. But the major work of a diocesan advisory service is obviously to meet the direct needs of the head and staff of a school. In some areas there is already extensive L.E.A. advisory work, including the services of an adviser on religious education. In such areas the work of the diocesan education committee will be to co-operate with and supplement the work of the L.E.A. In less well served areas the diocesan education committee must seek to provide some compensatory service for its church schools, both aided and controlled. It may prove to be more economical and also more effective to centre such advisory services on a unit larger than a single diocese, particularly if the number of church schools is limited.

553 Much of the work we envisage for these advisory services is already being tackled in some dioceses by diocesan inspectors, or advisers, or visitors, as they are being increasingly called. They should be able to help the head and staff over questions concerning the life of the school community, and also concerning relations between the school and the local community which includes, of course, the families of the pupils in the school. They should also attend to the equipment and facilities available in the school, and may possibly be able to obtain funds with which to supplement the L.E.A. provision of equipment. But diocesan advisers will probably feel a particular

concern for the worship and religious education being provided in their church schools. It goes without saying that where there is an L.E.A. adviser in religious education it is essential for close liaison to be maintained between him and the diocesan advisers. This is important both in controlled schools (where the religious education will be identical with that given in the best of the county schools, if our recommendations are accepted) and in aided schools, where the religious education will be related to the worship and teaching of the Church of England.

554 It is obviously necessary at this point to define exactly what we mean by the term "religious education which is related to the worship and teaching of the Church of England". What we do not mean is a purely domestic type of denominational instruction which starts with the assumption that all the pupils are committed members of the Church of England and which has as its sole purpose the strengthening of that commitment. It could well be argued that this closed type of religious education is not defensible even in a Sunday school context. We are fully persuaded that it is quite indefensible in the context of the Dual System. The purpose of religious education in an aided school must be as it was defined for the county school (see ch. 4), that is, to explore the place and significance of religion in human life and so to make a distinctive contribution to each pupil's search for a faith by which to live. Where it will differ from religious education in the county and controlled schools is in its freedom to achieve this purpose through involvement in one particular religious tradition. Insight can never be achieved without some measure of involvement; nor, of course, can it be achieved without some measure of objectivity. Owing to the suspicion that religious education in church schools has tended to lack objectivity, regulations governing religious education in county schools have tended to inhibit involvement. It is our hope that the aided school of the future will be enabled to achieve the right balance.

555 For example, through its links with the local congregations and the local clergy its pupils will be able to feel something of what it means to belong to a worldwide Christian society. This will enable them to study the Church from the inside, rather than from the outside. The phrase "This is what we do, what we believe" will be appropriate in an aided school. This is not to suggest that what others do or believe will never be studied; far from it. The comparative study of religions will play as great a part in the aided school, particularly at secondary level, as in any other. But the starting-point for study of the religious quest will be the Anglican tradition, as experienced within the local community. To say this is not to deny in any way that religious education must always be pupil-related, relevant, and open-ended (cf. paras 245–8 of ch. 4). It is in fact a reassertion of these principles, inasmuch as the aided school will be able to provide, through its general pattern of activities, many opportunities for gradually building up that experience which alone can make religious education relevant to the pupils' own lives.

556 Two practical steps need to be taken to underline this rather different view of Anglican teaching which we see as being necessary. One concerns the place of the Catechism; the other is the question of the inspection of religious education. Instruction in the Catechism as part of preparation for confirmation has been a regular feature in many church schools for a long time. This is, quite obviously, very much a domestic task performed in the school. As such we feel it to be quite inappropriate to the controlled school and not appropriate to the aided school if thought of as part of the school curriculum.

557 Because we are recommending that religious education, even in a church aided school, should not be seen in domestic terms, it is obviously no longer appropriate to remove it from availability to inspection by H.M.I. Clearly it was not right, and would not be right, for H.M.I. to pronounce upon the efficacy of religious education when it is conceived as a purely denominational exercise. But where religious education has the open, educationally defined aims which we have set forward, then it would be wrong, even in a church aided school, to single religious education out from every other subject by not opening it to the general oversight of H.M.I.

558 The diocesan advisers would therefore shed the last remaining vestiges of their earlier role as inspectors, and would have as their task in future both the general advisory role to the whole school, and the specific tasks of encouraging and stimulating new and better approaches in religious education, giving guidance in various aspects of the subject, providing information about materials and resources, organizing conferences for the interchange of ideas, and suggesting schemes of work. There may well be diocesan, or regional, handbooks of suggestions for religious education in church aided schools, but the days have long since passed when there was a rigid central syllabus and the inspectors' task was to check up on how closely and efficiently the syllabus had been followed by each class.

559 As many church aided schools as possible should also have definite, practical links with neighbouring church colleges of education, so that there can be cross-fertilization of ideas and particularly so that research and experimental projects can be mounted by colleges and schools working together. As Canon J. Gibbs has written in *The Communication of the Christian Faith*, "It is imperative that the Church recognizes the colleges as her educational laboratories. It is also imperative that the colleges realize their obligation to the Church and by bold experimentation provide her with centres of educational thinking and research."[1]

560 One final and most important aspect of all these diocesan and central support and advisory services must be mentioned, namely the opportunity for ecumenical co-operation which they provide. We recognize that there are at the moment many differences of emphasis, and indeed of aim, between the various bodies involved as partners in the Dual System, but we believe that there are already some signs of the development of a common mind on many issues, to an extent which would have been considered utterly impossible only ten or twenty years ago. Where there is the greatest chance of close ecumenical enterprise, we believe, is in the conduct of research and in the provision of certain advisory services. Roman Catholic catechetical centres are already widely used by Anglican and other teachers, and it would not be too large or sudden a step to develop some of these (or similar) centres on an ecumenical basis, jointly financed. It is obvious that thinking and planning about joint educational enterprise between the Anglican and Methodist Churches must be started immediately. We must also start thinking of joint colleges and schools on a wider ecumenical basis—jointly financed, jointly managed, and with a true ecumenical purpose and outlook (not the sort of compartmentalized hybrid which has been talked of in some areas, having what are virtually two denominationalist communities coexisting within one educational institution). Of course, such ecumenical schools would need to be established in areas where the Churches

[1] Report issued by the Church of England Board of Education 1967 (C.A. 1654), p. 40.

are already well established in ecumenical co-operation. There are, at present, many legal, financial, and administrative problems of the greatest complexity involved in this whole area of development, but we look forward ultimately to the development of a nation-wide pattern of ecumenical aided schools.

The Church's Central and Diocesan Educational Structures

561 It has already been stated in ch. 2 that the English educational system illustrates the principle of the distribution of power. Nowhere is this more clearly seen than in the administration of church schools. Almost all church schools have their own trust deeds, and their managers or governors have a high degree of legal autonomy. They are subject to control and direction by L.E.A.s and the Department of Education and Science, in common with all maintained schools. The authority exercised over them by diocesan and central church authorities is a mixture of the moral and the financial, and is limited by the policy of the Department of Education and Science and of the L.E.A. The *diocesan education committee* has wide duties and responsibilities, but few powers over individual schools except that which is enjoyed by any paymaster; its influence derives from the intrinsic wisdom of its decisions and the skill of its officers. The *Church of England Schools Council*, which antedates its superior body, the Board of Education, is concerned to negotiate conditions under which dioceses and schools may operate to the best advantage, but it has no power over either. Such success as it has had depended upon its ability to persuade the Department of Education and Science that it truly represents the mind of the Church at a financial and administrative level.

562 The *National Society* is in a constitutional relationship with many church schools, and is thus able to speak for individual schools and groups of schools in a way not at present open to a body ultimately answerable to the Church Assembly. It has, moreover, some knowledge of the management and development of church schools, which has been of value to the Church at large. The Church of England Schools Council, with its concern for the legal and constitutional conditions under which church schools may flourish, and the National Society, with its relationship of service to individual schools, have, so far, managed to coexist through cross-membership of committees and a shared staff. Neither the Church of England Schools Council nor the National Society has any powers of compulsion over dioceses or individual schools.

563 This extraordinarily Trollopian apparatus has produced a situation in which today we can consider the future of church schools. In 1944 many in the Church thought that there was no future for them at all. The achievement by which so much has been preserved and developed, and new schools started, is to be attributed to the skill and devotion of many diocesan directors of education—men for the most part without professional educational qualifications, no formal training in administration, exiguous staffs, and often with parochial responsibilities. Having in mind the circumstances under which most of these men have been expected to work, their achievement has been of great value to the Church's work in education.

564 It may well be that the emergence of synodical government will result in some restructuring of central bodies concerned with education, and a reappraisal of the relationship of the National Society to the more official bodies which the General Synod will set up. It is certainly no part of our function to prescribe in detail what should and should not be done, but certain general points need to be made. One of the tests of the wisdom of the General Synod will be the extent to which it can continue a policy of co-operation with the historic voluntary societies in the Church. It would be an impoverishment of the Church's work in education if means were not found by which the National Society and the General Synod's official bodies could work harmoniously together to advance the Church's concern for education. But whatever new structures and relationships are evolved, certain tasks will need to be continued in the future—the negotiation of conditions under which the Church may do its work in education, and the provision of services to dioceses and schools. It should not, however, be thought that the General Synod can devise a policy for church schools and then merely hand it down for implementation. Policy emerges as a consensus, as an amalgam of differing interests and insights, from every level of Church life. And it must not be forgotten that the major factors in the determination of a policy for church schools are the decisions taken by central government and local education authorities. It is, therefore, important that the General Synod should maintain a strong central negotiating body, which

10

can both make a positive contribution to national policy and represent the practicalities of the church's involvement in the system.

565 We recognize that the task of physically maintaining and developing church schools has consumed a quite disproportionate amount of the Church's effort in education since 1944. There has been very little of significance in the literature of religious education emanating from official or semi-official church bodies. If the primary function of the Church is to serve the national educational system and work within it, then it is desirable that the Church should initiate and encourage its members to make their full contribution to contemporary educational development. But it would be unfortunate if any kind of party line, or official doctrine, in matters of religious education were to be set forth from the centre. We see a need for a professionally competent advisory service in religious education, under the aegis of whatever body the General Synod charges with responsibility in this field. This advisory service would also be available for the work undertaken by diocesan education committees, and would act in association with official and unofficial agencies already at work. Even a small advisory staff would be costly, and the Church must realize that professional service can be obtained only if it is paid for at professional rates.

566 In a number of dioceses a reappraisal of the work sponsored by the diocesan education committee is already in hand, and we have been glad to note the setting up of an advisory service to schools in a few dioceses. It is urgently necessary that this should be much more widely accepted by diocesan education committees as a part of their normal work. We hope that the advisory service provided from the centre will be able to co-ordinate what is already being done and stimulate work in dioceses where the need has not yet been met at a professionally competent level. For we stress that the Church's contribution to religious education, both from the centre and where sponsored by diocesan education committees, must be of a quality to command the respect of colleagues on the staffs of local authorities and colleges of education, no less than of teachers in schools. We fully recognize that action at this level will call for increases in diocesan budgets, but it is futile in the extreme for the Church to continue providing school buildings without at the same time showing an active, professional concern for the general as well as the religious education given in them.

567 It is very questionable whether there will remain a place for the general duty diocesan director of education, who has a general responsibility for all areas of work undertaken in the name of the diocesan education committee and a particular responsibility for the administration of church schools. As dioceses reappraise their educational work, we hope they will be assisted by a development group sponsored from the centre, which will help them to move forward to new patterns more suitable to the existing and the emerging situations. At a time when the staffs of diocesan offices are assuming greater responsibility for administrative and financial matters, we question whether it is any longer appropriate to entrust the purely administrative work of maintaining church schools to clergymen whose professional training and experience has been in other fields. We see the diocesan director of education of the future as filling the role of pastor to teachers and clergy engaged in education, as colleague of the administrative secretary and the educational adviser, and as the interpreter of the Church's mind to the education service in his area. Because an adequate education staff to deal with religious education in schools will be costly to provide, we recommend that neighbouring dioceses consult as to how some of these services can be shared.

568 We have restricted ourselves in this section to recommendations of a very general kind, and we are not unmindful of the work already being done. Our profound conviction is that, whilst existing services are continued, the Church at large must either provide and pay for a more professionally competent advisory and administrative staff or be willing to see its influence diminished and its insights ignored, whatever it may have achieved by way of continuing provision of school places.

SPECIAL NOTE RELATING TO
THE CHURCH IN WALES AND ITS SCHOOLS

Inevitably the precise form of the argument put forward in the preceding chapter is expressed in terms of the established position of the Church of England familiar to the great majority of the members of the Commission, and in relation to the present or projected system of central and diocesan educational administration to serve church schools in England. The statistical charts and tables, however, take in church schools in Wales as well as in England. Although the position of the Church in Wales as a disestablished Church and its proportionately smaller involvement in the overall school system causes certain significant practical differences, the general approach of the Church in Wales in seeking to discharge and maintain its traditional responsibility and contribution within that system is very similar to that outlined for England.

During the long and bitter controversy over disestablishment the position of church schools in Wales provided a very sensitive topic for agitation and argument. At times the Church's protagonists were forced to defend what was made to appear to be a purely domestic concern with church schools and the religious teaching given in them. Nevertheless, the importance of the Church's contribution to the general educational task was never neglected and in the years following the setting up of the separate province in 1920 church leaders were constantly stressing this wider involvement. Amid all the post-war preoccupation with development plans and administrative issues, too, the traditional Anglican concern for national education has been maintained.

In Wales this general concern contains an important extra factor. The position of the two languages, Welsh and English, as the media of teaching and the Church's reconciling task in serving and bringing together the two linguistic elements in the nation are most relevant issues in the consideration of future policy development. This Report, however, is not the appropriate place to enlarge on these problems.

Like the Church of England, the Church in Wales has made her own assessment of her task, though in a somewhat differing social context and with less in the way of specialist resources, in studies such as the Report of the Manpower Commission of the Governing Body of the Church in Wales. In the strictly educational field the Church in Wales has to take into account the findings of the Gittins Committee, whose Report[1] reinforces and particularizes for Wales the general tenor of the Plowden Report in England.

In any proposed reorganization affecting the relationship between the central educational administration of the Church of England and the National Society, particular notice will have to be taken of the value and importance to the Church in Wales and her schools of the services of that Society and the continuing responsibilities which the National Society has towards church schools in Wales.

[1] *Primary Education in Wales* (H.M.S.O. 1967).

8
Recommendations

(1) General Introduction

569 In our earlier chapters we have tried to show how complex is the historical and political background in which religious education has emerged in this country, and how it has also taken its character from particular theological attitudes and particular stylings of the Christian faith, not always contemporary with the educational practice to which they gave rise. To attack or to defend religious education within the single perspective of a particular attitude to the Bible or Christian doctrine, especially if this were already outdated, or to see it as bound for ever to a particular historical and political settlement would be as inept as it would be naive, as narrow-minded as it would be insensitive. What we have rather tried to do has been to elucidate the theory and practice of religious education in a way which takes careful account of major developments in theological and philosophical studies over recent decades and of important developments in educational practice. We have also sought to remain alert to the practical context in which religious education takes place—e.g. contemporary questions about teaching methods, administration, and finance. This is the broad perspective in which we have set our inquiry, and while, whether in the documents submitted to us or otherwise, particular questions have arisen in relation to possible changes in the 1944 Education Act, we have from first to last conceived our task in far wider terms, terms more suited to the general importance and significance of the subject. Still less have we seen ourselves as having to take up negative defensive attitudes hesitant of novelty and nervous of anything which might disturb the *status quo*. It would be a poor argument for religious education if those who value it had to take up such attitudes as these.

570 Implicit throughout this Report has been our Christian concern with education as a whole, as a rounded process of which specifically "religious education" is only one part. Some of the reasons for this concern emerge in the final section of ch. 2 and are taken up again at the beginning of ch. 7. The Christian conception of man as "created in the image of God, redeemed by Jesus Christ and destined for eternal life" brings with it the inevitable corollary that Christian people are deeply concerned with the growth to maturity of "the whole man", "the healthy enlargement of men's minds and person- alities and the creation of truly human relationships and com- munities", all of which tasks fall to (or should fall to) a nation's educational system. The Church has naturally paid particular attention to the specific area of "religious education", which tends to be a neglected area in contrast with other subjects which have more obvious and immediate material benefits. But while our special con- cern in this final chapter is, therefore, with religious education, in- cluding school worship, this must be seen in the context of our wider concern with education in the fullest sense of that term.

571 We have, in our discussions, considered the clauses of the 1944 Education Act which relate to religious instruction and school wor- ship and we have, on a number of occasions, discussed the desirability or otherwise of their retention in any new legislation. It will be apparent from all that has gone before in the Report that we believe that the term "religious instruction" is no longer satisfactory, and that it should be replaced in official and in colloquial use by the term "religious education". It will also be recalled that throughout ch. 4 of this Report we have argued that school worship is an essential component of "religious education" and should be seen as included within that term. Moreover, in discussing what statutory regulation (if any) should relate to religious education, we have obviously borne in mind what we have stated earlier in our Report about the aims, methods, and content of religious education. We have also attended to the evidence presented to us. We have concluded that it is essential for administrators, educationists, teachers, and all others concerned with religious education, to examine the possibility of a more con- temporary and less restrictive approach in framing new legislation relating to this subject. But throughout all our discussions we have been conscious of the many educational, administrative, and indeed legal problems raised by this issue.

572 It is in this general context that we would like to see religious education acknowledged on educational grounds and not by singling it out and making it alone of all subjects legally "compulsory". Rather should it take its place alongside other studies without which a young person in our particular culture could hardly be said to be educated. We believe that it was unfortunate that the 1944 Education Act perpetuated the over-sharp distinction made by previous legislation between "secular instruction" and "religious instruction". Further, we think that the theological, educational, ecclesiastical, and cultural climate is now so far different from that prevailing in 1944 as to render the statutory regulations relating to religious education made at that time no longer appropriate. We also noted that the evidence presented to us gave us no ground for thinking that the preservation of the *status quo* is desired by most educationists.

573 But four considerations led us to conclude that some measure of statutory acknowledgement of the importance of religious education (in which we include school worship) is still required.

(*a*) The "free for all" which might result from a total and immediate abandonment of all forms of statutory provision would inevitably create confusion and uncertainty giving rise to misunderstanding among parents, teachers, and pupils.

(*b*) Total and immediate abandonment would suggest that the country as a whole shared the views of those who hold religious beliefs to be unimportant, false, or vacuous. We have no grounds for believing that this conclusion has any basis in fact.

(*c*) Head teachers might be exposed to local pressure groups, both secularist and sectarian.

(*d*) The subject is not yet sufficiently understood as an educational discipline; hence, in some schools religious education might disappear in whole or in part since it does not have the same obviously utilitarian and examination supports as are given, e.g., to English and mathematics.

574 In giving this issue further consideration we recalled that section 7 of the 1944 Education Act contained an introductory statement of general principles, viz:

The Statutory system of public education shall be organized in three progressive stages to be known as primary education, secondary education and further education; and it shall be the duty of the L.E.A. for every area so far as their powers extend, to contribute towards the spiritual, moral, mental and physical development of the community by securing that efficient education throughout these stages shall be available to meet the needs of the population of their area.

Further, we noted that in section 8 (Duty of L.E.A.s to secure provision of primary and secondary schools) the Act stated that

... the schools available for an area shall not be deemed to be sufficient unless they are sufficient in number, character, and equipment to afford for all pupils opportunities for education offering such variety of instruction and training as may be desirable in view of their different ages, abilities and aptitudes and of the different periods for which they may be expected to remain at school, including practical instruction and training appropriate to their respective needs.

575 Our discussion of this whole issue, not least in the light of these two sections, led us to formulate the following proposal which we offer for study and consideration by educationists and administrators. We suggest that any new Education Act should attempt to define more precisely, though only in brief outline, the essential basic components of the education to be given to all pupils at school and that religious education should be placed within this general educational context. The Act might, we think, lay down that *all pupils in county and voluntary schools shall be provided, according to their ages, abilities, and aptitudes, with education in the arts and sciences, in religion and morals, and in physical and practical skills.* In doing this the new Act, like the present one, could then place *a general duty upon L.E.A.s to ensure that such educational provision is made* without taking away from governors their traditional responsibility for the curriculum of their schools; though in exercising this responsibility governors are, of course, bound by the requirements of any legislation. *The governors of almost all voluntary schools, being bound by the terms of their trust deeds, would have that further legal support for the religious education provided in their schools.*

576 We fully recognize that there is a long and valued tradition in British education which militates against state control of the curriculum. We would argue that such a general specification of education as we have proposed above goes no further, though we would think it far clearer, than the phrases used in sections 7 and 8 of the 1944 Act. There is no detailed determination of the curriculum; that would be as objectionable to us as to any teacher. We also see this proposal as consistent with developments in present-day political philosophy. The planned society has come to stay, and if such a

society is to allow for a genuine expression of local opinion—and so to be a genuine democracy—then overall planning must be of sufficiently open texture to give a large, realistic, and effective place to local and personal initiatives. Further, we see this proposal as going far to place religious education in its true setting—as essential to each pupil's general education, and so within the normal framework of the curriculum.

577 We now set out our summary of recommendations. What detailed implications these recommendations may have for possible changes in a new Education Act is primarily the concern of the educationist, the administrator, and the legislator. We were not asked to make specific recommendations relating to the precise re-wording of educational legislation. We do not wish to formulate a detailed "standpoint" in such a way as to suggest that each point must somehow be "met". We think this neither courteous nor meaningful within the context of discussion and debate which lies behind the formulation of educational policy in this country.

(2) *Recommendations*

1 The term "religious instruction" should be replaced forthwith by the term "religious education". What we understand by "religious education" in the context of this recommendation is fully set out in ch. 4.

2 Religious education, including participation in school worship, should form part of the general education received by all school pupils.

3 The statutory provisions relating to religious instruction and school worship in the 1944 Education Act should not be continued in their present form in any forthcoming educational legislation.

4 Some degree of statutory acknowledgement is required with regard to religious education, including school worship, but such statutory acknowledgement should allow the schools a wider measure of flexibility than is provided by the existing legislation.

5 In relation to any new Education Act we hope that the proposals outlined in para 575 of the General Introduction to this chapter will receive serious study by educationists and administrators.

6 Our detailed recommendations relating to "The future pattern of

10*

school worship" are set out in paras. 309–320 of ch. 4, and should be read within the context of that chapter.

7 Conscience clauses for teachers and withdrawal rights for parents should be preserved, but on this matter see further, ch. 4, paras 317–8, especially as this issue is affected by the lowering of the age of majority.

8 Where religious education is time-tabled as a separate subject it should receive a minimum time-table allocation of two periods per week. Where religious education is part of integrated or combined studies, a comparable weighting of contribution should be ensured.

9 The existing machinery for the drawing up and adoption of an Agreed Syllabus by an L.E.A. should be abandoned.

10 Booklets, pamphlets, and other advisory material should be published regularly under the auspices of the D.E.S. and the Schools Council to assist teachers of religious education in schools of all kinds.

11 Each local education authority should ensure that a handbook of suggestions is available for teachers of religious education in its area. Some local education authorities will wish to draw up their own handbooks and so will call on theologians, educationists, and teachers with the relevant knowledge and experience. Handbooks should be regularly revised.

12 Local education authorities are urged to appoint an Adviser, or Advisers, in religious education. Such an official would assist in sponsoring the subject in schools within the normal processes of curriculum development.

13 So far as may be practicable, appropriate provision for religious education should be made available in all educational institutions providing full time education for students in the 16–18 age range.

14 Effective education, and therefore effective religious education, depends on the provision of a satisfactory general educational environment. In this context we endorse recommendations made by other committees, and particularly the Plowden Committee, with regard to

   (*a*) the need for adequate pre-school facilities in play groups and nursery classes;

(*b*) the need to give urgent attention to problems of staffing and school buildings in educational priority areas.

We also stress the need for the creation of a more informed public opinion in educational affairs. This is one of the essential pre-requisites to that increase in financial support without which these improvements will be impossible.

15 The religious education of immigrant children raises a wide variety of complex issues and should be the subject of a separate inquiry. In the present situation we recommend that this problem should be approached with care and sensitivity and decisions taken in the light of the particular needs of local areas. See further, para. 315 of part 3 of ch. 4.

16 An extensive research programme is required. There is a particularly urgent need for further research into:
(*a*) the religious education of children in the 5–13+ age group;
(*b*) the religious education of less able pupils of all age groups.

17 There is a need for more teachers of religious education for older pupils who are qualified to undertake the necessary specialist teaching. We would also encourage the appointment of teachers with special training in religious education at primary level. Such teachers could act in a consultant capacity within the school.

18 The number of one-year, full-time, Diploma in Religious Education courses should be increased. L.E.A.s should be willing to second serving teachers to attend such courses, as they do in other subjects. The relationship between these Diploma courses and the B.Ed. degree for serving teachers should be given careful scrutiny.

19 We welcome the setting up in 1969 by the British Council of Churches of a Working Party to inquire into the whole problem of the supply and training of teachers of religious education. In view of this Working Party we think that it would be inappropriate for us to make further detailed recommendations on this particular topic at the present time.

20 More attention requires to be given to the in-service training of teachers of religious education. We should like to see practical and effective co-operation between L.E.A.s, H.M.I., the Area Training organizations, the Churches, the university extra-mural

departments, the W.E.A., and a number of voluntary bodies such as the Christian Education Movement.

21 The claims of religious education in the development of the B.Ed. degree should be fully recognized.

22 Teachers of religious education should participate in further research and experiment with integrated studies.

23 We recognize the educational value of the discussion of moral questions by members of staff who hold different viewpoints and expound them with concern for responsible moral decision; but for reasons which we discuss in ch. 3 we do not regard the introduction of a separate subject called "Moral Education" on to the time-table as a desirable development.

24 Contemporary teaching methods at all levels of schooling presuppose the existence of high quality textbooks, reference books, filmstrips, films, and a wide range of other aural and visual aids. Authors, publishers, and manufacturers are encouraged to continue to attend to these developing needs, which exist in religious education as in all other subjects.

25 Research and experiment should continue into the applications for religious education of recent developments in educational technology—e.g. closed circuit TV, electro-video-recording, and video-tape recording techniques.

26 Religious education should continue to have its full place in radio and TV broadcasts for schools. It is important that those responsible for the planning and presentation of these programmes should continue to maintain a sensitive and informed awareness of contemporary educational developments.

27 We fully recognize that there is still a need for church-based voluntary religious education, e.g. in Sunday schools. We further recognize the importance of church-based adult religious education. We say no more about these subjects since both lie outside our terms of reference, but see further, evidence from the Church of England Children's Council, p. 330.

28 Those responsible for religious education and school worship in independent and direct grant schools, including preparatory schools, should develop contacts with their colleagues in maintained schools and in particular should keep in touch with developments in religious education in the maintained schools.

29 We consider that the appropriate central body within the Church
of England should examine the possibility of appointing a full-
time Moderator, to give some degree of pastoral and official care
to clergy working in schools (independent, direct grant, and maintained); to assist with their in-service training; to assist where
possible with appointments; and, in consultation with diocesan
bishops, to assist with their return to parochial work.

30 The Church of England's immediate and wholesale withdrawal
from the Dual System is undesirable. Even if it were thought to
be desirable, it would be impracticable (short of major parliamentary legislation) on account of the exceedingly complex administrative, legal, and financial negotiations and adjustments
involved.

31 The Church should for the present see its continued involvement
in the Dual System principally as a way of expressing its concern
for the general education of all children and young people rather
than as a means for giving "denominational instruction". See
further Recommendation 35.

32 On the assumption that voluntary aided schools have the educational outlook we have advanced and accomplish the integration of home, Church, and school which we see as their
particular value for both society and the Church, then it is our
view that the Church should continue to accept its commitment
to voluntary aided schools, but—because of the financial burden—
should plan to do so on a proportionately reduced scale.

33 Wholesale adoption of controlled status is not recommended.
The Church should see its concern for controlled schools not so
much in terms of "rights" as in terms of the responsibilities which
we set out in paras. 537–543 of ch. 7.

34 The status of the special agreement school is now anomalous and
such schools should be converted to aided schools.

35 A central body of the Church should be *immediately* charged with
the task of collecting detailed information about the financing of
church schools and colleges of education and should then attempt
to determine future policy both in the light of likely educational
developments and decisions about the Church's priorities. This
will be essential if the Church is to make responsible policy

decisions about any future commitment to the Dual System or further development of the Church's involvement in education. We view this as a task of *urgent necessity*.

36 The "spread" of church voluntary aided schools should so far as may be possible be more rationally distributed, both geographically and within the educational system. To achieve this end a greater degree of centralized co-ordination will be necessary.

37 Closer consideration requires to be given both by the Church and the education authorities to the employment of clergy within the education service, whether full-time or part-time, with particular reference to their theological and educational training, to their remuneration, and to their diocesan status. This should be the subject of *immediate* inquiry by the appropriate central body within the Church.

38 Diocesan education committees—perhaps working jointly in local co-operation—should ensure that a competent advisory service is available to teachers in church schools within their area. Each D.E.C. should also ensure that a regularly revised handbook of suggestions for religious education in voluntary aided schools is available.

39 Religious education in Church of England voluntary aided and controlled schools should be open to inspection by H.M.I.

40 General oversight of policy relating to church schools should be the duty of an appropriate central body and such a body should be responsible to the General Synod.

41 As a preliminary to more far-reaching inquiries into the Church's educational work, an *immediate* inquiry is needed into the functions of the "diocesan director of education" or "director of religious education". Such an inquiry should be conducted under the sponsorship of the appropriate central body, but should be carried out by a group consisting for the most part of lay people who are professional educationists. The inquiry should cover qualifications and experience; terms of reference; remuneration and administrative assistance; and range of duties performed.

42 In single-school areas, where the existence of a Church voluntary aided school is the subject of extensive local protest, the Managers of the school should consider exchanging aided status for controlled,

provided that appropriate legislation could be introduced to make possible the restoration of aided status should the local situation change, or should the provision of a county school make the area no longer single-school. (See further, ch. 7.)

43 Admissions policy for a church voluntary aided primary school should give priority to the children of the local area, whatever their denominational allegiance, assuming that their parents understand and accept the religious aims of the school.

44 We hope that, in accordance with the regulations of the Convocations, bishops will permit the admission of non-Anglican pupils and staff to services of Holy Communion conducted in voluntary aided schools.

45 Where a parish contains a church school, the patron should, whenever possible, take care to appoint only those clergy who have some educational competence and understanding and who may be expected to contribute to the life of the school. Training courses for such clergy should be provided by the diocesan education committee.

46 Diocesan education committees should run regular courses and conferences for the managers and governors of voluntary aided and controlled schools.

47 Working parties should be set up *without delay* both at national and local level to examine ways and means of realistic and practical ecumenical co-operation within the Dual System.

APPENDIXES

A
Evidence presented to the Commission

Evidence presented to the Commission is in two categories—general evidence and questionnaire evidence.

General Evidence

In the autumn of 1967 the Chairman made a public appeal through the press for comments from the general public on the issues being examined by the Commission.

Questionnaire Evidence

In 1968 the Commission issued a questionnaire to seventy-five different educational and ecclesiastical organizations and to a number of other public bodies who might be expected to be concerned with religious education. Many of these replied formally, submitting statements on behalf of the organization concerned. Others preferred not to attempt to express a common mind, but distributed the questionnaire among their members and invited them to reply as private individuals. Altogether eighty-seven formal statements were received and 550 replies from private individuals.

The General and Questionnaire evidence was divided up into six representative sections. Each section was studied and assessed by a member of the Commission. A cross-section of all the evidence was circulated among all the members of the Commission. The final collation of the material was made by the Secretary and this summary of evidence was also circulated among the members. One full meeting of the Commission was devoted to the consideration and discussion of the evidence. We were primarily concerned to find where the weight of opinion lay and what were the main issues at stake.

In this Appendix we set out:

(1) A copy of the Commission's Questionnaire:
(2) List of Organizations submitting evidence:
(3) List of Persons submitting evidence:
(4) A Selection of the evidence received from various organizations.

QUESTIONNAIRE

Section A

1 Should Religious Education, however defined, form part of the curriculum of all types of primary and secondary schools?
2 If it should not form part of the curriculum of such schools what kinds of moral and ethical instruction, if any, should replace it?
3 If, on the other hand, it is a part of the curriculum, is it either desirable or essential that its position should continue, in any future legislation, to be supported by "compulsory" provisions similar to those of the 1944 Education Act?
4 If Religious Education continues to be "compulsory", how would you improve or modify existing safeguards for the rights of those parents who, on grounds of conscience, do not wish their children to receive it?
5 Are any additional safeguards required to protect the position of teachers who, on grounds of conscience, do not wish to take part in Religious Education and school worship?
6 In any future provision for R.E. (on a compulsory or non-compulsory basis) should anything be done to protect the rights of children (mostly immigrants) of other faiths? Should provision be made, in fact, where circumstances appear to justify it for religious education other than Christian education? (cf. some existing maintained Jewish schools.)
7 Should a daily act of corporate worship (subject to the conscience clause) be a statutory obligation upon all Primary and Secondary Schools?
8 If not, should all schools continue to make regular provision for acts of corporate worship e.g. on a weekly basis, or on an age-group basis?
9 Is there still a place within the English educational system for the continuance of denominational schools, e.g. Church of England Voluntary Aided and Voluntary Controlled Schools?
10 Would you favour a complete "secularization" of public education involving the progressive dismantling of the traditional "dual" system and the prohibition of religious teaching of all kinds?

Section B

Please give any further comments you wish to make:

NOTE

In the preparation of this Questionnaire the Commission acknowledges the assistance of Mr J. G. M. Allcock, C.B.E., M.A., formerly Chief Inspector of Schools of the Department of Education and Science. The Commission hoped that the degree of openness implicit in all the questions would encourage free, open, and thoughtful comment. The quality of the material received made it clear that this hope was largely fulfilled.

ORGANIZATIONS WHICH SUBMITTED EVIDENCE

Allied Schools; Assistant Masters Association; Association for Religious Education for Teachers and Lecturers; Association for Special Education (Branches of); Association of Assistant Mistresses in Secondary Schools; Association of Chief Education Officers; Association of Head Mistresses; Association of Headmistresses of Preparatory Schools; Association of Teachers in Colleges and Departments of Education; Association of Voluntary Aided Secondary Schools.

Baptist Union of Great Britain & Ireland; Blackheath Association for the Advancement of State Education; Blandford Press Ltd; British Humanist Association.

Campaign for Moral Education; Campaigners; Christian Education Fellowship; Christian Education Movement; Church Education Corporation; Church in Wales Provincial Council for Education; Church of England Children's Council; Church of England Schools Council; Churches' Fellowship for Psychical and Spiritual Studies; Congregational Church in England and Wales; Council of the Church Colleges of Education; County Councils Association.

"Education for Living" Workshop.

Faith Press Ltd; Free Church Federal Council.

R. Gibson & Sons (Glasgow) Ltd; Girl Guides Association; Girls' Public Day School Trust; Girls' Venture Corps; Godolphin and Latymer School; Headmasters Association; Humanist Teachers Association (Guildford, Hampstead, and Oxford University Groups).

Inter-School Christian Fellowship.

London Church Schools Association.

Methodist Education Committee; Methodist Publishing House & Epworth Press.

National Association of Divisional Executives for Education; National Association of Head Teachers; National Association for Teachers of Religious Knowledge; National Secular Society; National Society; Thomas Nelson & Sons Ltd.

Outward Bound Trust.

Presbyterian Church of England; Progressive League.

School Broadcasting Council for the United Kingdom; Scout Association; Socialist Educational Association; Southampton College for Girls; Southwark Diocesan Roman Catholic Parents and Electors Association.

Unitarian Religious Education Department.

Whitelands College, Putney; Woodard Schools.

Evidence was received from the following Diocesan Education Committees:
Bangor; Bath and Wells; Birmingham; Blackburn; Bradford; Bristol; Canterbury; Carlisle; Coventry; Derby; Ely; Exeter; Gloucester; Guildford; Hereford; Lichfield; Lincoln; Liverpool; London; Newcastle; Norwich; Oxford; Sodor and Man; Southwark; Southwell; Truro; Winchester; Worcester.

INDIVIDUAL PERSONS WHO SUBMITTED EVIDENCE

It should be noted that within this category are placed a number of persons who are official members of various educational or other organizations, but who could not guarantee to speak on behalf of or to represent any collective opinion within their organization.

Miss M. L. Abbot, Newfoundland Rd Primary Sch., Bristol; Mr D. Aird, Ely; Mrs E. Alexander, East Harting; Mr T. S. Alflatt, Uffculme Sch., Moseley; Mr N. Allcoat, Cardinal Wiseman S.M. Boys' Sch., Coventry; T. A. Allen, Fallowfield; Mr R. C. Anderson, Liverpool; R. O. J. Anderson, London W.C.; Mr J. C. Appleton, Hartlepool; Mr G. Appleton, Canterbury; Mrs M. J. Appleton, St Teresa's Inf. Sch., St Helens; Mr W. N. Archer, Mundella C.P. Sch., Folkestone; C. Arkwright, St Thomas More Girls' Sch., Newtown; Miss M. Armour and Mr T. Armour, St Mary's Jnr Sch., Fleetwood; Rev. G. L. W. Armstrong, Bagshot; Mr K. Arnold, Port Talbot; Mrs E. Ascroft, Sacred Heart Inf. Sch., Wigan; Mr S. F. Ashby, London; Miss Aspinall, St Peter's Sec. Sch., Orrell; N. Atherton, Sacred Heart Inf. Sch., Wigan; Rev. D. A. Atkinson, Newton Abbot; Mr M. B. Atkinson, Old Llutton C.E. Pr. Sch., Kendal; Rev. H. V. Atkinson, Rugby; Rev. D. Attfield, London; Mr J. G. Auton, Chigwell Sch., Essex.

Mr T. R. Babb, Redruth; Sister M. Baptist, St Vincent's Inf. Sch., St Helens; Mrs Bagnall, St Theresa's R.C. Sch., Sheffield; Mr K. Baisbrown, Warblington County Sec. Sch., Havant; Mr. D. G. Baker, Botswana, S. Africa; Mr W. Baker, East Dulwich; Dr D. Ball, Welling; Mr R. G. Ball, Swindon; Mr M. Balmer, Blackburn; Miss Banks, St Peter's Sec. Sch., Orrell; Mr M. Barnes, Cambridge; Rev. P. Barratt, Cambridge; M. Barry, St Albans Inf. Sch., Cardiff; C. F. Bartlett, London N.22; Mrs I. M. Bartlett; J. M. Barton, Horsham; J. D. Batten, Leigh Jun. Sch., Essex; Rev. G. Bates, Liverpool; Mr C. J. Beale, Outwood, Redhill; Mrs F. H. Belcher, Rhondda; R. A. Bell, London N.W; Mr E. E. Bellett, St Mark's C.E. Primary Sch., Farnborough; Mrs A. Bennett, Bournemouth; Mr J. A. Benstead, Ealing Grammar Sch. for Boys; A. H. M. Best, London W.C.2; Mr A. R. Bielby, Huddersfield New College; Mr R. Birch, Durham City; Canon K. M. Bishop, Deane; Mrs D. M. Blackburne, St Teresa's Inf. Sch., St Helens; Mrs D. L. C. Blake, St Peter's Jnr Sch., Gloucester; E. Blake, St Patrick's Inf. Sch., Wigan; Mrs M. Blan, Sacred Heart Inf. Sch., Wigan; Mrs S. Blanchard, Hallcroft Sec. Sch., Retford; Mr D. L. Bland, Hartlepool; Miss N. K. Blockley, Corpus Christi Sch., Portsmouth; T. Blockley, St Paul's J.M. and I. Sch., Paulsgrove; W. Boardman, St Cuthbert's Inf. Sch., Pemberton; Mr A. C. Body, West Harnham; Mrs M. D. Bolton, Paddock House Jnr Sch., Accrington; Miss K. Boulton, Our Lady's R.C. Sch., Dalton-in-Furness; Miss M. M. Bourne, Lincoln; Mr A. Braithwaite, Aspatria Jnr Sch., Cumberland; M. Braithwaite, Newcastle; Mr E. M. Brash, Woolton; Mr N. Brewster, Bishop Auckland; E. Brocklehurst, Edmund Arrowsmith Sec. Sch., Ashton-in-Makerfield; Mr A. A. Briggs, County Sec. Sch., Charlton Kings; Mr J. B. Brockington; A. Brown, St Edward's Inf. Sch., Wigan; W. Brown, St Wulstan's Primary Sch., Fleetwood; Mr A. J. Bryant, Oxford; Mr J. Buckle, C. E. Cont. Sch., Lincoln; Mr C. Buckley, Stockport; Miss L. M. Buckley Hunters Hill O.A.S., Bromsgrove; S. J. T. Buffey, Salisbury; B. M. Bull, Star Inf. Sch., London E.16; W. Bullin, Arnold County Sec. Sch., Nottingham; Rev. J. Bullock, Hartlepool; Mrs J. L. Burke, Pool Hayes Comp. Sch., Willenhall; Mr F. Burr, Leeds; Mrs Buttar, St Peter's Sec. Sch., Orrell; Mrs V. Byron, Bolton; Rev. L. W. Barnard, Winchester; Miss M. Buchan-Sydserff.

Mrs J. F. Cain, St Teresa's Jnr Sch., St Helens; Mr P. A. Caine, Redscope Jnr

Sch., Rotherham; Rev. G. M. Calder, Truro; Miss A. W. Callaghan, St Peter's Inf. Sch., Gloucester; J. Campion, St Joseph's P.S., Derby; Rev. N. Capey, York; J. F. Casey, St Wulstan's Primary Sch., Fleetwood; J. B. Carmel, Wembley; Mr R. B. Carter, Scissett C.E. J.M. and I. Sch., Clayton West; Rev. P. J. van de Castiele; Mr G. Cairns, Newcastle; A. A. Chappell, Smith Hospital Sch.; A. M. Chapman, London S.W; Mr S. Chappell, Sithney C.P. Sch., Helston; Mr C. R. Cheeseman, Biggin Hill; Miss D. B. Charnock, Highfield C.E. Inf. Sch., Pemberton; J. Charnock, St Mary's J.M. Sch., Standishgate; F.M. Cheers, Holy Family R.C. Sch., New Springs, Lancs; E. D. Cheshire, Compstall; S. E. Chew, Blackburn; Sister Christine, St John's R.C. Sch., Wigan; Mr P. Christopher, St Peter's Sec. Sch., Orrell; Mr V. Chipchase; M. L. Chivers, Lister St C.P. Sch., Hartlepool; Sister K. M. Clapham, St Stephen's P.S., Welling; Miss A. J. Clarke, St Cecillia's R.C. P.S., North Cheam; Mr D. K. Clarke, Slough Grammar Sch.; Mr G. Clarke, Richmond; Mr F. J. Clayton, Rollesby C.P. Sch., Norfolk; Miss M. Clifford, St Theresa's Sch., Sheffield; Mrs E. J. Cleggett, Cardiff; Miss M. G. Comont, Rockwell Green V.C. P. Sch., Wellington; Mrs M. Condon, St Theresa's R.C. Sch., Sheffield; M. J. Conlon, Paddock House Convent, Oswaldtwistle; Rev. D. Connelley, Doncaster; O. T. Connor, St Mary's R.C. Jnr Sch., Cardiff; Miss L. V. Conroy, Convent Grammar Sch., Bury; M. Conway, St. Joseph's R.C. P.S., Derby; I. Coomber, Canterbury; Mrs C. T. Cootes, Basingstoke; M. M. Corcoran, St Oswald's Primary Sch. and J. B. Corless, St Oswald's Jnr Sch., Wigan; Miss O. Corson, Huby; Mrs A. Cormino-James, Garrards Cross; Mr J. R. M. Cosser, Chichester; J. Craven-Griffiths, South Lambeth; E. Cronin, St Mary's R.C. Jnr Sch., Cardiff; Mr R. Crook, Moorend C.E. Jnr Sch., Cleckheaton; G. Crossley, Richworth St John's C.E. P.S., Nr Halifax; E. A. Croxford, Beckenham; M. C. Cummins, St Mary's R.C. Jnr Sch., Cardiff; Mrs M. Cutler, Kneller Sec. Girls' Sch., Twickenham; Sister M. Cyril, St Joseph's Jnr Sch., Cardiff; Col. J. H. H. Coombes, London.

C. M. Daly, St Teresa's Jnr Sch., St Helens; Canon A. H. Dammers, Coventry; Mr S. Dann, Crowborough; G. F. Divall, Wimborne County S.M. Sch.; D. A. Davies, Wembley Jnr H. Sch.; E. A. Davies, Birmingham; Mrs P. Davies, Carlson House Sch. for Spastics, Birmingham; A. Davison; Mr A. W. Davson, London S.W; Mr R. U. Dawes, Lichfield; Mr D. Day, Aspatria Jnr Sch., Cumberland; Miss G. S. Dearden, Douglas; Mrs D. M. Derbyshire, St Teresa's R.C. Inf. Sch., St Helens; Mr J. J. Derbyshire, St Edward's R.C. Jnr Sch., Wigan; A. K. Diamond, Liverpool; Deaconess A. Dixon, Durham; D. Doherty, St Mary's R.C. J.M. Sch., Wigan; Mrs M. Doncaster, Royston; A. C. Donovan, St Mary's R.C. Jnr Sch., Cardiff; Mrs A. Dooney, Sacred Heart Inf. Sch., Wigan; Mr A. A. Douglas, Hexham; C. E. Dove, South West Ham Tech. Sch.; Miss A. M. M. Dowell, South Shields; Mr C. W. Dowson, St Joseph's Comp. Sch., Swindon; J. L. Duckworth, Sowerby Bridge; Mrs V. Duffield, St Theresa's R.C. Sch., Sheffield; S. A. Duxbury, Edmund Arrowsmith Sec. Sch., Ashton-in-Makerfield; Mrs T. Dyson, St Theresa's R.C. Sch., Sheffield.

J. Edwards; Rev. P. J. Edwards, Mayfield; Mr R. Edwards, Croydon; Mr E. A. Egan and Mr J. M. Egan, St Joseph's Comp. Sch., Swindon; Mr J. C. Ellis, Frederick Gough Grammar Sch., Scunthorpe; M. M. Ellison, St Cuthbert's Inf. Sch., Wigan; Miss E. E. Ellsmore, Cleeve Comp. Sch., Cheltenham; Mr N. Ellwood, Bishop Middleham; Mr E. England, London E.C; Mr A. Evans, St Luke's C.E. Jnr Sch., Kingston-on-Thames; Mr A. N. Evans, Chichester; Mr J. H. Evans, Hallmoor P.S., Birmingham; K. M. Evans, St Marie's R.C. Jnr Sch., Rugby; Mr T. E. Evans, Gloucester.

Miss E. Falk, Croydon; N. T. Fallon, St Joseph's R.C. P. Sch., Wigan; Mrs D. Fantini, Cardiff; M. S. Fargus, Ripon; R. M. Faulkner, Maghull; Rev. R. S. Ferguson, St Mary's Sec. Sch., Richmond; T. Fielding, St Wulstan's P. Sch., Fleetwood; Mrs J. Fincham, Chelmsford; Mr M. Firrible, Edgbaston; Miss M. Fisher, Bristol; M. I. Fison, Salisbury; C. Fleming, St Patrick's Inf. Sch., Rochdale; Mr D. C. Flint, London W; The Lady Foot, Yelverton; E. M. Foster, St Cuthbert's Inf. Sch., Pemberton; B. Fox, St Mary's R.C. P. Sch., Enfield; L. Fox, Battyeford Jnr Sch., Mirfield; M. C. Fox, St Edward's Inf. Sch., Newton; C. N. Frank, Southampton; I. Frank, St Mary's R.C. P. Sch., Enfield; Mr J. Frian, London; Mr S. Frith, St Chad's C.E. J.M.I. Sch., Brighouse; C. H. Fullmer, Birmingham; Miss E. J. Funnell, Paddington and Maida Vale Sch., London; Mr A. Furniss.

Mr B. S. Gaffney, Gateshead; Mrs E. G. Gale, St Leonards; Rev. J. B. Gale, St Leonards; M. E. Gallagher, St Patrick's Inf. Sch., Wigan; D. Garnett, Ravensworth County Jnr Sch., Middlesbrough; M. T. Geering, St Mary's R.C. Jnr Sch., Standishgate; Mr I. E. Geffen, Walsall; Mr F. Gilbert, Thurleston S.M. Sch., Ipswich; R. S. Good, Canterbury; Mr D. F. Goodhead, Butts P. Sch., Walsall; M. A. Goffin, Testwood Sec. Sch., Totton; J. Gordon, Edmonton; M. D. Gore, Edmund Arrowsmith Sec. Sch., Ashton-in-Makerfield; Mr G. Goswell; I. Grahame, Berkhamstead; Miss B. Green, Sheepridge; Mrs F. M. Green, Rise Park Jnr Sch., Romford; Mr L. J. Green, Hargrave Park J.M. Sch., Islington; Mrs M. M. Green, St Vincent's Inf. Sch., St Helens; Mr W. N. Greenaway; Burnt Tree C.P. Sch., Tividale; Rev. E. B. Greening, Sale; J. A. Grees, Westbury; Mrs I. Grice, Brentwood; Mrs E. T. Griffiths, St Teresa's Jnr Sch., St Helens; Mrs M. Grisdale, Aspatria Jnr Sch., Cumberland; Mr R. E. Grout, St Paul's C.E. Sch., Tottenham; Mr J. D. Grey, Irthing Valley Sch., Brampton, Cumberland; Gloucester Teachers' Meeting.

Mr A. Hall; M. Hall, St John's R.C. Sch., Wigan; Mr R. J. C. Hall, St Albans; Misses A. and S. Halliwell, Preston; Miss A. Halpin, St Cuthbert's R.C. Sch., Pemberton; Mr E. Hambleton, St Paul's Sch., Brierley; Miss J. Hamer, Bexhill; Mr J. Hamilton; Mr P. Hammond, Hexham; Mr P. Hancock, Portsmouth; Staff of Hanging Heaton C.E. Sch., Batley; Miss G. Hanks, Sunbury; Mr J. W. Hanmer, Chipping Sodbury Grammar Sch.; Mr J. Hansford, Bury Grammar Sch.; Mrs D. Hard, Brighton; A. V. Harding, Edmund Arrowsmith Sec. Sch., Ashton-in-Makerfield; Rev. C. E. L. Harris, Sutton-by-Dover; Mr J. N. Harrison, Durham; T. Hart, Erith; Mrs M. B. Harvey, St Vincent's Inf. Sch., St Helens; Mr G. W. Hatfield, Brixham; Mrs T. R. Havens, London N; Mr D. Hawkes, Horsham; E. A. Hawkins and J. Hawkins, Edmund Arrowsmith R.C. Sec. Sch., Ashton-in-Makerfield; Mrs E. J. Hayes, Stoke Golding C.E. Sch.; Miss M. Hayes, Wells; M. A. Hayes, Bradford; Mr J. Haynes, Culloden Jnr Sch., London E.14; Mr P. Haynes, Bath and Wells; Mr and Mrs J. Hazel, London S.W; Mrs M. A. Hearn, Luton; G. M. Hedley, Sacriston; Mr J. Henriksen, Hoddesdon; Mr M. Herbert, Peterborough; Dr A. Herxheimer, London S.W; Mr J. G. Hewett, Storrington; Mr A. E. Hill, York; Mr M. Hill, Isleworth; Mr D. A. Hillman, Bushey Grammar Sch., Herts; A. C. Hilton, Stanton; G. Hilton, St Thomas More Sec. Sch., Newtown; Mr M. G. Hinton, Dover Grammar Sch.; Mr E. W. Hobson, Meltham C.E. P. Sch.; D. C. Hocking, Rushden; H. Hogan, St Cuthbert's Inf. Sch., Pemberton; S. Hogben, St Wulstan's P. Sch., Fleetwood; Mrs H. Hogg and Mr A. M. Hogg, Beckenham; Mr H. L. Hogg, Hartlepool; Mr Holden, St Mary's Sch., Fleetwood; E. Holland, St Edward's R.C. Jnr Sch., Marsh Green; W. E. Holland, Edmund Arrowsmith Sec. Sch., Ashton-in-

Makerfield; Mr R. Holley, Farnborough; Mrs D. Holloway, Carew Manor Sch., Wallington; J. Hoogerwerf, St Joseph's R.C. P. Sch., Derby; Mr T. M. Hope, Cardinal Wiseman S.M. Boys' Sch., Coventry; Mr J. H. Hopper, Grafton C.E. Sch., Marlborough; I. Hopwood, Winifred Cullis Sch., Gloucester; Rev. R. G. H. Horne, Hurstmonceux; G. W. Horrocks, St Thomas More Girls' Sch., Wigan; Sister M. Houghton, St Patrick's Inf. Sch., Wigan; O. Howell, Oxford; Miss V. Howell, St Stephen's P. Sch., Welling; Miss D. C. Howlett, Edgbaston; Mr E. Horwood, London; Mr J. F. Hudson, Earlsheaton C.E. Jnr Sch., Dewsbury; Mr T. Hughes, Yale High Sch., Wrexham; Mr A. E. Hunt, Fishponds, Bristol; Mrs C. Hunt, Buckland Monachorum; Mrs M. E. Hunt, St James Sch., Hereford; W. Hurst, St Thomas More Girls' Sch., Newtown; M. Hyatt, Parbold Sch., Standish; Mrs Hanron; Very Rev. H. C. L. Heywood, Southwell; Mrs Hooton and Mr Hickey, Irthing Valley Sch., Brampton, Cumberland; Mr John Hull; Mr G. L. Heawood, Midhurst.

K. F. Ireland, Hartshill High Sch., Warwickshire.

Mr D. C. James, Chiswick Comp. Sch.; Mr F. D. James, St Bedes Sch., South Shields; M. E. James, Heathfield House High Sch., Cardiff; Mrs E. Jans, Hose C.E. P. Sch.; Mr E. A. Jenkins, Rushden; Mr T. J. Johnson; M. Johnston, St Edward's Inf. Dept., Newtown; Mrs A. S. Jones, St Albans Inf. Sch., Cardiff; Mr G. H. Jones, Kingshurst, Birmingham; Mr H. Jones, Mold; Mr P. L. Jones, St Joseph's R.C. Comp. Sch., Swindon; F. G. Jordan, St Mary's R.C. P. Sch., Standishgate; Sister Joseph, Sacred Heart Inf. Sch., Wigan; Sister Josepha, St Wulstan's P. Sch., Fleetwood; M. Joyce, St Michael's Sch., Chatham; K. E. Jukes, Barnet; Sister Julie, St Thomas More Sch., Wigan; Rev. R. P. Johnston, Islington.

Mr H. Kelley, South Harrow; Dr E. L. Kendall, Canterbury; Miss J. M. Kendrick, Stockport; Mr J. Kennedy, SS. Peter and Paul R.C. Sch., St Helens; Mrs D. Kenniford, Paddock House Convent Grammar Sch., Oswaldtwistle; Mrs M. A. Kerr, Southbourne; J. Killaren, Our Lady and All Saints R.C. Sch., Parbold; Miss E. King, West Hampstead; Miss J. M. Kneale, London W; A. Kneen, Peel; Mr N. E. H. Knight, London W.C; Mrs R. Knight, Aberdeen; Rev. S. H. Knight, London W.C.

P. Lander, St Mary's Jnr Sch., Fleetwood; Miss B. Lanigan, Paddock House Sch., Accrington; W. Laxton, Southsea; Miss W. R. Lazzari, St Mary's P. Sch., Newcastle; Miss J. Leahy, St Patrick's Inf. Sch., Grangetown; Mr A. Ledger, Oxford; Mr E. W. Leggatt, Simms Cross County Jnr Sch., Widnes; V. Leleux, Northampton; Mrs S. Lemagnen, St Joseph's R.C. P. Sch., Derby; A. Lenagan, St Patrick's Inf. Sch., Wigan; Miss M. C. Lenton, St Michael's R.C. P. Sch., Chatham; Mr. J. Levitt, Leek; D. H. C. Lewis, Lichfield; B. Livesey, Holy Family R.C. Sch., Aspull; Mrs F. E. Lloyd, St Joseph's Comp. Sch., Swindon; G. Lloyd, Tonna, Neath; J. N. Lloyd, Barrow Hill J.M. Sch., London N.W; Miss S. Lloyd, Parkfield Cedars Girls' Grammar Sch., Derby; Sister M. Lomax, St Thomas More Sec. Sch., Newtown; M. W. Lonsdale, St Cuthbert's Inf. Sch., Wigan; Rev. A. G. Loosemore, Wakefield; Sister Mary Loyola, Paddock House Convent Grammar Sch., Accrington; A. Lund, St Cuthbert's R.C. Sch., Pemberton; Miss M. Lunn, Almondbury C.E. Sch., Huddersfield; Mr F. G. Lyne, Birmingham; Rev. J. Livingstone, London.

H. A. MacDonald, Bishop Wulston High Sch.; M. E. McAlpine, Walcot,

Swindon; Mr S. C. McCallion, Cardinal Wiseman Sec. Sch., Coventry; J. McCarthy, St Mary's R.C. Jnr Sch., Cardiff; Mr J. McCaughey, London S.W; Mrs M. A. McGawley, St Maries R.C. Inf. Sch., Rugby; Mr W. J. McKeough, Gravesend; Miss E. McNulty, Cadishead; Mr R. Y. McNulty, Northampton; N. M. McSweenup, St Mary's R.C. Jnr Sch., Cardiff; A. Madden, St Illtyd's R.C. Sch., Swansea; Mr M. Madden, London S.W; Mr N. B. Maginness, Cardinal Wiseman S.M. Boys' Sch., Coventry; Mrs V. M. Malley, Sacred Heart Inf. Sch., Wigan; Mr H. Malir, Blessed John Payne R.C. Sch., Chelmsford; Mr D. Marcus, Barnet; Sister Marie, St Wulstan's P. Sch., Fleetwood; M. C. Marsland, St Wulstan's P. Sch., Fleetwood; Brother Martin, s.s.f., Dorchester; Mr E. F. Masters, Orpington; Mr J. W. Makins, Saundersfoot; Mrs M. T. Matthews, Sacred Heart Inf. Sch., Wigan; Miss B. Mawby, Shenfield; Miss M. Maxwell, St Mary's Jnr Sch., Fleetwood; Lt C. May, Plymouth; A. Maybin, St Mary's R.C. P. Sch., Enfield; E. Mayo, Macefield C.S. Sch., Warley; Mr H. F. Mellon, S. S. Fisher-More R.C. Sec. Sch., Widnes; Mrs V. E. Mercer, St Theresa's Inf. Sch., St Helens; W. Metcalfe, Bradford; Mrs A. E. Milan; Mr E. R. Milford; M. E. Miller, St John's R.C. Sch., Wigan; Mr H. Milne, Edinburgh; Mr R. G. Mitchell, Upper Poppleton; M. M. Molloy, St Mary's Jnr Sch., Fleetwood; Miss J. Molyneux, Micklefield Sch., Reigate; A. Moore, St Oswald's P. Sch., Ashton-in-Makerfield; Mr J. Moore, Coventry; D. Moran, St Illtyd's R.C. Sch., Danygraig; Miss E. Morgan, Selattyn C.E. Sch., Salop; E. D. Morgan, Newcastle; Mr G. R. Morgan, Colwyn High Sch., Colwyn Bay; Mrs M. Morley, Oadby; R. W. Morley, Queen Edith S.M. Sch., Cambridge; Mr T. W. Morley, Canada; Mr B. Morris, Monkton Combe Jnr Sch., Bath; Mrs K. Mouat, Cuckfield; Miss A. Mulholland, St Bede's Inf. Sch., Jarrow; C. Mullaghy, Paddock House Convent, Accrington; Mrs D. Munday, Wheathampstead; Mr S. Munns, Derby; A. Murphy, St Illtyd's R.C. Sch., Swansea; Mrs P. MacNair, London.

Mr P. M. Newton, Birmingham; A. Nelson, St Anne's County Sec. Girls' Sch., Fareham; Rev. C. M. G. Nesbitt, London N.W; J. Nettleship, West Bromwich Grammar Sch.; B. Nevin, Edmund Arrowsmith Sec. Sch., Ashton-in-Makerfield; Miss F. E. A. Newbigin, Newcastle; Mr T. W. Nightingale, Bishop Auckland; Deaconess A. L. M. Nokes, Portsmouth; Mr R. H. Norbury, St Edmundsbury & Ipswich; Mr A. K. Northey, Edmund Arrowsmith Sec. Sch., Ashton-in-Makerfield; Lord Nugent of Guildford, London S.W; Professor W. R. Niblett, London.

Sister C. O'Brien, St Patrick's Open Air Sch., Hayling Island; H. C. O'Donnell, Paddock House Grammar Sch., Accrington; C. O'Keefe, St Illtyd's R.C. Sch., Swansea; D. and J. M. O'Keefe, Ealing; E. O'Neil, St Joseph's R.C. Sch., Wigan; Mr G. Oliver, Southend High Sch.; Mr F. B. Olney, St Mary's R.C. Boys' Sch., Burnley; Mr E. M. Osman, St Wulstan's Primary Sch., Fleetwood; Mrs U. Ouley, Girls' County Sec. Sch., Arnold; Our Lady of Mount Carmel, St Helens (Head and 20 staff); Canon H. S. O'Neill, Derby.

D. J. Phillpot, Hereford; Mr John Prickett, B.C.C. London; Very Rev. P. Pare, Wakefield; Mrs K. Palmer, London W.11; K. W. Palmer, Aspull Holy Family, Wigan; Miss F. Parker, Stoneleigh W. County Jnr Sch.; J. R. Parkin, New Close Primary Sch., Warminster; M. Parry, Manchester; Mr B. Partington, Sodor and Man; Rev. C. T. L. Payne, London S.W.2; M. V. Pearson, Muswell Hill, London N.10; Mr R. Peck; Mrs A. Pennington, Aspatria Jnr Sch., Cumberland; Mr B. Perry, Lady Bay County Jnr Sch., Nottingham; Miss E. M. Peters, Darland Sec.

Sch., Rossett; Mr R. S. Peters, Malvern Link; M. C. Petersen, St Patricks Inf. Sch., Grangetown; Miss E. P. Phenis, St Albans Inf. Sch., Cardiff; Mr G. B. Phillipson, Canterbury; Mrs B. Pilbeam, Chester; Mr A. I. Polack, London S.W.3; M. Poulton, Parbold R.C. Sch., Wigan; Mrs J. Pratt, East Suffolk Inf. Sch.; F. Price, St Thomas More Sch., Wigan; Miss M. Priest, Girls' County Sec. Sch., Arnold; I. M. Prior, St John's R.C. Primary Sch., Wigan; Mr R. H. Pryke, Leicester; Mrs S. Purdue, Bengeo, Hertford; Mr C. D. Pugh, Tilney All Saints P. Sch., Kings Lynn; Mrs I. Querfurth, Barnet; G. Quinn, Sodor and Man.

Mr G. H. Rackham, Abbotswood County Primary Sch., Southampton; M. V. Radclyffe, Lydney; Mr P. J. Rainsford, Langley Sch., Sutton Coldfield; C. B. Raithby, Mrs Mary King's P. Sch., Lincoln; S. Ramsdale, St Edwards Jnr Sch., Newtown; Mr P. B. Rance, Hertingfordbury Primary Sch., Hertford; Miss T. Rawcliffe, Paddock House Grammar Sch., Oswaldtwistle; K. W. Reed; Mr R. D. Reed, Ulcombe; Mrs A. W. Reilly, St Vincents Inf. Sch., St Helens; Miss M. Rein, St Patrick Inf. Sch., Cardiff; Mr D. H. Renhard, Halesowen; Miss M. J. Renton, Port Erin; Miss J. R. Reynolds, Dukeries Comp. Sch., New Ollerton; Miss P. Richards, Grove Park Grammar Sch., Wrexham; Rev. D. Richard, Durlaston; Mr G. Richardson, Paddock House Convent Grammar Sch., Accrington; M. Richardson, Arnold County Sec. Sch., Nottingham; P. Richardson, Guildford; F. M. Rimmer, St Cuthberts Inf. Sch., Pemberton; G. Robertson, London N.12; A. C. Robinson, St Joseph's Comp. Sch., Swindon; Mrs L. Y. Robinson, Hipperholme Inf. Sch., Brighouse; Mrs M. Robinson, Aspatria Jnr Sch., Cumberland; Mr P. Robinson, Wollaston; B. G. Robson, Doncaster; Mr W. E. Rogers, Hose C.E. Sch., Leicestershire; H. J. Rooney, Minster in Sheppey; E. Rourke, St Patrick's Inf. Sch., Wigan; Mr A. J. Rowe, Nicholas County Sec. Sch., Basildon; K. A. F. Ruddy, St Theresas R.C. Sch., Sheffield; H. Rushforth; Mr G. Rust, King Edward VI Sch., Southampton; T. A. Ryan, St John's R.C. Primary Sch., Wigan; Mr K. J. Ryder, Welling; Mr H. W. Rye, Oxford; P. Reeves.

St Mary's C.E. Sch., Barnsley; Mr W. J. Samuda, Harwich; Lt Col. G. A. I. Sanders, Wells; Miss M. Sattersfield, Holy Family Sch., New Springs, Wigan; Mr C. E. Savage, Shipley; Mr R. Schofield, Criggleston Sch., Wakefield; Mrs J. Schrecker, West Twerton Girls' S.M. Sch., Bath; E. R. Seeds, Plymouth; D. Selmer, Bebington County Sec. Sch. for Girls, New Ferry; Rev. A. Shackleton, Middleton Junction, Manchester; Miss J. M. Shandley, St John Fisher Girls' Sch., Wigan; B. Shanks, Barnards Green; Mrs E. M. Sharratt, Upper Basildon; Mr J. P. Shaw, Cardinal Wiseman Sec. Sch., Coventry; Miss D. B. Shea, St Francis R.C. Sch., Caterham; M. J. Shepherd, St John's Inf. Sch., Wigan; M. A. Sherriff, Holy Family Sch., Aspull, Wigan; Bishop of Sherwood; Miss G. Sinfield, Knowle, Bristol; Mr H. Shipley, Ilford; C. B. Short, St Alban's R.C. Inf. Sch., Splott, Cardiff; Mr P. Sills, Wimbledon; G. E. M. Simmons, London E.C.2; W. Sing. Paddock House Grammar Sch., Oswaldtwistle; Mr C. J. Skews, Twickenham; Mr A. Simpson, Flixton, Manchester; Mr B. F. Slater, Henley; Miss D. C. Slee, Bolton; Mr Smail; Headmaster and Staff, St Peter's Day Sch., Mansfield; M. A. Smart, Batley Birstall Raikes Lane C.E. Inf. Sch.; A. J. Smith, Chicester; Mr B. J. Rushby-Smith, Southwell; M. Smith, St Thomas More Girls' Sch., Wigan; Mrs D. Speakman, Morecambe; M. H. Spear, St Patrick's Inf. Sch., Grangetown; Mr R. Speer, Horesehouse; N. V. Spencer, Darlington; J. T. Spence, Hereford; Mr D. Staples, Sheffield; Mr I. A. Stapleton, London N.W.3; Sister Stephanie, St Joseph's R.C. Primary Sch., Dorking; Mr D. Stephens, Blue Coat Sec. Sch., Dudley; Mr B. Stigant, Laxey; Miss J. Straker,

Secular Humanism Promotion Unit; Mr S. Street, Leominster; Miss D. Stucky, St Mary's R.C. Sch., Enfield; Mr R. A. Summers, Maidstone; P. W. Sutcliffe, St Joseph's R.C. Primary Sch., Derby; M. Sutton, Gillingham; Mr W. Swift, Addington Park; W. Swift, St Oswald's Primary Sch., Ashton-in-Makerfield; Mrs J. Symons, Paignton; Sister M. Syra, St Mary's R.C. Sch., Cardiff.

Mr R. H. Tasker; Mr R. G. Tee, Calverley; Mr D. W. Thacker, Willerby County Sec. Sch.; J. Thomas, St Wulstan's Primary Sch., Fleetwood; V. C. Thomas, St Joseph's R.C. Primary Sch., Derby; T. Thomlinson, Lichfield; Mr G. V. Thompson, Aldersbrook County Sec. Sch., London E.12; Mrs J. M. R. Thompson, Twigworth; Mr R. D. Thompson, Sladen C.E. Sec. Sch., Kidderminster; A. Thompson; J. Thomson, Dundee; Mrs M. Thorpe, Paddock House Convent Grammar Sch., Oswaldtwistle; Mrs E. Titheradge, Barnet; Mr W. N. Todd, Burnham-on-Sea; K. M. Tolfree, Quarles Girls Sec. Sch., Romford; Miss M. Tolfree, Romford; Mr R. Townsend, St Joseph's R.C. Comp. Sch., Swindon; Mr T. Toman, Clough Hall Comp. Sch., Kidsgrove; Miss N. Traynor, Eldon Sec. Sch., London N.9; R. Troll, St Joseph's Comp. Sch., Swindon; Rev. A. E. F. Trotman, Salisbury; D. H. Turner; Mr J. Turner, St Peter's Sec. Sch., Orrell.

M. C. Upton, Rochester; Miss M. A. Urquhart.

Mr J. Van Hear, Falmouth; Rev. R. P. Vaizey, Bocking; M. M. Veasey, St Patrick's Inf. Sch., Wigan; H. M. Venables, Southwell.

K. Waddington, Edmund Arrowsmith Sec. Sch., Ashton-in-Makerfield; A. M. Wade-Dutton, Ramsey; Mr D. Wainman, Knaphill; S. G. Walker, Bridgwater; Mr A. Walsh, Bristol; Mr A. St G. Walsh, King's Sch., Chester; Mr E. G. Ward; Miss K. Warren, Cheam County Jnr Sch., P. T. Watson, Richmond C.P. Sch.; Sheerness; Mr D. Webb; Mr J. A. Webb, St Joseph's Comp. Sch., Stratton St Margaret; Mrs J. R. Webster, St Vincent's Sch., St Helens; Mr M. E. Webster, Manchester; Mr E. N. Wellington, Birchwood C.P., Sch., Swanley; G. F. Westcott, Sutton; Mr J. Whettem, Bristol; Mrs M. Whetton, Knowsley Longview Jnr Sch., Liverpool; Mr R. B. White; Mr H. White, St Teresa's Jnr Sch., St Helens; M. Whittle, Edmund Arrowsmith Sec. Sch., Ashton-in-Makerfield; Mrs C. Wild, East Suffolk Inf. Sch., Mrs D. Wild, Aspatria Jnr Sch., Cumberland; Mrs M. E. Wilkes, Islington, London; J. I. M. Wilkinson, Immaculate Conception Sch., Chelmsford; M. Wilkinson, Kinver; Mr A. Williams, St Thomas More Girls' Sch., Wigan; Mr A. W. Williams, Llangollen; Mr D. Williams, St Thomas More Girls' Sch., Wigan; Mrs M. Williams, Girls' County Sec. Sch., Arnold; M. G. Williams, St Joseph's Primary Sch., Derby; Mrs S. E. Williams, Frinton-on-Sea; Mr E. Wilmore, Canberra Jnr Sch., London W.12; Mr J. A. Wilson, Clarence Jnr Sch., Swindon; M. P. Wilson, Sacred Heart Primary Sch., Barrow; Sister Winifred, St Teresa's Inf. Sch., Newtown; R. M. Winter, Norwich; G. R. Wiskin; Mrs A. Wood, Belle Vue Inf. Sch., Wordsley; Mr D. Wood, C.E. Sch., Royston; Mr D. A. Wood, Newcastle; W. Wood, St Mary's Primary Sch., Newcastle; Miss T. Woodhall, Littleborough; Mr A. F. Woodhurst, Romford Tech. High Sch.; Mr S. R. Woods, Epsom; Miss M. N. Woolfe, Old Hutton Ch. Sch., Westmorland; Mrs J. Worsley, St Vincent's Inf. Sch., St Helens; Chief Education Officer, Wiltshire.

Mr B. R. Youngman, Brooke, Norwich.

F.M.J., W.J.C., D.A.B., and 43 unsigned or with illegible signatures.

A SELECTION OF EVIDENCE RECEIVED
FROM VARIOUS ORGANIZATIONS

ASSOCIATION OF CHIEF EDUCATION OFFICERS

Introduction

In submitting their views on religious education in schools in reply to the questionnaire circulated by the Commission, the Association wish to state that they welcome the opportunity of expressing their views on this important part of the curriculum and life of the schools in this country. The Association recognize that the Education Act of 1944 gave to local authorities a difficult task when it told them to foster the spiritual and moral development of children in the schools. They would like to state at the outset, however, that the Association firmly believe that religious education should continue to form part of the curriculum of primary and secondary schools. The Association recognize that in submitting this view they are also representing the view of the majority of parents who wish to retain religious education in the school curriculum even though the motives of many parents in this connection are very mixed. The conservative among parents largely support an evangelical approach, while others are less clear in their motives. It should be recognized, however, that there is a minority who would wish to see religious education taken out of the curriculum with its place taken by general moral and ethical teaching.

The Association would draw the attention of the Commission to changes in the approaches to this subject which have occurred in the country generally since the war, changes which are perhaps exemplified by many of the recommendations of the Newsom Report of 1963 and the Plowden Report of 1966. The changes in the moral attitudes of society as reflected in the schools have made the work of the teacher of religious education much more difficult than in the past. While pupils in primary schools can accept teaching that depends largely on an authoritarian approach, when children reach the secondary stage and are mature enough to be critical, the young person is likely to reject all religious values which seem to depend on an undisputed authority. The Association recommend the need for change brought about by the increased numbers of pupils who remain at school until they are 16, 17, or 18 years of age.

The Association would suggest that it is almost impossible to change religious education in schools without having parallel changes in the religious education and teaching offered by the Churches to adults; and that what happens in the schools must be reflected in what might be called the adult concept of religious education, and, if the schools are asked to be realistic in their approach to the subject, this will have its effect upon the wider teaching practice of the Churches.

Section A

1 With reservations about the use of the words "should" and "however defined", the Association would strongly support the view that religious education should form part of the curriculum of all types of school. The question, however, cannot be fully answered without defining what is meant by the term "religious education" and without defining how

the subject is approached in the class-room. The Association would wish to emphasize that they do not see religious education in denominational terms, neither do they see it as being solely concerned with the Christian doctrine. As far as teaching is concerned, the Association would emphasize the necessity for voluntary specialization at the primary school level, and at the secondary stage the necessity for a complete reappraisal on the lines of ch. 7 of the Newsom Report, "Spiritual and Moral Development".

2 With an affirmative answer to Question 1, there would appear to be no need for an answer to this question. Perhaps it may, however, be emphasized that the affirmative answer to Question 1 envisages a much wider interpretation of religious education than many have placed upon it in the past. The Association would draw the Commission's attention to paras. 165 and 166 of the Newsom Report.

3 The view most widely held by the Association is that compulsion results in unwilling teachers being involved in the subject. The Association feel that the compulsory provisions of the 1944 Act may well have lessened the influence of religious education in the schools. While the Association are inclined to the view that religious education should cease to be legally compulsory, they would firmly maintain that it must be recognized as an essential component part of the curriculum.

4 The Association feel generally that the existing safeguards are satisfactory. Some members feel that the attention of parents should be drawn more positively than hitherto to the provision for opting out. The Association recognize that there is a danger that any attempt to modify existing safeguards might be interpreted as an encouragement to avoid the general rule. The Association emphasize, however, that, where children are withdrawn from religious education, the schools should provide some other useful educational activity for the children concerned.

5 The Association do not consider that any additional legal safeguards are necessary.

6 The Association would answer in the affirmative to both parts of this question. Immigrants of other faiths should be treated as parents who withdraw their children on conscientious grounds. Where it is possible for reasonable special arrangements to be made, this should be adopted. At the same time the Association considers that the Religious Education syllabus of schools in this country should remain Christian and undenominational.

7 The majority view of the Association is that a daily act of corporate worship should not be a statutory obligation. The Association recognize, however, the difficulty in which the removal of obligation would place many headmasters and headmistresses. The Association endorse the views as set out in para. 174 of the Newsom Report and affirm that many of the Association's members are impressed by the reality which regularly marks many school services. They would also endorse paras.

570 and 571 of the Plowden Report. They would suggest that the fact that for many young people school assembly and corporate worship has little meaning is more due to the individuals who are taking the assembly than to the fact of the assembly itself.

8 The Association entirely endorse the suggestion made in the question and would support any encouragement of experiment and variety in the ways in which schools might organize alternatives to the corporate act of worship.

9 The majority view is that there is still a place for voluntary aided schools, although it seems that there is less support for the retention of controlled schools. It should, however, be stated that there is a strong minority view in the Association expressing doubt as to the need for the retention of denominational schools in the educational system. It is, however, emphasized that this is a minority view which has not taken full account of the views of parents who often at some inconvenience elect to send their children to a denominational school.

It is difficult to argue for the retention of voluntary controlled status.

10 The Association is strongly against the complete secularization of public education and are of the opinion that the legal prohibition of religious teaching would be more dangerous than the present legal compulsion. The Association would endorse the recommendations of the Newsom Report set out at the conclusion of ch. 7.

Section B

Among comments made by members under this section were those expressing approval of the latest agreed syllabus being published and they indicate that more are being considered by L.E.A.s generally. In general the majority of the comments which the Association would make under Section B are to be found in ch. 7 of the Newsom Report and section A of ch. 17 of the Plowden Report. The Association would support the recommendations at the end of each of these sections.

NATIONAL ASSOCIATION OF
DIVISIONAL EXECUTIVES FOR EDUCATION

N.A.D.E.E. is a body concerned with the administration of education. It is questionable how far it is competent to comment on the major policy problems involved in the religious settlement embodied in the law of education. The Executive Committee decided however that an effort should be made to contribute to the enquiry being undertaken by the Commission on Religious Education.

The Executive have confined themselves to the questionnaire as submitted, although they have found the terms of the questionnaire sometimes very difficult to answer and considered that the complete statement made in reply to the questionnaire inevitably gave an inadequate expression to the issues involved in religious education in schools.

Answers to the Commission's questions (p. 288 above) are as follows:

1 The Committee were unanimous in their view that religious education, however defined, should form part of the curriculum of all types of primary and secondary schools. "However defined" covers an enormous range. "Religious education" as stated could embrace a complete survey of the religions of the world, and certain conditions arise even in this country where religious education means education in a faith that is non-Christian. For the purposes of this paper, however, religious education may be taken to mean instruction in the beliefs and practices of the Christian Church. This involves the presentation at a level the pupil can understand of its forms of worship and of its basic philosophic principles. It is almost impossible to produce a lowest common measure of Christian doctrine but for school purposes it includes belief in:

(a) Fundamental creation by a person, in the sense we understand "person", for a good purpose, in the sense we understand "good". Without the concepts of God, creation, purpose, good, the world has no meaning. In general religion we are concerned with these concepts at all levels of human experience; in religious education we are concerned with them to the extent that they can be understood by pupils in primary and secondary schools.
(b) The exemplification of creation, purpose, and moral values in the life of Christ, as recorded in the New Testament.
(c) The association of the Christian belief and way of life with personal and social moral qualities. The acceptance that the highest level of human moral achievement is reached in Christian experience.

The case for teaching religious knowledge and worship in schools is based on the assumption that it can help pupils to find a faith to live by—that there is a purpose in living. The Newsom Report put it that education is a task in fostering spiritual and moral development. "Most boys and girls want to be what they call 'being good' and they
11

want to know what this really implies in the personal situations that confront them." "They also want to know what kind of animal man is and whether ultimately each one of them matters and if so why and to whom."

The case for religious education being part of the curriculum of all schools rests on this well-being of individual children rather than the wishes of their parents or the need to strengthen religious institutions. But the deep concern of parents that their children shall receive the spiritual benefits of a religious education, and the widely accepted view that by so doing, moral standards (both individual and communal) will be raised, are important reasons. Schools generally claim some measure of responsibility for the moral standards and welfare of their pupils (or at least, putting it negatively, they rarely disclaim such responsibility). Similarly, however much or little practised, religious activity is an integral part of the school life and any scheme of education which deliberately ignored it would of necessity be distorted.

2 If the first question is answered in the affirmative, the second does not arise logically. But if it is in this way suggested that moral and ethical instruction can be given only as part of a curriculum of religious education, and that moral and ethical instruction is something which can be provided either in religious education or by some other method, the conception must be denied. It may be true that religious education affords a way of developing moral and ethical ideas but it is not the only way. It has no monopoly of virtue. The words "not form" and "replace" are loaded. If all Christian teaching in schools were banned, qualities such as truth, integrity, moral grandeur would not cease to be important nor cease to be taught. It may well be that the most satisfactory way of approaching moral and ethical training is through the inculcation of religious beliefs supported by a high standard of performance in school and at home, but it is not exclusive. A saint can grow up despite a vicious home and a pagan education. So that although the answer to the second question as framed is "no", the question carries overtones which ought to be resisted.

3 If the answer to Question 1 is in the affirmative, then some form of compulsion is implicit. One cannot assert that religious education should form part of the curriculum of all types of schools and go on to say that it is optional. But once the attitude of compulsion is emphasized, the value of religious education is weakened. If it is to be part of the curriculum of all schools, then someone has got to frame the curriculum, someone has got to teach it, and the pupils have got to receive it. "Compulsion" and "moral values" are ill bedfellows. The more the element of compulsion has to be retained, the less it is likely to achieve its purpose. The present law divides religious instruction from religious worship in such a way as to encourage pupils to believe that an act of worship is sharply distinct from the study of religious ideas. However, there is a world of difference between the formulated settlement expressed in the Education Act of 1944 and the actual

practice in the schools. If the terms of the Act were carried out in detail, the education service would come to a grinding halt. Fortunately the good sense of authorities and teachers and the invaluable capacity of children to "switch off" prevents a chaotic situation arising. Section 25 of the 1944 Education Act would be unworkable if it were followed literally. The Department of Education, for example, allows the building of new schools and the continuance of older ones where a single act of worship by all pupils is impracticable. Section 25(3) states that it shall not be required as a condition of any pupil attending any county school or any voluntary school that he shall attend or abstain from attending any Sunday school or any place of worship, but in circumstances of pressure on accommodation this happens frequently. In practice the legalistic statement contained within the Education Act has softened into a general toleration. Reserve powers are effective provided they are never invoked. The real difficulty in advocating any change is that none would be workable if enforced. The weakness of leaving matters as they are is that the legislative sanctions have degenerated into an archaic pretence inconsistent with the vital importance of the subject they regulate.

4 Assuming religious education continues to be compulsory, it is essential that the rights of parents and of senior pupils should be respected. At present the law provides that the parents can withdraw their children from religious worship and instruction. Now that large fifth and sixth forms have been established, it would be reasonable to extend the right to young people on their own account. It is essential that head teachers and governing bodies should make the opportunity of withdrawal real and yet unobtrusive. Just as a head teacher ought not to be allowed to decide against the inclusion of religious education in the curriculum which would result in a personal decision overriding a majority one, so a head teacher ought not to be in a position to make withdrawal from religious education a calculated and obvious defiance of the school practice. At the earliest possible age the wishes of young people themselves ought to be respected. Nothing is more damaging to religion than compulsory religious instruction taught by indifferent teachers to sceptical young people.

5 There should be a clear statement in the Education Act that no teacher (in other than an aided school—see 9) should be required to undertake the teaching of religious instruction as a subject or to participate in acts of corporate worship. We ought to move away from the idea that Religious Education is the only compulsory subject on the time-table and move towards the acceptance of it as a subject in its own right in the same way that we accept English, Mathematics, Science. Compulsion by legislative decree in matters of religion in the end defeats itself. On the positive side there should be greater opportunities for the subject to rank as a major one, in respect of number of specialists, heads of departments, equipment and allowances, and in the facilities for courses and in-service training. If a teacher takes a post specifically

advertised as one for the teaching of religious education, he should expect to undertake the specialist training and become highly competent in the discipline and teaching methods appropriate, but no teacher, as a condition of his appointment to the staff of a school, should be required to undertake the teaching of the subject. The difficulty about this matter is that one cannot legislate about the exceptional. The normal arrangements which now apply are generally accepted.

6 It seems obvious that any future legislation relating to religious education should protect the position of immigrant minorities.

7 It would be an advantage to remove the obligation for a daily act of worship while at the same time giving every encouragement to a higher standard of performance. A central place designed for worship by a few is better than a vast concert-cum-gymnasium-cum-dining-cum-assembly hall which lacks all religious character. Nothing could be worse than a perfunctory or obviously rushed religious observance in which the notices, admonitions, and injunctions dominate the proceedings. At all costs a daily religious service with a mechanical ring about its formality ought to be avoided. If it degenerates into an irksome daily task, it is worse than useless—it is insidiously destructive of faith.

In many new schools it is physically impossible to assemble all the pupils, and despite the reservations in section 25 it is noticeable that the Department has approved new constructions in which compliance with the Act is impossible. This does not mean that in church voluntary schools it should not be retained as a major feature, nor that the staff of local authority schools should not be encouraged to consider an act of religious worship as a highly desirable feature of school life. But if it has to be enforced by statutory obligation in order for it to take place at all, the contribution it makes to spiritual welfare is likely to be very low.

8 It is equally undesirable to impose a standard pattern of weekly assembly, house assembly, form room assembly, in substitution for the daily act of worship. It does not become better by being intermittent or selective. Quality is likely to be achieved in an atmosphere of permissive striving for high standards rather than rigorous requirement. There is, however, a great deal to be said for the inspiration that comes to the school from a well-led and devotionally sincere act of common worship.

9 There is still a place within the English educational system for denominational schools of the aided type, but only provided there is genuine alternative accommodation available for parents who do not wish their children to attend them. Such schools should continue to function as part of local authority schools provision. Since their pupils come in the main from religious minded homes, the link between home and school in these church schools should be exceptionally close. There

is no case on essentially religious grounds for continuing the "controlled" school as it has been known. The elaborate checks and safeguards of reserved teachers have been largely forgotten. Very rarely does a teacher receive appointment as, or think of himself as, a "reserved" teacher. In many instances the link between Church and school has remained, but it has come to be based upon common service to the local community rather than the statutory provisions of the Education Act. The enthusiasm of the diocesan authorities to replace older controlled schools has been very limited.

Some of our members, however, consider that, religious principles apart, there is a case for retaining controlled schools despite the anomalies of the scheme and its unenforceable provisions. Its advantages to the local education authority are (1) the limited church access, where the Church holds few rights but retains some opportunities, avoids divided command in appointments and day to day direction; (2) its physical maintenance is not limited by church financial shortages nor confused by shared responsibilities.

10 We would not favour a complete secularization of public education at the primary and secondary stage, although it has become a feature of the further education institutions (other than the Church founded colleges of education) that they have few facilities for religious teaching. There appears to have been very little pressure from church authorities towards the introduction of more organized emphasis on religious education in colleges of further education.

ASSOCIATION OF HEADMASTERS

Before the Commission under the Bishop of Durham had been formed, the question of religious education in schools had been considered by the Joint Council of Heads, consisting of members of the Headmasters' Association, the Headmasters' Conference, the Association of Head Mistresses, and the National Association of Head Teachers. A statement was drawn up in 1966 and finally approved by the four constituent members of the Council at the beginning of 1967 in the following terms:

We, the representatives of the undermentioned associations, constituting the Joint Council of Heads, are strongly of the opinion that the criticism of Religious Education which is being expressed in some quarters represents the views of a vociferous minority and does not represent the views of the majority of teachers and parents.

We accept the need for the possible revision and adaptation of the Agreed Syllabus, in those areas where such review has not already been or is not at present being carried out, but we are convinced that the teaching of religion is an essential part of education. We also believe that the majority of parents wish it to be included in the school curriculum, whether they claim to be Christian themselves or not. Moral teaching is not enough.

We recognize:
1 that the relevant sections of the 1944 Education Act need some revision and amendment;
2 that there is a need for more specialists in religious education in all types of school and, therefore, for increased facilities for training;
3 that religious advisers can give considerable help to teachers and should be appointed in all areas.

We believe:
1 that religious education is a most important part of the curriculum and of school life;
2 that Christianity, a precious part of our heritage, should be taught not only as a study of a major world religion but as a way of life;
3 that the Morning Assembly can be a vital and real experience in the daily life of the School and as such should be preserved.

THE HEADMASTERS' CONFERENCE
THE ASSOCIATION OF HEAD MISTRESSES
THE HEADMASTERS' ASSOCIATION
THE NATIONAL ASSOCIATION OF HEAD TEACHERS

Section A

It will be evident that this statement covers some of the topics which are the concern of the Commission; but, as the whole question is of such importance, affecting the deepest beliefs of men and women, we have consulted our members again and the questionnaire has been sent out to the eighteen Divisions in England, Wales, and Northern Ireland which constitute the Association. We should be less than frank if we did not say at the outset that, having studied the questionnaire, many of our members have been surprised and disturbed by what they consider to be its inadequacy.

In the words of one of our Divisions in the North of England, "particular objection was taken to the key Question 1". It is just not good enough for the Commission to put "however defined" after "Religious Education" when they ask whether or not it should form part of the curriculum of schools. A question left without definition becomes meaningless. Members of the Commission are better informed than most people about the wide connotation that can be given to the word "religious", and, if the definition is left vague enough, it is possible to say that no school claiming to be a community can avoid some form of religious education even though the common convictions binding its members together need not be those of the Christian faith. The use of the word "curriculum" in this question would almost suggest that the Commission has confused "religious education" with "religious instruction". It would seem to be inapt, if not inept, to talk about religious education almost as if it were a subject on the time-table when everyone knows that, in so far as it takes place in a school, religious education arises out of the whole way of life and the personal relationships which go to make the school what it is. The fact that all this has been discussed at great length in many books, notably *Christian Education in a Secular Society*, by W. R. Niblett (O.U.P. 1960), makes us all the more surprised to find the question put in such terms in 1968. From these comments on Question 1 it will be obvious that we do not consider it profitable to say anything further in reply to Question 2.

The confusion becomes really serious in Question 3. The word "it" can only refer back to "religious education" in Question 1, and, as every schoolmaster knows, religious education has never been and in the nature of things never could be compulsory by law. About the compulsory provisions in the 1944 Act for Religious Instruction in School we are divided. Not only the humanists but some of the staunchest Christians among us are deeply unhappy about a situation in which Christian teaching is a legal requirement. Nevertheless, for two main reasons the majority of us would not favour a mere rescinding of the law as it now stands. The civilization to which we belong has been profoundly affected by Christian belief and in such circumstances it is a proper part of the education of any boy or girl to be made aware of what Christian belief is. Secondly, as headmasters responsible for the drawing up of a time-table, we know how easy it is to overestimate the significance of a phrase such as "the compulsory provisions of the Act". There are many forms of compulsion exerted on a school time-table and the clauses on religion in the 1944 Act are only one of them. New subjects are continually clamouring for a place while old subjects demand more time and devices such as a six-or ten-day week are hardly adequate to provide space for the multitudinous demands. Pressures such as those exerted by university entrance faculty requirements or those of professional bodies are no less compelling because they are not incorporated in an Act of Parliament.

The next three questions, 4, 5, and 6, are fairly close linked and we do not think that any legal changes are required in respect of any of them. What can be done in school will depend on the facilities available to the headmaster and, above everything else, on the number of boys and girls who wish to withdraw. It is surely unnecessary to remind members of the Commission that the Act does not require schools to give Christian teaching. What is to be included under the term "religious instruction" is decided by the Committee constituted according to the terms laid down in Schedule v of the Act. There is nothing to prevent the inclusion in an Agreed Syllabus of the study of Buddhism or Hinduism or the Muslim religion in any area where such teaching was deemed more appropriate than a study of the Bible.

Like Question 3, Question 7 revealed deep differences of opinion among our members. Most of us still think that it would not be wise to have a "free for all" among schools in the provision of a daily act of worship, but the majority is smaller than in the answer to Question 3 and there is a general desire for a more flexible approach. We can see no good reason why a headmaster should need to break the law if he wishes on occasions to have his school assembly at the end rather than the beginning of the day. As the size of secondary schools increases, the proportion of them without a hall capable of accommodating all the pupils is becoming so great that, of itself, it is an argument against continuing the requirements for "a single act of worship attended by all such pupils", but apart from the merely physical difficulties we do not think it educationally desirable always to have the same assembly for boys and girls of eleven and young men and women of 18 or 19. We think there is everything to be said for separate assemblies at the discretion of the Head of the school and indeed this has become a common practice in spite of the law. It is also to be noted that, when the 1944 Act was promulgated, no one envisaged the enormous increase in the size of the sixth form, which has been one of the typical developments of the post-war years, and the presence of such a large number of young adults can create special problems in a school if they begin to feel resentment against coercion. One of the arguments for compulsory attendance is that all children should have the opportunity of experiencing an act of worship; but sixth-formers are not children and we think that the provision of an act of worship for young men and women above the age of compulsory attendance should be at the discretion of the school.

In this year when we are celebrating the Universal Declaration of Human Rights we can hardly call for the abolition of denominational schools in view of Article 26 (3): "Parents have a prior right to choose the kind of education that shall be given to their children." Nevertheless, we are aware that there can be a great deal of hypocrisy in the suggestion that parents are choosing to send their children to certain schools on religious grounds when in fact it is other characteristics of the life of the school which are the real attraction. The existence of denominational schools can also cause an unhappy limitation of the Christian concern of the Church, so that it concentrates too much of its attention and resources on the schools of its own denomination and shows too little concern for the religious education of children in county schools.

To Question 10 we give almost a unanimous "no". Divisions of the Association which by a majority vote wished to see the abolition of the compulsory clauses governing religious instruction and the act of worship were unanimous in rejecting a concept in this country of a purely secular public education system on the lines of that in the U.S.A. As one division put the point:

This would be compulsion in reverse and would raise more problems than it would solve. The real question is not whether the subject should be taught but what form it would take . . . the majority of Heads in the Division believe that Religious Education has an important part to play in helping children to come to grips with the meaning of life. This does not mean that we shall teach what we believe the answers to be but that we shall leave pupils to make their own judgements.

Section B

As some of our answers have indicated, we cannot help wondering whether the Church of England has come to grips with the situation created by the 1944 Act. Is its policy to cultivate its own garden in the development of its own denominational schools or to go out into the highways and by-ways and actively involve itself in the provision of the best kind of religious education for all children? Very often what is the matter with religious instruction in school is not that it is religious but that it is not particularly good teaching. There is a dearth of what Dr Hilliard has called "informed enthusiasts" to make a centre for the religious education of a school.

There is an intractable problem here. The late Archbishop William Temple once wrote: "A statesman who supposes that a mass of citizens can be governed without appeal to their self-interest is living in a dreamland and is a public menace. The art of government in fact is the art of so ordering life that self-interest prompts what justice demands." This general principle can be applied to the smaller world of a school, and divinity teachers as a group suffer serious professional disadvantages that must deter many from joining them. In the majority of schools divinity has only one period a week on the time-table of most forms and two periods a week would be considered a generous allocation. This means that a divinity specialist may have to take responsibility for the teaching of as many as 600 or more children and this is an impossible load for anyone to carry. Whether the load can be spread depends on the availability of other members of staff willing to teach the subject, but, even when they are willing, they are not by any means always well informed. Religious Instruction is a subject which, more than most, cries out for part-time assistance, and we should like to call the attention of the Churches to this need. As we know from the report *Theological Colleges for Tomorrow*, ordination training is at present under review, and we very much welcome the suggestion in the report that the training of some ordinands should be associated with the colleges of education. If it could become part of the pattern of the training of ordinands that a proportion of them with the

11*

necessary gifts should be qualified to teach in schools for something like two days a week, then the Churches would have made a distinctive contribution to the needs of the schools and, although this is not part of our brief, we might venture to hope that the experience of teaching in a school would not be without its value to those whose prime duty it will be to communicate with a congregation.

Additional Note

One of our members, the headmaster of a well-known Roman Catholic school, made a personal comment which we think of such interest that we give it an addendum to the collective reply.

"I have not answered all these questions because I think there is a fundamental question which underlies them:

"If religion is the revelation by God to men, then it is something certain and sure, and something which interprets and makes sense—though in a mysterious way—of all human experiences. On this ground, it is a question of—as our Lord said—'we speak what we know, we bear witness to what we have seen'. On the other hand, many people think religion and its moral consequences are a matter of opinion. If religion is merely a matter of opinion, then it is unjust and intolerable that anybody's opinions should be foisted upon the young or upon anyone else. Whether this is in the realm of faith or of morals, all your questions seem to me to involve this. If we *know* something to be so, we must teach it, for otherwise we are not only concealing the facts but giving the impression that we do not *know* and have nothing to say and that the salvation of God is not only certain and sure but it is the sole guide to human happiness. If, on the other hand, we teach religion and morals as if they were opinions, we must necessarily alienate—and rightly alienate—those who see no reason at all why they should put themselves out or be incommoded for the mere opinions of other people.

"I do not think therefore that there is any need for me to reply to your questionnaire in detail as to my mind everything must be judged by this: if religion is merely an opinion, compulsory worship of any kind is an outrage."

ASSOCIATION OF HEAD MISTRESSES

Answers to the Commission's questions (p. 288 above) and comments prepared by a Working Party are as follows:

Section A

1 We agree that Religious Education, however defined, should form part of the curriculum of all types of primary and secondary schools. Religious Education is concerned with the basic questions which have exercised mankind from the beginning of time—"Who am I? Where do I come from? Where am I going? What is the meaning of life?" Education is concerned with helping young people to discover and to choose their direction in a meaningful way and therefore it must include religion, which professes to offer solutions to these questions. Most parents (according to national opinion polls and Mr May's survey in the North East the figure is 90%) want their children to be taught Religious Education even if they themselves have no religious affiliations; to be able to make a choice when they are of age to do so, young people must be taught about Christianity. As the N.A.H.T. Council said in April 1966, "Christianity should be taught not only as a study of a major world religion but particularly as a way of life."

On educational grounds there seems no justification for leaving out a large and vitally important sphere of human knowledge and experience from young people's general education. To omit Religious Education from the curriculum would give a very restricted understanding of civilization and of our cultural heritage since religious attitudes have at all stages been bound up with its growth and development. (One member has personal knowledge of the difficulties of teaching English and History in a school where there were no Religious Education lessons at all.)

2 While some moral and ethical instruction can of course be given outside a religious context it was generally felt that it could not replace the teachings of Christ, and that to be taught in a meaningful way it often needed to be related to religious beliefs about the nature and purpose of human existence. The implied suggestion of this question that Christian education is primarily concerned with teaching morals and ethics is surely a misconception. Christianity is not a set of rules and customs that are binding on Christians; concerned as it is with the development of the whole person, it offers grounds for faith in a relationship with God which colours all life's relationships. One member who has studied the Humanist booklets in detail feels that the chief fallacy of their proposed syllabus for ethical teaching is their assumption that, given the right teaching and stimuli, people will acquire "along with the personal capabilities of a mature adult" equally mature moral capabilities. Christian education offers a more realistic assessment of human nature and is therefore more hopeful in its promise of redemption.

3 It was generally agreed that this was a very difficult question. Most of us dislike the word compulsory and several members pointed out that English and Mathematics are not described as compulsory subjects, yet no one plans a curriculum without them or suggests that either parents or children shall decide whether they are to be studied or not. In the present climate of opinion there might well 'be the danger that some schools would economize on Religious Education teachers or yield to parental pressure for more Arithmetic or English instead of Religious Education. There is an *a priori* argument that if a compulsory system was thought reasonable in 1944, how much more is it reasonable now that (i) there has been so much further thinking on agreed syllabuses and methods of teaching; (ii) denominational rivalry and sectarianism are so much less evident; (iii) the withdrawal procedure does safeguard those who do not wish their children to take part. On balance it seemed that most of us favoured the retention of the compulsory provisions at present, but several thought that the schools should be free to arrange courses which were not necessarily continuous with more periods in some years and fewer (or none) in others.

4 We felt that existing safeguards were sufficient. It is important to respect the minority view and at the same time to ensure the integration of the child in the school community. Provision for the excluded child should be of a sympathetic and positive rather than of a negative nature (e.g. project work or alternative Scripture for schools with, for example, a large Jewish community). Members of other faiths—Hindu, Parsee, Buddhist, and Jewish—often wish to take part in Religious Education in order to learn, while remaining firm in their own religious persuasion. We would stress the need for education and not indoctrination.

5 We thought that the existing safeguards were sufficient in secondary schools, but some headmistresses felt it should be more clearly stated that no teacher should be required to take part in Religious Education or school worship who on grounds of conscience does not wish to do so. There is a problem for Heads, who are generally associated with the school's worship, but we felt that it should not prevent the appointment of someone who could not on grounds of conscience take Assembly. An even greater problem faces the primary school as Religious Education is usually taken by the class teacher; but it should be possible to arrange for the interchange of classes so that the class teacher need not teach Religious Education if it is against her conscience to do so. Alternatively, in any kind of school, team teaching where Religious Education is linked with Art, Music, Drama, History, Literature, or Science could be helpful. The problem of a Head who on grounds of conscience did not wish to take Assembly might be solved by inviting the Religious Education specialist, or other members of staff who were willing, to be responsible for days or weeks at a time. The growing practice of having more than one Assembly, and of

having prayers chosen and conducted by girls and boys themselves would help, and a greater use could be made of the clergy of all denominations and of B.B.C. services. We hope that the wider and more flexible approaches to school assembly will enable more staff and Heads to take part.

6 See 4. On the whole, separate schools for particular faiths tend to prevent integration, particularly for immigrants; but while it is not the duty of the State to provide education in every faith, it should be prepared to do so if there is a sufficient demand. Every effort should be made to find meeting-points; the practice of some schools which have weekly joint prayers for Christians and Jews emphasizes what we have in common and enhances the spirit of community. It should be possible to extend this practice, without neglecting the needs of the smaller number of committed Christians.

7 There was some difference of opinion here. Some thought that the
8 word "regular" rather than "daily" should be used, and that it should be possible for the Head to vary the time (some schools already do this), the age range, and the form of service. Many of those who do not in fact attend public worship in the churches would, in spite of this, still wish to have the act of worship retained in the schools. They recognize the fundamental need for a sense of awe and reverence in the face of transcendental truths. Granted that there are many deficiencies and inadequacies in institutional religion and its expression in worship, both in the Churches and in the schools, it would be a grave mistake to cut young people off from a corporate act which at its best is capable of teaching them to reflect on their own nature and discover themselves, if only occasionally and in glimpses, at a deeper level and in relation to God. It is important, however, that the act of worship should be varied and imaginatively conceived, giving opportunities for silence and thought at some times and at others showing involvement in world problems and making full use of speech, music, and sometimes movement and the visual arts.

It might be a help, especially to new Heads, if the Department of Education and Science would run courses on Assemblies, for the preparation of them is a time-consuming work, and Heads are not always aware of all the new and excellent material available or of all the valuable experiments which are taking place in so many schools today.

9 We thought that as long as parents wanted denominational schools they should be available (perhaps the day may come when more of them should be Christian rather than of a special denomination). One or two members were concerned about the situation in a village where the Church of England school (generally controlled status) is the only one. It is of paramount importance that there should be tolerance and understanding in such cases.

10 We were against such a prohibition: one member said that she felt as strongly against prohibition as others do about compulsion.

Section B

The very name the "National Society for the promoting of Religious Education according to the principles of the Church of England" may provoke the kind of attitude which makes some people want to "secularize" schools. What is needed is in all subjects and aspects of school life a feeling of respect for other people (real *caritas*), a genuine search for truth which may begin by leading thoughtful adolescents away from religion; but often these are the very ones who later become deeply and satisfyingly convinced. It would be a pity if a vocal but comparatively small number of secular Humanists should make the demand for abolition of Religious Education and school Assembly appear more general than it actually is.

All who are concerned that the old agreed syllabuses did not meet the religious needs of children in schools will welcome the much more lively, imaginative, and up-to-date publications such as the West Riding Syllabus. It was recently commended in the House of Lords debate as likely to stimulate young people into thinking about religion for themselves, so that they can reach their own conclusions basing them on more adequate knowledge than they have sometimes had in the past.

To improve Religious Education there is a great need for more teachers of knowledge and understanding, not only in the schools but in the colleges of education which should prepare young men and women to contribute to the "spiritual, moral, mental, and physical development of the community". More in-service training and the appointment of Religious Education advisers in all authorities should also help to improve staffing.

We hope that out of the present Commission's work some lively thinking will come on what should be taught and in what ways it can be related to the questions young people ask about relationships and life in general. Although we are not at all complacent about the present situation in schools, we would like to remind the Commission of the following additional points:

(i) the improvement in the status of Religious Education, as a subject, especially in girls' schools, as a result of the increasing number of candidates who are now taking Religious Knowledge to Advanced Level; some of these are reading the subject at the Universities or taking it as a specialist subject at Colleges of Education.

(ii) The great potentiality of the schools to contribute to the Church's work since they have access to every child in the population, whereas only a small number go to Sunday schools (it is estimated to be only 5%).

(iii) Many of the objections to Religious Education are based on memories of indifferent Scripture teaching in the past, whereas in many schools today the approach is quite different; teachers are aware of the new thinking and prepared to make a more open and ecumenical approach to the whole field of Religious Education.

May 1968

ASSOCIATION OF ASSISTANT MASTERS
IN SECONDARY SCHOOLS

It must be recognized that in the Association there is a wide divergence of views on the subject of Religious Education. What follows is an attempt to give some idea of what these views are: it is not possible to say to what extent the different opinions are held. Answers to the Commission's questions (p. 288 above) are as follows:

Section A

1 We believe there should be a clear distinction drawn between Religious Knowledge offered as a subject for examination and Religious Education as the broader subject taking its place with others in the school curriculum.

Very few parents indeed withdraw their children from Religious Education. Whether this is due to a desire that their children should have some measure of instruction in religious matters or to ignorance of the "conscience clauses" in the 1944 Education Act is an arguable point, and indeed some members maintain that the attention of parents should be specifically drawn to these clauses. We believe that Religious Education should be available in the curriculum. A number of teachers, who wish Religious Education to remain in the curriculum, believe that it should be broadly defined—more especially for those pupils who do not wish to prepare for examinations. It is probable that because of the traditions and heritage of this country Christian teaching would form the basis, but Religious Education should include the comparative study of other religions and also of modern philosophies. The purpose of education is to enable a young person to come to an honest decision having considered all the facts. While the teacher in charge would have his own religious commitment, there should be an opportunity for some of the work to be done by those of other commitments or of no commitment at all.

We note that there are some who would wish Religious Education to be withdrawn from the curriculum, some because of antipathy to religious beliefs, others because they consider that a State system of education should be entirely neutral towards religious matters; among these latter are some teachers of Christian conviction who would not wish to propagate their faith from a privileged position.

2 The answer to Question 1 largely deals with this question. Three comments, however, may be made:

   (i) In a good, well-run school with a healthy tradition behind it moral and ethical behaviour is acquired unconsciously without formal instruction.

   (ii) Some schools are experimenting with courses in "Personal Relationships and Personal Responsibility" separated from Religious Instruction and dealing with such topics as Family Life, Adolescence, Social Behaviour, Racial Problems, and the like.

The idea is that teachers whose personal beliefs may prevent them from taking part in Religious Education may nevertheless make a useful contribution to the moral development of their pupils. The results of such courses have yet to be fully assessed. It seems unlikely, however, that such courses could proceed far without some reference—most likely by the pupils themselves—to philosophic or religious criteria, and therefore might just as well come under the purview of Religious Education.

(iii) It may also be noted here that research is being conducted into the possibility of combining such subjects as English, History, and Religious Knowledge into one branch of study to be termed "Humanities". Again results must be awaited. It might well work in the junior stages of a school, but in the senior stages there would be grave danger of both teacher and taught falling between three stools.

3 It should be emphasized that we are concerned particularly with pupils of secondary age, that is, 11 and beyond, in whatever type of school they may be among the many in the different developing patterns of secondary education.

We feel that Religious Education should not be supported by the compulsory provisions of an Act of Parliament. The existence of a subject which is compulsory is alien to the principles and practice of English education in which it is left to each individual school to make decisions for itself. Moreover, the compulsory provision is a serious handicap to the subject and operates strongly against its acceptance by the pupils.

It is only fair to add that some teachers would prefer that the compulsory requirement of an Education Act be retained arguing that optional continuance would tend to eliminate the subject from the curriculum.

4 The present safeguards are considered adequate by some, inadequate by many others. The latter consider that parents should regularly be informed of their rights under the 1944 Education Act. We entirely disapprove of pupils sitting in the class-room and not taking part in the lesson.

We feel that, if Religious Education continues to be "compulsory", it should be enforced and not simply given a place in the time-table. Equally, we feel that the safeguards should be properly provided and not treated casually.

5 It is true that sections 25 (1) and 25 (2) of the 1944 Education Act, which require a daily assembly for worship and the giving of religious instruction, could come into conflict with section 30 of the same Act which exempts teachers on conscientious grounds from taking part in either, and also in conflict with the well-established tradition of the teaching profession that no qualified person shall be excluded from a teaching post by reason of his political or religious opinion.

If sections 25 (1) and 25 (2) were repealed, it would still be necessary to make sure that a teacher could not be required to take part in

Religious Education or acts of worship even though these might be on a purely voluntary basis in the school.

Difficulty arises in schools where the old tradition lingers that the form-master or class teacher shall give Religious Instruction. Refusal to do so, or to answer questions as to his willingness, may prejudice a candidate's appointment. The growing tendency to appoint Religious Education specialists offsets this difficulty to some extent, but it does exist.

There is some unease in the teaching profession that on occasion questions on religious matters are improperly asked at interviews by the interviewing authority. It is felt that interview etiquette and professional etiquette after appointment need considerable tightening, though whether this is better done by regulations agreed between teachers and the Department of Education and Science and enforced by the Department or by a code of conduct drawn up by teachers and honoured by them is a debatable point.

Questions should not be asked at interviews which call for a statement of religious opinions and willingness to attend worship. Questions on willingness to teach Religious Education should be asked only where reference has been made in the relevant advertisement.

In particular, candidates being interviewed for a post of Head-teacher should not be asked questions calling for a statement of religious opinions or willingness to take morning service, although it would be reasonable to ask the candidate for an objective statement on the place in the curriculum of Religious Education. We feel strongly that a candidate's religious commitment, or lack of commitment, should in no way bar him from appointment to a post of Head-teacher.

It is relevant to refer to clause 7 of the Recommendation of the Intergovernmental Conference on the Status of Teachers, to which Britain was a party. This states:

All aspects of the preparation and employment of teachers should be free from any form of discrimination on grounds of race, colour, sex, religion, political opinion, national or social origin, or economic condition.

6 The answer to Question 4 deals with safeguards. The A.M.A. has no evidence of any demand for the instruction of "immigrant" faiths in school. The Jewish faith is already provided for in schools where circumstances so require.

If the principles which we have set out in our answer to Question 1 on the content of Religious Education as we have defined it, were accepted, there would be no need of any specific safeguards.

7 There is a considerable difference of opinion about these questions.

8 Some teachers, and, indeed, many senior pupils, think that the act of worship would gain if it were held less often. It would then become a meaningful occasion rather than a mere routine. The first and last days of the school week have been suggested.

We believe that a distinction should be drawn between, on the one hand, an assembly of the school and, on the other, acts of worship for those who wish to attend. Morning service is a reasonable school activity, but it should not be obligatory in provision nor compulsory in attendance.

9 There seems to be no professional objection to the continuance of such schools. Sections 28 and 30 of the 1944 Act appear to be working satisfactorily and safeguard both pupils and teachers.

10 Complete "secularization" of public education would involve altering the trust deeds of many schools, and this could be construed as an attack on liberty.

"Secularization" might put present difficulties into reverse. Now, children whose parents do not wish them to receive religious instruction have to be safeguarded; under "secularization", it would be the children whose parents do. A strong view is that Religious Education should no more be prohibited than compelled, though many would like to see a more historical and comparative approach than is often common and a setting perhaps in a broader historical background.

Conclusion

We believe that if our suggestions are accepted and acted upon, the result would be to raise quite considerably the status of the subject of Religious Education in schools.

ASSOCIATION OF ASSISTANT MISTRESSES
IN SECONDARY SCHOOLS

The Executive Committee of the A.A.M. has given careful consideration to the questionnaire on Religious Education sent to the Joint Four by the Commission, and to the replies from the members of the Association whom they consulted. These replies show that opinions on this important topic are very varied. It is therefore impossible to provide simple answers representative of the views of the Association as a whole.

While a number of members would wish to see Religious Education continuing as part of the curriculum for secondary schools, there are others who would wish it to become optional or to be replaced by the study of ethics and social and international problems. Some members believe that religion is too important an aspect of human life to be ignored, and they therefore would wish it to remain as part of the curriculum. It is suggested that there should no longer be agreed syllabuses, which are unrealistic and limiting. A number of members point out the need to include some comparative study of world religions in the syllabus.

There is division of opinion amongst members about the desirability of continuing to support the teaching of Religious Education by such "compulsory" provisions as those in the 1944 Education Act.

There is general agreement that parents should be made aware of their right to withdraw their children from Religious Education. While some believe that no further steps need be taken to inform parents, others feel that parents should be regularly informed of their rights and that there should be a well-publicized system for dealing with complaints, with scope for appeals.

It is felt that there is need to ensure that no teacher is subject to pressure to take part in the teaching of Religious Education, or to attend an act of worship. The freedom of Heads of schools in this matter is thought to be in particular need of protection. Teachers should have the same rights as children and parents, and the teaching of Religious Education should, it is thought, be in the hands of those who wish to participate.

Where there are sufficient numbers and a sufficient demand, members would wish to see provision for Religious Education for children of other faiths. Some feel, however, that all sectarian teaching should take place outside school, Religious Education in school being broadly based, bringing in the study of other faiths as well as Christianity.

A number of members would wish to see the daily act of corporate worship remaining as a statutory obligation. Others believe that this obligation should be removed, leaving the schools with more freedom. A corporate act of worship is thought to be less relevant in large schools with pupils of widely differing age and ability.

Some members see a continuing place for denominational schools, though they are anxious that they should not be over-sectarian in their outlook. Other members would prefer these schools to disappear, since they tend to create divisions between young people.

There was little support for the complete "secularization" of public education. Most members see a continuing place for Religious Education, in an atmosphere which provides greater freedom and more limited compulsion for the schools. Many saw the need for more well-trained and imaginative specialist teachers of the subject, especially in secondary schools.

4 July 1968

BLACKBURN DIOCESAN COUNCIL
FOR RELIGIOUS EDUCATION

Answers to the Commission's questions (p. 288 above) and comments are as follows:

Section A

1 Religious Education in the sense of making pupils sufficiently knowledgeable about, and interested in, religion to make up their own minds about the Christian faith, should form part of the curriculum of all secondary schools. The justification of this lies in the fact that it stands as a "subject" fully in its own right comparable with any other in the curriculum; any education which were to omit this facet of human experience would be defective.

At the primary stage, some would hold that religious education should be ideally in the hands of the family and the Church, but this might well result in depriving a majority of young children of any training in Christian faith and practice. Further, to introduce a subject into the secondary curriculum which had no place at the primary stage might well cause resentment, particularly in the case of those who through the failure of the Church and the family had had no contact with it. We would emphasize the need to use experienced teachers in the primary schools, so that no ideas should be given to the child which would create a mental blockage and so prevent the normal development of religious understanding.

2 On the basis of the answer to Question 1 there is no further answer needed. We do not believe that there is any firm foundation for moral and ethical instruction apart from a religious faith, which for the majority will be the Christian faith. Any other basis is bound to be subjective, particularly in these days when the recognized moral standards which have been traditional are being called into question.

3 The use of the word "compulsory" in connection with the teaching of the Christian faith is abhorrent to many of us, and so would lead us to hold that this teaching is not in any way advanced by "compulsory" provisions such as now exist in the 1944 Education Act. On the other hand, we are fully aware of the dangers inherent in abolishing such compulsory provisions in the sense that it can leave too much to the individual Head to decide according to his personal predilections. So, while deprecating compulsion, we fear that it may be most inexpedient to open the door to any who have such a narrow view of education that they would exclude anything that could not be defined as purely "secular".

4 If religious education continues to be "compulsory", we believe that the facilities for withdrawal should be such as to place no child at a disadvantage. Withdrawal should in no sense involve any punitive

aspect; it should, on the other hand, provide a positive opportunity to employ the time constructively.

Attention is drawn to the Plowden recommendation that parents should be given more general information when their children enter a school. Attention could be drawn to the opportunity of withdrawal in such typed or printed material provided for new parents.

5 The safeguards already existing appear adequate. Teachers should certainly have the right to opt out of religious instruction. But it should be noted that experience has shown how many teachers benefit from taking part in it.

6 Children of other faiths are already protected by the right of withdrawal. If the numbers in a school seem to justify it, we would support some provision for the teaching of another faith by an experienced believer in that faith who should, if possible, also be a qualified teacher.

7 We believe that compulsory acts of worship for the whole school at the
8 beginning of the school day are now unsuited to the circumstances of many schools; because of their size and the scattered nature of some of their buildings it has become impracticable to have the whole school together. But we stress that any attempt to teach the Christian faith divorced from its expression in worship is a mere travesty and would totally fail to impart any real knowledge of its meaning. Experience has so often shown that the morning act of worship can set the tone for the whole day, so that this beginning to the day should never be lightly abandoned. Hence, where a morning assembly for the whole school is impossible, acts of worship on a house or year basis should be arranged. In the case of very young children, however, other religious considerations may call for a deviation from the norm. "Prayers" can often follow more naturally after an activity or a story and teachers should feel free in such cases to reorganize the timing of worship.

9 We believe that there is a very strong case for continuing Church of England voluntary aided and voluntary controlled schools. The recognition of parental rights in connection with the choice of school, and at the same time of the rights of Churches and other bodies to establish schools provided that educational standards are maintained seems to us to be of the essence of any society which values freedom! And for such purposes financial resources should be made available.

10 Answered in previous paragraphs.

Section B

THE CHURCH'S RESPONSIBILITIES

We believe that the Church must become increasingly alive to its responsibilities in the field of education and seize the opportunity provided by the present ecumenical climate to see that Religious Education is taught divorced from the old denominational approach.

It would seem that the Church which has for so long been the pioneer in religious education needs to take a long hard look at her education programme at both national, diocesan, and parochial level. There is a desperate need for more and more liaison between those engaged in statutory and those in voluntary religious education at all levels. It is true also to say that this is where we stand on common ground with so many of the other denominations, and maybe we, as members of the Anglican Church, ought to be doing much more to initiate training courses, etc. on the practice, principles, and techniques of communicating the Christian faith.

1. Teaching

There must be even greater attention paid to the training and provision of teachers of religious education in day schools. The following are some suggestions we have received.

In Colleges of Education
(i) Joint courses or "teach-ins" for those responsible for the religious education departments in both denominational and state colleges.
(ii) With the co-operation of the Department of Education and Science to make places available for "crash" courses for qualified and experienced teachers wishing now to specialize in Religious Education.
(iii) The Church to explore the possibilities *re* the suggestion above (ii) being implemented within the setting of existing training courses (e.g. Cranmer Hall, Selly Oak) for these specialized courses. In both (i and ii) there would be a case for pressing for grant aid and/or secondment on full salary during training.

Teachers in Day Schools
(i) More advisers in religious education to be appointed by L.E.A.s for work among serving teachers. (It need hardly be stated that advisers are rampant for practically every other subject on the time-table) The bishop's visitors (or inspectors) should then be prepared together with the diocesan director of religious education and his assistants to work very closely with these advisers in their own particular areas.
(ii) More training courses organized by local Councils of Churches in co-operation with the L.E.A. are needed to bring day school teachers and others up to date with the latest developments in religious education.
(iii) Need for more articles written by serving teachers giving account of experiments, etc. in various schools in the field of religious education. These to appear in all educational periodicals.
(iv) More posts of special responsibility to be made available to the divinity specialist.

Sunday Schools
The Church must be increasingly alive to the need of adequate training for those engaged in voluntary work in the field of religious education. It is vitally important that Sunday school work should measure up to the latest insights into religious education; therefore, training courses for Sunday school teachers should be frequent and exacting. Further, such

groups as the Mothers' Union and Young Wives should share in the responsibility for religious training.

Theological Colleges
The lack of adequate training in educational methods in our theological colleges is disturbing. Theological colleges could be linked with colleges of education and university departments of education so that clergy who are now largely trained as priests and pastors, may be adequately trained to be teachers as well.

Clergy and Parish Workers
More adequate training of clergy and parish workers through post-ordination courses. This applies particularly to those who regularly teach not only in Church schools but in other types of schools in the parish.

2. The Management of Schools

The managers and members of governing bodies of Church schools should become more aware of their responsibilities, and dioceses should be encouraged to arrange training courses to further this end.

3

The clergy should become more conscious of their pastoral responsibilities in connection with all types of schools and show a willingness to help Heads and teachers, so that a real dialogue may be established between Church and school.

4

In any new Education Act which might lack compulsory provisions
(a) controlled schools must have the right to retain "reserved" teachers;
(b) the rights of parents to withdraw their children for religious education and worship must be safeguarded.

OUR ATTITUDE TO "COMPULSORY" LEGISLATIVE PROVISIONS

It must be evident from reading our answers to the questionnaire that, while we find it difficult to justify the compulsory provisions of the 1944 Act, we have grave fears of the effects on *society* if they are removed.

While we do not think that the protection of legislative clauses is what we as a Christian body should seek, we realize that many children from Christian homes and many from homes which, though only nominally Christian, desire Christian *teaching* for their children, will be pupils in "maintained" schools. In these schools, even where the head is a Christian and anxious that he and his staff should reflect the Christian way of life, and give every facility for religious education *and worship*, he may be subject to intolerable pressures from certain groups. In this connection it has to be remembered that even the support of a strong body of governors may be lacking as many such schools have merely nominal "governors" with little real power.

Where the head is a professed atheist there will be nothing, in the absence of compulsory provisions, to prevent a totally secular atmosphere being developed—a situation which individual members of staff who are Christian may find impossible.

Therefore, we feel bound to say that, starting from our view that there is no sure basis for morality apart from a religious faith, the compulsory provisions, though difficult to justify logically, appear to be a necessary, if unwelcome, safeguard that the moral values which seem to us essential for the stability of society are not further undermined. So our ultimate conclusion is that we cannot recommend the abolition of the compulsory provisions of the 1944 Act.

BRITISH HUMANIST ASSOCIATION

Answers to the Commission's questions (p. 288 above) and comments are as follows:

Section A

1   *Religious Instruction*, with its suggestion of inculcation or indoctrination, can, of course, have no place in modern education. We think that religion should be dealt with in secondary schools in an open way as teaching *about* religions. We do not think that it should be a part of the curriculum in primary schools, but information should be given and questions answered as occasion requires.

2   Once again, we reject the concept of "instruction" in this context. Every subject taught and every school activity does have a moral aspect, and moral education itself is rooted in the child's experience of the school as a community, and therefore depends on the school's quality as a community. When moral questions arise, they should be dealt with and not passed over as irrelevant. There should be ample time for life-centred courses which would include discussion of personal and social issues.

3   It is neither desirable nor essential that the position of Religious Instruction and the act of worship should continue to be supported by "compulsory" provisions. As well as the moral content which arises from the subject areas, at least as much time as is now given to Religious Instruction should be devoted to life-centred courses.

4   (i) Parents should be informed of their rights and required annually to state whether or not they wish their children to attend the act of worship and/or receive Religious Instruction.
    (ii) Proper provision should be made for those who are excused, and parents informed of this.
    (iii) The right should be exercised by the child concerned from the age of 14, and not by the parents.
    N.B. A modern integrated curriculum makes it impossible to exercise these rights.

5   Adequate safeguards against the consequences of the Act are not possible. In the present unsatisfactory circumstances, questions concerning school assembly or any other oblique question to which the answer is calculated to reveal the candidate's religious opinions should be prohibited at interviews for appointment to school posts, not least to headships. Heads of schools should inform their staff that they are not required to attend assembly nor to take Religious Instruction.

6   We regard segregation of schoolchildren on religious lines as educationally and socially intolerable, especially as in most cases religious would coincide with racial segregation.

7   No.

8 Schools should not make official provision for acts of corporate worship, but such worship could be allowed as an extra-curricular activity.

9 Humanists argue that the State should not be involved either in sponsoring the non-denominational Christian teaching of the county schools or—still more—in financing and recognizing the religious teaching of individual Churches or religious bodies. This should be left to the home and the Church, without either support or interference from the State. Humanists also regard it as actively harmful that children should be segregated into different religious groupings, not merely for specific religious instruction but for their school life at large; in preparation for an open society all alike would gain from sharing a common school experience. Under whatever auspices, exclusive experience of a closed school community is a wrong basis for education in what society has in common.

We would hope that in due course denominational schools will be given up on the ground that they are no longer necessary for the defence of the faith and no longer desirable because educational segregation is unacceptable. What is now totally unjustifiable is the continued existence of areas in which the only available school is a Church of England voluntary aided or voluntary controlled school.

10 Yes and no. Yes, because the "dual" system involves educational segregation. No, in the sense that we do *not* advocate "the prohibition of religious teaching of all kinds", but only the use of the authority of school and State to make the Christian faith the compulsory basis of moral education. We are not against education of any kind; we are totally opposed to indoctrination and the limiting of a child's religious knowledge to almost total emphasis on one faith.

Section B

This statement applies particularly to county schools because they include 84.6% of the nation's children, and because the regulations governing religion in these schools are far less justifiable than in the denominational schools. The argument against the voluntary aided schools is different.

The United Kingdom is acknowledged to be a plural society, and is increasingly so. In such a society the State does not have the moral authority to impose on the county schools public education in, and practice of, a particular faith. If it is objected that the evidence of opinion polls is a warrant for the action of the State, the answer is (quite apart from a sociological critique of the polls) that, when what was formerly a common faith has been seriously put in question by a substantial number of responsible citizens, it is no longer available as the assumed basis of society, and to present it in the schools as if it were is dishonest in itself and confusing to the children.

If justification is sought on the ground that the Act provides options and makes discrimination illegal, the objection must be made that these provisions have proved unworkable and unfair in practice and have put many parents and teachers in a dilemma. Worse than that, by founding the school as a community on a false unity, they complicate and confuse human relations in the school, and in a bad case can poison the whole atmosphere. The existing regulations encourage pretence on the part of the teachers which is not missed by the pupils. A school needs an ethos, but this can be valid and effective only when drawn from values held in common.

Although indoctrination is explicitly and repeatedly disavowed, under the present regulations it is unavoidable. The Plowden Report on the curriculum explicitly stated that children should be taught to know and love God, and not be confused by being taught to doubt before faith is established. In *The Communication of the Christian Faith* it is regarded as the job of the primary school to send children on with Christian belief as an "assimilated assumption". Many of the agreed syllabuses proclaim openly that the aim of religious education in the schools is the full commitment of the pupils to the Christian faith and way of life. Even the West Riding syllabus, generally regarded as one of the most enlightened, insists that worship is the most important of school activities. In any case, the imposition by the State of an act of worship on the county schools at the beginning of each day is in itself an act of indoctrination. Children sense and resist indoctrination so that the moral purpose which indoctrination seeks to serve is defeated by the method.

A most serious result of the regulations is that moral education is assumed to be taken care of by religious education. This may mean (1) that the Religious Education teacher is looked upon as chiefly or solely responsible, and (2) that moral standards are so identified with religious beliefs that the one is abandoned with the other. Moral education is a complex matter—as the Farmington Research Unit has already pointed out—which is hardly likely to be seriously tackled so long as the false assumptions of the existing regulations remain.

For all these reasons we think that the religious clauses of the 1944 Act are unwise and have had deplorable consequences for education, for morals, and for religion.

Having stated our very strong objections to the regulations under which religion is at present in the county schools, we should like to indicate what we think would be reasonable.

1 Christianity is the long-standing European tradition and a thorough understanding of the basis of the faith and the record of the Church has a necessary place in general education in this country.

2 Many teachers are believing Christians, and there is every educational reason why they should be fully free as individuals to bear witness to their faith in the opinions they express and the stands they take; as should other teachers whose views are different.

3 Although there is objection to an official act of worship in the county school in which the whole school is involved, there can be no objection to worship as an extra-curricular activity, participated in by believing Christians and offering the experience to others.

4 An assembly, not necessarily daily, of an inspiring and uplifting

character, but free from the limitations now imposed upon it, has a part to play in unifying and reinforcing the personal and social values of the school community and extending the outlook of the children.

5 As recommended by the Crowther Report, education can and should play some part in the search of young people for a way of life. Christianity offers one such way and should have its due part in the orientation programme implied in this recommendation. We do not want Humanist voluntary aided schools nor Humanism substituted for Religious Instruction. Any sectarian approach is obviously educationally improper today.

6 The kind of life-centred courses we recommend should blend subject discovery with self discovery, and enable the pupil to see himself and his society in the vast context of biological evolution and cultural history. Such courses, centred in "situational teaching", could draw in teachers of conflicting outlooks and different specializations, with their own contributions to make, and draw upon disciplines for which there is no formal place in the curriculum, such as psychology, anthropology, and sociology, which are rich in human interest and insight. We believe that in the frame of general studies of this character young people today are likeliest to be stimulated and helped to find their bearings for a choice of life.

CHURCH OF ENGLAND
BOARD OF EDUCATION CHILDREN'S COUNCIL

The Children's Council recognizes that the primary task of the Durham Commission is to consider Religious Education in the day school. The terms of reference for the Children's Council make it necessary that our main consideration should be religious education in the voluntary sector. We nevertheless believe that there is a close and very necessary association between the two whereby they interact upon one another and cannot be understood fully if looked at separately. Education is all of a piece, and, while we focus attention upon one sector or another, nevertheless all sectors impinge on each other, for the child is a whole, and education is about the development of the child.

During the past decade attention has been given to the study of children's learning and the teaching methods that should be used in the light of the findings of leading psychologists, most particularly Professor Piaget. The Children's Council has paid close attention to the work that has been done and its implications for the whole field of religious education. The work of Dr Goldman, Harold Loukes, Violet Madge, Kenneth Hyde, and Colin Alves, has been carefully followed, and in many instances direct co-operation with research workers has been undertaken. In 1968, after two years of preparatory thought and experiment, the Children's Council published *Alive In God's World*. This publication has received wide acceptance in schools as well as in the voluntary sector. Its publication makes clear that the same research work, the same techniques and methods are applicable in work of both voluntary and statutory teachers and no sharp division can be made between these two spheres.

The important factor to which the Council would like to draw the Commission's attention is that throughout this period of research we have been increasingly aware of the need for religious education of any sort to be closely related to the experience of the children, and to be as much concerned with the formation of attitudes as the giving of instruction, though we fully recognize the place for the latter.

Both experience and attitudes arise from within the home and the community to an equal, if not greater, extent than from the school. It is therefore quite clear to us that the many voluntary agencies concerned with the religious education of the child outside the school, the child's own home and the life of the local community, all affect very strongly the way in which the child is able to receive religious education in school. We would also stress the immense importance of the first five years of the child's life; attitudes formed during this period are formed from home and community and represent the foundation upon which the school will be able to build. This fact emphasizes even further, the tremendous importance of the work done by supportive agencies outside the school for the experiential approach to religious education.

During the past twelve months considerable interest has been taken not only by the D.E.S. (Education Survey 5—Parent/Teacher Relations in Primary School), but also by research workers and practising teachers in the relationship of home to school (*Learning Begins at Home,* by Michael Young and Patrick McGeeny; *Linking Home and School,* ed. Maurice Craft; *Parents and Teachers, Partners or Rivals,* by P. Green; *All Our Future,* by J. W. M. Douglas—all these follow up to home and school). This recognition of the need for partnership clearly imposes upon all educationists the need to pay close attention to the development of supportive agencies outside the school which can reinforce and supplement the learning that goes on within it. The co-ordination of these agencies and the linking of them and of the work of the teacher in school with worshipping groups in the community is a difficult, perhaps insuperable task, but one that cannot be allowed to be disregarded simply because of the difficulties and tensions inherent within it.

We feel that there can be little need to stress all this before such a body as the Durham Commission, but we fear that there is a danger that, in the concentration upon the school situation, the part played by those who work within the community may be overlooked. If this happens, whatever may be done in the classroom may be easily negatived or made irrelevant by lack of support outside, or by failure to relate what is done in one part of the child's life to what is done in another.

Michael Young, in his description of research work on parent relationships in a London primary school, points out that in ordinary educational matters the attitude of the teacher must change from thinking of himself as *in loco parentis* to recognizing himself as a "partner *cum parente*" in the education of the child. It is this concept of partnership which is absolutely vital if religious education in school is going to have any meaning in the future.

COUNTY COUNCILS ASSOCIATION

Answers to the Commission's questions (p. 288 above) and comments are as follows:

Because of the very great importance which the Association attach to religious education in schools and because of their desire to strengthen and enrich religious education in all its aspects, they believe that they should contribute to this attempt by the Commission set up by the Church of England Board of Education in association with the National Society to make a searching reappraisal of this vital question. It must, however, be clearly understood that the Association will wish to give further consideration to the whole matter (and, in particular, to the "compulsory" issue) in the light of the Commission's report, when available. There is no question at this stage of their giving formal support to early proposals for the amendment of existing legislation.

Preliminary Considerations

While it would not be appropriate to preface the replies to this questionnaire with a statement *in extenso* of the complex and continuously changing background against which the current problems and opportunities of religious education must be considered, it seems nevertheless important to emphasize that there have been, in this context, significant changes in the climate of public opinion in this country since the 1944 Education Act. How far these have been due to such factors as the changes in the position of Christianity as a world religion; the loss of Empire and the decline in the political/economic strength and international influence of Great Britain; the growth of a relatively affluent, Welfare State society; the development of mass communications and mass entertainment; the reactions of the organized Churches themselves; the ecumenical movement; the rise of Humanism, the problems of immigration and racial discrimination, etc., it is hard to say. But it is difficult to deny that, judged in such terms as church attendance and active involvement in avowedly Christian activities, there has been a continuing decline in Christian belief, particularly among young people, in the last twenty-four years. During the same period denominational differences between the Christian Churches have lessened appreciably. Moreover, there has been, in addition to much indifferentism and some active hostility to Christian religious education, a significant growth in the number of people who profess and practice non-Christian beliefs of many kinds. Yet again, there have been important changes during the last twenty-four years in the legal and financial position of church schools in this country—so that (*inter alia*) the promoters of voluntary aided schools now contribute substantially less in proportion (and public funds correspondingly more) to their provision and maintenance than was formerly the case.

Though the attitudes and pressures which surround it are altering all the time, the "religious question" in relation to the public system of education remains a peculiarly difficult and sensitive one. Sharply differing views are held with deep sincerity and conviction. Paradoxically the more *concerned* people are about the fundamental purposes of Religious Education, the more likely they are to disagree about the methods by which those purposes can best be achieved. Disagreement of this nature is bound to be reflected in the internal discussions of a representative body like the Association.

Two other points should perhaps be made at the outset. First, the Commission's questionnaire is not explicitly confined to the public system of education, but the answers given exclude consideration of schools outside the public system. Second, while there are few aspects of the problem which could be regarded as distinctively "County" (i.e. not equally affecting County Boroughs), it is true to say that county councils generally have a higher proportion of voluntary church schools (often small, often old-established) and that they also have a substantial number of "single-school areas" where parental choice of school, whether on religious or other grounds, is in practical terms non-existent.

Section A

1 The key words here are "should" and "however defined". The questions of compulsion and of denominational versus undenominational religious education do not appear to be involved at this stage.

This question cannot be answered without some attempt to define what is meant by "religious education". The 1944 Education Act explicitly embraces within the term "religious education" both "religious instruction" (i.e. religious education in the Commission's questionnaire) and the act of worship, and in what follows the term "religious education" is used in its wider sense.

It is our view, first, that the influence of Christianity on the development of western civilization has been so immense that some understanding of what Christianity stands for and of its historical and cultural significance over the centuries is an essential part of every child's education. It is also our view that all schools at all stages must be concerned with the education of every child at three levels—with facts, with value judgements, and with what has been called "the level of ultimate significance". The second of these may, the third in our view must, involve questions of religion (not necessarily Christianity and not necessarily related to individual acceptance of any particular set of religious beliefs).

In the sense in which we have now defined it, we affirm that religious education should most emphatically form part of the curriculum of all types of primary and secondary schools. We maintain very strongly that, whether compulsory or not, Religious Education (which for most schools in most circumstances will remain wholly or predominantly *Christian* religious education) must be recognized as a normally essential component of the curriculum of all schools—at least as essential as English or Mathematics. Moreover, we believe that it will be found that the vast majority of parents (often in contrast to their own attitudes and practices) want religious education for their children.

12

We cannot wholeheartedly endorse the "traditional" approaches to religious instruction particularly in primary schools because we think they have all too often been authoritarian, unimaginative, and unrelated to the child's level of understanding. But some of the newer approaches seem to us thoroughly desirable and comprehensible at all stages.

We recognize the very great value and importance of corporate acts of worship in very many schools, though we cannot claim that corporate worship is well conducted in all schools or that it has real meaning and enduring significance for all children.

We should like to feel that "religious education" was not so much a subject of the curriculum as an aspect of every subject and an attitude informing the whole life of the school. At the same time, in practical terms, we think that all local education authorities should ensure (as they do for other "basic" subjects) that there are sufficient teachers of religious instruction (including, where appropriate, teachers with specialist qualifications) to meet the demand. We would therefore stress the importance of due attention to religious education in the training of teachers.

2 In view of the answer to Question 1, this question is strictly speaking inapplicable. However, we should like to make two points here:

(i) Much of the difficulty in judging the merits of the "humanist" case seems to us to lie in the fact that no one has yet, to our knowledge, produced in detail a practical and satisfying syllabus of "moral and ethical instruction" to replace religious education.

(ii) The idea that one can teach ethics successfully outside a religious context to the whole ability range at all stages of primary and secondary education (as opposed to the very intelligent few in the later stages of secondary education) seems to us, to say the least, not proven.

3 We have already stated our view that religious education must, like English and mathematics, be regarded as an essential component of the curriculum of all schools. But religious education is also unique in the sense that it involves, for each individual, issues of fundamental belief (hence, among other things, the need for conscientous safeguards for parents and teachers).

Whether religious education is "compulsory" or not, the extent and quality of the work done will depend on there being enough teachers with the skill, imagination, and devotion which are needed more perhaps for this than for any other "subject".

The vital questions therefore are: "Would the removal of the compulsory provisions affect the attitude of children throughout their school careers to religious education as a normal part of the school curriculum in such a way as to increase the number of students entering colleges of education and universities who are, potentially, future teachers of religious education of the kind we would like to see?"

and "Would their removal make it easier for colleges and departments of education to bring that potential to fruition?".

We are impressed by the arguments of those who believe that the answer to both these questions is "Yes". Many of us find ourselves in general agreement with the comments in the Gittins Report, for example:

If the teacher feels free, he is in the best state of mind to give of his best and, in education, it is only the best that should interest us. We feel that compulsion weakens rather than fortifies attitudes towards religion in school (p. 369).

and

We recommend a relaxation of the statutory position which enforces religious education and an act of worship in schools. There is a strong tradition and conviction about the place of religious education in the work of schools and we believe it to be preferable to rely on and strengthen this tradition rather than rely on compulsion (p. 377).

We do not think there is much historical evidence for the view that Christianity *as a living faith* has been strengthened by the support of the law. Many of us believe that the "compulsory" provisions of the 1944 Act have probably detracted from, rather than added to, the prestige and influence of religious education in schools, and are therefore inclined to the view that religious education should cease to be legally compulsory.

At the same time, we recognize the deep concern of those who feel that the removal of the "compulsory" provisions would lead to a decline in religious education in maintained schools and possibly to their complete "secularization". We also appreciate the viewpoint of those who, while they probably would not wish to introduce "compulsory" provisions for religious education *de novo*, would nevertheless think it wrong to repeal them at this juncture because they are apprehensive about the unintended implications which such a national decision might carry, especially if this were done as an isolated act in the legislative process.

We conclude, therefore, that, if the compulsory provisions are to be repealed, this should be done as part of a major new Education Act and should be coupled with a reaffirmation and amplification of the duty now placed on local education authorities (1944 Education Act, section 7) to "contribute towards the spiritual, moral, mental and physical development of the community . . .". It would then be clear that all local education authorities, governors, managers, and head teachers (whatever their personal views) must continue to accept the obligation to provide religious education for all children whose parents want it (i.e. do not opt out) and to use their best endeavours (particularly in relation to the staffing resources available, both quantitatively and qualitatively) to ensure that it is as well taught as its central importance demands.

4 If compulsory religious education continues, we think the existing safeguards for parental rights are legally adequate, though they are very

often imperfectly understood. We think that in view of the cardinal importance of the subject the principle of "opting out" rather than "opting in" should continue to apply; the possibility that some parents who do not "opt out" will be motivated more by indifference or a desire to conform than by religious conviction must in our view be accepted.

We think that, for children who are withdrawn from Christian religious education by the exercise of their parents' option, more should be done, wherever practicable, to provide satisfying alternative programmes of study, possibly in other Christian denominational or in non-Christian religions if their parents so wish, or at least in "moral and ethical instruction". The practicability of this will depend on the numbers of children for whom particular alternative programmes are desired and the availability of staff and accommodation. We think that more use could be made of "voluntary" teachers (i.e. not paid by the local education authority) for denominational Christian religious education and instruction in non-Christian religions, and that the alternative programmes should take place, again wherever practicable, on school premises at both the primary and secondary stage. (This is possible under present law at the secondary but not at the primary stage.) We also think that "voluntary" religious education teachers would need to be properly accredited and very thoroughly trained in modern teaching methods.

5 The legal position (1944 Education Act, section 30) is already quite clear and we do not think that any additional legal safeguards are necessary or desirable.

6 The 1944 Act does not specifically require Christian religious education though it has been widely assumed to do so. Non-Christian voluntary aided schools (e.g. Jewish) can be conducted as maintained schools under the existing law.

We have already indicated that we would favour arrangements in school for education in other religions wherever there is a demand which in practical terms can be met. The need for such arrangements is greater than in the past as a result of the settlement of certain immigrant communities. Schools in the areas concerned have a duty to respect non-Christian beliefs sincerely held and to facilitate instruction in those religions. At the same time, it seems to us clear that the religious education syllabus for most schools in this country will and should remain Christian and undenominational.

7 We recognize the value of "school assemblies" (particularly for juniors and seniors) when the whole school is gathered together for a signified, serious purpose and its members experience a real sense of community. But we recognize that assemblies of the whole school may in some cases be difficult, even impossible, for practical reasons and we think there is at least equal value and appropriateness, on occasions and for particular groups of children, in house, group, or class assemblies.

We attach great importance to regular corporate acts of worship *provided* they are well conducted and involve the children at *their* level of understanding. Where the importance of religious education is recognized and expressed in a school's daily act of worship, the requirement may well be thought unnecessary. Where it is not, the statutory requirement could well be counter-productive.

It is our hope and belief that, whether or not the compulsory provisions are repealed, the act of worship will be increasingly seen as a fundamental part of religious education, demonstrating that religious education cannot be confined to the class-room but involves opportunities for Christian practice which include corporate worship.

8 See 7. If the element of compulsion is removed, we think that the vast majority of governors, managers, and heads will wish their schools to provide regular and, we hope, varied and imaginative opportunities for corporate worship, and we think they should.

9 Despite the steadily increasing, and now very substantial, proportion of their costs borne by public funds, we would not argue for the abolition of aided schools as such, though we note the special difficulties of certain "single-school" areas where there is no real freedom of choice for parents except the freedom to "opt out".

In the limited context of this inquiry, some may feel that it is more difficult to argue for the retention of "voluntary controlled" status. The voluntary controlled schools (often old foundations, mostly Church of England) are evidence of the debt that the English system of education owes to the Churches and private charities, but the differences between voluntary controlled and county schools seem now more historical than real. Both are wholly maintained by public funds, and if the more flexible approach to religious education and corporate worship which has been advocated above were adopted for all maintained schools, voluntary controlled status would, we think, appear more than ever an anachronism. There are, however, practical reasons why voluntary controlled schools should continue to be a recognized part of the system. They have in the past proved a useful half-way stage between the aided school and the county school and we believe that they will continue to do so in the foreseeable future.

10 We emphatically would not favour a complete secularization of "public education" because we think that this would be to deny a basic part of each child's nature. We feel bound to add that the preservation of the "traditional 'dual' system" does not seem to us an essential condition for avoiding complete secularization.

We would regard legal prohibition of religious education as a great deal more damaging than legal compulsion could ever be. Our view in brief is that, in our rapidly changing society, the schools should be as free as possible to make their distinctive contribution to religious as to other aspects of education and that, if this freedom is given, it will be used responsibly in a Christian setting for the general good.

Section B

A brief further note is perhaps appropriate on agreed syllabuses. We do not very much like the complicated and cumbersome legal paraphernalia of agreed syllabuses. We would like to see (and we expect to see) in Religious Education as in other "subjects" more experimental work, more specimen syllabuses, teaching guides, working/research papers, etc., and more lively informal discussion among teachers. On the other hand, we think that, in the absence of any directly expressed parental preference, religious education in local education authority-maintained schools should be *both* Christian *and* not distinctive of any particular denomination. We find great merit in some of the more recent agreed syllabuses and commend their imaginative educational and interdenominational approach. And we are doubtful whether general acceptance of a non-denominational approach (which we still wish to see) would be secured without very close consultation between all interested parties on much the same lines as, but without the statutory authority of, the Fifth Schedule of the 1944 Education Act.

FREE CHURCH FEDERAL COUNCIL

Answers to the Commission's questions (p. 288 above) are as follows:

Section A

1 The short answer to this question is "In principle, yes", but this must be qualified by the answers given to the subsequent questions and by the meaning to be attached to the words "however defined". They are here taken to mean "of some kind or another".

2 A good deal more attention needs to be given to this question than heretofore, not only in anticipation of possible changes in the Education Acts, but in deference to the position of non-Christian elements in the community, and also to that of the humanists.

It would be helpful if the humanists produced some suggestions in this field. Even if this is done, the teaching of ethics, philosophy, and the comparative study of religions will raise problems of teacher-supply as acute in their way as any we know in the present situation. It is difficult, however, to see how moral and ethical teaching can be formulated in isolation from some recognized standards. If these are not the standards of the Christian faith, then the danger is that some conception of "national interest" may be set up as a criterion. (See article in *Times Educational Supplement* (10 November 1967), "The Secular Approach to Morals in Japan", by E. M. Pye.)

3 It is not *essential* but it is *desirable* that Religious Education should be written into legislation in some way. Religious Education is more likely than other subjects to be the victim of unfavourable attitudes on the part of those responsible for curricula. The notion of compulsion, however, is foreign to the teaching and practice of religion. In the sense in which the idea is used by objectors, it is doubtful whether it represents either the intention of the 1944 Act, or what in fact takes place in the great majority of schools. If Religious Education is the only subject named in the Act as required, it is also the only one out of which teachers and pupils may contract on grounds of conscience. In any objectionable sense of the word it is less compulsory than any other subject.

4 The existing safeguards are adequate, but more could be done in many instances to acquaint parents of their rights in this matter and to provide constructive alternatives. There is some force in the contention that "withdrawal" from Religious Education puts the individual child in an invidious position. It is possible to exaggerate this point, but in so far as it is valid, it reflects as much as anything the fact that such children are not given constructive alternative work to do.

5 The existing safeguards are adequate in theory, but in practice the teacher who "contracts out" often finds himself at a disadvantage. This applies especially in applying for headships.

6 Certainly the rights of children of other faiths must be safeguarded and

are by the existing conscience clauses. In some areas, however, the numbers of such children are considerable. There would seem to be no logical reason in these instances why the present provisions made for Jewish children should not be extended. Against this, however, must be set the fact that the parents of many such children seem to wish their children to receive Christian instruction. There is also a danger of fragmentation that would be bad educationally and socially (and burdensome economically) and a possibility that provisions made to help clearly defined religious communities might be exploited by Christian "sects".

7 It is a weakness in the present provisions that religious education and worship are dealt with as if they were the same thing. The opportunity to participate in school worship, however, is an important part of religious education. Many teachers also feel it is an important element in a school's corporate life. Worship should be dealt with separately from religious education and far more option given as to when and by whom it should be conducted and, at the secondary stage, pupils should be free to express their own conscientious view points.

8 If "worship" were excluded altogether from the statutory obligations, many, perhaps most, schools would continue to hold it and should certainly be encouraged to do so. But apart from a statutory requirement who is to say they *should* continue to do so?

9 Denominational schools have a place in the educational system by historical evolution. They represent the conviction of many Christians that the Churches should be actively involved in educational provision. These facts must be accepted and respected. The situation, however, is not homogeneous. Church of England schools exist for somewhat different reasons from Roman Catholic or Jewish schools. The idea of denominational enclaves is not a good one socially or educationally (and probably not denominationally). But if church schools can be "Christian" first and "denominational" second, there is still a valuable role they can play in serving the community. Single-school areas must not be created and religious tests for admission to church schools, though not unreasonable, are a source of misunderstanding and friction.

The situation also is not static. The growing degree of aid from public funds that the voluntary schools have been justly given and the changing pattern of secondary education raise the question whether the Churches' participation in education must not in future take some other form than the provision of buildings.

10 If it were possible to start *de novo*, a system of state schools only would probably be best, but not a system that was "secularized". It is possible that present trends will lead to a "progressive dismantling of the traditional dual system" (see answer to question 9) and this would not be distasteful to Free Church opinion in the main, so long as it was *progressive* and the best in the voluntary school contribution was preserved in the new system. Any "secularization" of education would, however, remove from it one of its most important elements and be

contrary to the traditions of our country and to the mass of public opinion.

Section B

The Free Church Federal Council, while supporting in principle the provisions of the current Education Acts, is none the less aware of the need to rethink both the policy and the method of religious education. The former it is actively engaged in doing through the Central Joint Education Policy Committee and the tripartite consultations known as "The Nine". The latter is the active concern of the youth and education departments of our several denominations and of the British Lessons Council (an associated body) whose recently published syllabus *Experience & Faith* marks a new beginning in the children's work of the Free Churches and is also creating considerable interest in the day school situation.

Without being committed to any extreme positions, the F.C.F.C. accepts the general findings of recent investigations into the religious understanding of children and young people. It believes that the application of these ideas to religious education in schools can not only greatly facilitate religious education itself, but also by virtue of its "open-endedness" remove at least some of the problems and anomalies faced by the uncommitted teacher of the subject.

The Council is anxious to see Agreed Syllabuses rewritten to take account of recent research and to see more of its fruits made available to teachers through publications and in-service training schemes. The Council would like to see the appointment of standing advisory councils for religious education made mandatory. It also believes the appointment of L.E.A. advisers in religious education can be of great value.

The Council believes that the problems of religious education in schools cannot be solved apart from the problems of teacher supply and training. These problems are not only, or even primarily, a matter of money and buildings, but reflect the need for a much more systematic and vigorous programme of education in the Church both among its children and its adults. It is ultimately from an alert and informed church membership that the necessary supply of teachers must come. The Churches must constantly keep before their people the challenge of the teaching profession as a way of fulfilling a sense of Christian vocation.

May 1968

NATIONAL SOCIETY

Prefatory Note

The Commission on Religious Education was set up by the National Society in association with the Church of England Board of Education. When the Commission reports, it will be the duty of this body to consider the Commission's recommendations and to advise their officers what steps should be taken to implement any part of the recommendations. It is thought desirable that the National Society, because of its special experience of schools in the voluntary sector, should make a contribution to the evidence, but it must be stated at the outset that the National Society must be free to express its view on the final report which it is presumed will be made in the light of the evidence available. The evidence submitted now, therefore, in no way binds the National Society to any view on the final report.

Answers to the Commission's questions (p. 288 above) and comments are as follows:

Section A

1 The National Society gives an unambiguous "yes" as the answer to the first question. It does so because of its own convictions about religious education and its own commitment to the teaching of the Christian faith, which runs deeply in our culture, of which "organized" Christianity is still a part. The Society's conviction about the religious dimension of life plainly indicates its attitude to the part which religious education should play in the curriculum, and it considers it unnecessary to resort to what might be termed "fringe" reasons for the affirmative answer it gives.

2 N/A.

3 The compulsory (or universal) provision for religious and moral education should be retained. This ought to ensure proper teaching of the Faith and a place for religious education on the time-table. This provision accords with, and in this respect fulfils, the general principle laid down in section 7 of the 1944 Education Act.

4 The existing safeguards are adequate.

5 The position of such teachers is adequately safeguarded (*a*) by statutory provision; and (*b*) by professional associations.

6 Certainly. There are no difficulties of principle here.

Existing practice should continue. Pupils of other faiths should have, where practicable, opportunity for systematic instruction in their own faith. This should apply equally to church schools and county schools. Attention should also be paid, however, to the necessity for such pupils to be made aware of, and given an understanding of, the cultural heritage of the Christian faith.

7 No.

8 While recognizing the importance of daily prayer and worship, and urging in any case the need for statutory provision for regular and frequent worship, the National Society does not suggest the continuation of the precise requirements of the Education Act as it now stands. The form and timing of acts of worship will depend to some extent on the organization of the school and on age groups. Greater flexibility, however, does not imply any diminution of the value of corporate worship. We emphasize the correlation of instruction and worship.

9 Yes. The voluntary schools not only ensure a wholesome variety in the maintained system, but also provide opportunities for the full implementation of the principle stated in the answer to question 1 above. Furthermore, the Church cannot survive unless it is genuinely involved in the world in which we live. Having its own schools presents the Church with an essential sphere of involvement and at the same time enables it to serve.

10 No—as indeed is implied by the foregoing.

Section B

The National Society wishes to make the following observations:

1 Everything possible should be done to secure an adequate supply of qualified teachers of religious education. The possibilities of such supply need to be further investigated—for instance, in the increasing number of theological students in certain universities and among the students in church colleges of education. The likely number of teachers is related to the quality of the teaching they themselves have had; thus the growth in the number and quality of convinced teachers will itself be the seed-ground of future supply. The clergy should be encouraged to foster teaching as a vocation.

In-service training of teachers of religious education should be developed and extended. L.E.A.s should encourage this, and should co-operate with Institutes of Education to achieve it. The provision of training in the Institutes themselves should also be expanded. The National Society welcomes the appointment by some L.E.A.s of religious education advisers, and hopes this practice may be extended.

The content of training for Religious Education teachers should not be limited to the bare bones of the Bible, doctrine, and church history, *but should also include the study of the relationship of faith and culture.* The Christian doctrine of man is the root of the Christian's approach to education, but he must see man against the realities of his cultural background. Without this he cannot understand the apparent godlessness of the age; without this he cannot begin to reawaken the (essentially biblical) realization that this is God's world. Without this, too, he cannot see how to achieve constructive relationships, for example, with humanists, who share a caring and sensitive approach to the education of children.

2 An intensified programme of research in the field of religious education

is necessary with the dual aim of assessing and analysing the present
position, and also of looking forward to future possibilities. That is to
say, research should be concerned not only with what is happening
now, but also with what ought to happen and with what could happen;
and it should be continuous. There is danger in the notion that there is
a "church view" of religious education, but churchmen should be
made aware of what is going on and of what developments are possible
and desirable. Accurate knowledge must always inform Christian
thinking.

Research should be undertaken not simply by people who are ex-
ponents of psychological, sociological, and educational techniques,
however expert they may be, but by a team which includes competent
theologians and biblical scholars.

In this connection the National Society wishes to observe that the
revised Catechism is in a form inconsistent with widely accepted methods of teaching.

3 The Church's work in education should, in every way possible, be
undertaken on an ecumenical basis. The real reason for this is not to
strengthen the voluntary sector in the maintained system but to share
Christian experience in this field and to foster and demonstrate a common Christian concern for what education is about. Christians in
education, and particularly in teaching, do not shelve their religious
convictions, but neither do they see them as inimical to the freedom of
the pupil. The unity of all Christians should be evident in that authoritative (not authoritarian) approach which is the outcome of genuine
conviction, which itself emerges from a common Christian experience;
if it is authentic, it is plainly seen to be such, and is free alike from the
arrogance of self-assertiveness and the oppressiveness of religiosity.

Practical projects in education and research should also, where
possible, be ecumenical in character.

4 The need for in-service training of the clergy cannot be overstressed.
Teaching is part of their ministry; many of them have official positions
in the educational structure or are employed professionally as teachers.
Far more should be done to inform and train them.

Much greater attention should be paid to these matters in preparation for ordination, and there is much to be said for at least some of
that preparation taking place in a college of education. The theory and
practice of education, with particular reference to religious education,
should be part of the normal initial training of every ordinand. Attention is drawn in this connection to para. 74 of the de Bunsen Report,
Theological Colleges for Tomorrow. If some of the training of ordinands
took place in colleges of education, the Church would have to face the
cost, and would have also to ensure that courses were of adequate
length. But such a scheme would be a two-way benefit—an advantage
to both ordinands and future teachers.

NATIONAL SECULAR SOCIETY

Answers to the Commission's questions (p. 288 above) are as follows:

1 Religious education in the form of a series of propositions about the existence and attributes of God should not be given. However, it is desirable that school leavers know what members of different religious groups believe. This information could be given either in a course on comparative religion, or as part of history, literature, or social studies courses.

2 The most important contribution the school can make to moral education is through example by teachers, and the fostering of an atmosphere of generosity and consideration for others in the school. In the secondary school there should be plenty of free discussion of moral questions. Fund-raising for charities and practical help for local old or blind people should be encouraged.

3 There should be no compulsion.

4 Parents should be asked in a neutral way whether or not they wish their children to have Religious Instruction. Schools should be required to provide adequate accommodation for withdrawn children, who are at present too often left standing in a draughty corridor. Assemblies should be split into a religious and non-religious part, and withdrawn children brought in for sports notices, etc. Fifth and sixth form pupils should make their own decision as to whether they will attend religious assemblies.

5 Appointing committees should be forbidden to ask candidates questions about religious affiliation. Genuine protection for teachers is virtually impossible as long as there are legal requirements regarding assemblies and religious instruction which make it inconvenient to have heads or junior class teachers who will not participate.

6 The best safeguard would be to remove religion from school altogether. Otherwise the proposals under 4 above are the best that can be done. The idea of setting up special schools for children of other religions is appalling. Children should never be segregated according to their parents' religion.

7 No. (One of our members writes: "Invite the Archbishop to sit in mufti at the back of the hall and watch a secondary school audience, bored stiff or actively defiant.")

8 No.

9 No. We consider that denominational schools are inherently wrong, as they mean the segregation of children by religion, and the religious training given in them usually takes the form of indoctrination. We are particularly concerned at the position in single-school areas, and feel that schools in these areas should be transferred to local authority control immediately.

10 We do favour complete secularization, but prohibition of religious teaching of all kinds would be wrong. We want teachers and pupils of all religions and none to be able to express their opinions, and to compare and contrast views in an atmosphere of freedom.

SOUTHWARK DIOCESAN CATHOLIC PARENTS' AND ELECTORS' ASSOCIATION

We submit this Memorandum as lay members of the Roman Catholic community—a community which has long had a substantial and special stake in the state system of education in this country—a community more-over, which by the efforts of its members has shown a determination, despite at times an almost crippling financial burden, not merely to main-tain, but steadily to increase that stake.

This has not been achieved by or for denominational pride, or in a spirit of separatism, but rather because of the deep concern of Catholic parents for the moral and spiritual welfare of their children. As evidence of that concern, our voluntary aided schools, almost without exception, are filled and over-full, and in those rare instances where it is otherwise there are clear and special reasons why this should be so.

Again, almost invariably in our primary and secondary schools, cer-tainly in those within the Southwark archdiocese, written applications for admission (frequently in excess of the places available) are received by the head teacher each year long before the opening of the September term. The number of such applications increases annually. As a typical example we cite a one-form entry (40) primary school in an outer London borough, opened only last Easter (1967), where fifty-seven such applications for admission in the coming September are already in the hands of the managers.

We think it relevant here also to mention a sample survey carried out recently by members of this Association in four contiguous parishes, based on a substantial but completely random selection from the names recorded some three years previously in the baptismal registers of the four parishes. Of these families (about 300) still residing at their original addresses, 98% of those approached returned signed declarations expressing a desire that their children should be educated in a Catholic school. We would not claim to be unique in this respect, indeed we gladly acknowledge and are happy to know that others, not of our faith, under like circumstances have shown a similar determination to the same end.

In so far as we wish our children to be instructed, wherever possible, in their own faith, in Catholic schools and by Catholic teachers, it might perhaps be supposed that we have little interest in the practice in state or county schools and because many, if as yet by no means all, of our children are so educated, that we might have small concern with that issue. The case is far otherwise. As Christians we cannot disregard the spiritual well-being of all our fellow-Christians. As citizens, on the other hand, we are both involved in, and concerned for, the general moral spirit of our country. None, we believe, will question our right to express that concern.

We turn now to the nature and purpose of education, as we regard it. Every human personality contains many potentialities, some of them for good and some for evil. It is surely, therefore, the business of education to foster and develop the first and, so far as may be, to correct or eradicate the second. If this is true, then the end of education is to achieve a balanced development of the whole person, body, mind, and spirit. It must follow that moral training, by instruction and example, is therefore an integral part of education and any form of education is distorted and incomplete if such training is excluded from it.

We cannot believe that this view of education and of the obligations arising from it are in any way peculiar to ourselves or to those who think as we do. It would, for example, be hard to discover a school which would deliberately disclaim any responsibility for the moral care and development of its pupils. It would be even more difficult, we believe, to find responsible parents who would willingly commit to such a school the care and training of their children; to go further, fewer still who would knowingly place the instruction of their children, even to the extent of a single specialized subject, in the hands of a teacher of whose moral integrity there was doubt. It is no disproof of this definition of education, as it is still less a reason for avoiding the grave implications which arise from it, to ask, as many of those who oppose Religious Instruction in state schools do ask—"but what is good?" Such a question has not even that small merit which may lie in novelty; the Pilates of every age have sought to avoid responsibility by posing it.

Clearly there are those who, after honest and serious consideration, have grave doubts of, or complete disbelief in, Christianity, as there are also men of other faiths—Jews, Moslems, etc. It seems equally apparent, however, that the great majority in this country still retain a sincere, if often vague, belief in Christian truths. Moreover, however much they may go by default or omission, there can be little doubt that for most of our countrymen the accepted standards of conduct and morals are those contained and expounded in the New Testament. It is, therefore, not surprising that recent tests of public opinion have revealed an overwhelming majority in favour of retaining Religious Instruction on the curriculum of state schools, for it can hardly be questioned that Christianity is the religion which that majority had in mind; or that they envisaged such instruction as the basis for the moral training of their children.

In considering this issue we see it as relevant and important to remember also that the development and structure of society in this country is Christian. Down the centuries our customs, conduct, and laws have been formed in the Christian mould, as also has our culture. Indeed, it could well be argued that the democratic way of life itself, based as it is on the principle of equality of all men, has no logical or reasonable justification outside the concept of Brotherhood as Sons of God; for, apart from the common experiences of birth and death, it is self-evident that in no other respect, physical, intellectual, or moral, is one man the equal of another.

There remains one further fundamental consideration. Under natural and moral law, indeed also under civil law, parents have the prime responsibility for the education of their children. Within that responsibility is the duty also to provide, in so far as they are able, the best education as they see it. In a complex civilization such as our own the majority of parents are obliged to delegate a large part of that education to others. They do not, however, thereby relinquish or even dilute their duty to seek and to choose that type of education which they conceive to be best for their children. As they retain the duty, so also do they acquire the right of choice. In no sector of education is this right more valid and sacred than in that which concerns the conscience.

For all these reasons we hold, not alone, that it is reasonable and entirely appropriate to retain Instruction in Christianity in schools and that the State has in fact an obligation to do so.

5 May 1968

Note 1

EXAMINATION OF THE MAIN OBJECTIONS RAISED TO
RELIGIOUS INSTRUCTION

There are, without question, a number of minorities in this country who, for reasons of conscience, would not wish their own children to receive that form of religious instruction, which, since 1944, has been given in state schools.

Many Anglican and almost all Roman Catholic parents find the agreed syllabus less than acceptable. Jews and atheists also, among others, and presumably parents in the recent immigrant groups who are of non-Christian beliefs, would not wish their children to be instructed in the Christian faith—an attitude which must attract our sympathy and merit our support. There are, moreover, those other sincere Christians who may not question the need for such instruction but doubt its value in its present form.

Of all these minorities, however, of whom almost certainly the Anglican and Roman Catholic are the largest, the secular humanist group (perhaps the smallest) is unique in actively and vociferously campaigning for the total abolition of any form of Christian instruction and worship in any school financed wholly or in part from public funds. It is not appropriate here—nor would it be perhaps—for us to argue the truth of Christianity. It is, however, relevant to point out that Humanism rests entirely upon belief. Even in purely materialistic terms it is not possible to disprove the existence of a Creator. On the other hand, to credit a universe, the very bounds of which are a mystery—a universe manifestly governed by order, law, and design—entirely to blind chance or to some unreasoning and unspecified force, most surely demands a faith equivalent to that of any believer in Christ. It is fair, then, for us to single out their objections and contentions for a special comment.

As we have said, we are in complete accord with parents of the Humanist persuasion in their desire that their children should not receive instruction in a faith they do not hold. Catholics, after all, are in a similar position; indeed, we have been at pains to prove the widespread and deep concern of our parents on this very issue, but we do not and we would not believe ourselves thereby justified in proposing that the present system should be scrapped.

13

Neither the Humanists nor ourselves are under compulsion; the same options which are open to us are there also for them to exercise if they so wish. We agree that the right of withdrawal is hardly ideal, but it would in great measure meet their just requirements. Moreover, an alternative exists in the voluntary aided school, built now with very substantial aid from state funds and an option, incidentally, which is exercised for more than 15% of the state system.

It could be argued, perhaps, that this as an alternative is almost closed to the Humanist because parents holding such views are relatively few and dispersed and therefore, in most areas, unlikely to be able to establish schools with a pupil entry large enough to qualify for aided status. The opinion polls strongly indicate that it is so; but if it is so, there is then even less justification for demanding that the entire state system should be remoulded to conform with the beliefs of such a tiny minority; and this, by requiring that no school in the public sector should teach or acknowledge the existence of God, is in effect what the Humanists do demand.

There remains, of course, also the alternative suggested by the Humanists themselves for parents with strong religious convictions; that is, to build and maintain schools at their own expense entirely outside the state system. Certainly, we would view such a solution in a tax-paying community as less than democratic. Moreover, from the Humanists' point of view, we would have thought also illogical and unjust; for if it is essentially and gravely wrong to "indoctrinate" a child in a school maintained by the State, as they so vigorously contend, then clearly that wrong is not lessened nor justified, merely because the parent is prepared and able to pay. Nevertheless, if the Humanists see such an alternative as valid for religious-minded parents, they cannot reasonably maintain that it is not also valid in their own case.

We have no quarrel with the Humanists' concept of school as a place where a child should learn self-respect, confidence, and consideration for others and acquire a sense of responsibility and community; but such an idea is hardly novel, indeed it is no more than is commonly expected of any school. It is, rather, the methods and means advocated by the Humanists to achieve these desirable ends which we find inadequate and misdirected. Despite the claims made for it, the basic syllabus recommended by the British Humanist Association is very far from being objective. This is hardly surprising for it is a very open question whether any form of instruction or training in "what is right and what is wrong" can, in fact, ever be objective.

Formed as it is on Humanist belief it is, of course, nothing less than "indoctrination" in Humanism. It is legitimate, therefore, to speculate how far the virtues which it advocates, but fails logically to justify on rationalist grounds, are in fact "left overs" from a second or third generation Christian background and even more is it right to ask how long such virtues would continue as accepted standards if unsupported by Christian doctrine.

Where it is positive the recommended curriculum is obviously based on the precept that "honesty is ultimately the best policy", which may be true but is very poor morality, if indeed, it is not mere expediency: for, by implication, that precept must also carry its own consequential sanctions untempered, be it said, by divine mercy. Strictly applied it excludes love, charity in its wide sense, and also hope.

On the other hand, where it is not positive, the syllabus proposes, during that period of its life when it instinctively seeks firm guidance and naturally and fruitfully responds to kindly authority, to present the child with a series of religious options. These, surely in the absence of clear instruction, can only lead to confusion or to worse.

We cannot accept that adequate and truly moral training can be given outside the concept of a source of positive Goodness and for the sake of that Goodness. Reason is an uncertain guide; we know full well that man, when he silences his conscience, can all too easily find reasons compatible with, and satisfying to, his intelligence, to justify any variation of conduct or misconduct. Intelligence, moreover, even of the highest calibre, is no measure at all of man's integrity.

Note 2

THE CONTENT OF THE AGREED SYLLABUS

The submission of proposals about the content of an agreed syllabus by members of a religious body which consistently withdraws its children from any instruction given according to an agreed syllabus may appear presumptuous. We contend, however, that as taxpayers and as ratepayers we can be as much concerned with the preservation of a Christian way of life in this country, which is the heritage of our forefathers, Protestant and Catholic alike, as with the maintenance of a moral order founded upon a code of Christian ethics, the consequence of a belief in God and his Son, Jesus Christ.

We submit that an agreed syllabus of religious instruction in the Christian faith should contain instruction in those tenets of faith which are held in common by the Christian denominations whose children attend the school. It follows that there should be no one rigidly adhered-to syllabus imposed on all schools belonging to one particular education authority, but rather a variety dependent upon the religious convictions of the parents whose children attend the school at a particular time, or upon the particular religious suasions of a certain district. Instruction in the fundamental tenets of Christian belief supported by relevant scriptural references would give a child knowledge of the main Christian truths, leaving the acceptance or rejection of them, as advocated by the Humanists, to the child himself. Such instruction, linked to a consequential study of Christian ethics would not only give a child some fundamental values upon which to order its life, but would also offer a more logical basis upon which to show Christian charity towards its fellows than the vague fraternal beneficence recommended by Secular Humanism.

There has been much criticism of the content of agreed syllabuses. From a perusal of several, it seems that the compilers had drawn up a complete theological course. Emphasis seems to have been placed too heavily upon the Old Testament to the neglect of the New. Children have been known to have left school with the idea that Christianity consists of belief in certain stories from the Old Testament, the credibility of which they find hard to accept. A more positive attention to the life of Christ and the New Testament would be more in keeping with the objective of the 1944 Act, namely that of presenting the child with religious instruction in the Christian faith.

B

"Indoctrination"

by B. G. Mitchell

Nolloth Professor of the Philosophy of the Christian Religion
University of Oxford

The word "indoctrination" has strong pejorative force and its use belongs most naturally to the realm of polemics. In a reasoned treatment of religious education one would like for that reason to avoid it. Nevertheless, it does draw attention to a genuine problem, which needs to be faced. The charge is often made that religious education involves "indoctrination" and that this is enough to condemn it. In reply it is often argued that religious education need not and should not involve "indoctrination". Can we do anything to clarify this controversy?

It is, as we have remarked, the critic of religious education who tends to introduce the word into the discussion. For him it means the inculcation of (especially religious) doctrines in a manner that is objectionable. The problem for him is to specify more precisely *what* it is that he feels to be objectionable. In the literature attempts have been made to locate this in (1) a certain *method* of teaching; (2) a certain *content* of teaching; (3) a certain *aim* in teaching.

1. *Method* In this sense A indoctrinates B in respect of *p* (a belief) if A brings it about that B believes *p* otherwise than by enabling B to understand the reasons for *p*. Indoctrination in this sense is unavoidable. Every teacher, at every stage in the educational process, with every subject, has to some extent to "indoctrinate" his pupils. No one can always produce sufficient reasons for every statement he gets others to believe—(*a*) because they cannot always understand the reasons; (*b*) because he does not always know the reasons; he himself accepts a good deal on authority; (*c*) because life is too short. As Willis Moore writes,

What I propose . . . is that we frankly admit that learning necessarily begins with an authoritative and indoctrinative situation, and that for lack of time, native capacity or the requisite training to think everything out for oneself, learning even for the rationally mature individual must continue to include an ingredient of the unreasoned, the merely accepted. The extent to which every one of us must depend, and wisely so, on the authoritative pronouncements of those who are more expert than are we in most of the problems we face is evidence enough of the truth of this contention. It would seem to be more in accord with reality to consider the "indoctrination" and the "education" of the earlier liberal educators to be the polar extremes of a continuum of teaching method along which actual teaching may move in keeping with the requirements of the situation. With infants in nearly everything and with mature, reasoning adults in very little, the teacher will use indoctrinating procedures. Between the two extremes the proper mixture of the one method with the other is appropriately determined by the degree of rational capability of the learner with regard to the subject matter before him and the degree of urgency of the situation.[1]

Since it is impossible to dispense with indoctrination conceived merely as a method, the critic of indoctrination (who wishes the word, so far as possible, to have pejorative force in all contexts) proceeds to introduce some limitation as to *content*.

2. *Content*   In this sense A indoctrinates B in respect of *p* if A brings it about that B believes *p* otherwise than by enabling B to understand the reasons for *p*; *where* p *is a debatable or controversial statement*. The objection now is to "teaching of reasonably disputatious doctrines as if they were known facts".[2] Flew argues that the right way to meet Moore's point is by introducing into the concept of indoctrination some appropriate essential references to content; "or, as the case may be, by recognizing that these are already there. . . . The notion must be limited first to the presentation of debatable issues; and then further perhaps to the would-be factual, as opposed to the purely normative. Once some such limitation, or limitations, have been made it ceases to be necessary to allow that any indoctrination at all is 'inevitable'."

Flew's inclination to exclude "the purely normative" is presumably due to his recognizing the force of the argument (advanced in our chapter on Moral Education), that some "norms" at least must be accepted by the child before he is capable of understanding the reasons for them. Flew's argument assumes (*a*) that it is possible to delimit the class of "controversial" or "debatable" would-be actual beliefs and (*b*) that it is never necessary to use "indoctrinatory procedures" (as set out in 1. above) in respect of them. With respect to (*a*) how is this requirement to be satisfied? We might say (i) that a belief *p* is "controversial" if it is possible for a reasonable man to believe not-*p*. This would seem to be much too wide. There must be very few serious opinions which have not, at some time or other, somewhere or other been held by reasonable men. We might amend this to (ii) ". . . if there are today reasonable and reasonably well-informed men who believe not-*p*". This might do and should not be too difficult to apply. Flew might think it still too wide, and there are indications that he is looking for a different *sort* of distinction. "For surely, we cannot out of hand dismiss basic differences of *logical status* [my italics] in the content of what is taught as irrelevant to the question of how, if at all, these different

---

[1] "Indoctrination as a Normative Concept", in *Studies in Philosophy and Education*, vol. IV, no. 4, p. 401.
[2] Anthony Flew, commenting on Moore, in *Studies in Philosophy and Education*, vol. V, no. 2, p. 277.

sorts of thing ought to be taught." This suggests that, perhaps, e.g. historical questions are not, in his sense, "debatable", although they do provoke a great deal of debate, while religious or "metaphysical" questions are. So perhaps we might try, instead of (ii), (iii) ". . . if it belongs to a class of beliefs whose logical status renders them (in some way to be elucidated) essentially controversial". It is not at all clear that one can, in the way proposed, draw a clear line between e.g. history and metaphysics and Flew has not done it for us, but I propose to try out both definitions (ii) and (iii) in relation to (*b*)—whether one can altogether avoid "indoctrinatory procedures" in respect of them.

Willis Moore in his article seeks to distinguish between "education" and "indoctrination". He makes the illuminating point that:

The supporting philosophies of man whence flow these two methods of teaching provide the basic distinction we seek. The liberal believes in a latent rationality in every normal infant, a capacity for reasoned decision-making that, under careful cultivation and through practice, can be enhanced and developed. The authoritarian holds that the vast majority of mankind remain indefinitely juvenile in their responses, hence indefinitely in need of restrictive guidance and management in all important areas of behaviour. *Most liberals feel, however, that man is innately either biased in favour of the good and the right or, at worst, neutral with respect to them* [my italics]. The authoritarian suspects man of a bias in favour of the evil and wrong or that he is possessed of an original sin from which only a miracle can save him. The difference between the two philosophies and consequent methods of teaching should be seen not as the absolute white versus black of the older liberalism but as one of degree only, yet a very significant degree.

There can be no doubt, I think, that this liberal "philosophy" (as Moore significantly terms it) is "controversial" according to both definitions (ii) and (iii). There are reasonable men who do not accept it and it has a "metaphysical" character. It is, or is part of, a "philosophy of life".

The first thing to notice, then, is that the entire *liberal approach to education* (let alone the particular methods its protagonists choose to employ) depends on a "controversial" or "debatable" position. So equally does the authoritarian approach. But the relevant question for our present purpose is: "Can or should the liberal refrain altogether from using 'indoctrinatory procedures' in conveying this liberal attitude to his pupils?" Must he refrain from doing anything, whether by word or example, to bring it about that a child believes that other children in the school are "innately biased in favour of the good", without at the same time providing the child with evidence sufficient to convince a reasonable man of the truth of this controversial proposition? If Johnny is being consistently beastly to Tommy and Tommy is tempted to condemn Johnny out of hand, must the teacher avoid saying anything like "Johnny is really good at heart" because he cannot there and then convince Tommy by rational means of the truth of this apparently implausible and certainly disputable assertion? It seems to me perfectly clear that the liberal teacher in a liberal school will do everything in his power to communicate by persuasion, by his own personal example and by choice of other exemplars, indeed by the whole ethos of the school, this liberal attitude. He will, of course, endeavour, as soon as it is possible and so far as it is possible, to enable the child to see for himself how and why men are basically good, etc., but unless he has devised an environment in which "actions speak louder than words" he is going to find this difficult or impossible. The liberal is likely also to be a believer in democracy and he will presumably presuppose in his ordering of the school, and teach by word and example, etc. those fundamental beliefs about human beings (their rationality, their need to participate in decisions affecting themselves) upon which democratic institutions rest, beliefs which are certainly "controversial" and which he can only adequately justify at a comparatively late stage in the educational process.

Flew resists this conclusion: "Even if it were the case—and I do not myself admit that even this is proved—that democratic institutions somehow presuppose the general acceptance of some similarly disputatious would-be factual beliefs, it still would not follow that it is in the interests of such deservedly cherished institutions either necessary or prudent to indoctrinate our children with these congenial beliefs." We might consistently and properly insist, with Dewey and his followers that "The means is constitutive with respect to the end: authoritarian methods tend to create authoritarian products . . ."

It seems to me that Flew is here confronted by a dilemma. He can *either* refuse to adopt *any* "indoctrinatory procedures", like the more extreme liberals who, as Moore puts it, "took the bull by the horns by advocating a nearly total permissiveness in the earliest learning situations, thus eliminating indoctrination in teaching by doing away with teaching"; *or* deliberately attempt by manipulating the child's environment in different ways to induce in him attitudes and beliefs favourable to democracy. If he adopts the former policy, it is highly improbable that he will succeed in producing the sort of democratic personality he wishes; if the latter, he is engaged in indoctrination as he has defined it.

It is at this point that I might usefully turn to the definition of indoctrination in terms of *aims*, as well as *method* and *content*.

3. *Aims* The suggestion now is that "A indoctrinates B in respect of *p*, if he brings it about or seeks to bring it about that B believes *p* in such a way that he is unable subsequently to believe not-*p*". In order not to convict of indoctrination the teacher who produces in his pupils an unalterable conviction that $2+2=4$, we should perhaps add "even if presented with sufficient reasons for believing not-*p*". In other words, to indoctrinate with respect to *p* is to produce an entirely closed mind with respect to *p*. Something of this sort is probably what many people have in mind when they object to "indoctrination". "Indoctrination" of this extreme kind is, alas, not unknown in religious education, but the most conspicuous contemporary examples are to be found amongst fanatical nationalists or communists. We could, of course, regard as "indoctrination" an educational process whose aims are less extreme than this, not to make it impossible, but merely more or less difficult for the individual to change his

mind if given good reason; which aims to give him a permanent *bias* in a particular direction.

If we do relax the definition in this way, can we still condemn "indoctrination" unreservedly? This may well depend on where we find ourselves along the liberal–authoritarian axis. The liberal aims at enabling the individual to realize his potentialities as a rational, autonomous adult. He will use indoctrinatory procedures as little as he can and he will regard his teaching as successful to the extent that his pupil comes to think entirely for himself. He is confident that, when this happens, his pupil will be as well equipped as anyone else to make wise decisions.

An educator will tend to move away from the liberal towards the authoritarian pole of the axis to the extent that he doubts the possibility or the desirability of the liberal's aim. "The authoritarian", says Moore, "holds that the vast majority of mankind remains indefinitely juvenile in their responses, hence indefinitely in need of restrictive guidance and management in all important areas of behaviour." In other words, the authoritarian doubts whether people who think for themselves will necessarily think for the best. The classical exponent of the extreme form of this position is Plato, whose philosopher-kings would select those capable of "education" and "indoctrinate" the rest. It can safely be said that none of our own contemporary educators would take such an extreme position seriously. A more powerful challenge to the extreme liberal view is that of Burke when he recommends adherence to "prejudice with the reason involved", rather than relying simply on "the naked reason", because

prejudice with its reason, has a motive to give action to that reason, and an affection that will give it permanence. Prejudice is of ready application in the emergency; it previously engages the mind in a steady course of wisdom and virtue, and does not leave the man hesitating in the moment of decision, sceptical, puzzled, and unresolved. Prejudice renders a man's virtue his habit; and not a series of unconnected acts. Through just prejudice, his duty becomes a part of his nature.[1]

Burke's argument may be developed as follows:

1. The liberal ideal of the wholly autonomous rational individual subjecting all his beliefs to criticism and retaining only those that survive the test cannot be realized. Every individual grows to maturity in a cultural tradition and cannot produce a rational "philosophy" of his own from scratch.

2. It is not only false but dangerous for the individual to *think* he is capable of doing this. Society depends for its proper functioning upon a multiplicity of shared beliefs, values, and attitudes, and will suffer to an indefinite extent, if the individual feels that these have no claim upon him except in so far as he can independently validate them.

3. To the extent that these shared beliefs, etc. are eroded by "rational" criticism, their place in the life of the individual and society will be taken

[1] *Reflections on the Revolution in France*, World Classics edition of Burke's Writings, vol. IV, p. 95.

13*

not by beliefs, values, and attitudes that are (for the first time) based on good reasons, but by ideas that are largely the product of current fashions. Educators who scrupulously refrain from introducing any bias into the educational process will not thereby ensure that their pupils escape bias, only that the bias is imparted by other agencies.

In the light of this discussion it would appear that neither the extreme liberal nor the extreme authoritarian thesis is at all plausible and that the sensible educator will take up some sort of intermediate position. He will not use "indoctrinatory procedures" more than is necessary (and he will always respect the personality of the pupil), but he will not feel guilty about using them when they *are* necessary. He will not expect or intend to produce an educated adult who has no beliefs, values, or attitudes, which he cannot rationally defend against all comers and who is incapable of settled convictions, deep-seated virtues, or profound loyalties. But neither will he treat his pupils in such a way as to leave them with closed minds and restricted sympathies. The process of being educated is like learning to build a house by actually building one and then having to live in the house one has built. It is a process in which the individual inevitably requires help. The extreme authoritarian helps by building the house himself according to what he believes to be the best plan and making the novice live in it. He designs it in such a way as to make it as difficult as possible for the novice to alter it. The extreme liberal leaves the novice to find his own materials and devise his own plan, for fear of exercising improper influence. The most he will do is provide strictly technical information if asked. The sensible educator helps the novice to build the best house he can (in the light of accumulated experience). He strikes a balance between the need to produce a good house and the desirability of letting the novice make his own choices; but he is careful that the house is designed in such a way that it can subsequently be altered and improved as the owner, no longer a novice, sees fit.

This analogy is simply an elaboration of Aristotle's remark that "men become lyre-players by playing the lyre, house-builders by building houses and just men by performing just actions".[1] Aristotle saw the need for the individual to grow into a desirable pattern of intellectual and moral dispositions whose rational basis he learns as he develops, but could not learn unless the underlying dispositions were already there. Aristotle, no doubt, makes too little provision for originality. This defect is made good by Gilbert Murray's comment on Euripides: "Every man who possesses real vitality can be seen as the resultant of two forces. He is first the child of a particular . . . tradition. He is secondly, in one degree or another, a rebel against that tradition. And the best traditions make the best rebels."[2] The liberal wants to make sure that we produce rebels; the authoritarian that we do not produce rebels. The sensible educator is concerned to produce good rebels.

[1] *Nicomachean Ethics*, 1103 A.33.
[2] *Euripides and his Age*, p. 6.

C

The Changing Scene since 1950

by P. W. Kent

Dr Lee's Reader in Chemistry, Christ Church, Oxford

The coming of the 1950s saw the beginning of a period of intense scientific development, especially in those regions linking biology and the physical sciences. The great progression of exact scientific thought which, originating centuries before in the rigorous methods of mathematics, extended through physics and chemistry, now made its impact on biological phenomena of the most fundamental kind. Biochemical investigations in the earlier decades of the twentieth century had done much to identify processes of living cells, for example energy yielding reactions, pathways of metabolic changes, in terms of the then current chemical theory. Already a number of the enzymes catalysing specific reactions had been isolated, some in a crystalline form, and the principal characteristics of enzyme activity were known. The living cell had come to be recognized as a dynamic organization in which equilibrium takes the form of an elaborate network of simultaneous enzyme reactions, some synthetic, others degradative. In other directions, physiological and behavioural investigations had gone far in providing detailed information about characteristics of whole organisms. The most dramatic advance was made, however, in the molecular basis of genetics. In 1953 Watson and Crick for the first time described the three-dimensional structures of deoxyribonucleic acid, as comprised of a double spiral of two interlocked molecules, one complementary to the other. To this substance, present in all cell nuclei, is ascribed the coding properties by which fundamental biochemical processes are mediated. It is responsible first for the transmission of genetic information to progeny cells arising from cell divisions, and secondly for the translation of the genetic information of the nucleus into the characteristic reactions and behaviour of the cell. The impact of these discoveries on ways of thinking about biology cannot be overestimated. Henceforth, all is new, and entirely fresh vistas at once become available for speculation and investigation. Important results[1] followed swiftly, including mechan-

[1] Foundation papers have been reprinted and collated in a single volume by J. H. Taylor, *Selected Papers on Molecular Genetics* (Academic Press, New York and London 1965).

isms of protein synthesis (including enzymes), Jacob and Monod theories
of gene action, role and coding information carried by ribonucleic acids.

Out of these findings there has emerged a generalized biological theory
"The Central Dogma"[1] which can be summarized diagrammatically:
the arrows indicating the direction of transfer of genetic information:

(duplication)   (transcription)   (translation)

D N A   ———→   R N A   ———→   protein

The underlying statements of the dogma require that
1. deoxyribonucleic acid (DNA) is a template for its self-replication
   (duplication);
2. all cellular ribonucleic acid (RNA) is constructed on DNA templates;
3. all protein is determined by RNA templates;
4. the "flow" of information is unidirectional, i.e. protein never provides
   templates for RNA, nor RNA for DNA.

In effect, it is implied that the living cell may not gather genetic information
from its environment. Adaptability, where a living system adjusts (if it can
do so) to variations in the environment, is achieved by implementation of
information already present in a latent form. Alternatively, mutations may
occur by occasional modifications of DNA, some of which may confer
survival value. The latter considered as random events, extrapolated over
successive generations, are of great importance as the basis of natural
selection.

This new approach to biology has led to considerable speculation about
wider issues. Writing in 1963 Gunther Stent[2] claimed that "the understanding of biological self-replications in molecular terms marks another
milestone in the march against vitalism". This view reasserts in a new
style the belief that the phenomena of life can be explained in purely
mechanical terms.

The final blow would appear to have been given to any lingering doubt
regarding the existence of any mystical forces characteristic of life. Other
authors have extrapolated further, maintaining that all information about
life is contained in DNA; the present laws of physics and chemistry are
adequate to explain the living state. No further laws ("biotonic laws")
exist nor are required.[3] Sections of opinion, including scientific humanists,
have seen these advances in molecular biology as arguing powerfully for a
deterministic view of the whole of living experience, which, it is asserted,
evolved out of the material and non-living by solely "natural" means.
Life may be an automatic and inevitable consequence of creation, given
the prevalance of suitable conditions of matter and time. The aggressive
scepticism of the supernatural and of spiritual attributes, regarded as

[1] J. D. Watson, *Molecular Biology of the Gene*. (W.A. Benjamin Inc., New
York and Amsterdam 1965).
[2] G. S. Stent, *Molecular Biology of Bacterial Viruses* (W. H. Freeman & Co.,
San Francisco and London 1963).
[3] F. H. C. Crick, *Of Molecules and Men* (Washington University Press, Seattle
1966).

superfluous and outdated notions, has been as enthusiastically promoted in this century as in the last.[1]

Impressive as are the current developments, molecular biology is still only in its early stages, and few would hold that a final statement has been achieved. Bernal,[2] in a recent work, has reviewed some unsolved problems which confront a materialistic view of life and its origin. Other bodies of scientific opinion maintain a more critical approach to the assessment of molecular biological findings.[3]

Sir Alistair Hardy, in his Gifford Lectures in 1964–5, points to the problem of a material world which at the same time knows of its own existence.[4] For Hardy, as for Julian Huxley, the elements of mystery remain—the mystery of existence and the mystery of mind. Yet, if mind is an emergent property of living matter, it too must have evolved in all its complexity. Few philosophers concern themselves with the possibility that "human sensory and intellectual apparatus have developed by evolutionary processes, adapted best to suit the environment. Nor can we exclude the possibility that these apparatus are still susceptible to evolutionary change."

The features discussed thus far are amongst those associated with an essentially pragmatic view of the world, regarding it as an object for human manipulation.[5] Other world views which contemplate any element of purpose or identity must include, almost inevitably, senses of mystery and wonder. In general, however, such problems are not restricted to scientists themselves, and one has to consider the position of the majority who are not scientists but who have grown up in a world built up and dominated by technology. Increasingly for some, the only realities are those of the material world (with the technologist and scientist their interpreter and custodian). For others, the realities are those of feeling rather than knowing. Polanyi[6] has pointed out that mechanisms, man-made or morphological, are boundary conditions harnessing the laws of inanimate nature, and being irreducible to those laws.

In recent years, the striking achievements in space exploration must be reckoned as factors now significantly influencing public outlook. Apart from the magnitude of the technological aspects of the achievement, in setting himself on the moon, man has placed himself exterior (though perhaps scarcely by a hairsbreadth in the cosmic scale) to the world in which his life evolved. As this form of research advances, its impact must also increase. It may be expected to contribute in satisfying man's curiosity about his uniqueness, about the existence of life outside the world which he knows.

It is perhaps not emphasized sufficiently that, were a deterministic explanation of life or its origins to be conclusively established, the argument for the existence of God would not be diminished. It might serve to

[1] J. Tyndall, *Fragments of Science* (Longmans 1872).
[2] J. D. Bernal, *The Origin of Life* (Weidenfeld and Nicolson 1967).
[3] W. H. Thorpe, *Science Men & Morals* (Methuen 1965).
[4] A. Hardy, *The Divine Flame* (Collins 1966).
[5] E. L. Mascall, *Concilium* (1967), 6, 60.
[6] M. Polanyi, *Science* (1968) 160, 1303

extinguish certain ideas about the ways in which God may be present in creation (ideas which, for the most part, theologians discarded long ago). Taken to the limit, the reduction of the whole of life and human experience to the kinetic properties of atomic or sub-atomic structures would leave questions of purpose, destiny, and inspiration, and there would remain the paradox of the origin of the first hydrogen atom.

Future developments in the biological field, recent researches on organ transplants, on sub-cellular transplantation, and the possibilities of personality modification, indicate areas of even greater complexity than the present. With these developments will come the need to make moral decisions, which pale those of the moment into insignificance and which will make even greater demands on the integrity and fullness of stature of civilization.

The educational aspects of the new situation for the individual can be broadly summarized under three headings. Firstly, it involves preparedness for change, the ability to adjust to new knowledge and new avenues of experience which may become open to man. Secondly, it has concern for the integration of experience and in its wholeness is subsumed material, the spiritual and the psychological. The debate about the existence of God is really a confrontation between the undoubted givenness of that with which the scientist deals and the meaning of existence, as David Jenkins puts it. In this context, the debate can be considered as a continuing exercise in integration of givenness and experience. Thirdly, it is concerned with the basis for decision-making.

D

Independent School Chapels

a legal note by B. Ludlow Thorne

Legal Adviser to the National Society

This appendix is concerned with such questions as "Who is the Ordinary of a chapel of an independent school? Is it the bishop or the headmaster?" "Who decides whether the attendance of pupils at chapel services shall be compulsory or voluntary?" "Who decides the types and forms of service, the vestments and the ornaments in the chapel? Is it the headmaster or the chaplain?"

A bishop is appointed by the Crown and is "chief in superintendency" in matters ecclesiastical within his diocese. Taking this definition with the definition of a chapel, which in strict legal terms is a building consecrated for the purposes of divine worship in accordance with the tenets of the Church of England, not being a parish church or cathedral, there is no doubt that the Ordinary of an independent or direct-grant school chapel is the bishop.

There are three statutory provisions relating to school chapels. The first is section 31 of the Public Schools Act 1868 (the 1868 Act) which applies to seven named schools. The chapel of every such school is deemed to be a chapel dedicated and allowed by ecclesiastical law for the performance of public worship and the administration of the sacraments according to the liturgy of the Church of England, and to be free from the jurisdiction or control of the incumbent of the parish in which such chapel is situate. Nothing is laid down as to who may officiate.

The second statutory provision is section 53 of the Endowed Schools Act 1869 (the 1869 Act) which does not apply to the schools which are subject to the 1868 Act. The section provides that the chapel of an endowed school which has either before or after the commencement of the 1869 Act (2 August 1869) been consecrated according to law, or is authorized in writing by the diocesan bishop to be used as a chapel for such school, shall be deemed to be allowed by law for the performance of public worship and the administration of the sacraments according to the liturgy of the Church of England. Such a chapel shall be free from the jurisdiction and control of the incumbent of the parish in which it is situate. The main difference between the two Acts mentioned is that in the 1868 Act the chapel is deemed to be dedicated whereas in the 1869 Act the chapel must either be consecrated or authorized in writing by the bishop.

The last statutory provision is The Extra-Parochial Ministry Measure 1967 (the 1967 Measure). This applies (*inter alia*) to any school, and permits the diocesan bishop to licence a clergyman of the Church of England to perform such offices and services as may be specified in the licence on any premises forming part of, or belonging to, the school in question. No such licence shall extend to the solemnization of marriage, and the performance of offices and services in accordance with any such licence shall not require the consent or be subject to the control of the minister of the parish in which they are performed. The alms collected shall be disposed of in such manner as the licensed clergyman may determine subject, however, to the directions of the bishop. Any licence granted under the 1967 Measure may be revoked at any time by the bishop. Nothing in the 1967 Measure shall affect the 1868 or 1869 Acts.

The 1868 and 1869 Acts are virtually the same in their effect. The exemption from the jurisdiction of the parish priest attaches to the building, which is stated to be a place of public worship. The school governors, or their agent, the headmaster, are free to choose any clergyman to officiate. Provided that the liturgy of the Church of England is complied with, it is a matter for agreement between the headmaster and the chaplain what the religious practices in the chapel are. If they disagree, the chaplain cannot be compelled to do as the headmaster wishes, unless he has signed a contract to that effect. But there will be no need for the headmaster to consult any ecclesiastical authority before getting another chaplain.

Under the 1967 Measure the approach is different. The exemption from control by the parish priest arises out of the licence granted by the bishop to the individual clergyman. If the headmaster and the chaplain do not see eye to eye, there will again be no question of compelling the chaplain, unless he is under contract. In this situation the headmaster is powerless to get any clergyman, other than the parish priest, to officiate until another chaplain has been licensed to the school by the bishop. The 1967 Measure contains no directions as to how the services and offices are to be performed, but obviously they must not be contrary to law.

It is not altogether clear what the liturgy of the Church of England is for the purposes of school chapels. The terms of some recent Church Assembly Measures dealing with liturgical questions give rise to doubt. One example will suffice. The Prayer Book (Alternative and Other Services) Measure 1965 provides that the new forms of service may not be used "in any church in a parish" without the consent of the Parochial Church Council, and a church is defined as including any "chapel or other place of public worship which is not a cathedral and in which the Book of Common Prayer is required by the Act of Uniformity 1662 to be used". Section 1 of the 1662 Act refers to any "chappell or other place of publique worship". It seems possible, therefore, that chapels subject to the 1868 and 1869 Acts are not free from the jurisdiction of the Parochial Church Council in this and possibly other matters. The position may well be the same where a clergyman licensed under the 1967 Measure is officiating in a school.

This is not the place to set out when a school is subject to the Endowed Schools Act and each school must decide that for itself.

The fabric and ornaments of the chapel are provided and maintained at the expense of the school governors, who will therefore have the last word in many decisions affecting them.

E

Religious Education in
Special Schools
by the Rev. A. H. Denney

Research Officer, Church of England Children's Council

Religious education in the special school presents a number of problems which make it rather different from religious education as practised in an ordinary school. In the first place the special school contains children who, regardless of the particular handicap from which they may be suffering, will almost certainly present learning difficulties of one sort or another. Most special schools are free from the restrictions of a subject-based curriculum and an examination syllabus; for this reason special education has often tended to be in advance of normal educational methods because of the advantage of flexibility and the opportunity for experiment.

By the regulations of 1959 children in special schools, which number approximately 408 (284 day, 124 residential, catering for about 40,000 children) are divided into seven main groups of handicap, namely, blind and partially sighted; deaf and partially deaf; educationally subnormal; epileptic; physically handicapped and delicate; maladjusted; and with speech defects. Of these the E.S.N. group is by far the largest. It is estimated that about 10% of the total school population is E.S.N., that is to say about 700,000 children. Of these, however, less than 40,000 are in special schools, probably about 10,000 await places, and the remainder are catered for in various parts of the ordinary school system. Religious education in the special school therefore refers to a comparatively small proportion of these children who do in fact need special consideration.

Since the special school avoids a subject-based approach to learning, the communication of the Christian faith is something that permeates all the school activities and is mediated through far less tangible factors than in the ordinary school situation. The relationships of staff to one another and to the children is reflected in the relationships of the children to one another; these together determine the atmosphere in which the children live and work. This means that the attitudes adopted by the children are very much a reflection of what they find in those with whom they are closely associated throughout their school lives. The same principle holds with the way in which religious education is integrated into the school activities. When not seen as a subject to be taught, it is discovered and is an expression of a way of life intimately related to class-room, community, and home. In no other teaching situation is the relationship of teacher and pupil so vital for a child's understanding of the person of Christ. No other group of children are, generally speaking, so sensitive or so vulnerable in their relationships with the adult world. The high quality of teachers involved in special education and its vocational nature accounts for the quite striking concern among teachers for the communication of a spiritual interpretation of life to the children in their care. In conjunction with this the influence of the home and the need for community acceptance and support cannot be too strongly emphasized.

During the past five years the Children's Council has concerned itself very closely with the needs of special categories of children; in two cases these categories include children in special schools. In 1967 we published a small book entitled *All Children are Special*, which was the result of the consultations of a group of people personally involved in work with educationally subnormal children. The following quotation from ch. 3—Communicating the Faith—will indicate the prerequisites for religious education in the special school.

In religious education children will learn far more from the persons by whom they are surrounded than they will by the formal transmission of information, although one must necessarily accompany the other. The atmosphere at home and at school, the attitudes of parents and teachers to worship, private prayer, the study of the Bible, relationships between children and children and between staff and children, will all strongly colour a child's understanding of the person of Christ and the content of the Gospel. Since spiritual development is intimately bound up with the development of personality, so the involvement of the child in activities which are appropriate to his age and experience and which deepen his understanding of the world in which he lives and of the problems, worries, fantasies and hopes which he has of it, will provide material for his Christian interpretation of both himself and his world.

The writers made it clear in describing various practical projects which were part of school activities that religious education can be woven into the children's lives and be associated with many other aspects of learning and seen to be relevant to the whole of life.

In 1969 there appeared *Seeing in the Dark*, a booklet which is the work of a group of involved persons dealing with the religious education and pastoral care of blind and partially sighted children. Here again we have been made aware of the absolute necessity for beginning all our thinking with an understanding of the children's needs and limitations, and with understanding religious education as something which is communicated from teacher to child within the life of the school itself. Again we have been made aware of the two guide-lines of all religious education—the exploration of the child's world in partnership with his teacher and the communication of attitudes within a person-to-person relationship.

Children at Risk was published by the Children's Council in 1968 and is concerned with children who are delinquent, deprived, or maladjusted. In one chapter, contributed by Brother Leo of the Franciscan School for Maladjusted boys at Hooke, the problem of involvement, especially as it affects a "religious", is discussed. Brother Leo sums up:

Relationships can be seen then as delicate and subtle affairs which are continually changing, and always demanding of those involved. Here is a task which calls for considerable committal on the part of the residential worker, but a task which contains material of tremendous value for him as well as for those for whom he is responsible.

There are no church special schools though there are many of church foundation or management such as that mentioned above at Hooke. There is, however, opportunity for the Church through her involvement in education to provide skills and foster vocation. The service of children with special educational needs is a matter to which trainers at all educational levels should give particular attention.

BIBLIOGRAPHY
INDEX

Bibliography

GENERAL BOOKS

ACLAND, R., *We Teach Them Wrong*. Gollancz 1963
—— *Curriculum or Life?* Gollancz 1966
ALVES, C., *Religion and the Secondary School*. S.C.M. 1968
ARCHAMBAULT, R. D., ed., *Philosophical Analysis and Education*. R.K.P. 1965
BALLARD, P. H., et al., *Man in Society*. Congregational Church in England and Wales. 1967
BANDER, P., ed., *Looking Forward to the Seventies*. Colin Smythe 1968
BEREDAY, G. Z. F., and LAUWERYS, J. A., ed., *Church and State in Education*. Evans Bros. 1966
BLACKHAM, H. J., *Religion in a Modern Society*. Constable 1966
BOVET, P., *The Child's Religion*. Dent 1928
BROPHY, B., *Religious Education in State Schools*. Fabian Society 1967
BROTHERS, J., *Church and School*. Liverpool University Press 1964
BRUCE, V. R., and TOOKE, J., *Lord of the Dance*. Pergamon 1966
BULL, N. J., *Moral Education*. R.K.P. 1969
CASTLE, E. B., *Moral Education in Christian Times*. Allen & Unwin 1958
CHURCH OF ENGLAND BOARD OF EDUCATION, *The Communication of the Christian Faith*. C.I.O. 1967
CLIFF, F., and P., *A Diary for Teachers of Infants*. Rupert Hart Davis 1967
COUSINS, P. *Why we should keep Religion in our Schools*. C.P.A.S. 1969
—— *Education and Christian Parents*. Scripture Union 1969
COUSINS, P., and EASTMAN, M., ed., *The Bible and the Open Approach in Religious Education*. Tyndale 1968
COX, E., *Changing Aims in Religious Education*. R.K.P. 1966
—— *Sixth Form Religion*. S.C.M. 1967
CRUICKSHANK, M., *Church and State in English Education*. Macmillan 1963
DAINES, J. W., *Abstracts of unpublished theses in Religious Education: Part I 1918–57; Part II 1958–63*. University of Nottingham Institute of Education 1963–4
—— *Meaning or Muddle?* University of Nottingham Institute of Education 1966
DEARDEN, J., *The Philosophy of Primary Education*. R.K.P. 1968
DEPARTMENT OF EDUCATION AND SCIENCE, *Children and their Primary Schools* (Plowden Report). H.M.S.O. 1967
—— *Religious Education, Present and Future*. (Report on Education, No. 58). H.M.S.O. 1969
DEWAR, D., *Backward Christian Soldiers*. Hutchinson 1964

ELVIN, H. L., *Education and Contemporary Society*. Watts 1965

ERIKSON, E., *Childhood and Society*. Penguin 1965

FERGUSON, J. A., *To Do and to Know*. R.E.P. 1968

GALLUP POLL, *Television and Religion*. U.L.P. 1964

GOLDMAN, R. J., *What is Religious Knowledge?* National Froebel Foundation 1959

—— *Religious Thinking from Childhood to Adolescence*. R.K.P. 1964

—— *Readiness for Religion*. R.K.P. 1965

GRAY, J., *What about the Children?* S.C.M. 1970

GREELEY, A. M., and ROSSI, P. H., *The Education of Catholic Americans*. Aldine Publishing Co. (Chicago) 1966

GUNDRY, D. W., *The Teacher and the World Religions*. Jas. Clarke 1968

HAMILTON H. A., *Religious Needs of Children in Care*. National Children's Home 1963

HEARN, R., *Modern Psalms by Boys*. U.L.P. 1966

HEAWOOD, G., *The Humanist–Christian Frontier*. S.P.C.K. 1968

HEMMING, J., and MARRATT, H. W., *Humanism and Christianity: The common ground of moral education*. Available from Borough Road College, Isleworth 1969

HILL, M., *R.I. and Surveys*. National Secular Society 1968

—— *Surveys on Religion in Schools*. National Secular Society 1968

HILLIARD, F. H., *Teaching Children about World Religions*. Harrap 1961

—— *The Teacher and Religion*. Jas. Clarke 1963

HILLIARD, F. H., et al., *Christianity in Education*. Allen & Unwin 1966

HINDLEY, A. H., *A New Kind of Teaching*. R.E.P. 1968

HINNELLS, J. R., ed., *Comparative Religion in Education*. Oriel Press 1970

HOWKINS, K. G., *Religious Thinking and Religious Education*. Tyndale 1966

HUBERY, D. S., *Teaching the Christian Faith Today*. Chester House 1965

—— *Christian Education and the Bible*. R.E.P. 1967

HYDE, K. E., *Religious Learning in Adolescence*. Oliver & Boyd 1965

—— *Religion and Slow Learners*. S.C.M. 1969

INSTITUTE OF CHRISTIAN EDUCATION, *Religious Education of Children in the Nursery and Infants Schools*. C.E.M. 1964

—— *Religious Education of Children in the Junior School*. C.E.M. 1964

—— *Religious Education of Pupils from Eleven to Sixteen Years*. C.E.M. 1962

—— *Religious Education of Pupils from Sixteen to Nineteen Years*. C.E.M. 1962

INNER LONDON EDUCATION AUTHORITY, *Learning for Life*. I.L.E.A. 1968

JAMES, C., *Young Lives at Stake*. Collins 1968

JEBB, P., *Religious Education*. D.L.T. 1968

JEFFREYS, M. V. C., *Glaucon*. Pitman 1955

—— *Religion and Morality*. R.E.P. 1967

—— *Truth is Not Neutral*. R.E.P. 1969

JONES, C. M., *Worship in the Secondary School*. R.E.P. 1969

KAY, W., *Moral Development*. Allen & Unwin 1968

KENT COUNTY COUNCIL, *A Handbook of Thematic Material*. Kent County Council 1968

KENWRICK, J. G., *The Religious Quest*. S.P.C.K. 1955

KNEALE, J., *Religious Education for Today's Children*. Blandford 1968
LANCASHIRE EDUCATION COMMITTEE, *Religion and Life*. Lancashire County
  Council 1968
LEE, R. S., *Your Growing Child and Religion*. Penguin 1965
LEWIS, E., *Children and Their Religion*. Sheed & Ward 1962
LOUKES, H., *Teenage Religion*. S.C.M. 1961
—— *New Ground in Christian Education*. S.C.M. 1965
MACLURE, J. S., *Educational Documents, England and Wales 1816–1967*.
  Chapman & Hall 1968
MACY, C. J., ed., *Let's Teach Them Right*. Pemberton Books 1969
MADGE, V., *Children in search of Meaning*. S.C.M. 1965
MARRATT, H. W., et al., *Religious and Moral Education*. Available from
  Borough Road College, Isleworth 1965
MARTIN, D., *A Sociology of English Religion*. S.C.M. 1967
MATHEWS, H. F., *Revolution in Religious Education*. R.E.P. 1966
MAY, P. R., and JOHNSTON, O. R., *Religion in our Schools*. Hodder 1968
MINISTRY OF EDUCATION, *15 to 18* (Crowther Report). H.M.S.O. 1959
—— *Half our Future* (Newsom Report). H.M.S.O. 1963
MORAN, G., *God Still Speaks*. Burns & Oates 1967
MORAY HOUSE, *Curriculum and Examinations in Religious Education*.
  Oliver & Boyd 1968
NIBLETT, W. R., *Christian Education in a Secular Society*. O.U.P. 1960
NIBLETT, W. R., ed., *Moral Education in a Changing Society*. Faber 1963
NORTHAMPTONSHIRE EDUCATION COMMITTEE, *Fullness of Life*. Northants
  Education Committee 1968
—— *Life and Worship*. Northants Education Committee 1968
PEACHMENT, B., *The Defiant Ones*. R.E.P. 1969
PETERS, R. S., *Ethics and Education*. Allen & Unwin 1966
PETERS, R. S., ed., *Perspectives on Plowden*. R.K.P. 1969
PIAGET, J., *The Child's Conception of the World*. R.K.P. 1929
—— *The Child's Construction of Reality*. R.K.P. 1955
REES, R. J., *Background and Belief*. S.C.M. 1967
ROTHWELL, J., *Nine o'clock on a Wet Monday Morning*. R.E.P. 1967
RUSSELL, and TOOKE, J., *Learning to Give*. Pergamon 1967
SACKS, B., *The Religious Issue in the State Schools of England and Wales*.
  University of New Mexico Press 1961
SCHOOLS COUNCIL, *Raising the School Leaving Age*. H.M.S.O. 1965
—— *Society and the Young School Leaver*. H.M.S.O. 1967
—— *C.S.E. Trial Examinations: Religious Knowledge*. H.M.S.O. 1967
—— *Community Service and the Curriculum*. H.M.S.O. 1968
—— *Enquiry 1: Young School Leavers*. H.M.S.O. 1968
—— *Humanities for the Young School Leaver: An approach through
  religious education*. Evans/Methuen Educational 1969
SMART, N., *The Teacher and Christian Belief*. Jas. Clarke 1966
—— *Secular Education and the Logic of Religion*. R.K.P. 1968
SMITH, J. W. D., *Religious Education in a Secular Setting*. S.C.M. 1969
SMITH, K. N., *Themes in Religious Education*. Macmillan 1969
STANFORD, E. C. D., *Education in Focus*. R.E.P. 1965

STRAWSON, W., *Teachers and the New Theology*. Epworth 1969
TILLICH, P., *Theology of Culture*. O.U.P. (N.Y.) 1964
TIRRELL, L., *The Aided Schools Handbook* (revised). N.S.: S.P.C.K. 1969
TRIBE, D., *Religion and Ethics in Schools: The case for secular education*. National Secular Society
TUCKER, B., *Catholic Education in a Secular Society*. Sheed & Ward 1968
UNIVERSITY OF SHEFFIELD INSTITUTE OF EDUCATION, *Religious Education in Secondary Schools*. Nelson 1961
VAN BUREN, P., *Theological Explorations* (chapter on "Christian Education in a pragmatic age"). S.C.M. 1968
WAINWRIGHT, J. A., *Church and School*. O.U.P. 1964
WALTON, R. C., ed., *A Source Book of the Bible for Teachers*. S.C.M. 1970
WEDDERSPOON, A. G., ed., *Religious Education 1944–84*. Allen & Unwin 1966
WEST RIDING EDUCATION DEPARTMENT, *Suggestions for Religious Education*. W.R. Education Committee 1966
WILLIAMS, J. G., *Worship and the Modern Child*. S.P.C.K. 1957
WILSON, J., *Education and the Concept of Mental Health*. R.K.P. 1969
WILSON, J., et al., *Introduction to Moral Education*. Penguin 1968
WILTSHIRE EDUCATION COMMITTEE, *Agreed Syllabus of Religious Education*. Wiltshire County Council 1967
YOUNG, T. R., *A Basis for Religious Education*. Colin Smythe 1967

JOURNALS

Catholic Education Today. 6 issues a year—Burns & Oates. (First published January 1968.)
Learning for Living. 5 issues a year—S.C.M. Press. (First published September 1961.)
Moral Education. 3 issues a year. Pergamon. (First published May 1969.)
Spectrum. 3 issues a year. I.S.C.F. Education Trust. (First published September 1968.)

It should be noted that the list of text books which follows is selective. A full Religious Education Text Book Bibliography is published by the Christian Education Movement, Annandale, North End Road, London, N.W.11. Price 4s 6d

THE RELIGIOUS EDUCATION OF CHILDREN AND PRE-ADOLESCENTS 5–13+
A SHORT SELECTION OF SUITABLE TEXTBOOKS

BULL, N. J., *Great Christians*. Hulton Educational Publications 1960
BULL, N. J., and WHITBURN, Y. D., *Primary Bible Readers*. Hulton Educational Publications 1957
DOBSON, H. W., *Quest: Activity books*. C.I.O. 1967
DOBSON, H. W., *Quest: Teacher's handbook*. C.I.O. 1967

GOLDMAN, R. J., ed., *Readiness for Religion Series* (thematic material). Rupert Hart Davis 1966–8
HENDERSON, R., and GOULD, I., *Life in Bible Times.* Chambers 1968
HILLIARD, F. H., *Behold the Land* (Pictorial Atlas of the Bible). Philip 1963
HOLM, J. L., and MABBUTT, G. C., *Phoenix series.* Schofield & Sims 1964
KLINK, J. L., *The Bible for Children.* Burke 1968
PRICKETT, D. J., and TAYLOR, D. J., *Topic books.* Lutterworth 1970
WADDERTON GROUP, *Alive in God's World.* C.I.O. 1968

THE RELIGIOUS EDUCATION OF ADOLESCENTS 13+–18
A SHORT SELECTION OF SUITABLE TEXT BOOKS

ALVES, C., *The Scriptures.* C.U.P. 1962
BENFIELD, G., *Things They Say.* Arnold 1967
BIRNIE, I., *Encounter.* McGraw-Hill 1967
—— Focus on Christianity series. Arnold 1969
BROWN, B., *Making Sense of Living.* Arnold 1969
—— *Making Sense of Loving.* Arnold 1969
CHAMBERLAYNE, J. H., *The Quest of Faith.* R.E.P. 1969
CHRISTIAN EDUCATION MOVEMENT, *Probe: Population and Family Planning; Drugs; Racial Discrimination; Human Rights.* S.C.M. 1969
DALE, A., *New World.* O.U.P. 1966
DENNEY, A., *World Faiths and Modern Problems.* Hamish Hamilton 1969
DINGWALL, R., *Relationships.* R.E.P. 1969
ELLIOTT, J., *Me, Other People and God.* Mowbray 1966
GUY, H. A., *Landmarks in the Story of Christianity.* Macmillan 1949
HILLIARD, F. H., *How Men Worship.* R.K.P. 1965
HODGSON, C., *Genesis in the Dock.* R.E.P. 1964
LANCE, D., 11–16 series (esp. Year 5 material). D.L.T. 1967
LORD, E., *Family Life.* Longmans 1966
—— *Look into Life.* Denholm House 1966
MARTIN, C. G., ed., General Studies series. Longmans 1968
MILLER, P. F., and POUND, K. S., *Creeds and Controversies.* E.U.P. 1969
PARRINDER, E. G., *A Book of World Religions.* Hulton 1965
S.C.M. SERIES, *Thinking Things Through.* 1958 onwards
SHAW, W. A., *The Living Bible.* Holmes McDougall 1965
SHEWELL, H. E. J., ed., *The Story of the Scriptures*, Bks. 1–8. Schofield and Sims 1960
YOUNG, R. W., *Everybody's business.* O.U.P. 1968
VARIOUS, Connexions series. Penguin Educational 1968
WIGLEY, B. *From Fear to Faith* (Developing World Series) Longman 1970

SCHOOL WORSHIP

BACON, C., and M., *Praying with Beginners.* Chester House 1969
BANYARD, E., *Word Alive.* Belton Press 1969
BIELBY, A. R., *Sixth Form Worship.* S.C.M. 1968
—— *Education through Worship.* S.C.M. 1969

BUCKMASTER, C., *Give Us This Day*. U.L.P. 1967
CAMPLING, C., and DAVIS, M., *Words for Worship*. Arnold 1969
COX, L. E., *Gateways to Worship*. R.E.P. 1965
CRELLIN, V., *Tongues of Men*. Hutchinson 1966
DAFFERN, T. G., *Poems for Assemblies*. Blackwell 1963
GODWIN, E., *Child of God*. R.E.P. 1969
GRIFFIN, G., *Praying with Seniors*. Chester House 1969
HILTON, J. T., *Manual of Morning Worship*. Schofield & Sims 1953
—— *Starting the Day*. Pitman 1965
HOBDEN, S. M., *Explorations in Worship*. Lutterworth 1970
HODGETTS, C., *Sing True*. R.E.P. 1969
KITSON, M., *Infant Prayer*. O.U.P. 1964
O'BRIEN, I., *Poems for Worship*. Blackwell
PRESCOTT, D. M., *The Senior Teacher's Assembly Book*. Blandford 1955
QUOIST, M., *Prayers of Life*. Gill (Dublin) 1965
ROSE, M. E., *The Morning Cockerel Book of Readings*. Hart Davis 1967
—— *The Morning Cockerel Hymn Book*. Hart Davis 1967
SCOTTISH CHURCHES' HOUSE, *Dunblane Praises*. Scottish Churches' House 1969
SELLICK, D., *Christianity and the Teenage Thinker*. Mowbray 1969
SMITH, P., ed., *Faith, Folk and . . .* series. Galliard 1967+
SWANN, D., *Sing Round the Year*. Bodley Head 1965
THOMSON, I., *Two hundred School Assemblies*. Mowbray 1966
TREW, B. G., *Assembly Alphabet*. R.E.P. 1965
YOUNG, J. and E., *Praying with Young People*. Chester House 1969
100 Hymns for Today. Wm. Clowes 1969

Index

Only the text of the Report is indexed. References are to pages.